This monograph is the second in a series issuing from the Center for the Study of Gender, Education and Human Development in order to make ongoing research and evolving theory available to colleagues. Other monographs in the series, listed below, can be obtained by writing to the Study Center, Harvard Graduate School of Education, Cambridge, MA. 02138.

Monograph 1: *A Guide to Reading Narratives of Conflict and Choice for Self and Moral Voice*, Lyn Mikel Brown, Editor.

Monograph 3: *Moral Voice, Adolescent Development, and Secondary Education: A Study at the Green River School*, by Carol Gilligan, D. Kay Johnston, and Barbara Miller.

Monograph 4: *Psyche Embedded: A Place for Body, Relationships and Culture in Personality Theory*, by Carol Gilligan, Lyn Mikel Brown, and Annie G. Rogers.

Monograph 5: *Making Connections: The Relational Worlds of Adolescent Girls at The Emma Willard School*, Carol Gilligan, Nona P. Lyons, and Trudy Hanmer, Editors (in preparation).

Monograph 6: *Translating the Language of Adolescent Girls: Themes of Moral Voice and Stages of Ego Development*, by Annie G. Rogers and Carol Gilligan.

# Mapping the
# Moral Domain

# Mapping the Moral Domain

## A Contribution of Women's Thinking to Psychological Theory and Education

Edited by
Carol Gilligan, Janie Victoria Ward, and Jill McLean Taylor
With Betty Bardige

CENTER FOR THE STUDY OF GENDER, EDUCATION AND HUMAN DEVELOPMENT
Harvard University Graduate School of Education, Cambridge, Massachusetts

Distributed by Harvard University Press

**Library of Congress Cataloging in Publication Data**

Main entry under title:
  Mapping the moral domain.

  Bibliography: p.
  Includes index
  1. Women—Psychology. 2. Moral development.
3. Developmental psychology. I. Gilligan, Carol.
HQ1206.M342   1988      305.4'2      87-72418
ISBN 0-674-54832-9 (cloth)
ISBN 0-674-54831-0 (paper)

*Dedication by Marilyn Brachman Hoffman to the memory of Margaret Collins Sullivan, teacher of English and Dean of Girls, McLean Junior High School, Fort Worth, Texas, from the 1940's through the 1960's,*

*Herself the embodiment of the highest moral development, and for generations of her adolescent students, a role model for their development of the ethic of care and responsibility.*

We acknowledge with special gratitude the intellectual and material encouragement and support of Marilyn Brachman Hoffman.

# TABLE OF CONTENTS

*Slightly different versions of the following chapters have previously appeared in other publications.*

Prologue, "Adolescent Development Reconsidered," Carol Gilligan. In C. E. Irwin, ed., *Adolescent Social Behavior and Health: New Directions for Child Development*, 37. San Francisco: Jossey–Bass, Inc., 1987, 63–92. Also published as the Gisela Konopka Lecture, University of Minnesota, 1987.

Chapter 1, "Remapping the Moral Domain: New Images of the Self in Relationship," Carol Gilligan. In T. C. Heller, M. Sosna, and D. E. Wellbery, eds., *Reconstructing Individualism: Autonomy, Individuality, and the Self in Western Thought*. Stanford, Calif.: Stanford University Press, 1986, 237–350. Copyright © 1986 by the Board of Trustees of the Leland Stanford Junior University.

Chapter 2, "Two Perspectives: On Self, Relationships, and Morality," Nona Plessner Lyons. In *Harvard Educational Review*, 53(2), May 1983, 125–145. Copyright © 1983 by the President and Fellows of Harvard College. All rights reserved.

Chapter 4, "Two Moral Orientations," Carol Gilligan and Jane Attanucci. To appear in *Merrill–Palmer Quarterly*, July 1988.

Chapter 6, "The Origins of Morality in Early Childhood Relationships," Carol Gilligan and Grant Wiggins. In J. Kagan and S. Lamb, eds., *The Emergence of Morality in Young Children.* Chicago: University of Chicago Press, 1987, 277–306.

Chapter 7, "Exit–Voice Dilemmas in Adolescent Development," Carol Gilligan. In A. Foxley, M. McPherson, and G. O'Donnell, eds., *Development, Democracy and the Art of Trespassing: Essays in Honor of Albert O. Hirschman.* Notre Dame, Ind., University of Notre Dame Press, 1986, 283–300.

# ACKNOWLEDGMENTS

In our efforts to bring questions about moral voice and gender to the attention of developmental psychologists and people working to promote human development, we have depended on the generosity of others. Our center at Harvard would not have been possible without the support and encouragement of Patricia Albjerg Graham, Dean of the Graduate School of Education. From the beginning, Marilyn Brachman Hoffman has encouraged our efforts to bring the results of our research to the attention of the scientific and educational community by providing support for graduate students and funding for the preparation of this monograph. In addition, the Mailman Family Foundation both encouraged our vision of a center that would give form to our collaboration, and funded that vision when it was more of a dream than a certainty. Initial support for our research was provided by the National Institute of Education and the Geraldine Rockefeller Dodge Foundation. Grants from the Esther A. and Joseph Klingenstein Fund, the Rockefeller Foundation, and the Lilly Endowment made it possible for us to extend our research in vital ways--from single-sex to coeducational schools, from the suburbs to the inner city. And many people helped in essential ways: Edith Phelps, our administrative director and head of school projects, Markie Trottenberg, our administrative assistant, who has sustained us in a variety of ways, Sue Christopherson, who reviewed and critiqued many of the earlier drafts of these articles, and Lynn Hamilton, our editor, who in the course of editing also became our teacher and our collaborator.

# CONTRIBUTORS

Jane Attanucci, Ed.D.

> Associate in Education, Harvard Graduate School of Education, Cambridge, Mass.; Instructor, Wheelock College, Boston, Mass. Research interests include self and morality in adolescence and adulthood, the parent–child relationship, and quantitative and qualitative research methodologies.

Betty Bardige, Ed.D.

> Vice-President of Learning Ways, an educational software firm; Trustee of the Mailman Family Foundation. Current interests center around students' responses to educational materials designed to support their moral thinking.

Susan Christopherson, Ed.M.

> Doctoral candidate, Harvard Graduate School of Education, Cambridge, Mass.; Intern at Tufts University Counseling Center, Medford, Mass. Research interests are adolescent development and children from alcoholic families.

Gina Cohen, Ed.M.

> Law student, University of Pennsylvania, Philadelphia, Pa.

Carol Gilligan, Ph.D.

> Professor of Education, Harvard Graduate School of Education, Cambridge, Mass. Continuing research on adolescence, moral reasoning and conflict resolution, identity development, and the contribution of women's thinking to psychological theory.

Dana Jack, M.S.W., Ed.D.

> Lecturer, Fairhaven College/Western Washington University, Bellingham, Wash.; part-time private psychotherapist. Ongoing research on depression in women, achievement/ relational conflicts in women, and divorce decisions (with Carol Gilligan).

Rand Jack, J.D.

> Professor, Fairhaven College/Western Washington University, Bellingham, Wash. Research interests involve the application of learning styles to jury deliberations and trial strategy, and ethical dilemmas among practicing lawyers.

D. Kay Johnston, Ed.D.

>    Assistant Professor of Education, Colgate University, Hamilton, N.Y.;
>    Research Associate, Harvard Graduate School of Education, Cambridge, Mass.
>    Ongoing research on adolescent and women's development, education, and
>    moral development.

Nona Plessner Lyons, Ed.D.

>    Lecturer on Education, Harvard Graduate School of Education, Cambridge,
>    Mass. Current research examines the following: conflict negotiation and
>    ethical decision making of girls; men and women managers; and ways in
>    which teachers make choices in the practice of their craft.

Susan Pollak, Ed.D.

>    Associate Psychologist, Mount Auburn Hospital, Cambridge, Mass.; frequent
>    contributor to *Psychology Today*; co-editor with Merry White of *The Cultural
>    Transition* (Routledge & Kegan Paul, 1986).

Jill McLean Taylor, Ed.M.

>    Doctoral candidate, Harvard Graduate School of Education, Cambridge, Mass.
>    Currently directing study in Cambridge school system examining adolescent
>    decision making. Continuing research on school-age pregnancy, adolescent
>    development, and moral development.

Janie Victoria Ward, Ed.D.

>    Assistant Professor of Education and Human Services, Simmons College,
>    Boston, Mass. Ongoing research focus on minority adolescent development,
>    particularly racial identity and its relationship to moral development.

Grant Wiggins, Ed.D.

>    Director of Research, Coalition of Essential Schools, Brown University,
>    Providence, R.I. Research interests in secondary school reform and
>    "thoughtfulness."

Ann Willard, Ed.D.

>    Staff Psychologist, Eliot Mental Health Center, Concord, Mass.; private
>    practice in Wellesley, Mass. Current research interests focus on decision
>    making in women's lives.

# PREFACE

**Carol Gilligan**

In the fall of this year, a woman from Memphis sent me a letter with a newspaper clipping. Children had been asked to write essays on how to improve their city, and the journalist noticed a difference between essays written by boys and by girls. To the boys, improving the city meant urban renewal as we generally conceive it: more parks, new buildings, renovations, better streets, more lighting. Girls, however, wrote about improving the city in a way the reporter found surprising. They suggested strengthening relationships between people: responding to people in need and taking action to help them. Now a professor of law, the writer of the letter explained that she had read *In a Different Voice* at Yale Law School and thought I would appreciate the illustration.

Such evidence, sometimes called "anecdotal," sometimes "naturalistic," poses a quandary for psychologists: how to interpret this difference or what to make of such observations? Differences in the way people speak about themselves, their lives, or their city may make little difference in how they live or have little impact on what they do. But the example contained in the newspaper clipping raises a further question: why do the same words (such as "improving the city") have different meanings for different people? Whose meanings will prevail and be taken as "right" or definitive? What are the implications of seeing or speaking in what is considered to be the "right" language?

The essays brought together in this volume examine a difference in moral voice and moral orientation. This shift in voice and perspective, initially described in *In a Different Voice*, affects the language of psychology and education. What is at stake is the meaning of such key words as "self," "relationship," "morality," and "development." The differences between a "justice perspective" and a "care perspective" are explored here in a variety of studies undertaken in different contexts. A common finding of these studies is that two voices can be distinguished by listening to the ways people speak about moral problems. These voices suggest different ways of experiencing oneself in relation to others. The observation that only one voice is acknowledged and well delineated within the fields of psychology and education as presently constituted draws attention to the fate of the other. The association of moral voice with gender, as in the opening example of the children's essay contest, renders the subject matter of these essays both political and controversial.

The papers here represent a collaborative effort to bring to bear considerations of moral voice and gender on discussions of psychological development and education. Identifying a justice perspective and a male speaker as normative within the fields of psychology and education, we sought to explore the implications for theory and practice of listening to girls and women and including a care perspective. For this purpose, we formed a center at the Harvard Graduate School of Education. The work of the center as it evolved over time--one study building on another-- suggests a new mapping of the moral domain, a new framework for theories of psychological development, and new directions for the practice of psychotherapy and education. But it also suggests a variety of questions for future research and points out the need for new research approaches and strategies.

In presenting the work of an ongoing research project, we hope that others will benefit from our insights and learn from our errors. To this end, we have included here both reports of individual studies and essays summarizing these studies and considering their implications. Throughout, the relationship between justice and care voices or perspectives is examined and reconsidered, and the relationship that emerges between moral voice, moral orientation, and gender becomes progressively clearer and more refined.

The essays in Part I demonstrate how the voices of justice and care define the coordinates for a new theoretical framework. These two moral voices draw attention to the vulnerability of people to oppression and to abandonment--vulnerabilities which are built into the human life cycle and constitute grounds for moral concern. The first essay, "Remapping the Moral Domain," establishes the close relationship between conceptions of self and conceptions of morality, linking the ethics of justice and care to different ways of imagining the self in relation to others. These different images of self in relationship create a genuine sense of moral ambiguity. In the essays that follow, two moral voices and perspectives are explored systematically in an effort to create a standard method for assessing moral voice and establishing moral orientation. Lyons' work represents the first step in that direction, a breakthrough which opens the way for subsequent work. Johnston carries this effort further by demonstrating that a person's spontaneous response to a moral problem is not necessarily the one which she or he deems best or preferable. By the age of eleven, most children can solve moral problems both in terms of rights (a justice approach) and in terms of response (a care approach). The fact that a person adopts one approach in solving a problem does not mean that he or she does not know or appreciate others.

The essay, "Two Moral Orientations," carries this discussion further by delineating the "focus phenomenon," the tendency for people to focus either on considerations of justice or considerations of care when describing an experience of moral conflict and choice. This work clarifies the "different voice" phenomenon. A care focus in moral reasoning, although not charac-teristic of all women, was almost exclusively a female phenomenon in three groups of educationally advantaged North Americans. Bardige's essay then raises the question: is a care perspective at risk in early adolescence, during the shift from primary to secondary education? Bardige's work suggests that girls who *appear* to exemplify lower levels of cognitive functioning in early adolescence, in fact, may be *resisting* the detachment which characterizes abstract or formal reasoning. In Bardige's study, this resistance consists of taking evidence of violence at face value. The issue of violence remains central in the final essay of Part I: "The Origins of Morality in Early Childhood Relationships." The skepticism with which psychologists greet reports of sex differences in empathy or moral reasoning is examined here against the evidence of stark sex differences in such morally relevant behavior as the incidence of violent crime and the care of young children. A new theoretical framework is seen as necessary if psychologists are both to embrace sociological facts and general observations and yet not promulgate a simplistic view of "male" and "female" behavior. Justice and care as two ideals of human relationship provide the coordinates for a new theory of human development. Two ways of thinking about moral reasoning and moral emotions when taken together can account for observed similarities and differences between males and females.

In Part II, the two-voice framework defines a new approach to the question: what constitutes development in adolescence and adulthood and to the related question: what are the goals of secondary and professional education? The initial essay, "Exit-Voice Dilemmas in Adolescent Development," written as part of a *festschrift* for the economist, Albert O. Hirschman, notes the parallel between theories of economic development and psychological development. Hirschman's analysis of different responses to decline in social organizations is transposed to the domain of adolescence where the drama between "exit" and "voice" solutions draws attention to new meanings of loyalty. The concern with faulty models of development then becomes directed to the consideration of inner city youth. Psychologists typically report a correlation between social class and moral development--a correlation that has been passionately attacked by Robert Coles. Here Ward's study of urban adolescents' reflections on violence they have witnessed provides evidence that urban teens reason in terms of both justice and care and that these moral voices carry different perspectives on violence. Ward's study opens the way to further research, by providing new categories of analysis (combinations of care and justice) and by suggesting that care reasoning may forestall violent responses to violence or violation.

Two chapters on adult development by Attanucci and Willard focus specifically on the experience of mothers. These essays examine the nature of care as well as misrepresentations of care, especially the concept of care that is linked to conventional conceptions of feminine "goodness." Both essays stress the terms in which mothers describe themselves as mothers, underscoring the difference between mothers' "own terms" and the terms of mothering which are embedded in current cultural scripts for women, such as psychologists' scripts for good or "good enough" mothers and media images of modern "superwoman." In the final two chapters, issues of care and justice are considered within the current practice of law and medicine, and questions are raised about the practice and the goals of medical and legal education. Both essays challenge the developmental model which equates adulthood with a justice perspective, and maturity with separation, self-sufficiency, and independence. Medical students and lawyers, speaking from a care perspective, with its underlying premise of connection or inter-dependence between self and others, draw attention to the ways in which people affect and are moved by one another--both wittingly and unwitting-ly. The vulnerability or openness of people to one another enables people to wound one another and also creates a powerful channel for help. Such openness, thus, is both a mark of human frailty and a source of human strength.

A word, finally, about the politics and the controversy of this research. The stark fact of the all-male research sample, accepted for years as rep-resentative by psychologists studying human development, in one sense speaks for itself. That such samples were not seen long ago as problematic by women or men points to different blindnesses on the part of each sex. The fact that these samples passed the scrutiny of peer review boards, and that studies of adolescence, moral development, and identity formation using all-male samples were repeatedly funded and widely published in pro-fessional journals indicates that the psychological research community needs to reexamine its claims to objectivity and dispassion. If the omission of half the human population was not seen, or not seen as significant, or not spoken about as a problem (by women or men), what other omissions are not being seen? On the simplest level, this collection of essays can be read as one answer--and a preliminary one at that--to the question: was anything missed by leaving out girls and women? The contribution of women's thinking, explored here in a variety of research contexts, is a different voice, a different way of speaking about relationships and about the experience of self. The inclusion of this voice changes the map of the moral domain. Listening to girls and women, we have come to listen differently to boys and men. And we have come to think differently about human nature and the human condition, and in turn, about psychology and education, disciplines devoted to understanding and improving human life.

# PROLOGUE

## ADOLESCENT DEVELOPMENT RECONSIDERED

### Carol Gilligan

In an essay, "On the Modern Element in Modern Literature," Lionel
Trilling writes of his discomfort in teaching the course in modern literature at Columbia College. No literature, he observes, "has ever been so
shockingly personal as ours--it asks every question that is forbidden in
polite society. It asks us if we are content with our marriages, with our
family lives, with our professional lives, with our friends . . . It asks us if
we are content with ourselves, if we are saved or damned." How is one to
teach such literature? After addressing the technicalities of verse patterns,
irony, and prose conventions, the teacher must confront the necessity of
bearing personal testimony, "must use whatever authority he may possess to
say whether or not a work is true, and if not, why not, and if so, why so"
(Trilling, 1967, pp. 164-165). Yet one can do this only at considerable
cost to one's privacy. What disturbs Trilling is that in the absence of such
personal confrontation the classroom lesson exemplifies the very problem
displayed in the novels--the costs of detachment and dispassion in the face
of what is most intensely passionate and personal.

To talk about the health of adolescents raises a similar problem.
Once we have covered the technicalities of physical disease and psychic
mechanisms, how will we respond to the adolescent's questions, or the
questions behind the questions: What is true? What is of value? Who
am I now? and Where is my home? I have studied identity and moral

development by listening to the ways in which people speak about themselves and about conflicts and choices they face. In this context, I have
thought about the nature of psychological growth as it pertains to questions
of truth and of value. Adolescence is a naturally occurring time of transition, a period when changes happen that affect the experience of self and
relationships with others. Thus, adolescence is a time of epistemological
crisis, an age when issues of interpretation come to the fore. The turbu-
lence and indeterminacy of adolescence, long noted and often attributed to
conflicts over sexuality and aggression, can also be traced to these interpretive problems. In this chapter, I will join concerns about the development of contemporary adolescents with concerns about questions of interpretation within psychology. I will begin by specifying four reasons for
reconsidering the psychology of adolescence at this time and then offer a
new framework for thinking about adolescent development and secondary
education.

## FOUR REASONS FOR RECONSIDERING ADOLESCENT DEVELOPMENT

The first reason for reexamining adolescent development is that our
view of childhood has changed. Since adolescence denotes the transition
from childhood to adulthood, what constitutes "development" in adolescence
hinges on how one views the childhood that precedes it and the adulthood
which follows. Recent research on infancy and early childhood reveals the
young child to be far more social than psychologists previously imagined,
calling into question most descriptions of the beginnings or early stages of
cognitive, social, and moral development. Daniel Stern's recent book, *The
Interpersonal World of the Infant* (1985), and Jerome Kagan's *The
Nature of the Child* (1984) document the interpersonal capabilities and
the social nature of young children: their responsiveness to others and
their appreciation of standards. Previously described as "locked up in
egocentrism," as "fused" with others, as capable only of "parallel play," the
young child now is observed to initiate and sustain connection with others,
to engage in patterns of social interaction with others, and, thus, to create
relationships with them. Robert Emde's research shows that nine-month-
old babies prefer mothers to respond to their actions rather than to mimic
or "mirror" their behavior (Emde *et al.*, 1987). In addition, infants by this

age have established specific patterns of social interaction with others, so
that their relationships with mother, father, caretaker, sibling, etc. can be
differentiated in these terms--by the researcher, and presumably by the
baby, since the patterns repeat. Thus, relationships, or connections with
others, are known to the young child as patterns of interaction that occur
in time and that extend through time: themes and variations.

It may well be that the tension between this felt knowledge of human
connection, this earliest grasp of what relationship means, and the ability
to represent this knowledge in language underlies many psychological
problems people experience and also many problems within the field of
psychology itself. Despite the fact that psychologists constantly talk about
interaction or relationship--between self and others, between person and
environment--the language of psychology is filled with static images of
separation. Thus, psychologists delineate borders and boundaries in an
effort to classify, categorize, and ultimately, to predict and control human
behavior, whereas behavior, especially when observed in its natural settings,
often resists such classification. At present, Martin Hoffman's (1976)
observations of empathy and altruism in young children and John Mordecai
Gottman's monograph, *How Children Become Friends* (1983), challenge
existing stage theories of social and moral development. These studies,
which derive from watching children in the natural settings of their daily
lives, reveal the disparity between the stage theory description of the young
child as "asocial" or "amoral," and the intensely social and also moral nature
of the young child's relationships with others. Like John Bowlby (1973,
1980), who observed the young child to grieve the loss that separation
entails, Hoffman saw young children perceive and respond to the needs
of others and Gottman saw children remember their friends, even after
surprisingly long intervals of physical distance and time.

These changes in the view of childhood necessitate a revision in the
description of adolescent development, since they alter the foundation upon
which psychologists have premised development in the teenage years. If
social responsiveness and moral concern are normally present in early childhood, their absence in adolescence becomes surprising. Rather than asking
why such capacities have failed to emerge by adolescence, implying that the
child is "stuck" at some earlier or lower stage, one would ask instead, what
has happened to the responsiveness of infancy, how have the child's capac-

ities for relationship been diminished or lost? This change in perspective also offers a new way of thinking about resistance, especially about signs of resistance on the part of adolescent girls (Gilligan, 1986). Rather than signalling conflicts over separation, such resistance may reflect a perception that connections with others are endangered for girls in the teenage years on a variety of levels.

The second reason for reconsidering what is meant by development in adolescence follows directly from this observation. Repeatedly (Bettelheim, 1965; Adelson & Doehrman, 1980), the inattention to girls has been noted as a lacuna in the literature on adolescence, which raises the question: What has been missed by not studying girls? The answer generally is felt to be something about relationships, and those who have studied girls and women confirm this speculation. Gisela Konopka entered the locked world of delinquent girls to learn their "own stories" and found that these stories were centrally about "loneliness accompanied by despair," a desperation of loneliness "based on a feeling of being unprotected, being incapable of making and finding friends, being surrounded by an anonymous and powerful adult world" (Konopka, 1966, p. 40). Konopka observed that although the need for connection with others, which means involvement with others who are "real friends" or with an adult who appears as "a person," is unusually intense among delinquent girls, the "need for *dependence* . . . seems to exist in all adolescent girls" (pp. 40–41, emphasis in original). Jean Baker Miller, writing in the mid-1970s about women who came for psychotherapy, noted that women's sense of self is built around being able to make and then maintain connections with others and that a loss of relationship is experienced by many women as tantamount to a loss of self (Miller, 1976). Listening to girls and women speaking about themselves and about their experiences of conflict and choice in a variety of situations, I heard conceptions of self and morality that implied a different way of thinking about relationships, one that often had set women apart from the mainstream of Western thought because of its central premise that self and others were connected and interdependent (Gilligan, 1977, 1982, 1984, 1986).

Thus, to say what is true--that girls and women, as the 1980 *Handbook of Adolescent Psychology* (Adelson & Doehrmann) put it, "have simply not been much studied"--is only to begin to appreciate what such study might entail. To reconsider adolescent development in light of the inattention to girls and women is to hold in abeyance the meaning of such key terms of psychological analysis as "self" and "development" and perhaps above all, "relationship."

For the present, to take seriously psychologists' past omission of girls and women in the formulation of developmental theory, and to see this absence as potentially significant, means to suspend for the moment all discussion of sex differences until the standards of assessment and the terms of comparison can be drawn from studies of girls and women as well as from studies of boys and men. The deep sense of outrage and despair over disconnection, tapped by Konopka, by Miller, by me, and by others--the strong feelings and the judgments often made by girls and women about being excluded, left out, and abandoned, as well as the desperate actions girls and women often take in the face of detachment, indifference, or lack of concern--may reflect an awareness on some level of the disjunction between women's lives and Western culture. Yet the equally strong judgments made by girls and women that such feelings are illegiti- mate and that their exclusion is justified or deserved serve to undercut this awareness. What the *Handbook of Adolescent Psychology* calls "the inatten- tion to girls and to the processes of feminine development in adolescence" (Adelson & Doehrmann, p. 114) tacitly supports the suspicion of girls and women that nothing of importance or value can be learned by studying them. In the moral conflicts adolescent girls and women describe, a central and searing dilemma concerns this problem of disconnection: Is it better, women ask, to turn away from others or to abandon oneself? This question --whether to be "selfish" or "selfless" in choosing between self and others --rests on the premise that genuine connection must fail. One reason for reconsidering the psychology of adolescence is to examine this premise.

The third reason for reconsideration pertains specifically to cognitive development and involves the definition of cognition, what knowing and thinking mean. Following Sputnik in the late 1950s, Americans became concerned about the state of math and science education as part of an effort to "catch up with the Russians." The revival of Jean Piaget's work in the early 1960s provided a psychological rationale for this endeavor, since in Piaget's view, cognitive development was equivalent to the growth of mathematical and scientific thinking (see, for example, Inhelder & Piaget, 1958). This conception of cognitive development conveys a view of people as living in a timeless world of abstract rules. Within this framework, there is no reason for teaching history or languages or writing or for paying attention to art and music. And in fact, the flourishing of Piagetian theory within psychology over the past two decades has coincided with the decline of all these subjects in the secondary school curriculum.

Educators looking to psychology to justify curriculum decisions still can find little basis for teaching history or for encouraging students to learn more than one language or for emphasizing complex problems of interpretation and the strategies needed for reading ambiguous texts. In the timeless world of "critical thinking," the fact that one cannot say exactly the same thing in French and in English becomes essentially irrelevant to the development of intelligence. Diane Ravitch (1985) recently has chron-icled the decline of historical knowledge among high school students and lamented the transposition of history into social science. Yet the human-ities, in order to gain funding or to defend their place within the curric-ulum, have often had to justify their educational value in terms derived from analyzing the structure of mathematical and scientific reasoning.

The ahistorical approach to human events also underlies the fourth reason for reconsideration: namely, the overriding value psychologists have placed on separation, individuation, and autonomy. To see self-sufficiency as the hallmark of maturity conveys a view of adult life that is at odds with the human condition, a view that cannot sustain the kinds of long-term commitments and involvements with other people that are necessary for raising and educating a child or for citizenship in a democratic society (see Arendt, 1958). The equation of development with separation and of maturity with independence presumes a radical discontinuity of generations and encourages a view of human experience that is essentially divorced from history or time. Psychologists in characterizing adolescence as a time of "second individuation" (Blos, 1967) and in celebrating an identity that is "self-wrought" (Erikson, 1962), have encouraged a way of thinking in which the interdependence of human life and the reliance of people on one another becomes either problematic or tacit. The way in which this value framework influences the interpretation of research findings is apparent in an article on adolescents which recently appeared in the *Journal of Personality and Social Psychology* (Pipp *et al.*, 1985).

Pipp *et al.* set out to discover how adolescents view their relationships with their parents over time--what changes they see in such connections from early childhood to late adolescence. Thus, college sophomores, those venerable stalwarts of psychological research, were asked to indicate in drawings and questionnaires the nature of their relationship with their parents at five points in time ranging from early childhood to the present. The authors note two distinct trends. One trend was expected and is familiar to anyone conversant with developmental theory. It consists of a linear progression whereby incrementally over time child and parent move from a relationship of inequality toward an ideal of equality. Thus, adolescents portray themselves as gaining steadily in responsibility, dominance, and independence in relation to their parents who, over time, decline on all these dimensions. With this shift in the balance of power, child and parent become increasingly alike or similar. The second trend noted was unanticipated and showed "a striking discontinuity." With respect to variables pertaining to love and closeness, college sophomores saw their relationships with their parents as closer at present than in the years preceding and as more similar in this respect to the relationships which they remembered having with their parents in early childhood. In addition, differences emerged along these two dimensions between the ways students represented their relationships with their mothers and fathers. They felt "more responsibility" toward their mothers, whom they perceived as "especially friendly," and they felt more similar to their fathers, whom they perceived as more dominant.

The unexpected findings of two asymmetrical lines of development tied to different experiences of self and relationship is of great interest to me because it corroborates the developmental model I have derived from analyzing the ways people describe themselves and make moral judgments, a model built on the distinction between equality and attachment as two dimensions of relationship that shape the experience of "self" and define the terms of moral conflict. For the moment, however, I wish to focus on the way Pipp *et al.* interpret their findings and specifically to note that in discussing their results, they collapse the two trends they report in a way that reveals an overriding concern with equality and independence. Thus, they take the fact that 19-year-olds describe themselves as their parents' children as a sign of limitation, an indication that the process of individuation is not yet complete.

> Although [our subjects] felt themselves to be more independent of the relationship than their parents were, there were indications that they still felt themselves to be their parents' children . . . The results suggest that the individuation process is still ongoing at the age of 19. It would be interesting to see whether it continues throughout adulthood. (Pipp *et al.*, 1985, p. 1001)

With this interpretation, the authors align themselves with the field of psychology in general. Viewing childhood attachments as leading developmentally toward separation, they portray continuing connections between adolescents and parents as a sign of dependence, negatively valued and considered as a source of limitation.

To summarize this first section, the need to reconsider adolescent development at present stems from changes in the understanding of infancy and childhood, the recognition that girls have not been much studied and that the studies of girls that do exist are often overlooked or not cited, the observation that Piagetian theories of cognitive development provide no rationale for roughly half of what has traditionally been regarded as the essence of a liberal arts or humanistic education, and the fact that a psychology of adolescence, anchored in the values of separation and independence, fails to represent the interdependence of adult life and thus, conveys a distorted image of the human condition, an image that fosters what is currently called "the culture of narcissism."

I take from these observations several cautions: that there is a need for new concepts and new categories of interpretation; that the accumulation of data according to old conceptual frameworks simply extends these problems; that the assessment of sex differences cannot be fully undertaken until female development is better understood; that such understanding may change the description of both male and female development; and that the approach to the psychology of adolescence and to subjects pertaining to adolescent development and education must be informed by the insights of such disciplines as anthropology, history, and literature. Specifically, psychologists need to incorporate the anthropologist's recognition of the dangers in imposing one set of ethnocentric categories on another population and take on the concerns of anthropologists, historians, and literary critics with the complexity of interpretation and the construction of alternative world views.

## FORMULATING AN APPROACH

In an issue of *Daedalus* (1971) devoted to the subject of early adolescence, several articles addressed the question of values. If the high school does not have a coherent set of values or a moral philosophy, Kagan argued, as did Lawrence Kohlberg and I, it cannot engage the commitment of its students. The school and the culture-at-large must offer some justification for learning to adolescents who are distracted by other concerns, who are capable of spotting contradiction, who have a keen eye for adult hypocrisy, and who are unwilling to put their self-esteem on the line when failure seems inescapable. Bruno Bettelheim some years earlier had linked the problems of youth to the problem of generations: "Whenever the older generation has lost its bearings," he wrote, "the younger generation is lost with it. The positive alternatives of emulation or revolt are replaced with the lost quality of neither" (1965, p. 106). Erik Erikson, writing at a time when the dissent of contemporary youth was rising, noted that for adults "to share true authority with the young would mean to acknowledge something which adults have learned to mistrust in themselves: a truly ethical potential" (1975, p. 223). To Erikson, ethical concerns were a natural meeting ground between adults and adolescents, both rendered uncertain by the predicament of modern civilization.

Yet if ethical questions are inescapable in relations between adults and adolescents, if the problems of adolescents are in some sense a barometer of the health of civilization and a measure of the culture's productive and reproductive potential, the issues raised by Trilling become central: How are adults to address the ethical problems of modern society? What claims to moral authority do the teachers of adolescents possess? The great modern novels that Trilling was teaching had as a central and controlling theme --"the disenchantment of our culture with culture itself . . . a bitter line of hostility to civilization" (p. 60). Thus, the urgency of the questions: Are we content with our marriages, our work, and ourselves? How do we envision salvation? What wisdom can we pass on to the next generation? Twentieth century history has only heightened ambivalence toward the life

of civilization by demonstrating in Germany, one of the most highly
educated and cultured of nations, a capacity for moral atrocity so extreme
as to strain the meaning of words.  In light of this history, any equation of
morality with culture or intelligence or education is immediately suspect,
and this suspicion may have opened the way for the current revival of
religious fundamentalism and of terrorism, as well as for the present
skepticism about nineteenth century ideas about development or progress.
The idea of "surrendering oneself to experience without regard to self-
interest or conventional morality, of escaping wholly from the societal
bonds, is," Trilling notes, "an ' element ' somewhere in the mind of every
modern person" (p. 82).  This element is manifest in one form or another
in many of the problems of today's adolescents.

The awesome power of the irrational in human behavior is the subject
of both classical tragedy and modern psychology, each attempting in different ways to untangle and explain its "logic," to understand why people
pursue paths that are clearly marked as self-destructive.  Why, for example,
do teenagers stop eating, abuse drugs, commit suicide, and in a variety of
other ways wreak havoc with their future?  Two approaches currently
characterize the response of professionals to these signs of disease.  One
approach relies on the imposition of control and seeks to override a tortu-
ous reason with behavior modification and biofeedback, to focus attention
on physical survival by teaching skills for managing stress and regulating
food and alcohol consumption.  The other approach reaches into reason and
joins the humanistic faith in the power of education with the insights of
modern psychology.  Positing human development as the aim of education, it
turns attention to the question:  What constitutes and fosters development?

My interest in adolescence is anchored in this approach.  It was
spurred by Erikson's attention to the relationship between life history and
history and by two insights in the work of Kohlberg:  first, that following
the Nazi holocaust, psychologists must address the problem of moral relativism, and second, that adolescents are passionately interested in moral
questions.  Thus, adolescence may be a critical time for moral education.
Erikson's study of Martin Luther highlighted the central tie between questions of identity and questions of morality in the adolescent years.  But it
also called attention to a set of beliefs that extend from the theology of
Luther's Reformation into the ideology of contemporary psychology:

a world view in which the individual is embarked on a solitary journey toward personal salvation, a world view that is centered on the values of autonomy and independence. Luther's statements of repudiation and affirmation, "I am not" and "Here I stand," have become emblematic of the identity crisis in modern times, a crisis that begins with the separation of "self" from childhood identifications and attachments and ends with some version of Luther's statement: "I have faith, therefore I am justified." In a secular age, the faith and the justification have become psychological. The limitations of this vision have been elaborated by a variety of social critics and are closely connected to the reasons I have given for reconsidering the psychology of adolescence: namely, the view of childhood attachments as dispensable or replaceable, the absence of women from the cosmology, the equation of thinking with formal logic, and the value placed on self-sufficiency and independence. Such criticisms are augmented by the facts of recent social history: the rise among teenagers of suicide, eating disorders, and educational problems. The need at present for new directions in theory and practice seems clear.

## TWO MORAL VOICES:  TWO FRAMEWORKS FOR PROBLEM-SOLVING

My approach to development is attentive to a moral voice that reveals the lineaments of an alternative world view. Seemingly anomalous data from studies involving girls and women called attention to moral judgments that did not fit the definition of "moral" and to self-descriptions at odds with the concept of "self." The data that initially appeared discrepant, thus, became the basis for a reformulation, grounds for thinking again about what "self" and "morality" mean (Gilligan, 1977, 1982).

Two moral voices signalled different ways of thinking about what constitutes a moral problem and how such problems can be addressed or solved. In addition, two voices draw attention to the fact that a story can be told from different angles and a situation seen in different lights. Like ambiguous figure perception where the same picture can be seen as a vase or as two faces, the basic elements of moral judgment--self, others, and the relationship between them--can be organized in different ways, depending on how "relationship" is imagined or construed. From the perspective of someone seeking or loving justice, relationships are organized in terms of

equality, symbolized by the balancing of scales. Moral concerns focus on
problems of oppression, problems stemming from inequality, and the
moral ideal is one of reciprocity or equal respect. From the perspective of
someone seeking or valuing care, relationship connotes responsiveness or
engagement, a resiliency of connection that is symbolized by a network or
web. Moral concerns focus on problems of detachment, on disconnection
or abandonment or indifference, and the moral ideal is one of attention
and response. Since all relationships can be characterized both in terms of
equality and in terms of attachment or connection, all relationships--public
and private--can be seen in two ways and spoken of in two sets of terms.
By adopting one or another moral voice or standpoint, people can highlight
problems that are associated with different kinds of vulnerability--to
oppression or to abandonment--and focus attention on different types of
concern.

A series of studies produced systematic evidence that people raise both
justice and care concerns in describing moral conflicts and that these concerns organize people's thinking about choices they make. In these studies,
people were asked to discuss conflicts and choices that they actually faced.
By asking people to speak about such conflicts, it was possible to examine
how people think about the age-old questions of how to live and what to
do. Most of the people who participated in these studies, primarily North
American adolescents and adults, raised considerations of both justice and
care when describing an experience of moral conflict. Yet they tended to
focus their attention on either justice or care concerns, elaborating one set
of concerns and minimally representing the other. The surprising finding
of these studies was the extent of this "focus" phenomenon. For example,
with focus defined as 75 percent or more concerns raised pertaining to
issues of justice or to issues of care, fifty-three out of eighty educationally
advantaged adolescents and adults, or two-thirds of the sample, demonstrated focus. The remaining third raised roughly equal numbers of justice
and care considerations (Gilligan & Attanucci, see Chapter 4).

The tendency for people to organize experiences of conflict and choice
largely in terms of justice or of care has been a consistent finding of research on moral orientation, ranging from Nona Lyons' (1983) and Sharry
Langdale's (1983) reports of orientation predominance, to the more strin-
gent analysis of orientation focus (Gilligan & Attanucci, this volume), to

the more interpretative analysis of "narrative strategies" (Brown *et al.*, 1987). The narrative strategy approach takes into account not simply the number or proportion of justice and care considerations raised but also the way in which concerns about justice and care are presented in relation to one another and in relation to the speaker or narrator of the dilemma; that is, whether justice and care concerns are presented separately or integrated, whether one or both sets of concerns are aligned with the narrator's voice (the "I") or claimed as the speaker's "own terms" (see Brown *et al.*). The fact that two moral voices can repeatedly be distinguished in narratives of moral conflict and choice, together with the fact that people tend to focus their attention either on problems of unfairness or on problems of disconnection gives credence to the interpretation of justice and care as distinct moral voices and as organizing frameworks for thoughts and feelings. The focus phenomenon, furthermore, suggests that people tend to lose sight of one perspective or to silence one voice in arriving at decisions or in justifying choices they have made.

The tendency to focus was equally characteristic of both the men and the women studied, suggesting that loss of perspective is a liability that both sexes share. There were sex differences, however, in the direction of focus. Of the thirty-one men who demonstrated focus, thirty focused on justice; among the twenty-two women who demonstrated focus, ten focused on justice and twelve on care. Care focus, although not characteristic of all women, was almost exclusively a female phenomenon in three samples of educationally advantaged North Americans. If girls and women were eliminated from the study, care focus in moral reasoning would virtually disappear.

With this clarification of the different voice phenomenon (the thematic shift in outlook or perspective, the change in the terms of moral discourse and self description, and the empirical association of these differences with women), it becomes possible to turn to new questions about development in adolescence and about psychological interpretation, as well as to concerns about moral relativism and moral education. It is noteworthy that both sexes raise considerations of care in describing moral conflicts they face and thus, identify problems of care and connection as subjects of moral concern. Yet it is women's elaboration of care considerations that reveals the coherence of a care ethic as a framework for decision. Women's think-

ing reveals how concerns about responsiveness and human relationship co-
here to form a world view or way of constructing social reality, as well as
a problem-solving strategy--a focal point for thinking about action and
choice. The description of care concerns as the focus of a coherent moral
perspective rather than as a sign of deficiency in women's moral reasoning
(or a subordinate set of moral concerns within an overarching justice
framework, such as concerns about special obligations or personal dilemmas) recasts the moral domain as one comprising at least two moral orientations. Moral maturity then presumably entails an ability to see in at
least two ways and to speak at least two languages, and the relationship
between justice and care perspectives or voices becomes a key question
for investigation.

The significance of the concept of moral orientation for thinking
about development in adolescence is illuminated by a study designed and
conducted by Kay Johnston (1985). Johnston set out to examine Michael
Polanyi's (1958) suggestion that there are two conflicting aspects of
formalized intelligence, one that depends on the acquisition of formalized
instruments (such as propositional logic), and one that depends on the
"pervasive participation of the knowing person in the act of knowing."
Polanyi considers the latter kind of intelligence to rest on "an art which is
essentially inarticulate" (Polanyi, 1958, p. 70). Johnston's question was
whether this way of knowing could be articulated. Her approach to this
question was informed by Lev Vygotsky's theory that all of the higher
cognitive functions (voluntary attention, logical memory, formation of
concepts) originate as actual relations between individuals, so that in the
course of development "an interpersonal process is transformed into an
intrapersonal one" (Vygotsky, 1978, p. 57). Vygotsky's theory allows for
individual differences that are not developmental differences and offers a
way of explaining how different experiences of relationships might lead to
different ways of thinking about a problem. According to Vygotsky's
theory of cognitive development, the sex differences in early childhood
relationships which Nancy Chodorow (1978) describes would set the
stage for differences in cognition and, thus, moral reasoning. Furthermore,
groups like women whose experience has been neglected in defining cognitive and moral proficiency may exemplify ways of thinking or know-

ing which appear, in the present context, to be inarticulate. Johnston's question was whether tacit knowledge or "intuitive" forms of knowing-- what Mary Belenky *et al.* (1986) have subsequently called "connected knowing"--might appear as different forms of moral problem solving.

Thus, she asked sixty eleven- and fifteen-year-olds from two schools in a typical middle-class suburb to state and to solve the problem posed in two of Aesop's fables. Of the sixty children, fifty-four (or fifty-six, depending on the fable) initially cast the problem either as a problem of rights or as a problem of response, framing it *either* as a conflict of claims that could be resolved by appealing to a fair procedure or a rule for adjudicating conflicting claims, *or* as a problem of need which raised the question: Was there a way to respond to all of the needs? Each way of defining the fable problem was associated with a different problem-solving strategy, suggesting that each moral orientation facilitates the development of a different kind of reasoning. For example, in the fable, "The Moles and the Porcupine" (see Chapter 3, Appendix), a justice orientation focused on identifying and prioritizing conflicting rights or claims ("The porcupine has to go definitely. It's the moles' house"). In contrast, a care orienta- tion focused on identifying needs and creating a solution responsive to the needs of all involved ["Cover the porcupine with a blanket" (so that the moles will not be stuck and the porcupine will have shelter) or "Dig a bigger hole"]. It is important to stress that these two approaches are not opposites or mirror images of one another (with justice uncaring and care unjust). Instead they constitute different ways of organizing the problem that lead to different reasoning strategies, different ways of thinking about what is happening and what to do.

An innovative aspect of Johnston's design lay in the fact that after the children had stated and solved the fable problems, she asked, "Is there another way to think about this problem?" About half of the children, somewhat more fifteen- than eleven-year-olds, spontaneously switched orientation and solved the problem in the other mode. Others did so fol- lowing a cue as to the form such a switch might take ("Some people say you could have a rule," or "some people say you could solve the dilemma so that all of the animals will be satisfied"). Then Johnston asked, "Which of these solutions is the best solution?" With few exceptions, the children answered this question, saying which solution was better and explaining the reasons why.

This study was a watershed in my thinking about developmental theory and research practices. The fact that people solve a problem in one way clearly does not mean that they do not have access to other approaches. Furthermore, a person's initial or "spontaneous" approach to a problem is not necessarily the one which he or she would deem preferable after more consideration. Eleven- and fifteen-year-olds were able to explain why they adopt problem-solving strategies that they see as problematic and to give reasons why they put aside ways of thinking which in their own eyes seem preferable. Whether there are reasons other than the ones they cite is, in this context, beside the point. The fact that boys who choose justice strategies but say they prefer care solutions consider care solutions to be naive and unworkable is in itself of significance. For example, in one high school, students of both sexes tended to characterize care-focused solutions or inclusive problem-solving strategies as utopian or outdated; one student linked them with impractical Sunday school teachings, another with the outworn philosophy of "hippies." Presumably, students in the school who voiced care strategies would encounter these reactions from their peers.

The tendency for children to define the fable problem in terms either of rights or of response, combined with their ability to switch orientations, heightens the analogy to ambiguous figure perception but also raises questions. Why do some people focus on justice and some on care when considering the same problem? Furthermore, why do some people see rights solutions as better and others see response solutions as preferable in the same situation? Johnston found sex differences in both spontaneous moral orientation and preferred orientation, with boys more often choosing and preferring justice formulations and girls more often choosing and preferring care strategies. In addition, she found differences in solutions to different fables, indicating that moral orientation is associated both with the sex of the reasoner and with the problem being considered (see Langdale, 1983, for similar findings).

Since people can adopt at least two moral standpoints and can solve problems in at least two different ways, the choice of moral standpoint, whether implicit or explicit, becomes an important feature of moral decision

making and of research on moral development.  The choice of moral standpoint adds a new dimension to the role commonly accorded "the self" in
moral decision making.  Traditionally in moral theory, the self is described
as choosing whether or not to enact moral standards or principles, as having or not having "a good will."  Yet the self, when conceived as a narrator of moral conflict or as a protagonist in a moral drama, also chooses,
consciously or unconsciously, where to stand, what signs to look for, and
what voices to listen to in thinking about what is happening (what is the
problem) and what to do.  People may have a preferred way of seeing,
listening, and speaking, so that one voice is more readily heard or understood by them.  Johnston demonstrated that at least by the age of eleven,
children know and can explain the logic of two problem-solving strategies
and will indicate why they see one or the other as preferable.  In adolescence, when thinking becomes more reflective and more self-conscious,
moral orientation may become closely entwined with self-definition, so
that the sense of self or feelings of personal integrity become aligned
with a particular way of seeing or speaking.

But adolescence, the time when thinking becomes self-consciously
interpretive, is also the time when the interpretive schemes of the culture,
including the system of social norms, values, and roles, impinge more
directly on perception and judgment, defining within the framework of a
given society what is "the right way" to see and to feel and to think, the
way "we" think.  Thus, adolescence is the age when thinking becomes
conventional.  Moral standpoint, a feature of an individual's moral reasoning, is also a characteristic of interpretive schemes, including the conventions of interpretation or the intellectual conventions that are taught
in secondary education.  A justice focus, which is explicit in theories of
moral development (Freud, 1925; Piaget, 1932; Kohlberg, 1969), also may
characterize other psychological theories and, thus, may in part explain the
correlation between tests of moral development and tests of cognitive,
social, and emotional development.  Although measuring different things,
all these tests may be measuring from the same angle.  Thus, a care focus,
which otherwise can be viewed as one aspect of moral reasoning, becomes a
critical perspective on an interpretive level, challenging the prevailing world
view.  Here the questions raised by Trilling become especially pertinent
because they articulate a central theme in modern culture that is at odds

with the dominant viewpoint in contemporary psychology, the theme of disenchantment. Psychology's response to the moral crisis of modern civilization has become a kind of heady optimism, reflected in the language of current stage theories of development and in educational or therapeutic interventions which convey the impression that the nature of moral maturity is clear and the road to development apparent. To bring in a standpoint missing from such theories enlarges the definition of cognition and morality and renders the portrayal of human development and moral dilemmas more complex.

## AN EXAMPLE OF ALTERNATIVE WORLD VIEWS

The following example of moral reasoning taken from a study of high school students, speaks directly to the matter of missing standpoint and suggests how a prevailing justice orientation may impinge on the judgments adolescents make, influencing the concerns that they voice and also what concerns they hold back or keep silent. The example contains both a theoretical point and a methodological caution: two judgments, one directly stated and one indirectly presented, highlight a developmental tension between detachment and connection and underscore the limitations of data gathered without attention to the issue of standpoint or the possibility of alternative frameworks or world views. At the heart of this illustration of alternative world views and the problems they pose is a critical but subtle shift in perspective, caught colloquially by the difference between being "centered in oneself" and being "self-centered."

A high school student, Anne, was attending a traditional preparatory school for academically talented and ambitious students, a boys' school which in recent years had become coeducational. When asked to describe a moral conflict she faced, Anne spoke about her decision not to buy cigarettes for someone who asked her to do so. Her reasoning focused on considerations of justice: "If I am against smoking, but yet I buy cigarettes for a person, I think I am contradicting myself." Non-contradiction here means reciprocity in the sense of applying the same standard to herself and to others, treating others as she would treat herself or want to be treated by them, and thereby showing equal respect for persons. Asked if she thought she had done the right thing, she answers: "Yes . . . I think it was, because I did not contradict myself, because I held with what

I believed." Thus, she assesses the rightness of her decision by examining the consistency between her actions and her beliefs, justified on grounds of respect for life and valuing health. Then she is asked: "Is there another way to see the problem?" and she says:

> Well, no. I mean, yes. It is not as simple as buying cigarettes or not. It has a lot to do with everything that I believe in . . . In another sense, it repre- sents how I just, how I deal with what I believe. I try not to break down be- cause somebody pressures me, but I don't feel like I get into situations like they always write about in books . . . I don't think people are represented the way they are sometimes.

It is important to emphasize that this intimation of another way of seeing and the suggestion that the way people and situations are commonly represented may not be an accurate representation, occur only after the interpretive question is raised: "Is there another way to see the problem?" And the interpretive question leads to confusion, to a dense statement that appears to alternate between two perspectives, one elaborated and one implied. The implied perspective, which "has a lot to do with everything that I believe in," is only clarified when Anne speaks about a friend whom she characterizes as "self-centered." In this context, the meaning of being "self-centered" shifts from "holding with what I believed" to "not thinking about how one's words or actions affect other people." With this shift, the alternative world view and the problem posed by alternative world views become clear.

Anne says that her friend does not recognize how what she says affects other people. "She does not think about how it affects them, but just about the fact that she told them." In other words, she acts as if speaking could be divorced from listening, or words from interpretation. Because her friend is inattentive to differences in interpretation, she "does not always recognize that what she likes to hear is not what other people like to hear, but may hurt their feelings." She is self-centered in that she does not realize that "other people are not all like her."

Attention to differences in interpretation, thus, is central to making connection with others. The interpretive question raised by the researcher that leads Anne to attend to the issue of perspective also leads her into a way of thinking where the failure to see differences becomes morally problematic, signifying carelessness or detachment (being self-centered) and creating the conditions for the unwitting infliction of hurt. This is a very different set of concerns from the concerns about non-contradiction and acting consistently with her beliefs which characterized Anne's justice reasoning. With the shift in perspective, the word "autonomy" takes on different connotations: to be self-regulating or self-governing can mean being centered in oneself but it also can mean not attending or responding to others. The tension between these two ways of seeing and listening creates a conflict which, as Anne says, is "not as simple as buying cigarettes or not," a conflict which, in addition, is not well represented by the common depiction of adolescent moral conflicts as "peer pressure" problems.

Asked if she had learned anything from the experience, Anne speaks in two voices. She asserts her satisfaction with her ability "to stay with what I believe, and as far as learning something from it, I was able to say 'no' and so I could say it again." But she also asserts her unease about shutting herself off from others, about becoming impervious to the changing circumstances of her life and unresponsive to the people around her:

> . . . but I don't know that I will always say "no" to everything. You can't all the time, and as you can make better friends and as you are under different circumstances and different situations, I think my answers will change--as I become more like the people in this school. Because no matter where you are, you tend to become at least a little like the people around you.

Anne does not doubt the wisdom or the rightness of her decision to say "no" in this instance, but the incident raises a further question: How can she stay with herself and also be with other people? Viewing life as lived in the changing medium of time and seeing herself as open to the people around her, she believes that in time she and her answers will change. The dilemma or tension she faces is not that of peer pressure --how to say "no" to her friends or classmates. Instead, it stems from a different way of thinking about herself in relation to others, a way that leads into the question of what relationship, or in this instance friendship, means.

The ability to sustain two perspectives that offer divergent views of a scene or to tell a story from two different angles can be taken as a marker of cognitive and moral growth in adolescence, a sign perhaps, in the context of ordinary living, of what Keats called "negative capability," the ability of the artist to enter into and to take on ways of seeing and speaking that differ from one's own. For example, with respect to the question of separation or individuation as it pertains to adolescents' perceptions of their relationships with their parents, one teenager says: "I am not only my mother's daughter, I am also Susan." Another, describing her anger at her holding-on mother, recalls herself as saying to her mother: "You will always be my mother . . . I will always be your daughter, but you have to let go." These "not only . . . but also" constructions used by teenage girls in describing themselves in relation to their mothers hold two perspectives (their own and their mothers') in tension and convey a view of change as occurring in the context of continuing attachment or connection. Thus, these teenagers imply that development need not entail detachment, in part perhaps because they recognize that relationships cannot be replaced. From this standpoint, the moral problems engendered by the transformations of relationships in adolescence pertain not only to injustice and oppression but also to abandonment and disloyalty. Thus seen, the psychology of adolescence takes on new dimensions. The much discussed problem of moral relativism is joined by the problem of moral reductionism, the temptation to simplify human dilemmas by claiming that there is only one moral standpoint.

## CONNECTION IN ADOLESCENCE

A study conducted at a high school for girls revealed that moral conflicts involve both problems of unfairness and problems of disconnection. As the balance of power between child and adult shifts with the child's coming of age, so too the experience and the meaning of connection change. What constitutes attachment in early childhood does not constitute connection in adolescence, given the sexual changes of puberty and also the growth of subjective feelings and reflective thought. Thus, the question arises: What are the analogues in adolescence to the responsive engagement which psychologists now find so striking in infancy and early childhood? What constitutes genuine connection in the adolescent years?

I raise this question to explicate a point of view which at first glance may seem inconsequential or even antithetical to concerns about adolescent development and health. One can readily applaud Anne's decision not to buy cigarettes for another (argued in terms of justice) and see her ability to say "no" as one that will stand her in good stead. My intention is not to qualify this judgment or to diminish the importance of this ability but to stress the importance of another as well. Like concerns about yielding to

pressure from others, concerns about not listening or becoming cut off
from others are also vital. The ability to create and to sustain human
connection in adolescence may, however, hinge on the ability to differentiate true from false relationship, to read the signs that distinguish authentic
from inauthentic forms of connection and thus, to protect the wish for
relationship or the willingness to be open to others from overwhelming
disappointment or defeat. The capacity for detachment in adolescence,
heightened by the growth of formal operational thinking and generally
prized as the hallmark of cognitive and moral development, is thus, double-
edged. It signals an ability to think critically about thinking but also has a
potential for becoming, in Anne's terms, "self-centered." Although detachment connotes the dispassion which signifies fairness in justice reasoning,
the ability to stand back from oneself and from others and to weigh
conflicting claims even-handedly in the abstract, detachment also connotes
the absence of connection and has the potential to create the conditions
for carelessness or violation, for violence toward others or toward oneself.

The adolescent's question, Where am I going?, is rendered problematic
because adolescents lack experience in the ways of adult work and love.
High school students, including inner city youth living in poverty, often
speak about their plans to work and to have a family. Yet even if such
goals are clearly envisioned, teenagers have no experience in how to reach
them. When you don't know where you are going or how the route goes,
the range of interpretation opens up enormously. If, for example, you are
going to the store, all signs read "to the store." But if you have never
been there before, even if you know you are looking for the store, the
signs may be unclear. The adolescent's question, Where is my home?, is
commonly raised by college students who wonder, is it here at school, or
back in Ohio or Larchmont? Where will it be in the future? How do I
interpret whatever new moves I make in my life? (Kaplan, 1985).

These interpretive questions fall on the line of intellectual and ethical
development that William Perry (1968) has traced, a line leading from
a belief that truth is objective and known by authorities to a belief that
truth is contextually relative and responsibility for commitment inescapable.
Yet Perry, although addressing the existential dilemma, leaves open the
issue of detachment that bothered Trilling, posing the teaching quandary he
raised: What commitments can one defend as worth making and on what

basis can one claim authority? Erikson (1968) wrote about the penchant of adolescents for absolute truths and totalistic solutions, the proclivity to end, once and for all, all uncertainty and confusion by seizing control and attempting to stop time or blot out or eliminate in one way or another the source of confusion, in others or in oneself. Many destructive actions on the part of adolescents can be understood in these terms. Because adolescents are capable not only of abstract logical thinking but also of participating in the act of knowing, because they are in some sense aware of subjectivity and perspective or point of view, because they are, therefore, able to see through false claims to authority at the same time as they yearn for right answers or for someone who will tell them how they should live and what they should do, the temptation for adults dealing with adolescents is to opt for the alternatives of permissiveness or authoritarianism and to evade the problems that lie in taking what Diana Baumrind (1978) has called an "authoritative" stance.

## RESISTING DETACHMENT

One problem in taking an authoritative stance with adolescents is that many of the adults involved with adolescents have little authority in this society. Therefore, although they may, in fact, know much about teenagers' lives, they may have little confidence in their knowledge. Rather than claiming authority, they may detach their actions from their judgment and attribute their decisions to the judgments of those who are in positions of greater social power. But another problem lies in the perennial quandary: what actions to take in attempting to guide teenagers away from paths clearly marked as destructive and how to read the signs that point in the direction of health. To reconsider the nature of development in adolescence itself raises a question of perspective--from what angle or in what terms shall this reconsideration take place?

Recent studies of adolescents in families and schools have found that adolescents fare better in situations where adults listen, and that mothers and teachers are centrally important in teenagers' lives. Mothers are the parent with whom adolescents typically have the most contact, the one they talk with the most and perceive as knowing most about their lives (Youniss & Smollar, 1985). Most researchers consider it desirable for fathers to be more involved with adolescents, but they find, in general, that fathers do not spend as much time or talk as personally with teenage children as mothers do. In studies of schools, teachers are cited as central to the success of secondary education. The good high schools identified by Michael Rutter and his colleagues (1979) and by Sara Lightfoot (1983) are characterized by the presence of teachers who are able, within the framework of a coherent set of values or school ethos, to assume authority and to take responsibility for what they do. Yet increasingly, mothers of adolescents are single parents living in poverty, and teachers at present are generally unsupported and devalued. Psychological development in adolescence may well hinge on the adolescent's belief that her or his psyche is worth developing, and this belief in turn may hinge on the presence in a teenager's life of an adult who knows and cares about the teenager's psyche. Economic and psychological support for the mothers and the teachers who at present are the primary adults engaged with teenagers, thus, may be essential to the success of efforts to promote adolescent development.

The question of what stance or direction to take is focused by the concept of moral orientation and also by the research findings that suggest two lines of development and their points of tension. If a focus on care currently constitutes a critical interpretive standpoint and highlights problems in schools and society which need to be addressed, how can a care perspective be developed and sustained during adolescence? The evidence that among educationally advantaged North Americans care focus is demonstrated primarily by girls and women raises questions about the relationship between female development and secondary education. But it also suggests that girls may resist the prevailing ethos of detachment and disconnection and that this resistance has moral and political as well as psychological implications. Thus, the question arises: how and at what cost can this resistance be educated and sustained.

In analyzing women's thinking about what constitutes care and what connection means, I noted women's difficulty in including themselves among the people for whom they considered it moral to care. The inclusion of self is genuinely problematic not only for women but also for society in general. Self-inclusion on the part of women challenges the conventional understanding of feminine goodness by severing the link between care and self-sacrifice; in addition, the inclusion of women challenges the interpretive categories of the Western tradition, calling into question descriptions of human nature and holding up to scrutiny the meaning of "relationship," "love," "morality," and "self."

Perhaps for this reason, high school girls, describing care focus dilemmas, will say that their conflicts are "not moral problems" but "just" have to do with their lives and everything they believe in (Brown, 1986) --as Anne said when she intimated that, in fact, she had another way of seeing the dilemma which she had posed in justice terms. From a care standpoint, her otherwise praiseworthy ability to say "no" to others seemed potentially problematic; what had seemed a valuable ability to stay centered in herself, to hold with what she believed, now seemed, in part, self-centered, a way of cutting herself off from the people around her. Thus, "development" for girls in adolescence poses a conundrum. At the center of this puzzle are questions about connection: how to stay in touch with the world and with others and also with oneself. What are the possibilities for genuine connection with others? What are the signs that distinguish true from false relationship? What leads girls to persist in seeking respon- sive engagement with others? What risks are attendant on this quest? And finally, what are the moral, political, and psychological implications of resisting detachment? If one aim is to educate this resistance, secondary education may play a critical role in this process.

Betty Bardige (1983, and this volume) analyzed the journals kept by seventh and eighth graders as part of the social studies curriculum, *Facing History and Ourselves: Holocaust and Human Behavior* (Strom & Parsons, 1982). She found evidence of moral sensibilities which seemed to be at risk in early adolescence. Specifically, she observed that the journal entries written by eight of the twenty-four girls and one of the nineteen boys showed a willingness to take evidence of violence at face value, to take one's response to the perception that someone is being hurt as grounds for taking action to stop the violence. Because this responsiveness to evidence of violence was associated with less sophisticated forms of rea- soning, and because detachment and dispassion were linked with the ability to see both sides of a story, the tension between responsiveness and de- tachment poses an educational dilemma: how to develop moral sensibilities anchored in common sense perception while at the same time developing the capacity for logical thinking and reflective judgment. The priority given in the secondary school curriculum to reasoning from premises and deductive logic, the importance placed on "critical thinking" (defined as the ability to think about thinking in the abstract), often leaves uneducated or undeveloped the moral sensibilities that rely on a finely tuned perception. The ability to respond to what is taken in by seeing and listening can form a basis for recognizing false premises as well as provide grounds for knowing what is happening and for thinking about what to do.

Given the heightened self-consciousness of teenagers and their intense fear of ridicule or exposure, secondary education poses a major challenge to teachers: How to sustain among teenagers an openness to experience and a willingness to risk discovery? The responsiveness of the relationship between teacher and student, the extent to which such connections involve a true engagement or meeting of minds, may be critical in this regard (see Wiggins, 1987). Yet when reliance on human resources is construed as a sign of limitation and associated with childhood dependence, the ways in which people can and do help one another tend not to be represented. As a result, activities of care may be tacit or covertly undertaken or associated with idealized images of virtue and self-sacrifice. This poses a problem for teachers, for parents, and for adolescents, one which for a variety of reasons may fall particularly heavily on girls.

Psychologists recently have sought to understand the terms in which girls and women speak about their experience and have drawn attention to terms of relationship which suggest both a desire for responsive engagement with others and an understanding of what such connection entails (see Surrey, 1984; Miller, 1984, 1986; Belenky *et al.*, 1986; Josselson, 1987). Catherine Steiner-Adair (1986), studying the vulnerability of high school age girls to eating disorders, found that girls who articulate a "critical care perspective" in response to interview questions about their own future expectations and societal values for women are invulnerable to eating disorders, as measured by the Eating Attitudes Test. The critical care perspective constitutes a standpoint from which girls can reject the media image of the "superwoman" and cultural values that link separation and independence with success. Steiner-Adair found that in the educationally advantaged North American population where eating disorders currently are prevalent, girls who implicitly or explicitly take on or endorse the superwoman image, who do not identify a conflict between responsiveness in relationships and conventions of femininity or of success, are those

who appear vulnerable to eating disorders. Thus, girls who show signs
of vulnerability seem to be caught within a damaging framework of interpretation; when discussing their own future wishes and societal values, they
do not differentiate signs of responsiveness and connection from images of
perfection and control.

Along similar lines, Jane Attanucci (1984) and Ann Willard (1985
and this volume), studying educationally advantaged North American
mothers of young children, note the disparity between mothers' "own
terms" in speaking about their experiences as mothers and the terms used
to characterize mothers and "mothering" in contemporary cultural scripts.
Mothers' own terms include terms of relationships which convey mothers'
experience of connection with their children, so that caring for children is
neither "selfish" nor "selfless" in these terms. In contrast, the terms used
by psychologists to describe "good" or "good enough" mothers convey the
impression that mothers, insofar as they are good mothers, respond to their
children's needs rather than to their own, whereas women, insofar as they
are psychologically mature and healthy persons, meet their own needs and
separate themselves from their children. Willard found that women who
draw on their own experience of connection with their child in making
decisions about work and family (whatever the specific nature of these
decisions) tend not to suffer from symptoms of depression. In contrast,
women who cast employment decisions in terms derived from cultural
scripts, whether for good mothers or for superwomen, often show signs
of depression, suggesting that cultural scripts for mothers at present are
detrimental to women. What differentiates these scripts for mothering
from mothers' own terms is the division made between the woman herself
and her child, so that mothers in essence are portrayed as caught between
themselves and their child. Resistance to psychological illness among
adolescent girls and adult women was, thus, associated with their ability
to define care in terms that reflect experiences of authentic relationship
or responsive engagement with others.

The importance of reconsidering what is meant by care and connection
as well as what responsiveness in relationship entails is underscored also by
recent studies of inner city youth (Gilligan *et al.*, 1985; Ward, 1986; see
Chapters 8 and 9). Teenagers living in the inner city reasoned about care
in ways that often were far more advanced than their reasoning about

justice; they observed both the necessity for care and the reliance of people on human resources. For example, a fifteen-year-old when asked to
describe a moral conflict he had faced, spoke of a time when he wanted
to go out with his friends after a dance but his mother wanted him home.
He decided to go home, he said, to avoid "getting into trouble with my
mother." However, when asked if he thought he had done the right thing,
he spoke about the fact that he knew, from watching what had happened
when his older sister stayed out late, that his mother would not sleep until
he came home. His reason for going home was not simply grounded in a
desire to avoid punishment (Stage I reasoning in Kohlberg's terms) but
also in a wish not to hurt his mother and not to "just think about myself."

> My mother would have been worried about me all night if I stayed out . . .
> [When] my sister used to do it to her, she didn't get any sleep all night . . .
> I would be pretty bad if I kept her up like that, you know, just thinking
> about myself and not thinking about her . . . Why should I just go off and
> not worry about her and just think about myself?

Hearing this teenager's concerns about avoiding punishment and
getting into trouble, the psychologist schooled in the conventions of
developmental psychology might well suspend further questioning, assuming a match with a codable, low-level classification, a match rendered plausible because of this teenager's low socioeconomic status. Yet when the
researcher, perhaps rejecting a Stage I depiction of a fifteen-year-old as
implausible, chooses another line of questioning and pursues the boy's
recognition that his actions can hurt his mother, his moral strengths appear.
He expresses concern about hurting his mother, and his awareness of how
he can do so reveals a care perspective. Furthermore, his knowledge of
what actions will cause hurt is based on his own observations. Thus, he
does not need to put himself in his mother's place (which would earn him a
higher score on stages of social, moral, and ego development) because he
knows from experience with his mother how *she* will feel.

The change in assessment that results from listening for two voices
in the moral conflicts related by inner city teens is further illustrated by a
twelve-year-old girl who described her decision to override her mother's
rules. Having laid out the moral world in terms of a stark contrast between "good guys" and "bad guys," she contrasts this moral language with
the language of "necessity." "Good guys," she explains, sustaining both
languages, "know what's wrong and what's right and when to do right,

and they know when it's necessary to do wrong." Her example of moral conflict involves precisely this judgment. A neighbor who had cut herself badly called because she needed bandages; the twelve-year-old had been told by her mother that she was not to leave the house. Discussing her decision to leave, she speaks repeatedly of the fact that she "had to," referring to the neighbor's "need" and to her own judgment that it was "absolutely necessary" to help: "She needed my help so much, I helped her in any way I could. I knew that I was the only one who could help her, so I had to help her."

This example also contains a contrast between a seemingly simplistic moral conception (here a notion of absolute rules that determine right and wrong irrespective of intention or motivation, a "heteronomous" morality in Piaget's terms or a low-stage morality in Kohlberg's terms) and a more sophisticated moral understanding, captured by the language of necessity: the need of people for help and the ability of people to help one another. Although the seeming inability of this girl to anticipate her mother's approval of her decision would qualify her for a low level of interpersonal perspective-taking in Robert Selman's (1980) terms, her insistence that "I did the right thing" and her belief that her actions would have been right even if her mother had disagreed with her decision, suggests a more "autonomous" moral sense. Her decision in the instance she describes was guided by her judgment that help must be provided when it is needed and where it is possible: "You can't just stand there and watch the woman . . . die" (Gilligan *et al.*, 1985). This disparity, between seemingly low stages of social and moral development as measured by conventional psychological standards and evidence of greater moral understanding and sensibility than the developmental stage descriptions imply, was encountered repeatedly in the study of inner city teens, raising the kinds of questions about the moral life of children that have been articulated so pointedly by Robert Coles (1986).

The implication of these studies, taken together, is that interpretive problems cannot be separated from the consideration of adolescent development and that these problems raise questions not only about adolescents but also about the society and culture in which they are coming of age. The observation often made by teachers that girls, in general, become less outspoken following puberty, less likely to disagree in public or even to participate in classroom discussions, together with the observation that school achievement tends to drop off in adolescence for the children of ethnic minorities, suggest that secondary education, or the interpretive frameworks of the culture, may be more readily accessible and comprehensible to those students whose experience and background are most similar to that of the framers.  If at present a care perspective offers a critical lens on a society which seems increasingly justice focused, it is also one that clarifies and makes sense of the activities of care that teenagers describe--not only helping others but also creating connections with others, activities which they link with times when they feel good about themselves (see Gilligan *et al.*, 1985 and also Osborne, 1987).

Gender differences along the same lines as those found among educationally advantaged teens were also observed among inner city teenagers. Nine of eleven boys who described moral dilemmas involving friends focused their attention on the question of resisting peer pressure, while six of the ten girls whose dilemmas involved friends focused on questions of loyalty in relationship, citing as moral problems instances of abandonment, disconnection, and exclusion.  In addition, girls in the inner city were more likely than boys to describe dilemmas that continued over time, rather than dilemmas portrayed as one-time occurrences or repeated instances of the same problem.  Perhaps as a result, girls were more likely to seek inclusive solutions to the problems they described, solutions that contributed to sustaining and strengthening connections in that they were responsive to the needs of everyone involved.  While girls were apt to talk about staying with a problem in relationships and with the people involved, boys were more likely to talk about leaving.  The one boy in the study who described a continuing dilemma to which he sought an inclusive solution spoke about his problems in maintaining a relationship with both of his divorced parents. Thus, the tendency to voice concerns about connection, to seek and to value care and responsiveness in relationships, was associated in these studies *both* with social class *and* with gender (see also Ladner, 1972; Stack, 1974). This is very similar to the findings of Johnston (1985) and Langdale (1983) that moral orientation or the standpoint taken in solving moral problems is associated both with gender and with the problem being considered.

The language of necessity which distinguishes the moral discourse of inner city youth offers a compelling rendition of a care perspective in an environment characterized by high levels of violence.  Janie Ward's (1986) study of the ways in which adolescents living in the inner city think about the violence they witness in the course of their daily lives reveals the strength of a focus on issues of care and connection, one that opens possibilities of non-violent responses to violence and of holding off violent response.  Ward's study also reveals the importance accorded by teenagers to mothers who label violence in the family *as* violence (rather than speaking about love or not talking about what is actually happening) and who take action to stop it.  The clear sex differences with respect to violent action and the effects of these differences on male and female adolescents are curiously overlooked in current discussions about sex differences in moral development.  Yet such differences pose major questions for theory and research.

Reconsidering adolescence from the two standpoints of justice and care, and thinking about what constitutes "development" in both sets of terms, also spurs a reappraisal of traditional research methods, specifically a rethinking of the detachment which has been embedded in research practice.  When interviewing pregnant teenagers who were considering abortion, I was struck by the fact that most of them knew about birth control.  Their pregnancies seemed in part to have resulted from actions that comprised sometimes desperate, sometimes misguided, and sometimes innocent strategies to care for themselves, to care for others, to get what they wanted, and to avoid being alone.  Engaging with these teenagers in the context of inquiring about their moral conflicts and interpretive quandaries raised a question about the effects of research as an intervention, with both clinical and educational implications.  What lessons are taught about connection and about detachment, about care and about justice, through the practice of asking teenagers, in the context of a research interview, about their experiences of moral conflict?

It may be that asking teenagers to talk about their own experiences of moral conflict and choice in itself constitutes an effective intervention, as some preliminary evidence suggests.  Such questioning may reveal to teenagers that they have a moral perspective, that something of value is at stake in the conflicts they experience, and thus, that they have grounds for action in situations where they may have felt stuck or confused or unable to choose between alternative paths. The efficacy of the interview as an intervention may depend on the responsiveness of the research relationship, on whether the researcher engages with the teenager, rather than simply mirroring or assessing his or her responses. For the adolescent, the realization that he, and perhaps especially she, has a moral perspective which an adult finds interesting, or a moral voice that someone will respond to, shifts the framework for action away from a choice between submission and rebellion (action defined in others' terms) and provides a context for discovering what are one's own terms. In adolescence, this discovery galvanizes energy and stimulates initiative and leadership.

But the same is true for teachers as well. The interpretive and ethical questions raised by considering adolescent development form a basis for genuine collaboration between psychologists and secondary school teachers. One teacher's reflections on such collaboration, appended to this chapter, provide a cogent description of the intentions and the aims of this way of working. In essence, the method joins a naturalistic approach to research with what is perhaps the oldest strategy of education: not to teach answers but to raise questions which initiate the search for knowledge, and, in the spirit of discovery, to listen for what is surprising. If the modern element in modern literature is the theme of disenchantment with the idea of culture or civilization, the challenge to those of us who would speak about development in adolescence or about psychological health or education, is to take seriously the questions about truth and values which are raised by adolescents coming of age in modern culture--and then, in responding to these questions, to imagine that this generation may hear different voices and may see from a new angle.

## APPENDIX

A teacher comments on participating in a study of adolescent development conducted at the Emma Willard School for girls.

I see a danger in "using" the study to confirm or to justify a previously existing agenda. I get nervous when someone claims that "this work corroborates what we've said about" a set of institutional rules or dictates. I would hate to think that a study which asks us to listen to the *questions* and self-talk which reflect complexities of *ways* of thinking might be reduced to prescriptive "givens" concerning *the way* all young women think; or the way we, as educators, *should* teach all of our subject matter, or the reasons why stereotyping of any sort should be fostered, though in an altered form.

I imagine an excited colleague talking about what has been gained from the study. Now, it is clear why instead of running over the goalie in order to score, female team members stop to pick their opponent up. The conclusion is that women need to learn "to play the game." What is not questioned is whether or not "the game" is meant to test ferocity or skill. What is not recognized is that this situation could lead us to question in at least three directions. Certainly, we might question what kind of "education" would teach women to trample a goalie in order to gain the point. We might also ask if a more skillful team might not be able both to pick up the goalie and gain the point. Or we might ask, as we need to of our school grading systems, if the scoring system and rules validate those abilities and behaviors we wish to reward. We need to consider the possibility that any situation which frames a conflict in these terms ought, itself, to be questioned. If we assume that structures (institutions, pedagogies, grading systems, whatever) precede rather than embody a particular perspective, we miss what has been for me one of the most significant aspects of this study.

## ACKNOWLEDGMENTS

Two institutions, created to welcome and support women scholars, provided the settings in which I began and completed the work of this essay: the Mary Ingraham Bunting Institute at Radcliffe College and the Blanche, Edith, and Irving J. Laurie New Jersey Chair in Women's Studies at Rutgers University. I wish to thank the Carnegie Corporation for the support of the Mellon Faculty Fellowship. Special thanks are due as well to Mary Hartman, Dean of Douglass College, and members of the Laurie Chair Seminars for a stimulating and responsive environment in which to work. For the invitations that encouraged both the writing and the rewriting of this essay, I am grateful to Robert Blum. Jim Gilligan, Jane Lilienfeld, Bernard Kaplan, and Diana Baumrind offered most helpful criticisms and comments.

# Mapping the
# Moral Domain

A Contribution
of Women's Thinking to
Psychological Theory and Education

# PART I

# Remapping Development:
## Creating a New Framework for Psychological Theory and Research

# 1

## REMAPPING THE MORAL DOMAIN:
## NEW IMAGES OF SELF IN RELATIONSHIP

Carol Gilligan

In Book 6 of the *Aeneid*, when Aeneas travels to the underworld in search of his father, he is startled to come upon Dido--to discover that, in fact, she is dead. He had not believed the stories that reached him. "I could not believe," he tells her, "that I would hurt you so terribly by going." (Virgil, 6:463-464, p. 176). Seeing her wound, he weeps, asking: "Was I the cause?" (Virgil, 6:458, p. 175). Yet explaining that he did not willingly leave her, he describes himself as a man set apart, bound by his responsibility to his destiny. Caught between two images of himself--as implicated and as innocent, as responsible and as tossed about by fate--he exemplifies the dilemma of how to think about the self, how to represent the experience of being at once separated and connected to others through a fabric of human relationship.

The representation of the self as both separate and bounded has a long history in the Western tradition. Consonant with, rather than opposed to, this image of individual autonomy is a notion of social responsibility, conceived as duty or obligation. Yet as Virgil tells this story in the *Aeneid*--of a man apart, devoted to his mission of founding a city and bringing home his gods to Latium--he shadows it with others that resist expression, of "a sorrow too deep to tell" and "a love beyond all telling" (Virgil, 2:3, p. 33; 4:85, p. 98)--Aeneas's story of the fall of Troy and Dido's of her passion. Stories of sorrow and love have generally been kept

apart from discussions of morality and the individual; as in the *Aeneid,*
they are considered *infandum,* told in private, known but unspeakable.
Interspersing these stories with the account of Aeneas's heroic and arduous
journey, Virgil, however, suggests a connection. The uncertainty created by
this conjunction emerges in the underworld meeting of Aeneas and Dido. In
this scene, described by T.S. Eliot as one of the most poignant and civilized
passages in poetry (Eliot, 1957, p. 63), an acute psychological wisdom
creates a profound sense of moral ambiguity.

Was Aeneas responsible for Dido's self-inflicted wound? Why
couldn't he believe that he would hurt her so terribly by leaving? These
questions, in their essential tension, reflect two ways of thinking about
the self in relationship. A psychology of love that can explicate the connection between Aeneas's departure and Dido's action, as well as her subsequent anger and silence, vies with the categories of moral judgment that
presuppose a separate and autonomous individual. The two images of
self anchored by these two conceptual frameworks imply two ways of
thinking about responsibility that are fundamentally incompatible. When
Aeneas encounters consequences of his action that he had neither believed
nor intended and Dido, once generous and responsive, is rendered by grief
cold and impassive, this disjunction momentarily surfaces. The detachment
of Aeneas's *pietas* becomes the condition for his ignorance of her feelings;
yet his adherence to his mission does not imply the indifference that she in
her responsiveness imagined. Thus, the simple judgment that would condemn Aeneas for turning away from Dido or Dido for breaking her vow
of chastity yields to a more complex vision--one that encompasses the
capacity for sustained commitment and the capacity for responsiveness in
relationships and recognizes their tragic conflict.

The two meanings of the word "responsibility"--commitment to obligations and responsiveness in relationships--are central to the mapping of
the moral domain put forth in this chapter.[1] Since moral judgments reflect
a logic of social understanding and form a standard of self-evaluation, a
conception of morality is key to a conception of self in relationships. By
asking how we come to hold moral values and by tracing the ontogenesis
of values to the experience of relationships, I will distinguish two moral
predispositions that inhere in the structure of the human life cycle. Predispositions toward justice and toward care can be traced to the experi-

ences of inequality and of attachment that are embedded in the relationship between child and parent. And since everyone, thus, is vulnerable to oppression and to abandonment, two stories about morality recur in human experience.

The different parameters of the parent-child relationship--its inequality and its interdependence or attachment--may ground different feelings which differentiate the dimensions of inequality/equality and attachment/detachment that characterize all forms of human connection. In contrast to a unitary moral vision and to the assumption that the opposite of the one is the many, these two dimensions of relationship provide coordinates for reimagining the self and remapping development. The two conceptions of responsibility, reflecting different images of the self in relationship, correct an individualism that has been centered within a single interpretive framework. At the same time, the identification of attachment or interdependence as a primary dimension of human experience ties the psychology of love to the representation of moral growth and self-development.

The haunting smile that Virgil suspends over the scene of the underworld encounter, comparing Aeneas seeing the wounded Dido to "one who sees, / Early in the month, or thinks to have seen, the moon / Rising through cloud, all dim" (Virgil, 6:450-452, p. 175), catches the uncertainty surrounding the perception of a reality that has been obscured or diminished. As the dim moon recalls the ideals of stoic detachment and heroic individualism, it also conveys the fragility of love and its vulnerability to loss and separation. Thus, two stories in their shifting configuration create a fundamental confusion; yet one story tends to get lost, buried in an underworld region.

In recent years, two classical scholars, W.R. Johnson and Marilyn Skinner, have noted the continuing tendency of critics to reduce the complexity of Virgil's poetic statement, to override ambiguity in an effort to resolve the central problem of competing loyalties (Johnson, 1975; Skinner, 1983, pp. 12-18). The same tendency to reduce complexity is evident in contemporary psychology as well, where the ideal of individual autonomy has rendered the reality of love evanescent. In this sense, the current readings of the *Aeneid* by Johnson and Skinner, which focus the significance of the underworld meeting, correspond to efforts within psychology to recover a story about love that is known but only dimly apprehended.  In both instances, this retrieval reveals an inherent complication by drawing attention to "the ethical dilemma, now perceived, in what formerly had been thought of as a right and proper, albeit painful, course of action" (Skinner, p. 16).  As the perception of this dilemma "requires of Virgil that he shape a new formulation of heroism" (Johnson, p. 153), it currently implies a change in our psychological theories about development and about the individual.

The individualism defined by the ideal of the autonomous self reflects the value that has been placed on detachment--in moral thinking, in self-development, in dealing with loss, and in the psychology of adolescence.  By reconstituting the tension between attachment and detachment, which is dissolved by this representation, I will describe two conceptions of morality and of the self that lead to different ways of understanding loss and thinking about the conflicts of loyalty that arise in the course of human life.  The close tie between detachment and dispassion reveals the problem I wish to address by showing how the recovery of a lost story about love changes the image of the self in relationship.

The definition of the self and morality in terms of individual autonomy and social responsibility--of an internalized conscience enacted by will and guided by duty or obligation--presupposes a notion of reciprocity, expressed as a "categorical imperative" or a "golden rule."  But the ability to put oneself in another's position, when construed in these terms, implies not only a capacity for abstraction and generalization but also a conception of moral knowledge that in the end always refers back to the self.  Despite the transit to the place of the other, the self oddly seems to stay constant.  If the process of coming to know others is imagined, instead, as a joining of stories, it implies the possibility of learning from others in ways that transform the self.  In this way, the self is in relationship and the reference for judgment then becomes the relationship.  Although the capacity for engagement with others--for compassion and for response to another's pleasure and distress--is observed in early childhood and even in infancy, this capacity is not well represented in accounts of human development, in part because it is at odds with the still image of relationships embedded in the prevailing concept of the self.

From George Herbert Mead's description of the self as known through others' reflection and Cooley's conception of the "looking-glass self," to Erikson's emphasis on the discovery of self in others' recognition, and the current psychoanalytic fascination with the process of "mirroring," the relational context of identity formation has repeatedly been conveyed. But the recurrent image of the mirror calls attention to the lifelessness in this portrayal of relationships. When others are described as objects for self-reflection or as the means to self-discovery and self-recognition, the language of relationships is drained of motion and, thus, becomes lifeless. The self, although placed by psychologists in a context of relationships, is defined in terms of separation. Thus, others disappear, and love becomes cast in the depersonalized language of "object relations."[2]

A different way of describing self, generally confused with a failure of self-definition, has been clarified in recent years by attention to the experience of women.[3] In this alternative construction, self is known in the experience of connection and defined not by reflection but by inter-action, the responsiveness of human engagement. The close tie I have observed between self-description and moral judgment illuminates the significance of this distinction by indicating how different images of self give rise to different visions of moral agency, which in turn are reflected in different ways of defining responsibility.

When asked "What does responsibility mean to you?" a high school student replied: "Responsibility means making a commitment and then sticking to it." This response confirms the common understanding of responsibility as personal commitment and contractual obligation. A different conception of the self and of morality appears, however, in another student's reply: "Responsibility is when you are aware of others and you are aware of their feelings . . . Responsibility is taking charge of yourself by looking at others around you and seeing what they need and seeing what you need . . . and taking the initiative."[4] In this construction, responsibility means acting responsively in relationships, and the self--as a moral agent--takes the initiative to gain awareness and respond to the perception of need. The premise of separation yields to the depiction of the self in connection, and the concept of autonomy is changed. The seeming paradox "taking charge of yourself by looking at others around you" conveys the relational dimension of this self-initiated action.

These two conceptions of responsibility, illustrated here by the definitions of two young women, were heard initially as a dissonance between women's voices and psychological theories (Gilligan, 1982). Exploring this dissonance, I defined new categories of moral judgment and self-description to capture the experience of connection or interdependence, which overrides the traditional contrast between egoism and altruism. This enlarged conceptual framework provides a new way of listening to differences not only between but also within the thinking of women and men. In a series of studies designed to investigate the relationship between conceptions of self and morality and to test their association with gender and age, two moral voices could reliably be distinguished in the way people framed and resolved moral problems and in their evaluations of choices they made. One voice speaks of connection, not hurting, care, and response; and one speaks of equality, reciprocity, justice, and rights. Although both voices regularly appeared in conjunction, a tension between them was suggested by the confusion that marked their intersection and also by the tendency for one voice to predominate. The pattern of predominance, although not gender specific, was gender related, suggesting that the gender differences recurrently observed in moral reasoning signify differences in moral orientation, which, in turn, are tied to different ways of imagining self in relationship.[5]

The values of justice and autonomy, presupposed in current theories of human growth and incorporated into definitions of morality and self, imply a view of the individual as separate and of relationships as either hierarchical or contractual, bound by the alternatives of constraint and cooperation. In contrast, the values of care and connection, salient in women's thinking, imply a view of self and other as interdependent and of relationships as networks created and sustained by attention and response. The two moral voices that articulate these visions, thus, denote different ways of viewing the world. Within each perspective, the key terms of social understanding take on different meanings, reflecting a change in the imagery of relationships and signifying a shift in orientation. As in the ambiguous figure which can be perceived alternately as a vase or two faces, there appear to be two ways of perceiving self in relation to others, both grounded in reality, but each imposing on that reality a different organization. But, as with the perception of the ambiguous figure, when one configuration of self emerges, the other seems to temporarily vanish.

The nature and implications of these differences are clarified by an example. Two four-year-olds--a girl and a boy--were playing together and wanted to play different games.[6] In this version of a common dilemma, the girl said, "Let's play next-door neighbors." "I want to play pirates," the boy replied. "Okay," said the girl, "then you can be the pirate that lives next door." By comparing the inclusive solution of combining the games with the fair solution of taking turns and playing each game for an equal period, one can see not only how the two approaches yield different ways of solving a problem in relationships but also how each solution affects both the identify of the game and the experience of the relationship.

The fair solution, taking turns, leaves the identity of each game intact. It provides an opportunity for each child to experience the other's imaginative world and regulates the exchanges by imposing a rule based on the premise of equal respect. The inclusive solution, in contrast, transforms both games: the neighbor game is changed by the presence of a pirate living next door; the pirate game is changed by bringing the pirate into a neighborhood. Each child not only enters the other's imaginative world but also transforms that world by his or her presence. The identity of each separate game yields to a new combination, since the relationship between the children gives rise to a game that neither had separately imagined. Whereas the fair solution protects identity and ensures equality within the context of a relationship, the inclusive solution transforms identity through the experience of a relationship. Thus, different strategies for resolving conflicts convey different ways of imagining the self, and these different forms of self-definition suggest different ways of perceiving connection with others.

In 1935 the British psychiatrist Ian Suttie called attention to the representation of love in modern psychology, asking, "In our anxiety to avoid the intrusion of sentiment into our scientific formulations, have we not gone to the length of excluding it altogether from our field of observation?" (Suttie, 1935, p. 1). Noting that science, as generally conceived, "is at a particular disadvantage in dealing with the topic of human 'attachments,'" Suttie observed that love is either reduced to appetite or dismissed as an illusion (Suttie, p. 2). Thus, he set out to reconstitute love within psychology, defining love as a "state of active, harmonious interplay" and tracing its origins to a "pleasure in *responsive* companionship and a correlative discomfort in loneliness and isolation" that are present in infancy (Suttie, p. 4, emphasis in text).

This understanding of love was substantially extended by the British psychoanalyst John Bowlby (Bowlby, 1969/1973/1980). As Freud found in dreams and free associations a window into men's souls, Bowlby discovered in children's responses to loss a way of observing relationship. From this angle of vision, he came to see in the sorrow of children's mourning a capacity for love that previously was unimagined. The knowledge that this capacity is present in early childhood required a transformation in the account of human development. Tracing the formation of attachment to care giving and responsiveness in relationships, Bowlby rendered the process of connection visible as a process of mutual engagement. On this basis, he challenged the value psychologists have placed on separation in describing normal or healthy development, arguing instead that in separation lies a pathogenic potential for detachment and disengagement. Thus, he asked how the capacity for love can be sustained in the face of loss and across the reality of separation.

Bowlby's method was essentially the same as the one Freud set forth in his *New Introductory Lectures on Psychoanalysis.* Relying on the magnification of pathology to reveal what otherwise was invisible, Bowlby viewed loss as a fracture that exposes the underlying structure of connection. As Freud observed the psyche fractured in neurotic symptom formation, Bowlby observed in traumatic separation the breaking apart of a relationship. Quoting Goethe's statement that "we see only what we know" and William James's observation that "the great source of terror in infancy is solitude" (Bowlby, 1980), he set out to describe the phenomena of human attachment and sorrow, to separate the account of loss, mourning, comfort, and love from orthodox psychoanalytic interpretations and to anchor it instead in direct observation. The unit of his analysis was the relationship rather than the individual.

In his essay "Mourning and Melancholia," Freud (1917) describes with a clarity that remains unequaled, the symptomatology of depression, attributing it to a failure of mourning, conceived as a failure of detachment.

Rather than withdrawing libido from a lost and irretrievable object, the depressed person, as it were, takes his stand against reality, digging his heels into the argument that the object, in fact, cannot be lost. The mechanism of this denial, Freud says, is identification, complicated by anger and consequently, leading to self-denigration. In an effort to ward off a seemingly unbearable sorrow, the depressed person becomes the lost object of his affections. Rather than abandon the other, he chooses to become the other and abandon himself. Thus, in Freud's exquisite statement, "the shadow of the object fell upon the ego" (Freud, 1917, XIV, p. 249), the self undergoes eclipse.

In charting the natural history of mourning from his observations of children dealing with loss and separation, Bowlby (1980) demarcates a three-stage sequence of protest, despair, and detachment. Seeing denial and anger as inevitable responses to loss--the concomitants of normal grieving--he reinterprets detachment as the sign of a pathogenic repression rather than as a signal of mourning completed. Although both Freud and Bowlby stress the importance of remembering, Freud emphasizes remembering the loss and coming to terms with its reality, whereas Bowlby focuses on remembering the love and finding a means for its representation. This divergence leads to opposing predictions about the capacity for love following loss. Freud implies that only when the last shreds of hope and memory have been relinquished will the libido be free to attach again (Freud, 1917, XIV, p. 248). Bowlby, proceeding from a different conception of relationships and a different model of psychic energy, describes the process of mourning in terms of a separation or tear that must be mended, tying the renewal of the capacity for love to weaving together the broken narrative. The story of love must be told not so that it can be forgotten but so that it can be continued into the present. Although "object-finding" may be "object-refinding," in Freud's famous phrase (Freud, 1905/1963, VII, p. 227), attachments--located in time and arising from mutual engagement--are by definition irreplaceable.

Thus, Bowlby introduces a new language of relationships into psychology and recasts the process of development as one of elaboration rather than of replacement. Pointing to the visible signs of human engagement, he records the interplay of attachment seeking and care giving by which human bonds are formed and sustained. Yet in drawing the underpinnings of his revised theoretical conception from ethology and the study of information processing, he moves away from the human world of love he sets out to describe. Using animal analogies and machine images, he aligns his work with the prevailing metaphors of science; the cost of this assimilation is a reduction in the portrayal of relationships. The mother, cast as "attachment-figure," is seen primarily through the eyes of the child, and the mutuality of relationships, although stated, is lost in the way they are presented.

In directing attention to the observable signs of human connection, Bowlby's work recasts the distinction between mourning and melancholia in terms of a distinction between real and fabricated relationships. Seen in this light, mourning signifies grief over the loss of an attachment whose felt reality can be sustained in memory; melancholia signifies the isolation felt when an attachment is found to be fragmentary. If separation exposes the nature of connection, then the melancholia of depression, with its endless argument of self-accusation, may be seen as a response to a failure of attachment rather than as a failure of separation. This interpretation offers a new way of reading the stories about sorrow and love in the *Aeneid.*

Dido, discovering that Aeneas is secretly planning to leave her, suddenly sees the love between them to have been imagined. Correcting for distance in light of this perception, she replaces the term "husband" first with "guest" and then with "deserter" (Virgil, 4:323, p. 107; 4:421, p. 111). Yet, driven by a wavering memory, searching wildly for support and finding only disconfirmation, she turns in the end to enact the destruction of the relationship upon herself. Aeneas's surprise at seeing her dead confirms the reality of his separation. Yet his belated expressions of sorrow reveal the love which he had previously kept hidden. In Book 4, two uses of the word "husband" convey a central misapprehension: Aeneas, saying "I never held the torches of a bridegroom, / Never entered upon the pact of marriage," refers to the absence of contract; Dido, "humbling her pride before her love," refers to the fact of conjugation (Virgil, 4:338–339, p. 107; 4:414, p. 110). In Book 6, these two perspectives begin to cross and intermingle.

By verbal echoes and situational reversals, Virgil spins a skein of ironic allusion that serves, as Skinner observes, "to recall prior tragedy and

examine it from an altered perspective" (Skinner, p. 12). The compelling
poignancy and ultimate futility of Aeneas's and Dido's last meeting arise
from the recognition that Aeneas's stoic detachment has lost its heroic
quality, "becoming instead pathetically defensive," and that Dido's death has
come to appear less tragically necessary, seeming a "wretched, preventable
accident" (Skinner, p. 12). Thus, the costs of detachment--whether undertaken out of a mistaken notion of *pietas* or arising from traumatic separa-
tion--become increasingly clear. While Aeneas stands pleading, Dido flees,
demonstrating her unwillingness now to respond and recognizing that again
he will leave her. Aeneas, his "once kindly ears" having been blocked by
divinely ordained duty, continues his mission of founding a city. At the
end of the epic, he appears "fierce under arms" and "terrible in his anger."
Driven by anguish and fury, he enacts a senseless retribution on Turnus in
the name of keeping a promise (Virgil, 12:938; 12:946-947, p. 402).

The image of a civilization built on detachment returns in Freud's
description of adolescent development, where he identifies as "one of the
most significant but also one of the most painful psychical accomplishments
of the pubertal period . . . detachment from parental authority, a process
which alone makes possible the opposition, which is so important for the
progress of civilization, between the old generation and the new" (Freud,
1905/1963, VII, p. 227). This view of detachment as a necessary,
although painful, step in the course of normal development casts problems
in adolescence as problems of separation. Observing that "as at every stage
in the course of normal development through which all human beings ought
by rights to pass, a certain number are held back, so there are some who
have never gotten over their parents' authority and have withdrawn their
affection from them either very incompletely or not at all," Freud concludes
that this failure of development occurs mostly in girls (Freud, 1905/1963,
VII, p. 227).

Seen from a different perspective, however, the resistance of girls to
detachment underscores the ethical dilemma that the orthodox account of
development obscures. Rather than signifying a failure of individuation, the
reluctance to withdraw from attachment may indicate a struggle to find an
inclusive solution to the problem of conflicting loyalties. Adolescent girls
resisting detachment generally have appeared in the literature on adolescence to illustrate the problems that arise when childhood forms of rela-

tionship are not changed.  But by drawing attention to the problem of loyalty and to a transformation of attachment that resists the move toward disengagement, the experience of girls in adolescence may help to define an image of the self in relationship that leads to a different vision of progress and civilization.

Psychological development is usually traced along a single line of progression from inequality to equality, following the incremental steps of the child's physical growth.  Attachment is associated with inequality, and development linked to separation.  Thus, the story of love becomes assimilated to a story about authority and power.  This is the assimilation I wish to unravel in remapping development across two dimensions of relationship and distinguishing inequality from attachment.  Starting from the child's position of inequality and attachment, one can trace the straight line that leads towards equality and increased authority.  But one can also trace the elaborating line that follows the development of attachment, depicting changes in the nature and configuration of relationships and marking the growth of the capacity for love.  This two-dimensional frame-work of interpretation clarifies the problems created by oppression and by detachment.  But the interweaving of the two lines of development reveals a psychological ambiguity and ethical tension, which is most sharply focused by two opposites of the word "dependence."

Since dependence connotes connection, it can be extended along both dimensions of relationship, leading in one direction to independence and in the other to isolation.  These contrasting opposites of dependence--independence and isolation--illuminate a shift in the valence of relationships that occurs because connection with others can both impede autonomy or freedom and provide pleasure, comforts, and protection against loneliness.  When dependence is opposed simply to independence, this ambivalence of relationship disappears.  Progress then becomes equated with detachment and may be seen as a sign of objectivity and strength; ambiguity vanishes and attachments may appear as an obstacle to the growth of the auton-omous self.

The opposition of dependence to isolation, retrieving the ethical prob-lem and the inherent psychological tension, was highlighted by adolescent girls' responses to a question about the meaning of dependence.  The girls were participants in a study designed to map the terrain of female development that remains largely uncharted in the literature on normal adolescence.[7] In an interview that included questions about past experience, self-description, moral conflicts, and future expectations, the question about dependence was asked at the end of a section about relationships. The study serves to underscore the contrast between the view of relationships conveyed by the opposition between dependence and autonomy-- which has structured the discussion of adolescent development and appears on most scales of psychological assessment--and the view of relationships conveyed by the opposition of dependence to isolation, implied in the following examples:

*What does dependence mean to you?*

I think it is just when you can be dependent on or you can depend on someone, and if you depend on someone, you can depend on them to do certain things, like to be there when you need them, and you can depend on people to understand your problems, and on the other hand, people can depend on you to do the same thing.

When you know that someone is there when you are upset, and if you need someone to talk to, they are there, and you can depend on them to understand.

Well, sometimes it bothers me, the word, because it means that you are depending on somebody to make things happen. But also that you are depending on someone else to help you, you know, either to make things happen for you that are good or just to be there when you need them to talk to and not feel that you are cutting into their time or that they don't want you there.

I wouldn't say total dependence but if we ever needed each other for anything, we could totally be dependent on the person and it would be no problem. For me, it means that if I have a problem, I can depend on her to help me or anything I need help with, she will be there to help, whether she can help me or not, she will try, and the same goes for me.

Caring. Knowing that the person will always be there. I think there is a word like "painstaking care." You know that the other person would go through all the pain . . . it is so rare, you are really lucky if someone is like that.

That I know if I go to her with a problem or something like that or not a problem but just to see her, even if she has changed and even if I have changed, that we will be able to talk to each other.

Dependence, well, in this case it would be just like I really depend on him to listen to me when I have something to say or when I have something I want to talk about, I really want him to be there and to listen to me.

Here, dependence is assumed to be part of the human condition, and
the recurrent phrases--"to be there," "to help," "to talk to," "to listen"--
convey the perception that people rely on one another for understanding,
comfort, and love.  In contrast to the use of the word "dependence" to
connote hanging from someone like a ball on a string, an object governed
by the laws of physics, these responses convey the perception that attachments arise from the human capacity to move others and to be moved by
them.  Being dependent, then, no longer means being helpless, powerless,
and without control; rather, it signifies a conviction that one is able to
have an effect on others, as well as the recognition that the interdependence of attachment empowers both the self and the other, not one person
at the other's expense.  The activities of care--being there, listening, the
willingness to help, and the ability to understand--take on a moral dimension, reflecting the injunction to pay attention and not to turn away from
need.  As the knowledge that others are capable of care renders them lov-
able rather than merely reliable, so the willingness and the ability to care
becomes a standard of self-evaluation.  In this active construction, dependence, rather than signifying a failure of individuation, denotes a decision
on the part of the individual to enact a vision of love.

> I would say we depend on each other in a way that we are both independent,
> and I would say we are very independent but as far as our friendship goes,
> we are dependent on each other because we know that both of us realize that
> whenever we need something, the other person will always be there.

> I depend on her for understanding a lot and for love and she depends on me
> for the same things, understanding and just to be there for each other, we
> know that we are there for each other.

These portraits of love reveal its cognitive as well as its affective
dimensions, its foundation in an ability to perceive people in their own
terms and to respond to need.  Because such knowledge generates power
both to help and to hurt, the uses of this power become the standard of
responsibility and care in relationships.  In adolescence, when both wanting
and knowing take on new meanings, conflicts of responsibility assume
new dimensions, creating conflicts of loyalty that are not easily resolved.
Seeking to perceive and respond to their own as well as to others' needs,
adolescent girls ask if they can be responsive to themselves without losing
connection with others and whether they can respond to others without
abandoning themselves.  This search for an inclusive solution to dilemmas

of conflicting loyalties vies with the tendency toward exclusion, manifest in the moral opposition of selfish and selfless choice--an opposition in which selfishness connotes the exclusion of others and selflessness the exclusion of self. Thus, the themes of inclusion and exclusion, prominent in the childhood games girls play and manifest in their strategies for resolving conflicts, come to be addressed consciously in adolescence, in a line of development that leads through changes in the experience and understanding of attachment.

Within this framework of interpretation, the central metaphor for identity formation becomes dialogue rather than mirroring; the self is defined by gaining voice and perspective and known in the experience of engagement with others. The moral passion that surrounds this quest for self-definition was evident when adolescent girls were asked to describe a situation in which someone was not being listened to. The acuity of their perceptions of not listening, their awareness of the signs of inattention, extended across examples that ranged from a problem in international politics to conflicts in personal relationships, making the public as well as the private dimensions of attachment or interdependence clear. The themes of silence and voice that emerge so centrally in female narratives convey the moral dimensions of listening, but also the struggle to claim a voice and the knowledge of how readily this endeavor is foiled. When someone refuses to listen--signalling a failure to care--adolescent girls speak of themselves as coming up against a wall. Silence can be a way of maintaining integrity in the face of such inattention, a way to avoid further invalidation. But the willingness to speak and to risk disagreement is central to the process of adolescent development, making it possible to reweave attachment and enabling the distinction between true and false relationships.

"I just wish to become better in my relationship with my mother, to be able more easily to disagree with her," one adolescent explained, and this wish to engage with others rather than "making myself in their image" may signify both her temptation to yield to others' perceptions--to become, as it were, the mirror--and her recognition that excluding herself renders relationships lifeless, dissolving the possibility of connection. With this dissolution, attachment becomes impossible. Given the failure of interpretive schemes to reflect female experience and given the celebration of selflessness as the feminine virtue, girls' resistance to detachment challenges two long-standing equations: the equation of human with male and the equation of care with self-sacrifice. At the base of this challenge lies a story about love that joins opposition and progress to attachment as well as a view of the self as an individual within the context of continuing relationship.

Jane Austen structures the plot of her novel *Persuasion* to reveal such a transformation in the understanding of love and duty--a transformation that hinges on a change in self-perception. Anne Elliot, the heroine, yields to the persuasion of her "excellent friend," Lady Russell, and breaks off her engagement to Captain Wentworth in the name of duty and prudence. The suffering brought on by this detachment is chronicled in the course of the novel, but the resolution takes an interesting turn. Anne Elliot reconstructs her understanding of relationships in light of her recognition that "she and her excellent friend could sometimes think differently" (Austen, 1964, p. 140) and Captain Wentworth comes to see the impediment to relationship created by "my own self." He explains, "I was too proud, too proud to ask again. I did not understand you. I shut my eyes" (Austen, p. 234). Two ways of defining the self--by submission and by detachment --have created an obstacle to attachment that begins to give way when dialogue replaces reflection and blind commitment yields to response. Like searchlights crossing, these transformations of self intersect to form a bright spot of illumination, making it possible to join self with other and other with self. In this novel, where the engagement of divergent perspectives defines happy marriage, new images of self in relationship open the way to a new understanding of morality and love.

## NOTES

1. A similar distinction is made by H. Richard Niebuhr in *The Responsible Self*, New York (1963).

2. The term "object" was first used by Freud in *Three Essays on the Theory of Sexuality* (1905) to distinguish sexual objects from sexual aims. It is now widely used by "object-relations" theorists--psychoanalysts following Melanie Klein and Margaret Mahler--who focus on the primacy of relationships. In both contexts the term refers to a person who has become the object of another's desire.

3. This difference was described in the mid-1970s by N. Chodorow, "Family Structure and Feminine Personality," in M. Z. Rosaldo and L. Lamphere, *Woman, Culture and Society*, Stanford, Calif. (1974); by J. B. Miller, *Toward a New Psychology of Women*, Boston (1976); and by C. Gilligan, "In a Different Voice: Women's Conceptions of the Self and of Morality," *Harvard Educational Review*, 47 (1977). The point has been extended by Chodorow, *The Reproduction of Mothering*, Berkeley, Calif. (1978); Gilligan, *In a Different Voice: Psychological Theory and Women's Development*, Cambridge, Mass. (1982); Miller, "The Development of Women's Sense of Self," Stone Center Working Paper Series, 12, Wellesley, Mass. (1984) as well as in a variety of other feminist writings.

4. These responses to questions about responsibility were given by students at the Emma Willard School for girls in Troy, N. Y. All such quotes in this chapter are from these girls.

5. See C. Gilligan, S. Langdale, N. Lyons, and M. Murphy, "The Contribution of Women's Thought to Developmental Theory," report to the National Institute of Education, Washington, D. C. (1982). See also S. Langdale, "Moral Orientations and Moral Development," in "References," this volume; and N. Lyons, "Two Perspectives: On Self, Relationships and Morality," *Harvard Educational Review*, 53(2) (1983).

6. For this example, I am grateful to Anne Glickman, the mother of the four-year-old boy.

7. The study was conducted at the Emma Willard School for girls and is part of a larger project on adolescent development. For omission of girls in the literature on adolescence, see J. Adelson, ed., *Handbook of Adolescent Psychology*, New York (1980).


## ACKNOWLEDGMENTS

I am grateful to Mary P. Chatfield, my guide to the *Aeneid* and to classical scholarship, as well as to Hilde Hein for her insights about dependence. The study of two moral orientations was supported by a grant from the National Institute of Education. The study at the Emma Willard School was made possible by the Geraldine Rockefeller Foundation, and I wish to thank Trudy Hanmer and Robert Parker of the school, Scott McVay and Valerie Peed of the foundation, and Sharry Langdale, Margaret Lippard, and Nona Lyons of the Harvard Graduate School of Education for their collaboration. I am indebted to Marilyn Brachman Hoffman whose generous gifts and encouragement have provided support at critical junctures, and to the Carnegie Corporation for enabling me to spend a year as a Faculty Fellow at the Bunting Institute of Radcliffe College. Susan Pollak's comments on an earlier draft of this paper and Eve Stern's careful reading were most helpful in its revision.

# 2

## TWO PERSPECTIVES: ON SELF, RELATIONSHIPS, AND MORALITY

Nona Plessner Lyons

Asked in the course of an interview to respond to the question, "What does morality mean to you?" two adults give different definitions.[1] One replies:

> Morality is basically having a reason for or a way of knowing what's right, what one ought to do; and when you are put into a situation where you have to choose from among alternatives, being able to recognize when there is an issue of "ought" at stake and when there is not; and then . . . having some reason for choosing among alternatives.

Another responds:

> Morality is a type of consciousness, I guess, a sensitivity to humanity, that you can affect someone's else's life. You can affect your own life, and you have the responsibility not to endanger other people's lives or to hurt other people. So morality is complex. Morality is realizing that there is a play between self and others and that you are going to have to take responsibility for both of them. It's sort of a consciousness of your influence over what's going on.

In contrast to the notion of morality as "having a reason," "a way of knowing what's right, what one ought to do," there is the sense of morality as a type of "consciousness," "a sensitivity" incorporating an injunction not to endanger or hurt other people. In the first image of an individual alone deciding what ought to be done, morality becomes a discrete moment of rational "choosing." In the second image, of an individual aware, connected, and attending to others, morality becomes a "type of consciousness," which, although rooted in time, is not bound by the single moment. Thus, two distinct ways of making moral choices are revealed.

The representation in psychological theory of these two different images and ideas of making moral choices is the concern of this article. One view has come to dominate modern moral psychology--the image of the person in a discrete moment of individual choice. The identification of a second image--the individual connected and attending to others--and the systematic description of both views from empirical data are presented in this work. In her critique of moral philosophy, Iris Murdoch (1970), the British novelist and philosopher, indicates the importance of this investigation. She elaborates two issues raised by this second image of the self which apply as well to moral psychology: the need for a conception of self not limited to that of a rational, choosing agent, and a concern for acknowledging a conception of love as central to people and to moral theory.

Describing present-day moral philosophy as "confused," "discredited," and "regarded as unnecessary," Murdoch focuses on philosophy's idea and image of the self. Believing that modern moral philosophy has been "dismantling the old substantial picture of the self," Murdoch sees the moral agent reduced to an "isolated principle of will or burrowing point of consciousness." The self as moral agent, "thin as a needle, appears only as the quick flash of the choosing will" (pp. 47, 53). Murdoch rejects this classic Kantian image of the self as pure, rational agent. For her, moral choice is "as often a mysterious matter, because, what we really are seems much more like an obscure system of energy out of which choices and visible acts of will emerge at intervals in ways that are often unclear and often dependent on the condition of the system in between the moments of choice" (p. 54).

The picture of the self as ever capable of detached objectivity in situations of human choice is, thus, rejected by Murdoch. Yet, this image is central to Kohlberg's (1969, 1981) model of moral development. That model, which is a hierarchically ordered sequence of stages of moral judgment making based in part on the pioneering work of Piaget (1932/1965), is the dominant model of modern moral psychology. In addition, Murdoch's challenge to philosophy, "that we need a moral philosophy in which the concept of love, so rarely mentioned now . . . can once again be made central," can also be directed to moral psychology

(1970, p. 46). Murdoch's assumption is that love is a central fact of people's everyday lives and morality. But modern moral psychology, grounded in the concepts of justice and rights, subsumes any notion of care or concern for another which we might call love. It was Gilligan (1977) who first revealed this distortion of moral psychological theory.

Gilligan (1977, 1982), listening to women's discussions of their own real-life moral conflicts, recognized a conception of morality not represented in Kohlberg's work. To her, women's concerns centered on care and response to others. Noting too that women often felt caught between caring for themselves and caring for others, and characterized their failures to care as failures to be "good" women, Gilligan suggested that conceptions of self and morality might be intricately linked. In sum, Gilligan hypothesized (1) that there are two distinct modes of moral judgment--justice and care--in the thinking of men and women; (2) that these are gender-related; and (3) that modes of moral judgment might be related to modes of self-definition.

The research described here includes the first systematic, empirical test of these hypotheses. This article reports on the identification, exploration, and description from data of two views of the self and two ways of making moral choices. The translation of these ideas into a methodology made possible the testing of Gilligan's hypotheses. The empirical data consist of responses of thirty-six individuals to questions asked in open-ended interviews designed to draw out an individual's conception of self and orientation to morality. The data were analyzed first for descriptions of self, then for considerations individuals presented from their own real-life moral conflicts, and finally for correlations between the two.

The first part of this article presents interview data on ways that individual males and females--children, adolescents, and adults--describe themselves. These data reveal two characteristic modes of describing the self in relation to others: a self separate or objective in its relations to others and a self connected or interdependent in its relations to others. Then, from individuals' discussions of their own real-life moral conflicts, two ways of considering moral issues are distinguished: a morality of rights and justice and a morality of response and care. These data are then used to develop two coding schemes, methodologies for systematically and reliably identifying people's modes of self-definition and bases of moral choice. Finally, results of the study designed to test Gilligan's hypotheses and a discussion of the implications of this work for psychological theory and practice are presented. Thus, this article moves between the discursive essay and the research report, to show the evolution of a conceptual framework based on people's real-life experiences, and the translation of that framework into a systematic methodology for analyzing data and testing hypotheses.

A social dimension emerges as central in this work: in each of the two images of people making moral choices, there is a distinct way of seeing and being in relation to others. Although Kohlberg has identified a developmental pattern of a morality of justice, he has not elaborated the connection between his conceptualization of moral development and an understanding of relationships. Because this present work assumes that an understanding of relationships is central to a conception of morality, it is not directly parallel to Kohlberg's work, yet it does maintain an indebtedness to it.[2]   Gilligan and her associates (Gilligan, 1977, 1982; Langdale & Gilligan, 1980; Lyons, 1980, 1981) have outlined, only broadly, the developmental patterns of an orientation to care. What remains, then, is the task of examining the developmental patterns of a morality of justice and of care within a framework of relationships. This present work supports, modifies, and elaborates Gilligan's ideas and confirms Piaget's central insight that "apart from our relations to other people, there can be no moral necessity" (Piaget, 1932/1965, p. 196).

## DATA: THE INTERVIEWS

When asked to talk about themselves, individuals differ in how they describe themselves in relation to others. Because these differences became central to the construction of the coding schemes for identifying modes of self definition and moral choice, it is useful to look closely at the differences in the responses of adolescents, children, and adults. These data reveal two distinct conceptions of relationships, each characterized by a unique perspective toward others. The choice of male/female examples here heightens the contrast and is useful for purposes of illustration. But it is important to emphasize that these few examples are not intended to represent men and women in general.

For two fourteen-year-olds taking part in an open-ended interview, the question was the same:  "How would you describe yourself to yourself?" Jack begins:

> What I am?  [pause]  That's a hard one . . . Well, I ski--I think I'm a pretty good skier.  And basketball, I think I'm a pretty good basketball player.  I'm a good runner . . . and I think I'm pretty smart.  My grades are good . . . I get along with a lot of people and teachers.  And . . . I'm not too fussy, I don't think--easy to satisfy, usually, depending on what it is.

Presenting ways by which he evaluates himself, Jack comments on how he measures up in terms of a ranking of abilities:  good skier, basketball player, runner, pretty smart.  Talking about his relations with others, Jack continues to focus on his abilities:  "I get along with a lot of people and teachers."

Fourteen-year-old Beth's response begins as Jack's did with the activities that engage her; however, she then tells of the network of relations that connects her to others:

> I like to do a lot of things.  I like to do activities and ski and stuff.  I like people.  I like little kids and babies.  And I like older people, too, like grandparents and everything; they're real special and stuff.  I don't know, I guess I'd say I like myself.  I have a lot of stuff going on.  I have a lot of friends in the neighborhood.  And I laugh a lot.

The interviewer asks, "Why do you like yourself?" and Beth replies:

> . . . I don't know.  I think it's the surroundings around me that make my life pretty good.  And I have a nice neighborhood and a lot of nice friends and older people . . . We visit new people everywhere we go.  And there's my grandmother, and every time I go to my grandmother's, she makes me see all her friends and stuff.  And I think that helps me along the line, 'cause you get to know them, and it makes you more friendly.

The contrast between these two responses may not at first glance seem striking, but there is a difference between the images and ideas of each person's relationships to others.  Jack connects himself to others through his abilities.  Like his ranking of himself as a "pretty good skier" and a "good runner," Jack's way of relating to others is another measure of his abilities:  "I get along with a lot of people and teachers."  Jack's perspective towards others is in his own terms, through the self's "I."  Beth's connection to others is through the people who make up her "surroundings"--nice friends, older people, little kids, and babies.  Her connection *through* others is, in turn, *to* others:  "My grandmother . . . she makes me see all her friends and stuff."  Thus, Beth's perspective toward others is to see them in their own terms. She sees, for example, her grandmother with her own friends, in her own context. Further, Beth seems to see a circle of interdependence in these relationships: "And I think that helps me along the line, 'cause you get to know them, and it makes you more friendly." Although both young people discuss relational topics that sound similar, they reflect different perspectives towards others: seeing others in their own terms, or through the self's perspective.

These different ways of seeing others also emerge in individuals' considerations when talking about moral conflict. When asked, "Have you ever been in a situation where you had to make a decision about what was right but you weren't sure what to do?" Jack relates an experience of being with a group of his peers who wanted to wax windows on Halloween. To an earlier question, "What makes something a moral problem?" Jack had replied, "Somewhere I have to decide . . . whether I should do this or not . . . whether it's right that I should do something or whether it's wrong." Now, talking about his conflicts about that Halloween, he echoes the earlier response: "I knew it wasn't right, but they, the kids, they would think, 'Oh, he's no fun, he doesn't want to do it, he's afraid he's going to get in trouble,' stuff like that." Urged by the interviewer to describe the consequences he considered when making his decision, Jack mentions "getting in trouble," "my mother and father would have been upset by something like that. They wouldn't like it," and "if I didn't go, some of my friends would think . . . 'Well, he's no fun.'" Jack also describes his major consideration in making a decision: "Well, you have to think about what would be right . . . and then . . . are you gonna stand up for what's right and wrong to your friends, or are you gonna let them get you into going." Revealing that in the end he didn't go with his friends, he elaborates why: "I didn't think it was right . . . and if somebody wanted to wax my windows, I wouldn't like it, so I wasn't going to do that to someone else."

Through reciprocity Jack resolves this moral conflict. Asked if he had made the right decision, Jack replies, "Well . . . my parents would have been pleased that I had not gone . . . If the kids had gotten into trouble, I would have known that I made the right decision, 'cause I wouldn't have wanted to have been in that group." When challenged, "What if no one knew about it?" Jack resorts again to his "principle" for choice: "I don't think you could think that was the right decision if you were to do that, to wax somebody's windows and go away thinking that was the right thing to do."

For Jack, the moral problem hinges on knowing what is right and acting on that in spite of pressures or taunts from his friends. Solving the problem, then, becomes a matter of thinking about what would be right and standing up for that. His reciprocity-based justification is derived from the self's perspective: "If somebody wanted to wax my windows, I wouldn't like it, so I wasn't going to do that to someone else." Like the measure of self in relation to others found in his self description, Jack sees and resolves moral conflict through the self's perspective.

Beth's moral problem arises from a different set of concerns as well as a different perspective towards others. She describes the conflicts in her situation.

> I had a decision to give up my paper route. And I had a decision over two people, like two people wanted it. And I didn't know what was the right decision . . . Well, some friends of the person that I said could not have the route were going against me and saying that, you know, "You did it" and "What a stupid thing to do, to give it to the other person." The person got kinda upset and kinda turned against me.

Reconstructing how she thought through the problem, Beth illuminates her way of thinking about the choice:

> [at first] I was trying to think mostly who I thought was going to do better at it. I don't know, it kinda got me all upset because I didn't want to hurt somebody, one person's feelings by telling them they couldn't have it. And going to the other person and saying you can. I think that's mostly what bothered me . . . And then it bothered me more when I thought of what person was mostly gonna get it. I was thinking, well, are they really gonna do a good job? . . . I didn't want anybody doing it that was gonna be nasty to anybody. Because I have some older people that I do on the route, and they like to talk to you and everything. And I didn't want to give it to anybody that was gonna walk away. I wanted them to get along . . . I didn't want anybody getting in fights or anything.

The moral problem hinges on seeing the possible fractures between people and trying to avert them. Caught between wanting someone good for the paper route job and not wanting to hurt the person she had to turn down or neglect the needs of the elderly persons on her route, Beth's concerns for relationships and for the welfare of others are in conflict.

Asked, "How did you know that it was the right decision?" Beth tells us how things worked out: "The person that was bad for the job finally realized that the person [chosen] was going to be a good person to do it."

She also describes how she evaluates the decision: "I told my friends about it and my parents, and they said, 'Yeah.' And I told my paper route people that there was gonna be a new person, and they said, 'Yeah,' they liked that person. And so I thought, 'Well, I think I did a pretty good job, if everybody's happy.'" Beth measures the rightness of her choice by how things worked out for the individuals involved. She finds in the restoration of relationships, the validation of her choice.

Although Jack and Beth both wrestle with issues raised by friendships, two different kinds of moral problems concern them. Through two different perspectives--the perspective of self and the perspective of others--different problems arise and different resolutions are sought. These distinctions are found in data from younger children and adults as well.

Two eight-year-olds are asked, "How would you describe yourself to yourself?" (see Gilligan, 1982). Jeffrey answers in the third person, saying that "he's got blond hair" and "has a hard time going to sleep." He also focuses on abilities: "He learns how to do things; when he thinks they're going to be hard, he learns how to do them." Describing his way of relating to others, Jeffrey says, "He bugs everybody and he fights everybody," concluding with, "That's it, I'm lazy."

To the interviewer's question, eight-year-old Karen replies in the first person, "I don't know. I do a lot of things. I like a lot of things." Adding, "I get mad not too easy," she comments that she has "made a lot of new friends" and concludes, "And, um, I don't know if everyone thinks this, but I think I tell the truth most of the time."

Echoing themes of Jack, the adolescent, Jeffrey presents a measure of himself by abilities: "He learns how to do things; when he thinks they're going to be hard, he learns how to do things." Karen's observation that she has "made a lot of new friends" echoes adolescent Beth's self description of her connection to the people surrounding her. It is in contrast to Jeffrey's "he bugs everybody and he fights everybody."

Themes in the real-life conflicts which the children report repeat those of the adolescents. Jeffrey talks with the interviewer about a real-life conflict. "Like when I really want to go to my friends and my mother's cleaning the cellar. I don't know what to do." Asked by the interviewer why this is a conflict, Jeffrey elaborates:

'Cause it's kinda hard to figure it out. Unless I can go get my friends and
they can help me and my mother clean the cellar.

*Why is it hard to figure it out?*

'Cause you haven't thought about it that much.

*So what do you do in a situation like that?*

Just figure it out and do the right thing that I should do.

*And how do you know what you should do?*

'Cause when you think about it a lot, then you know the right thing to do
first . . . I think about my friends and then I think about my mother. And
then I think about the right thing to do.

To the interviewer's question, "But how do you know it's the right thing to
do?" Jeffrey concludes, "Because usually different things go before other
things. Because your mother--even though she might ask you second--it's
in your (i.e., her) house." Like Jack's use of the Golden Rule, for Jeffrey,
having a rule--"different things go before other things"--allows him to
resolve the dilemma. For both Jack and Jeffrey it is through the self's
perspective, the self's rule or standard, that moral conflict is cast and
resolved.

Different issues concern eight-year-old Karen. She describes conflicts
with friends: "I have a lot of friends and I can't always play with all of
them, so I have to take turns. Like, they get mad sometimes when I can't
play with them. And then that's how it all starts." Asked what kinds of
things she considers when trying to decide with whom to play, Karen
replies, "Um, someone all alone, loneliness. Um, even if they are not my
friends, not my real friends, I play with them anyways because not too
many people do that . . . They never think of the right person."

Describing the "right person" as someone who is "quiet who . . .
doesn't talk too much, who doesn't have any brothers or sisters," Karen,
like Beth, tries to connect people to one another, "to make them feel more
like at home." Asked to elaborate, Karen responds: "If a person's all alone
. . . if that person never has anyone to talk to or anything . . . they are
never going to have any friends. Like when they get older they are gonna
have to talk. And if they never talk or anything, then nobody's going to
know them . . . If that person always stays alone, she's not going to have
any fun."

For Karen, as for Beth, moral conflicts arise from having to maintain connections between people, not wanting people to be isolated, alone, or hurt. For both, resolutions are found by considering the needs of those involved. Like their adolescent counterparts, these two eight-year-olds reflect different perspectives towards others. They see and attend to different things.

These distinguishing characteristics and different ways of seeing others are manifest in adulthood. John, the thirty-six-year-old professional educator quoted at the beginning of this article, reveals a "logic" consistent with that of Jack and Jeffrey. He describes the decision to fire a colleague as a personal moral conflict. Although believing that the firing breached a prior agreement, he describes his conflict as "lack of confidence in my own judgment . . . feeling like maybe the others were right." His co-workers had decided to fire the staff member. Describing how he felt, John says: "I felt I had a commitment to live with . . . [we] all had a commitment to honor . . . But for me it was a serious matter of principles."

Later, reflecting on his decision to offer his resignation in protest, he comments on how he thought about the decision:

> Well, I guess I will never know for sure . . . but I am comfortable with it . . . I don't feel I perverted any principle I hold now in making that decision. For me it was a test. In a way it became a symbol, because all this had been weighing on me. In a way the principle was commitment to principle, and I had to decide whether I had it or not, and if I let it go by, then maybe I didn't have the right to ever challenge anybody else.

Common among Jack, Jeffrey, and John is a line of thinking in which issues of morality hinge on "moments of choice" and "knowing how to decide," thus conjuring up Murdoch's image of the self in the "quick flash of the choosing will."

Answering the question, "How would you describe yourself to yourself?" John goes on to talk explicitly about his own perspective towards others. He acknowledges: "I happen to be a person who likes the world of ideas," who can "delight myself for hours on end reading and thinking, puzzling over things . . . I am not the sort of person who has a natural outreaching towards other people. That for me is always sort of an effort . . . an effort that I need to be nudged to do." Suggesting the importance of relationships to him, he continues talking about their difficulties and rewards:

> I am nudged [towards others] in several ways--by other people . . . but also
> by my convictions that tell me that I have responsibilities to other people;
> and, once nudged though, the interesting thing is that it is always rewarding.
> And I am grateful because most of the personal growth I have gone through
> has been through these other people and not through thinking about the world
> of ideas and that sort of stuff. But somehow I always retreat into the corner
> and want to be off by myself. It is a paradox about me, one that I still
> haven't fully understood . . . Gregarious people, I think, can't fully understand
> sometimes how hard it is for certain people to become involved with people
> because what they regard as either minor personal risks or non-risks alto-
> gether, can strike a person like me sometimes as insurmountable obstacles.
> So that is one aspect of myself that just happens to come to mind. This is
> interesting because I had never thought about this much.

John picks up the themes of relating to others from the self's perspective
heard earlier in the responses of Jack and Jeffrey. So, too, an adult
woman repeats themes found in the concerns of Karen and Beth.

Forty-six-year-old Sarah, a lawyer, who describes herself as "per-
ceptive" and "responsive" to others, tells about a moral dilemma she faced.
She discovered in the course of a contested custody case that her client's
boyfriend was an illegal alien. Although withholding this information
was not technically legal, she sensed that the information could affect the
judge's ruling. She asked herself if telling would really make a difference in the long run and decided that it would not. She concludes, "nobody is getting particularly hurt by this." Talking about her dilemma in a
larger context, she describes the conflict her role creates:

> I think that I run into a dilemma in doing domestic relations work in the
> sense that I am dealing with a legal system that is dealing with something that
> it doesn't know how to deal with very well and I get very distressed because
> it is hard for me to put together exactly what my role is supposed to be . . .
> you are presiding over some pretty emotional moments in people's lives, and
> I never know whether I should be sort of, here is the lawbook, and not do
> anything to try to do whatever kind of counseling, whatever kind of support
> one might provide for people without costing them a fortune . . . On the other
> hand, I think people need something like this. I end up in a dilemma in
> dealing with custody decisions, which are very messy. And God knows,
> there is no right and no wrong. It is a question of how can you work out
> something that is going to be the least painful alternative for all the people
> involved . . .

The ultimate principle for resolving moral conflict, for Sarah, seems to
be to work out "the least painful alternative for all the people involved."

From these examples we see that individuals describe different kinds
of considerations in moral choice tied to different ways of being with
and seeing others: to treat others as you would like to be treated or to

work out something that is "the least painful alternative for all involved." To treat others as you would like to be treated demands distance and objectivity. It requires disengaging oneself from a situation to ensure that each person is treated equally. In contrast, to work out the least painful alternative for all those involved means to see the situation in its context, to work within an existential reality and ensure that all persons are understood in their own terms. These two ways of perceiving others and being in relation to them are, thus, central both to a way of describing the self and to thinking within the context of moral choice.

## DEVELOPMENT OF THE CODING SCHEMES

When moving from data to the conceptual constructs on which a coding scheme is based, a circular interaction occurs: the data account for the constructs and are, in turn, explained by them. Indeed, as Loevinger (1979) argues, such circularity is necessary to validate the coding schemes and to build the theory of which they are a part. This interactive process is described below to illuminate how ideas about human relationships, identified first in the statements of individuals, were translated into systematic categories of a coding scheme, a methodology for analyzing data.

Many researchers (Freud, 1925/1961; Piaget, 1932/1965; Erikson, 1968; Broverman *et al.*, 1972) have commented on the relational bias of women's conceptions of self and morality. But it was Gilligan (1977) who first suggested that this relational bias might represent a unique construction of social reality. The study discussed below, designed by Gilligan, hypothesized that men and women do think differently about themselves in relation to others. That there is such a difference was supported in an examination of data--such as the comments of those quoted earlier--and then elaborated conceptually on the basis of that data. In that process two different ideas and ways of experiencing human relationships were revealed that seemed tied to two characteristic ways of seeing others. This distinction was then conceptualized as two perspectives towards others. Table 1 presents schematically the two modes of being in relation to others--separate/objective and connected--and their respective perspective towards others--reciprocity or response.

Each of these two ideas of relationships with their characteristic perspective towards others implies a set of related ideas. The perspective of

TABLE 1

*Relationships of Reciprocity Compared with Relationships of Response*

THE SEPARATE/OBJECTIVE SELF
(Autonomous in Relation to Others)

*Relationships:*

| *experienced in terms of* | *mediated through* | *and grounded in* |
|---|---|---|
| RECIPROCITY between separate individuals; a concern for others, considering them as one would like to be considered, with objectivity and in fairness | RULES that maintain fairness and reciprocity in relationships | ROLES which comes from duties of obligation and commitment |

THE CONNECTED SELF
(Interdependent in Relation to Others)

*Relationships:*

| *experienced as* | *mediated through* | *and grounded in* |
|---|---|---|
| RESPONSE TO OTHERS IN THEIR TERMS a concern for the good of others or for the alleviation of their burdens, hurt, or suffering (physical or psychological) | THE ACTIVITY OF CARE which maintains and sustains caring and connection in relationships | INTERDEPENDENCE which comes from recognition of the interconnectedness of people |

the separate/objective self--labeled "reciprocity"--is based on impartiality, objectivity, and the distancing of the self from others. It assumes an ideal relationship of equality. When this is impossible, given the various kinds of obligatory role relationships and the sometimes conflicting claims of individuals in relationships, the best recourse is to fairness as an approximation of equality. This requires the maintenance of distance between oneself and others to allow for the impartial mediation of relationships. To consider others in reciprocity implies considering their situations as if one were in them oneself. Thus, an assumption of this perspective is that others are the same as the self.

The perspective of the connected self--labeled "response"--is based on interdependence and concern for another's well-being. It assumes an ideal relationship of care and responsiveness to others. From this standpoint, relationships can best be maintained and sustained by considering others in their specific contexts and not always invoking strict equality.[3] To be responsive requires seeing others in their own terms, entering into the situaations of others in order to try to understand how they view their situations. Thus, an assumption of this perspective is that others are different from oneself.

In Table 2 the relationship between these conceptions of self and orientations to morality are presented schematically. The data revealed that a description of self as separate/objective is associated with a predominance of justice considerations, while a description of self as connected is associated with a predominance of care considerations.

The conceptions of justice and care and the perspectives towards others are constructs that represent ideals containing strengths and weaknesses. Equality is an ideal and a strength of a morality of justice; the consideration of individuals' particular needs--in their own terms--is both an ideal and a strength of a morality of care. An impartial concern for others' rights, however, may not be sufficient to provide for care, and caring for others may leave individuals uncaring of their own needs and rights to care for themselves. In addition, the response perspective may suggest an unqualified and overly emotional concern for meeting the needs of others;[4] however, the present research suggests a greater complexity of meaning. Response to another is an interactive process in which a developing and changing individual views others as also changing across the life cycle.

Within most psychological models the ability to see another's perspective is considered a cognitive capacity which gradually becomes more objective and abstract (Mead, 1934; Kohlberg, 1969, 1981; Selman, 1980). In contrast, the perspective of response described here emphasizes the particular and the concrete. While it is assumed that this perspective changes over the course of development, the nature of these changes is not yet known. It may be that in "maturity" one generalizes the particular, that is, one always looks at the particular, and *this* is the general principle. This research suggests that our current unitary models of perspective taking may

TABLE 2

*Conceptions of Self and Morality in Relation to Moral Choice*

A MORALITY OF JUSTICE

| | | | | |
|---|---|---|---|---|
| Individuals defined as SEPARATE/ OBJECTIVE IN RELATION TO OTHERS: see others as one would like to be seen by them, in objectivity; | tend to use a morality of *justice as fairness* that rests on an understanding of RELATIONSHIPS AS RECIPROCITY between separate individuals, grounded in the duty and obligation of their roles. | Moral problems are generally construed as issues, especially decisions, of con- flicting claims between self and others (including society); resolved by invoking impartial rules, principles, or standards, | considering: (1) one's role-related obligations, duty, or com- mitments; or (2) standards, rules, or principles for self, others, or society; including reciprocity, that is, fair- ness--how one should treat another con- sidering how one would like to be treated if in their place; | and evaluated considering: (1) how decisions are thought about and justified; or (2) whether values, principles, or standards were/are maintained, especially fairness. |

A MORALITY OF RESPONSE AND CARE

| | | | | |
|---|---|---|---|---|
| Individuals defined as CONNECTED IN RELATION TO OTHERS: see others in their own situations and contexts; | tend to use a morality of *care* that rests on an understanding of RELATIONSHIPS AS RESPONSE TO ANOTHER in their own terms. | Moral problems are generally construed as issues of rela- tionships or of response, that is, how to respond to others in their particular terms; resolved through the activity of care, | considering: (1) maintaining relationships and response, that is, the connections of interdependent individuals to one another; or (2) promoting the welfare of others or preventing their harm; or relieving the burdens, hurt, or suffering (physical or psychological) of others; | and evaluated considering: (1) what hap- pened/will happen, or how things worked out; or (2) whether relationships were/are maintained or restored. |

need revision.  Perspective taking and a "perspective towards others" conceptualized here are separate phenomena.

It is important also that the use of the word "response" or "reciprocity" in subjects' responses not be assumed to indicate automatically the possession of that particular perspective on morality or relationships.  For example, an individual using a morality of justice and having a perspective of reciprocity might state, as did fourteen-year-old Jack, "I would not do that because I would not like someone to do that to me."  However, an individual using a morality of care and having a perspective of response might use the *word* "reciprocity" but with a different meaning.  "I want to reciprocate because they will need that kind of help and I will be able to do that for them."  In a perspective of response, the focus is always on the needs of others; it is the welfare or well-being of others in their terms that it important, not strictly what others might do in return or what the principle of fairness might demand or allow.[5]

What follows from these distinctions is that the language of morality must always be scrutinized for differences in underlying meaning.  For example, words like "obligation" or "responsibility" cannot be taken at face value.  The moral imperatives of what one is "obliged" to do, "should" do, or what "responsibilities" one has are, in fact, shaped by one's perspective towards others.

Research is needed to elaborate the conceptualizations presented here--of two perspectives on self, relationship, and morality--across the life cycle, especially attending to the issues of change and development.  Research should also address potential interactions, that is, ways in which one orientation to morality may affect or be affected by the other.[6]  In addition, individuals' understanding and awareness of their own perspectives of themselves in relation to others needs to be elaborated.  The work presented here shows how the logic of each mode of morality and self description has been elicited from interview data.  The next section will describe how that logic was captured in a methodology, that is, in two coding schemes, and used to test a set of hypotheses.

## AN EMPIRICAL STUDY TESTING GILLIGAN'S HYPOTHESES

In this empirical study,[7] male and female subjects were interviewed in order to ascertain their modes of self definition and of moral choice, and to explore the connection between them.  If, as Gilligan suggested, the absence of women subjects in past research obscured an understanding of the morality of care, the inclusion of both men and women within this study might reveal its complexity for both sexes.  A secondary purpose of the study was to explore a suggestion of Kohlberg and Kramer (1969) that when women are engaged professionally outside the home and occupy equivalent educational and social positions as men, they will reach higher stages of moral development than the typical adult woman (stage 3--interpersonal mode) found in Kohlberg's six-stage system of moral judgment making.  Therefore, a sample of professional women was included in the study.

*Sample.*  The sample of thirty-six people consisted of two males and two females at each of the following ages:  eight, eleven, fourteen to fifteen, nineteen, twenty-two, twenty-seven, thirty-six, forty-five, and sixty-plus years.  The sample was identified through personal contact and recommendation, and all subjects referred met the sampling criteria of high levels of intelligence, education, and social class.

*Procedure.*  The data were collected in a five-part, open-ended interview which was conducted in a clinical manner, a method derived from Piaget (1929/1979).  The interview proceeds from structured questions to a more unstructured exploration and clarification of each person's response.  Interview questions were developed to illuminate how the individual constructs his or her own reality and meaning, in this case, the experience of self and the domain of morality.

*Data Analysis.*  The data were analyzed first for modes of self definition, then for the subjects' orientations within considerations[8] of real-life moral conflicts.  Finally, they were analyzed for correlations between the two (Lyons, 1981).

## Considerations of Justice or Care in Moral Conflicts

By examining the considerations individuals present in the construction, resolution, and evaluation of their resolution of real-life moral dilemmas, the relative predominance of justice or care orientations to morality was determined.  Considerations were categorized as either response (care) or rights (justice) (see Coding Scheme, Appendix A), and scored by counting the number of considerations each individual presented within either

mode. In addition to identifying the presence of justice or care considerations, predominance of mode within this scoring system was determined by
the higher frequency of one or the other mode in a subject's responses. Results were also expressed as percentages indicating the relationship of the
dominant mode to all considerations the individual gave.

Intercoder reliability was established by two additional coders for both
identification of considerations within real-life dilemmas (Step 1) and
categorization of considerations as belonging to response or rights modes
within the subjects' construction, resolution, and evaluation of their moral
conflict (Step 2). Agreements for Step 1 were 75 and 76 percent; for Step
2, 84 and 78 percent.

Table 3 summarizes the predominance of response and rights considerations in real-life moral dilemmas for both males and females. The table
shows that in real-life conflicts, while males and females use both kinds
of considerations (rights and response), women use more considerations of
response more frequently than rights and men use considerations of rights
more frequently than response. In some instances the reverse is true.

TABLE 3

*Predominance of Considerations of Response or Rights
in Real-Life Dilemmas by Females and Males*

| Sex | Response Predominating % (N) | Rights Predominating % (N) | Equal Response/ Rights Considerations % (N) |
|---|---|---|---|
| Females (N = 16) | 75 (12) | 25 (4) | 0 (0) |
| Males (N = 14) | 14 (2) | 79 (11) | 7 (1) |

*Note:* $\chi^2$ *(2) = 11.63, p < 0.001.*

Table 4 illustrates this pattern in another way, indicating that all the
females in this sample employed considerations of response, but 37 percent
(six) failed to mention any considerations of rights. Similarly, all the males

employed considerations of rights, but 36 percent (six) failed to mention any considerations of response. These findings show that, in real-life moral conflict, individuals in this sample call upon and think about both care and justice considerations but use predominantly one mode which is related to but not defined by or confined to gender.

TABLE 4

*Absence of Considerations of Response or Rights: Females and Males*

| Sex | No Considerations of Response % (N) | No Considerations of Rights % (N) |
|---|---|---|
| Females (N = 16) | 0 (0) | 37 (6) |
| Males (N = 14) | 36 (6) | 0 (0) |

Although this study did not specifically consider developmental changes in moral thinking and self definition, some results suggest possible developmental issues. It is clear that considerations of both response and rights are found across the life cycle. However, after age twenty-seven, women show increased consideration of rights in their conceptualization of moral problems or conflict, although they still use considerations of response more frequently than rights in the resolution of conflict. This may be related to a second finding: the disappearance of the response consideration of "care of the self" at the same age. These findings suggest the possibility of an interaction between the rights and response orientations for women in their late twenties. Another finding with implications for developmental change is the greater incidence of considerations of response among male adolescents than among the male sample at large. In general, however, across the life cycle men's considerations of rights maintain greater consistency than do women's considerations of response. Taken together, these findings suggest separate developmental shifts for men and women which deserve further study.

Keeping in mind that the sample is small (N = 36), the results reported here support the hypothesis that there are two different orientations to morality--an orientation towards rights and justice, and an orientation towards care and response to others in their own terms. Morality is not unitarily justice and rights, nor are these orientations mutually exclusive: individuals use both kinds of considerations in the construction, resolution, and evaluation of the resolution of real-life moral conflicts, but usually one mode predominantly. This finding of gender-related differences, however, is not absolute since individual men and women use both types of considerations.

### Modes of Self-Definition:  Separate/Objective or Connected

This study also tested the hypothesis that individuals use two distinct modes of self definition. Respondents were asked, "How would you describe yourself to yourself?" and responses were analyzed to determine the predominance of one of two modes of self definition--separate/objective or connected. In a manner similar to that used for the analysis of the moral conflict data, these self-descriptive responses were categorized according to four components:  general and factual; abilities and agency; psychological; and relational (see Coding Scheme, Appendix B). Each individual was scored by counting the number of separate/objective or connected relational characterizations, and then the predominant mode was determined.

Intercoder reliability for the self-description data was established using two independent coders in a two-step coding process which was more rigorous than most correlational reliability procedures. Every statement about self definition was coded. In Step 1, in which each idea about the self was identified, intercoder reliability was 70 and 71 percent. In Step 2, in which each idea was categorized according to specific aspects within components, intercoder reliability was 74 and 82 percent.

A summary of male and female modes of self definition is given in Table 5. As the table indicates, women more frequently use characterizations of a connected self, while men more frequently use characterizations of a separate/objective self. Although these different gender-related modalities occur systematically across the life cycle, they are not absolute; some women and some men define themselves with elements of either mode. In addition, and perhaps more striking, is the finding that both men and

TABLE 5

*Modes of Self Definition: Females and Males*

| Sex | Predominantly Connected % (N) | Predominantly Separate/ Objective % (N) | Equally Connected and Separate % (N) | No Relational Component Used % (N) |
|---|---|---|---|---|
| Females (N = 16) | 63 (10) | 12 (2) | 6 (1) | 19 (3) |
| Males (N = 14) | 0 (0) | 79 (11) | 7 (1) | 14 (2) |

*Note:* $\chi^2$ *(3) = 16.3, p < 0.001.*

women define themselves in relation to others with equal frequency, although their characterizations of these relationships are different.

### Relationship of Definitions of Self to Considerations in Real-Life Moral Choice

Some of the more provocative results of this study concern the testing of the hypothesis of the relationship between modes of moral choice and modes of self definition. Table 6 presents these findings. In this sample, regardless of sex, individuals who characterized themselves predominantly in connected terms more frequently used considerations of response in constructing and resolving real-life moral conflicts. Individuals who characterized themselves predominantly in separate/objective terms more frequently used considerations of rights.

Although these results do not allow us to claim a causal relationship between modes of self-definition and modes of moral choice, an important relationship seems to exist. Clearly, further research is needed to see if these results hold over larger samples of a broader socioeconomic status. Furthermore, research is needed to test the possibility that patterns of decision making in areas other than moral choice may also be related to these modes of self definition.

TABLE 6

*Modes of Self Definition Related to Modes of Moral Choice*

| PREDOMINANT MODES OF MORAL CHOICE | MODES OF SELF DEFINITION | | |
|---|---|---|---|
| | *Connected* | *Separate/Objective* | *Other (S/C or none)* [*] |
| Response N = 13 (1M, 12F) | 10 (10F) | 0 | 3 (1M, 2F) |
| Rights N = 16 (12M, 4F) | 0 | 13 (11M, 2F) | 3 (1M, 2F) |

*Note:* $\chi^2$ *(2)* = *15.77, p < 0.005. In order to calculate the* $\chi^2$ *statistic, 1 was added to each cell in order to eliminate 0 cells.*

[*]*S/C indicates individuals having an equal number of separate/objective and connected characterizations; none indicates an individual having no relational characterizations.*

## IMPLICATIONS

The development of the methodologies presented here--the coding schemes for identifying modes of self-definition and moral judgment--made possible the testing of a set of hypotheses important for theories of ego and moral development and for educational and clinical practice as well. Although all of the implications cannot be addressed fully here, some of the most important ones are identified as an invitation to others to join in further clarification.

1. For psychological theories of moral development, a morality of care appears to be a systematic, life-long concern of individuals. It does not appear to be a temporary, stage- or level-specific concern, or subsumed within a morality of justice, as Kohlberg's work posits.

2. For psychological theories of ego and identity development, a relational conception of self--the self in relation to others--is central to self definition. This concern for connection with others should not be considered as present only at particular stages or as an issue

pertaining only to women. Although men and women may tend to understand and define relationships in different ways, a definition of self in relation to others is found *in both sexes* at all ages.

3. For theories of cognitive and social development, the fact that individuals construct, resolve, and evaluate problems in different ways seems to reflect two different perspectives towards others. This suggests that theories of cognitive and social development built on unitary models of social perspective-taking should be reconsidered.

4. For counselors, teachers, and managers, it is necessary, when dealing with conflicts within relationships, to take into account that the language of morality in everyday speech has different meanings for different people and that these may carry behavioral implications. For example, the terms "obligation" and "responsibility" may be understood differently from a justice and/or a care perspective.

5. For psychological research, there is a need to reflect the centrality of attachment in human development and interpersonal interactions. This means research should focus not just on the individual but on both members of an interacting unit--husband and wife, friend and friend, mother and child, teacher and student, manager and staff, and so forth. There is a need to move from a psychology of the individual to a psychology of relationships.

6. Sex as a variable for study ought to be included in research designs and methodologies as a matter of course. This research suggests both the difficulty in understanding sex difference and their importance to an improved understanding of theory and practice.

To accommodate the problems of modern moral philosophy, Murdoch (1970) has called for psychology and philosophy to join in creating a "new working philosophical psychology" (p. 46). This paper offers to psychologists and philosophers alike some new premises and methodologies by which to explore further the meaning of morality in our lives.

## NOTES

1. Responses are taken from interview data of the Rights and Responsibility Study (1978) conducted by Carol Gilligan and Michael Murphy to test Gilligan's hypotheses of the relationship between gender and self-concept and between conceptions of self and of morality.

2. Kohlberg's coding scheme focuses on analyzing moral judgments. It does not analyze the construction, resolution, and evaluation of moral choices, or considerations other than judgments in the resolution of conflict. In addition, it does not deal with real-life data, focusing instead on hypothetical moral dilemma data.

3. A fourteen-year-old girl suggested the subtlety of the process of considering others in their terms. Asked by the interviewer, "How do you think about what someone else's reaction is going to be?" she says, "Well, first I look at the person and I think about what they are like and how they have reacted in similar situations and how they react in general and, then, I put myself . . . in that person and try to put together a way that they would feel about this and this and this with the ideas that I have." She continues her explanation, "I guess I put myself away from me for a minute, put myself in their--but I am not relating myself to the subject at all. I am not relating the way that I feel about it, what's important to me--to what I let them think, to what I think that they'll feel." (Emma Willard School Study, Troy, N. Y., through the support of the Geraldine R. Dodge Foundation and with the collaboration of Robert Parker, Principal, Trudy Hanmer, Associate Principal, and the students and staff.)

4. In considering the "emotional aspect of concern for another," it is useful to note Blum's work, *Friendship, Altruism and Morality,* Boston (1980). Blum argues for a second mode of morality concerned with the good of the other and challenges the dominant Kantian view to argue that altruistic concerns and emotions can be morally good. The work presented here assumes Blum's philosophical argument and demonstrates empirically the psychological phenomenon that individuals do act out of concern for the good of another.

5. "Response" is an ancient word in the English language meaning "an answer, a reply; an action or feeling which answers to some stimulus or influence." "Responsibility" is usually associated with moral accountability and obligation and most frequently with contractual agreements related to a morality of justice. "Responsibility" carried in its earliest meaning "answering to something." It was only in the nineteenth century that "responsibility" became attached to moral accountability and rational conduct. (*Shorter Oxford English Dictionary,* 3rd ed., s.v. "response," "responsibility.")

For a useful discussion of "responsibility" as a new symbol and image in ethics, see Niebuhr's *The Responsible Self,* New York (1963). Niebuhr makes the interesting argument that "responsibility" as a new image of man--"man the answerer, man engaged in dialogue . . . acting in response to action upon him"--when used to refer to the self as agent, as doer "is usually translated with the aid of older images [of man] as meaning directed toward goals or as ability to be moved by respect for the law." Further, Niebuhr says, "the understanding of ourselves as responsive beings who in all our actions answer to action upon us in accordance with our interpretation of such actions is a fruitful conception, which brings into view aspects of our self-defining conduct that are *obscured* when the older images are exclusively employed" (p. 57). Niebuhr's point is relevant to the argument here. The meaning of "responsibility" in its sense of "responsiveness" is, or may be, obscured by teleological or deontological conceptions of morality.

6. This interaction is not to be confused with the fact that an individual with a major or predominant orientation may call upon considerations within either orientation when dealing with moral choice. But how a major orientation is influenced by the other or minor mode in its own sequence of development has not yet been elaborated and requires future work.

7. See Note 1, this chapter.

8. A consideration--the unit of analysis of the coding scheme--is an idea presented by the individual in the framing, resolution, or evaluation of choice.

## APPENDIX A

*Morality as Care and Morality as Justice:*

*A Scheme for Coding Considerations of Response and Considerations of Rights*

I. *The Construction of the Problem*

A. Considerations of Response (Care)

1. General effects to others (unelaborated)
2. Maintenance or restoration of relationships; or response to another considering interdependence
3. Welfare/well-being of another or the avoidance of conflict; or the alleviation of another's burden/hurt/suffering (physical or psychological)
4. Considers the "situation vs./over the principle"
5. Considers care of self; care of self vs. care of others

B. Considerations of Rights (Justice)

1. General effects to the self (unelaborated including "trouble," "how to decide")
2. Obligations/duty/commitments
3. Standards/rules/principles for the self or society; or considers fairness, that is, how one would like to be treated if in the other's place
4. Considers the "principle vs./over the situation"
5. Considers that others have their own contexts

II. *The Resolution of the Problem/Conflict*

[same as part I]

III. *The Evaluation of the Resolution*

A. Considerations of Response (Care)

1. What happened; how worked out
2. Whether relationships maintained/restored

B. Considerations of Rights (Justice)

1. How decided/thought about/justified
2. Whether values/standards/principles maintained

# APPENDIX B

*A Scheme for Coding Responses to the "Describe Yourself" Question*

I. *General and Factual*

   A. General factual
   B. Physical characteristics
   C. Identifying activities
   D. Identifying possessions
   E. Social status

II. *Abilities and Agency*

   A. General ability
   B. Agency
   C. Physical abilities
   D. Intellectual abilities

III. *Psychological*

   A. Interests (likes/dislikes)
   B. Traits/dispositions
   C. Beliefs/values
   D. Preoccupations

IV. *Relational Component*

   A. Connected in relation to others

      1. Have relationships (relationships are there)
      2. Abilities in relationships (make, sustain; to care; to do things for others)
      3. Traits/dispositions in relationships (help others)
      4. Concern (for the good of another in *their* terms)
      5. Preoccupations (with doing good for another; with *how* to do good)

   B. Separate/objective in relation to others

      1. Have relationships (relationships part of obligations/commitments; instrumental)
      2. Abilities in relationships (skill in interacting with others)
      3. Traits/dispositions in relationships (act in reciprocity; live up to duty/ obligations; commitment; fairness)
      4. Concern (for others in light of principles/values/beliefs/general good of society)
      5. Preoccupations (with doing good for society; with *whether* to do good for others)

V. *Summary Statements*

VI.  *Self–Evaluating Commentary*

A. In self's terms
B. In self in relation to others

1. Connected self
2. Separate self

## ACKNOWLEDGMENTS

    I wish to thank Carol Gilligan for her continuing support and encouragement, and Jane Attanucci, Miriam Clasby, Maxine Greene, Kay Johnston, Lawrence Kohlberg, Sharry Langdale, Jane Martin, Michael Murphy, Erin Phelps, Sharon Rich, Linda Stuart, Sheldon White, Bea Whiting, and Robert Lyons for their help and insights in the development of this work. I want to acknowledge, too, the support and personal encouragement of Marilyn Hoffman. The National Institute of Education funded the research reported in this chapter. The Geraldine Rockefeller Dodge Foundation is presently supporting a study of adolescent girls, part of which is also reported.

# 3

## ADOLESCENTS' SOLUTIONS TO DILEMMAS IN FABLES: TWO MORAL ORIENTATIONS--TWO PROBLEM SOLVING STRATEGIES

D. Kay Johnston

Recent discussions of moral development have dealt with contro-
versies relating to sex differences in moral development (Kohlberg, 1984;
Baumrind, 1986; Walker, 1986), cultural differences (Snarey, Reimer, &
Kohlberg, 1985; Snarey, 1985), and socialization versus developmental
theories of morality (Gibbs & Schnell, 1985). In these discussions one
definition of morality is offered, that of Kohlberg who followed Piaget
(1932/1965); thereby a theory of morality as the development of justice
reasoning is, in essence, taken for granted.

Other work has identified two moral orientations (Gilligan, 1977,
1982; Lyons, 1982, 1983) and explored how these two orientations are
used in people's thinking about real-life moral conflict and in hypothetical
dilemmas (Langdale, 1983). This work offers a theory about the morality
of care.

These two moral orientations--one of justice and rights and one
of care and response--have been shown to be represented in people's
descriptions of moral conflicts, but people tend to focus their attention
either on considerations of justice or on considerations of care so that
one orientation is predominant and the other minimally represented. In
addition, it has been demonstrated that in descriptions of real-life moral
conflict "care focus" dilemmas are more likely to be presented by females

and "justice focus" dilemmas by males (Lyons, 1982, 1983; Gilligan & Attanucci, in press and see Chapter 4). The discovery and exploration of moral orientations has largely been confined to data in which subjects were interviewed and asked to discuss an actual moral conflict which they faced. This question and its elaboration generate data called "real-life moral dilemmas." The moral orientations of justice and care appeared spontaneously in these discussions, but there was no attempt to system-atically explore the person's understanding of the moral orientation that was not focused upon or used spontaneously.

The present study begins with the hypothesis that there is no reason to assume that because a person uses an orientation spontaneously, she or he would not use the other orientation if asked whether there is another way to see the problem. Thus, the study considers the question: Can both males and females understand both moral orientations? This question is addressed by using a standard method (Johnston, 1983) to investigate the ability of one person to use both orientations in solving moral dilemmas. The dilemmas used are embedded in fables.

The study varied age and gender to test the premise that eleven and fifteen-year-old boys and girls can use both the justice and the care orientations. Consistent questions were asked of each participant and elicited not only alternative ways to solve the problem presented but also the participant's evaluation of different ways of solving the problem.

## METHOD

The author used two of Aesop's fables ("The Porcupine and the Moles" and "The Dog in the Manger") in two previous studies (see Appendix for fables). One study focused on different definitions of the moral problems posed in the fables;[1] another showed that boys and girls tended to solve the problems differently.[2] These two studies also found that the two moral orientations identified by Kohlberg and Gilligan emerged in the solutions of the subjects interviewed. These two orientations are characterized here as "rights orientation" and "response orientation," reflecting that the solution focused on issues of justice or issues of care. Subjects interviewed had solved the fable dilemmas either in the rights orientations by applying a universal rule which was seen as the fair way of solving a problem of con-flicting rights or claims as, "it is the mole's house; therefore, the porcupine must leave," or in the response orientation by trying to attend to and re-spond with care to the needs of all the animals in the fable, for example, "the moles and the porcupine must talk and share the house."

Thus, the fables present a standard method for interviewing a subject about his/her understanding of the justice and care orientation. The meth-od is similar to that used in eliciting real-life dilemmas in that it engages a person in discussing a moral problem; however, it is different in three ways. First, the fable offers a constant context which is specific and consistent for all interviewees so that comparisons can be made among and between peoples' discussion of the same dilemma. In this way it is similar to stan-dard measures of moral development that use hypothetical dilemmas. Sec-ond, the fables were not a reconstruction of a difficult moral problem faced by the interviewee. Because these dilemmas were not as personal as the real-life dilemmas, this interviewer felt less constrained in challenging the interviewee's construction of the problem and in making counter-suggestions which indicated reasons why solutions offered by the interviewee might not work. Finally, in this method the interviewee constructed both the moral problem and the solution, since he or she first was asked to identify the problem posed in the fable story and then to solve that problem.[3]

## Subjects

The subjects for this study were sixty adolescents who live and attend public school in a middle class suburban community north of Boston. The subjects were equally divided between boys and girls who were eleven and fifteen years of age.

The students were volunteers from four sixth-grade classes in two different elementary schools and from mixed levels of sophomore English classes. These students were recruited by the author who spoke to several classes and asked for student volunteers. Parental permission was obtained for each participant.

## Task and Procedure

The interviews were conducted in the schools. Following a brief explanation of the purpose of the interview, the interviewer read either "The Dog in the Manger" or "The Porcupine and the Moles." Following the first fable and discussion, the second fable was read; the fables were alternated in their order of presentation.

After the first fable was read the interviewer began a technique of interviewing which utilized standard questions combined with the method Piaget called the "clinical examination" (1979, p. 10). The first standard question was, "What is the problem?" followed by questions (or probes) which clarified what the subject had in mind, and how the problem had been defined. Then the subject was asked, "How would you solve it?" During this phase of the interview, counter-suggestions were made in order to examine the student's commitment to her/his initial solution. Questions were also asked to clarify the solution the subject had in mind and strategies being used to reach the solution.

Two solutions to each fable were coded: the "spontaneous" solution and the "best" solution. The student's first solution was considered the spontaneous, and the preferred solution was the best. The codes were assigned to the answers to the question, "Why is that a good solution?" These codes made a distinction between answers in the rights orientation or in the response orientation by following the logic of the Lyons coding scheme (1983).

In the overview of Lyons' coding scheme, the two moral orientations of rights and response are presented. The logic of a morality of rights is defined as construing moral problems as "issues/decisions of conflicting claims between self and others (including society). These issues are resolved by invoking impartial rules, principles, or standards which consider one's obligations, duty, or commitment; or standards, rules, or principles for self, others, and society." The response logic is defined as construing problems as issues of how to respond to others in their situations. In order to do so one considers how to "maintain relationships" or "promote the welfare of others or prevent them harm or relieve their burdens, hurt, or suffering, physical or psychological" (Lyons, 1983, p. 134). The coding of the fables relied on this logic.

When the solution for the fable relied on a principle such as "the right to own property" or "the right to life" expressed as a universal or impartial understanding, the solution was coded in the "rights" mode. Some examples of answers coded in the rights mode are:

The porcupine has to go definitely. It's the mole's house.

It's their ownership and nobody else has the right to it.

Send the porcupine out since he was the last one there.

Answers which responded to the needs of both animals in the dilemmas were coded "response" mode. Examples of these solutions are:

Wrap the porcupine in a towel.

If there's enough hay, well, this is one way, split it. Like, if they could cooperate. Like, take some of the hay so the dog can rest on it and take some of the hay so the ox can eat it. That's the only way to work it out.

There'd be times that the moles would leave or the porcupines would stand still or they'd take turns doing stuff--eating and stuff and not moving.

The both of them should try to get together and make the hole bigger.

Answers to the dilemmas which incorporated elements of both orientations were coded "both." Answers including both typically tried to incorporate or integrate the ideas that relied on a principle with the idea that the needs of both the participants in the dilemmas must somehow be met. Examples of these solutions are:

If the porcupine used the mole's house for the winter, then went back to where he used to live.

They (moles) should help the porcupine find a new house.

I think the moles should just ask him again to leave and if he says no, they should ask him, why not. If he says, "I can't find another place to live," then they should maybe enlarge their home. If he says, "I just don't feel like it," then they should send him out.

While relying on Lyons' exposition of the logic of the rights and response orientation, the fable coding departs from the actual coding procedure outlined by Lyons. Unlike Lyons' method which identified distinct ideas (i.e., "considerations"), the unit of analysis in the fable coding is the entire solution offered by the subject. Similarly, in Lyons' procedure there is a delineation of separate ideas into "chunks" which fall under either the response or the rights orientation. In other words, the coder's task is to mark separate ideas presented by the interviewee and code each idea as either justice or care. This also is not done in the fable coding, since the concern is not to quantify the considerations which appear in one or the other orientation, but rather to ascertain whether each orientation is represented by each subject.

The final difference in this coding is a category called "both." "Both" indicates that the logics of both orientations were represented and/or integrated in the solution. Once the orientation of the solution was identified, it was coded either Response, Rights, or Both. It could also be labeled Uncodable, which meant the answer did not clearly represent any identified logic.

This four-category coding is desirable for two reasons: (1) the range of answers is represented and (2) the possibility of reducing these moral orientations to an either/or dichotomy is eliminated.

### Intercoder Reliability

Intercoder reliability was determined for two coding categories in the fable data. These two categories were: (1) orientation used spontaneously and (2) orientation used for best solution.

The criterion of agreement was that the two judges identically coded each participant's spontaneous solution and best solution. The reliability of this coding method is reported in Table 1. It is worth noting that the second coder had not been previously reliable on the Lyons real-life coding

TABLE 1

*Intercoder Reliability*

| Solution Coded | Agreement | Cohen's Kappa[*] |
|---|---|---|
| Spontaneous solution to The Dog in the Manger | 100 | 1.00 |
| Spontaneous solution to The Porcupine and the Moles | 90 | 0.81 |
| Best solution to The Dog in the Manger | 100 | 1.00 |
| Best solution to The Porcupine and the Moles | 100 | 1.00 |

[*]Cohen's Kappa is the measurement of agreement that takes chance into account (1960).

scheme. This suggests that this standardized fable method may be easily replicated.[4]

As the interview continued, the student was asked, "Is there another way to solve the problem?" This standard question began the process of discovering the interviewee's ability to switch orientations. When the subject offered an alternative solution, the questioning process was repeated. If the subject was unable to spontaneously switch orientations, the interviewer used the following procedure. If the spontaneous solution given had been in the rights orientation, the interviewer said:

> *Is there a way to solve the dilemma so that all of the animals will be satisfied?*

If this did not help the subject adopt the response orientation, the interviewer said:

> *Some people would say that you can solve this problem by having the animals talk together and decide on a way in which they could all be happy. What do you think of that?*

This question was followed by another standard question:

> *How do you think someone who solved the problem in that way would think about the problem?*

If the spontaneous solution had been in the response orientation, the interviewer said:

> *Is there a rule you could use to solve the problem?*

If this did not elicit a rights solution, the interviewer said:

> *Some people would say that you could solve this problem by using a rule such as "This is the mole's house (or the ox's stable), so the porcupine (or dog) must leave." What do you think of that?*

This question was followed by:

> *How do you think someone who solved the problem in that way would think about the problem?*

Each of the interviewer's questions more clearly defined the thinking inherent in the second orientation for the subject. The idea of asking for the second orientation assumed the interviewer recognized the spontaneous orientation while interviewing.  The author has had extensive experience coding the orientations in real-life dilemmas and did recognize the rights or response orientation while interviewing for the 1983 pilot study.  If there was any question about which orientation was used spontaneously, the interviewer went through both sets of standard questions to elicit the subject's thinking in both orientations.

Finally, the interviewer asked:

*Of all the solutions we discussed, which one is best?*

## RESULTS

The central question in this research is:  How do adolescents use and explain both moral orientations while discussing the problem in the two fables.  To address this question, this article will focus on results pertaining to:  (1) the use of moral orientation for the spontaneous solution and (2) the use of moral orientation for the best solution.

In addressing each question, age and gender differences will be discussed.  The results for each fable are presented separately because they were sometimes different.  These differences are important and in some cases lead to different interpretations and implications.  In the *Fable Effects* section there is an examination of the effects of discussing both orientations in one fable on the consideration of moral orientation in the second fable.  For the sake of brevity, "The Porcupine and the Moles" will be referred to as the Porcupine Fable, and "The Dog in the Manger" as the Dog Fable.

### Moral Orientation Used for Spontaneous Solution

Tables 2 and 3 show use of spontaneous orientation by gender for each fable.  These results are collapsed across ages, since there was no significant difference in the use of spontaneous orientation by eleven and fifteen-year-olds.

As can be seen in Table 2, the orientation used spontaneously in the Dog Fable was significantly related to gender.  The expected pattern is demonstrated with 73.3 percent of males using the rights orientation for their initial solution.  In contrast, 50 percent of the girls used the response

TABLE 2

*Moral Orientation of Spontaneous Solution for The Dog in the Manger Fable,*
*by Gender*

|  | Female | Male |
|---|---|---|
| Rights | 12 | 22 |
| Response | 15 | 5 |
| Both | 3 | 1 |
| Uncodable | 0 | 2 |

$\chi^2 = 10.94$, d.f. $= 3$, $p = 0.01$.

*Note: The expected values in the tables presented here are frequently lower than 5, the recommended minimum (Siegel, 1956). To check the significance of these tables, the categories Both and Uncodable were eliminated because they often had low frequencies. Statistics were then calculated on the resulting two–by–two tables. The results were virtually the same. The tables presented here were selected because they represent the complexity of the responses more adequately than the two–by–two tables.*

TABLE 3

*Moral Orientation of Spontaneous Solution for The Porcupine and the Moles Fable,*
*by Gender*

|  | Female | Male |
|---|---|---|
| Rights | 15 | 21 |
| Response | 10 | 7 |
| Both | 5 | 1 |
| Uncodable | 0 | 1 |

$\chi^2 = 5.20$, d.f. $= 3$, $p = 0.16$.

orientation, 40 percent used rights, and 10 percent used both orientations in their initial solution.

In Table 3, it can be seen that the use of spontaneous orientation had no significant relationship to gender in the Porcupine Fable. It is interesting that 60 percent of all subjects interviewed spontaneously solved this Porcupine Fable in the rights mode. This presents a difference in the spontaneous solutions to the two fables.

## Moral Orientations Used for Best Solutions

The following tables show the choice of moral orientation for the best solution by gender for both fables. Again, there was no significant relationship with age and the use of moral orientations for the best solutions; therefore, the results are not presented by age.

TABLE 4

*Moral Orientation of Best Solution for The Dog in the Manger Fable, by Gender*

|  | Female | Male |
|---|---|---|
| Rights | 3 | 13 |
| Response | 24 | 13 |
| Both | 3 | 3 |
| Uncodable | 0 | 1 |

$\chi^2 = 10.52$, d.f. = 3, p = 0.01.

Table 4 shows that 80 percent of the females chose the response orientation as the best way to solve the problem, and 10 percent decided that a solution which included both orientations provided the best solution. This finding confirmed initial predictions. For the males it can be seen that 43.3 percent used the rights orientation and 43.3 percent used the response

orientation for the best solution. This is different from the predicted outcome which was that males would use the rights orientation predominantly.

TABLE 5

*Moral Orientation of Best Solution for The Porcupine and the Moles Fable,
by Gender*

|  | Female | Male |
|---|---|---|
| Rights | 6 | 17 |
| Response | 18 | 5 |
| Both | 5 | 6 |
| Uncodable | 1 | 2 |

$\chi^2 = 13.03$, d.f. = 3, p = 0.0046.

The results for the use of moral orientation for the best solution to
the Porcupine Fable (Table 5) show a highly significant relationship between orientation and gender. Sixty percent of the females chose response
and 56.7 percent of the males chose rights as the orientation providing the
best solution. This is the pattern predicted by previous research (Gilligan,
Johnston, Langdale, Lyons). Also of interest here is that five females
(16.7 percent) and six males (20 percent) used both moral orientations
in their best solution, thus integrating the two orientations.

**Fable Effects**

Analysis was also done to determine if the discussion of both orientations in the first fable influenced the use of orientations in the discussion
of the second fable. For each order of presentation, contingency tables
were used to explore the associations between: the spontaneous orientation
used in the first fable and the spontaneous orientation used in the second
fable; the best orientation used in the first fable and the best orientation

used in the second fable; the best orientation used in the first fable and the spontaneous orientation used in the second fable. None of these associations were significant, regardless of which fable was discussed first.

## DISCUSSION

This study demonstrates that within the specific discussion of the two fables, the two moral orientations described by Gilligan and Kohlberg are used by adolescents of both ages to solve the fables' moral problems and can be reliably identified. Then the question becomes: What leads to the use of these orientations? These fable data suggest that both gender and fable speak to that question. These findings:

1. present gender differences in moral orientation
2. show the influence of context on use of orientation as shown by the fable differences
3. question the assumption that there is one problem-solving strategy for moral problems
4. point to avenues for further research

### Gender Differences

Age was not related to use of moral orientation but gender was. The pattern of girls using the care orientation and boys using the rights orientation was present in one of the spontaneous solutions and in both of the best solutions. The spontaneous solution to the Porcupine Fable did not replicate this pattern and will be discussed in the section *Fable Differences.*

Two aspects of the findings are of particular interest. All of the boys and girls represented the two orientations in some way. They either used both orientations in their varying solutions or they switched orientations spontaneously when asked, "Is there another way to solve the problem?" Thus, by at least eleven years of age, most children indicate knowledge of both orientations. This shows that the gender difference does not reflect knowing or understanding only one orientation, but rather choosing and/or preferring one over the other as a solution to a moral dilemma. Thus, the gender difference represents a relationship between gender and choice of moral orientation. This relationship arises from the fact that the girls as a group choose both orientations more frequently than the boys who tend as a group to use the rights orientation more exclusively. In other words, boys use the moral orientation of care much less often than girls use the moral orientation of justice. This is interesting because even though the boys know both moral orientations, they most often choose and prefer only the rights orientation, while girls choose and prefer both. This finding corroborates Gilligan's original hypothesis that if only males are studied there *is* a predominant voice of morality, but studying girls complicates a unitary view of morality. It also suggests that girls may learn the dominant voice of morality, that of justice, and be able to represent this culturally valued dominant voice (see Kohlberg and also Miller, 1976, for a view of dominance in culture), but in addition, may represent a less well articulated voice of morality and shift voices with greater flexibility than boys. This flexibility may be a strength which is more evident in girls' development than in boys, and it raises the question of whether this is a characteristic of girls in particular or of subordinate groups in general.

## Fable Differences

The context of the fables influences the choice of moral orientation in two ways. As previously noted, the spontaneous solution to the Porcupine Fable did not yield significant gender differences. Although males predominantly used the rights orientation, females did not use the care orientation predominantly but used the care and justice orientations equally. When the females are divided by age, it is the fifteen-year-olds who choose the moral orientation of rights, while the eleven-year-olds use the moral orientation of response. The data suggest two explanations for this finding. The greater frequency of the spontaneous use of rights solutions by fifteen-year-old girls in the Porcupine Fable may reflect the nature of the conflict presented in this fable: The moles' claim to property and the porcupine's claim to shelter can readily be construed in the rights mode, especially in a rights-oriented culture such as the United States. The older fifteen-year-old girls may be more aware of our cultural norms and values. Another explanation for this finding is that older girls may be afraid of looking naive when they propose an inclusive solution like "They could build a bigger house" to solve this conflict. This would explain their use of the rights orientation spontaneously in this dilemma.

The second fable difference is that the Dog Fable elicits more best solutions using the response orientation from the boys. In both fables if there is a change from the moral orientation used spontaneously to that used for the best solution, it tends to be from the rights to the response orientation or to a solution using both orientations. This suggests that a more circumspect appraisal of the dilemma produces a more inclusive solution.

TABLE 6

*Moral Orientation of the Spontaneous and Best Solutions to Both Fables*

|  | *Rights* | *Response* | *Both* | *Uncodable* |
|---|---|---|---|---|
| *Spontaneous Solution* | | | | |
| Dog | 56% (34) | 33.3% (20) | 6.7% (4) | 3.3% (2) |
| Porcupine | 60% (36) | 28.3% (17) | 10.0% (6) | 1.7% (1) |
| *Best Solution* | | | | |
| Dog | 26.0% (16) | 61.7% (37) | 10.0% (6) | 1.7% (1) |
| Porcupine | 38.3% (23) | 38.3% (23) | 18.3% (11) | 5.0% (3) |

One can see in Table 6 that there are not major differences in the use of response in the best solution. In both fables there is a trend toward using response after both orientations have been discussed, but in the Dog Fable the trend is larger.

In the Porcupine Fable almost half of the changes (seven of fifteen) are accounted for by the fifteen-year-old females. This is not the case in the Dog Fable, where males account for thirteen of the twenty-two switches. It is important in this context to keep in mind that a significant relationship exists between gender and use of orientation for both spontaneous and best solutions in the Dog Fable. Thus, females began in the response orientation and ended there as well. But many males moved from rights to response. The question regarding the Dog Fable, therefore, becomes: What is it about *this* fable makes the boys want to try to meet the needs of the animals in this problem more than in the porcupine problem?

Initially the author believed that although the dog in the fable is cast in the villain role by taking over the ox's stable, adolescents might feel benevolent toward the dog since they probably knew many dogs and possibly have had one for a pet. However, when asked at the end of the interview if their solution would have been different if the dog were a raccoon, almost all of the respondents answered, "No." In the words of a fifteen-year-old male, "Well, probably not, the same alternatives are there." So the simplistic notion that the fable difference comes from the knowledge and liking of a more familiar animal was dismissed.

A question was added to this study after the pilot was conducted to get at the issue of switching moral orientations. When an individual solved one fable by using the rights orientation and the other by using the response orientation, he/she was asked why. Over half of the eleven and fifteen-year-old male adolescents were asked this question because 59 percent solved the two fables differently. The boys that changed were like the fifteen-year-old girls who changed in the Porcupine Fable in that their discussion also began to include the needs of both parties involved. One of the fifteen-year-old males who exemplified this pattern explains:

> S: Realize one another's needs, I guess. It's hard to do with animals though.
>
> I: *How would they get to do that if they had all kinds of human power? How would they get to that point?*
>
> S: Well, like the ox has to realize that the dog wants a place to sleep, he's tired, and the dog has to realize that the ox wants something to eat. So if they compromise they can each have half the stall and some hay.
>
> I: *How do you compromise? What does that mean?*
>
> S: Each give in on what you think to, ah, don't take your own side, compromise and like something that both would be [think would be] pretty fair.

This quote represents the central idea expressed by all the male adolescents who change orientations. The idea is that this dilemma does not have to be seen in a way that only deals with the needs of one of the participants. Both male and female adolescents recognize that if one can respond to the needs of all involved one removes the dilemma.

The differences found appear to arise from the question of when or under what circumstances do males abandon a rights orientation to problem solving and choose to use a response orientation. The data suggest the answer to this question. The boys' responses imply that the fundamental difference between these two fables lies in the possibility of the animals getting along after the problem is solved. For example, the eleven-year-old boys specifically address the ability of the moles and the porcupine to have a continuing relationship as indicated in the following excerpts:

> They (moles) get scratched all the time.

> The moles might still be annoyed even after all of the [pause], even if they tried lots of solutions and most of them might not work.

One boy, in explaining why there was a difference in the way he solved the two fables, said that the porcupine was "bothering the moles" and the dog was "just kicking the ox out." It is not immediately apparent why these are different, but one can distinguish between the suggestion of an ongoing difficulty (bothering the moles) and one incident (kicking the ox out). The implication is that, once the problem is solved between the ox and the dog, the conflict will be over. In contrast, one boy says, even "if they tried lots of solution," the porcupine, because of his fundamental difference from the moles (i.e., his quills) will continue to bother them. This theme is elaborated by a fifteen-year-old male.

> I: *Why do you see a difference in those two problems--the first one to have sharing the best, and this one to have the porcupine leave?*

> S: I think it depends mainly on the people involved. The dog and the ox, you can see where they might be able to live together, but a porcupine and a mole, the porcupine could be dangerous, so I guess it depends on the parties involved.

> I: *How can you sort out the situation? Thinking about what the people are like and how they are in the situation? How do you learn to do that?*

> S: See beyond what they look like and see inside. Some people are harsh or kind. Some people are prejudiced and some aren't. You can't put, for example, a person who wants to save the whales with someone who wants to kill them. You can't put them together and expect them to get along all the time. They won't even get along, maybe, so one will have to go. There's no good reason why they should be roommates in the first place.

> I: *What would happen?*

> S: If they become roommates?

*I: Yes.*

S: It would probably be the worst thing that ever happened. They'd be
fighting, because like in the back of their mind, like that subject of killing
whales, for example, and other topics, they'd probably pick at it.

To those boys, the response orientation provides the best solution only
if there is the possibility of relationship beyond the conflict. They share
an implicit criterion which they use to judge whether the relationship will
continue over time. In the fables the impediment they see to a long lasting
relationship is one of differences. This is a fundamental divergence in the
problem solving of these boys and girls. By using the response orientation
significantly more than the boys, girls *assume* that the relationship exists
and can continue. The boys assume that the relationship does not exist
if the differences in those involved in the problem appear too great.
Gilligan's analogy to the figure/ground problem is helpful here in calling
attention to the fact that, looking at the same image, one can focus on
different aspects of it. Girls looking at the dilemma tend to see the relationships as prominent whereas boys tend to see the individual differences
in the participants rather than their potential relationship as salient. These
boys only focus on the relationship if the differences recede to the background.

Thus, the fable data have interesting implications for understanding
differences in moral judgments. If morality signifies the understanding of
relationships with other people and serves as a guide to solving problems in
relationships, then the fables pose a cognitive exercise in resolving conflicts
in relationship. The ways that differences are conceived lead to different
strategies for negotiating conflicts in these relationships. In contrast to a
simplistic representation of the theory which holds that the importance of
relationships is more salient to females than to males, is the idea that males
and females tend to negotiate conflict in relationship in different ways.
The clearest difference is that 70 percent of the boys initially negotiated
conflict by applying rules; when rules don't work or when counter-suggestions indicate rules will not work, they must make a choice. This choice
tends to center on whether to invoke power--"The porcupine just has to
go"--or whether to begin to talk and find a way to meet specific needs.
The data in this study suggest that talking may only make sense to the
boys if the possibility of a continuing relationship exists beyond the

conflict.  In the fables they tend to evaluate this possibility by judging how fundamental the differences in the participants are.  Girls, in contrast, use both strategies in negotiating conflict but frequently begin by trying to attend to specific needs.  When this seems to be unworkable, they then may resort to rules.  The idea of different assumptions regarding relationships is the most compelling explanation for the finding that more boys use response in the best solution to the Dog Fable than in any other solution.  However, future research should attempt to test alternative explanations of these data and examine whether assumptions about relationships are different for male and female adolescents when discussing other dilemmas.

## IMPLICATIONS

### Strategies for Moral Problem Solving

Past research on moral development assumes one theory of morality-- that of Kohlberg.  Implicit in this theory is that only one problem-solving strategy, "justice reasoning," is employed in moral problem solving.  This system is a hierarchical system like Piaget's description of cognitive operations.  It orders priorities in a moral problem with the goal of being fair and objective.  Like Piaget's exclusion of variables problems (Inhelder & Piaget, 1958/1983, p. 302), this problem-solving strategy excludes variables until the most important variable remains.  In other words, Kohlberg documents a formal system of thinking which systematically chooses the best solution to a problem by isolating the "most moral claim" (Colby *et al.*, 1986).

The fable data indicate a second problem-solving strategy for moral problems.  This system *includes* variables or needs of participants in the dilemmas until a solution which integrates these needs is reached.  Polanyi writes of two conflicting aspects of formalized intelligence: (1) acquisition of formal instruments and (2) the pervasive participation of the knowing person in the act of knowing by virtue of an art which is essentially inarticulate (Polanyi, 1958, p. 70).

This study begins to render Polanyi's second aspect of intelligence articulate.  One girl says that to reason one needs to "care," and "caring" means "understanding."  When the boys and girls in this study begin to understand the needs of all participants in the dilemmas, they begin to employ a logic which includes the moral claims of all involved in the dilemma. The subjects in this study described this logic as "seeing every-body's side" of the problem. This is not done intuitively; rather, it is done by attending to all the variables in a particular situation. This logic does not systematically discard variables, but integrates as many variables as possible. These data demonstrate that both male and female adolescents do this kind of reasoning within the context of the fables, but girls are more likely to rely on this logic to provide solutions for the fable problems.

Therefore, gender may be related to the use of the problem-solving strategies in the following way. Vygotsky presents a theory of thinking in which the learner interacts with the society in which she/he participates, and he emphasizes the influence of that society on the individual. He be-lieves children first learn in an interaction with adults and as this learning gradually becomes internalized, "an interpersonal process is transformed into an intrapersonal one. All the higher functions (voluntary attention, logical memory, formation of concepts) originate as actual relations between human individuals" (Vygotsky, 1978, p. 57). This theory allows for individual and group differences.

Keeping this idea that different interpersonal interactions may lead to different intrapersonal functions leads to the work of Chodorow. She suggests that men and women learn to relate differently. "Most generally I would suggest that a quality of embeddedness in social interaction and per-sonal relationship characterize women's life relative to men's" (Chodorow, 1974, p. 66). She states that men, in order to develop, must separate or deny their attachment to their mothers; women do not need to do either of these things in their development.

Chodorow's idea of developing in a separate way or in a connected way would clearly imply two different experiences of interpersonal func-tions. Then, following Vygotsky's idea of thinking being transformed from inter- to intrapersonal, it would follow that the intrapersonal thinking would be different for people who identify themselves through connection with others as opposed to those who identify themselves through separation from others.

This idea of different interpersonal interactions leading to different cognitive strategies would suggest patterns of gender differences in cog-nitive functioning. But this discussion differs from Chodorow in that, rather than defining these different cognitive strategies as absolutely associated with gender, it posits that these two strategies are used by both males and females. Gilligan suggests that both males and females have the experiences of connection and separation, so these two types of interpersonal interaction shared by both males and females lead to two types of interpersonal functions employed by both genders. The interesting question, then, becomes not how do females think and how do males think, but *when* do males and females use these strategies? This study suggests that the use of these strategies may be dependent on the problem solver's view of the relationship in the problem.

### Further Research Questions

Of interest in these data are the two unpredicted findings that older girls use the moral orientation of rights in the Porcupine Fable, and boys use response as frequently as rights for the best solution in the Dog Fable. Further research would investigate the development of the moral orientation of rights in girls between the ages of eleven and fifteen. Does this development of the rights voice silence the spontaneous voice of care? Is it a developmental gain or loss for these girls? Also of interest are the different assumptions about relationship made by boys and girls. Is it true that boys make different assumptions than girls? It is interesting that in these data boys speak of similarities between those involved when describing relationships and girls do not.

Finally, the problem-solving strategy that the data suggest needs to be carefully described. Is it a strategy that is more frequently associated with girls, and is it a strategy viable outside the domain of moral problem solving? Cunnion (1984) began this investigation in the field of abstract reasoning, but it is not described adequately in the psychological literature.

In summary, this study:

1. Supports Gilligan's original hypothesis that there is a gender difference in moral problem solving; therefore, recent questions (Walker, 1984, 1986; Pratt *et al.*, 1984) regarding whether gender differences in moral reasoning exist are answered in the affirmative.

2. Demonstrates that both genders employ both systems of reasoning, although they employ these systems differently. This differential use seems to be related to the context of the fables and the view of relationships held by the problem solver.

3. Begins to articulate a system of problem solving that is related to the logic of the moral orientation of response.

The results of the present study indicate that any description of moral development which omits either moral orientation is not a sufficient description of moral reasoning. Further, any description of moral development which either omits or oversimplifies the gender difference found in this study would not provide an accurate description of moral development in either sex. The fact that this study found gender differences using a standard research design is important. Of equal importance is the complicated way these differences appeared. The most general conclusion is that individuals use and understand both moral orientations; however, the use of these orientations is influenced by gender and by the context of the problem.

An interview which does not probe for a subject's understanding of both moral orientations will not provide adequate data for exploring the ways in which both moral orientations inform an individual's solution to a given moral problem. Furthermore, the assumption that the initial way a subject solved a moral dilemma is the only way or the best way to solve a problem cannot be held.

# NOTES

1. Johnston, D.K.  "Adolescents' Responses to Moral Dilemmas in Fables." Unpublished manuscript, Harvard Graduate School of Education (1979).

2. Johnston, D.K.  "Responding to Moral Dilemmas in Fables, Ages Six to Eleven: A Brief Study of Gender Differences."  Unpublished manuscript, Harvard Graduate School of Education (1982).

3. In Langdale's research (1983), the problem of "closed" research, or research directed by the interviewer's question, is addressed.  This problem is avoided in the fables.

4. Six people were trained to code the fables over a six-week period.  Reliability tests were run on the spontaneous and best solutions to both fables.  The average reliability score was 80 percent.

# APPENDIX

### Fables

*The Porcupine and the Moles*

It was growing cold, and a porcupine was looking for a home. He found a most desirable cave but saw it was occupied by a family of moles.

"Would you mind if I shared your home for the winter?" the porcupine asked the moles.

The generous moles consented and the porcupine moved in. But the cave was small and every time the moles moved around they were scratched by the porcupine's sharp quills. The moles endured this discomfort as long as they could. Then at last they gathered courage to approach their visitor. "Pray leave," they said, "and let us have our cave to ourselves once again."

"Oh no!" said the porcupine. "This place suits me very well."

*The Dog in the Manger*

A dog, looking for a comfortable place to nap, came upon the empty stall of an ox. There it was quiet and cool and the hay was soft. The dog, who was very tired, curled up on the hay and was soon fast asleep.

A few hours later the ox lumbered in from the fields. He had worked hard and was looking forward to his dinner of hay. His heavy steps woke the dog who jumped up in a great temper. As the ox came near the stall the dog snapped angrily, as if to bite him. Again and again the ox tried to reach his food but each time he tried the dog stopped him.

Both fables are adapted from *Aesop's Fables*, retold by A. McGovern, which is published by Scholastic Book Company, 1963.

# ACKNOWLEDGMENTS

I acknowledge the teachers and the administrators who allowed me to talk with their students. I thank Jane Attanucci for her help with reliability coding and data analysis. Many friends and my family encouraged my work, and I owe them more than thanks. Finally, and most important, I thank the adolescents with whom I spoke.

# 4

## TWO MORAL ORIENTATIONS

### Carol Gilligan and Jane Attanucci

Recent discussions of sex differences in moral development have confused moral stage within Kohlberg's justice framework with moral orientation, the distinction between justice and care perspectives. Studies by Kohlberg (1984), Walker (1984), Baumrind (1986), and Haan (1985) address
the question of whether women and men score differently in Kohlberg's
scale of justice reasoning and report contradictory findings. In the present
study, we address the question of moral orientation and examine evidence
of two moral perspectives in people's discussions of actual moral conflicts.
In addition, we ask whether there is an association between moral orientation and gender.

The distinction made here between a justice and a care orientation pertains to the ways in which moral problems are conceived and reflects different dimensions of human relationships that give rise to moral concern. A
justice perspective draws attention to problems of inequality and oppression
and holds up an ideal of reciprocity and equal respect. A care perspective
draws attention to problems of detachment or abandonment and holds up
an ideal of attention and response to need. Two moral injunctions--not to
treat others unfairly and not to turn away from someone in need--capture
these different concerns. From a developmental standpoint, inequality and
attachment are universal human experiences; all children are born into a
situation of inequality and no child survives in the absence of some kind of
adult attachment. The two dimensions of equality and attachment charac-

terize all forms of human relationship, and all relationships can be
described in both sets of terms--as unequal or equal and as attached or
detached. Since everyone has been vulnerable both to oppression and to
abandonment, two moral visions--one of justice and one of care--recur
in human experience.

This article reports the results of three studies undertaken to investigate the two moral orientations and to determine to what extent men and
women differentially raise concerns about justice and care in discussing
moral conflicts in their lives. Lyons (1983) operationalized the distinction
between justice and care in terms of the perspective toward others which
they imply, contrasting a perspective of reciprocity with a perspective of
response. Evidence of these perspectives appeared in the kinds of considerations people raised in discussing real-life moral dilemmas. Lyons created
a reliable procedure for identifying moral considerations and assigning them
to categories. She defines a morality of justice as: fairness resting on "an
understanding of relationships as reciprocity between separate individuals,
grounded in the duty and obligations of their roles." Reciprocity is defined
in terms of maintaining standards of justice and fairness, understood differently at different developmental levels (Kohlberg, 1981, 1984). A morality
of care "rests on an understanding of relationships as response to another
in their terms" (Lyons, 1983, p. 136). A care perspective involves the question of how to act responsively and protect vulnerability in a particular
situation.

The examples presented in Table 1, drawn from discussions of real-
life dilemmas, illustrate the concept of moral orientation. Each pair of
dilemmas reveals how a problem is seen from a justice and from a care
perspective. In each pair of examples, the justice construction is the more
familiar one, capturing the way such problems are usually defined from a
moral standpoint. In 1J a peer pressure dilemma is presented in terms of
how to uphold one's moral standards and withstand pressure from one's
friends to deviate from what one knows to be right. In 1C a similar
decision (not to smoke) is cast in terms of how to respond both to
one's friends and to oneself; the rightness of the decision not to smoke is
established in terms of the fact that it did not break relationships--"my
real friends accepted my decision." Attention to one's friends, to what

they say and how it will affect the friendship is presented as a moral concern.

In the second pair of examples, a dilemma--whether to report someone who has violated the medical school's alcohol policy--is posed differently from the justice and care perspectives; the decision not to tell is reasoned in different ways. A clear example of justice tempered by mercy is presented in 2J. The student clearly believes that the violator should be turned in ("I was supposed to turn her in") and justifies not doing so on the grounds that she deserved mercy because "she had all the proper level of contriteness" appropriate for the situation. In 2C a student decides not

TABLE 1

*Examples of Justice and Care Perspectives in Real–Life Moral Dilemmas*

| *Justice* | *Care* |
|---|---|
| 1J [If people were taking drugs and I was the only one who wasn't, I would feel it was stupid. I know for me what is right is right and what's wrong is wrong . . . It's like a set of standards I have.] (High School Student) | 1C [If there was one person, it would be a lot easier to say no. I could talk to her, because there wouldn't be seven others to think about. I do think about them, you know, and wonder what they say about me and what it will mean . . . I made the right decision not to, because my real friends accepted my decision.] (High School Student) |
| 2J [The conflict was that by all rights she should have been turned into the honor board for violation of the alcohol policy.] [I liked her very much.] [She is extremely embarrassed and upset. She was contrite. She wished she had never done it. She had all the proper levels of contriteness and guilt . . .] [I was supposed to turn her in and didn't.] (Medical Student) | 2C [It might just be his business if he wants to get drunk every week or it might be something that is really a problem and that should be dealt with professionally; and to be concerned about someone without antagonizing them or making their life more difficult than it had to be. Maybe there was just no problem there.] [I guess in something like a personal relationship with a proctor you don't want to just go right out there and antagonize people, because that person will go away and if you destroy any relationship you have, I think you have lost any chance of doing anything for a person.] (Medical Student) |

to turn a proctor in because it would "destroy any relationship you have" and therefore, would "hurt any chance of doing anything for that person." In this construction, turning the person in is seen as impeding efforts to help. The concern about maintaining relationship in order to be able to help is not mentioned in 2J; similarly the concern about maintaining the honor board policy is not mentioned in 2C. A further illustration of how justice and care perspectives restructure moral understanding can be seen by observing that in 2J the student justifies not turning in the violator because of questions about the rightness or justification of the alcohol policy itself, while in 2C the student considers whether what was deemed a problem was really a problem for the other person. The case of 2C illustrates what is meant by striving to see the other in the other's terms; it also exemplifies the contrast between this endeavor and the effort to establish, independently of persons, the legitimacy of existing rules and standards. It is important to emphasize that these examples were selected to highlight the contrast between the justice and the care perspectives and that most people who participated in this research used considerations of both justice and care in discussing a moral conflict they faced.

Validity for Lyons' distinction between justice and care considerations was provided by Langdale (1983), who adapted Lyons' procedure in order to code hypothetical dilemmas. Langdale found that Kohlberg's justice-oriented Heinz dilemma elicits significantly more justice considerations than either a hypothetical care-oriented abortion dilemma or subject-generated real-life moral dilemmas. Langdale demonstrated further that the hypothetical Heinz and abortion dilemmas as well as recurrent types of real-life dilemmas are construed by some people predominantly in terms of justice and by others predominantly in terms of care. This negates the suggestion that concerns about justice and care arise from different kinds of moral problems. Instead, Langdale's analysis of moral orientation indicates how the same problem can be seen in different ways. At the same time her study reveals that hypothetical moral dilemmas can "pull" for the justice or the care orientation.

In the present study, we ask the following three questions: (1) Is there evidence of both justice and care concerns in people's discussion of real-life moral conflict? (2) Do people represent both sets of concerns equally or do they tend to focus on one and minimally represent the other? (3) Is there a relationship between moral orientation and gender?

## METHOD

### Subjects

Subjects were drawn from three research studies conducted over the past six years. As part of each study, the subjects were asked to describe a real-life moral dilemma. All three samples consisted of men and women matched for levels of education; the adults were matched for professional occupations. The decision was made to sample from an advantaged population, since sex differences in adult moral reasoning have been attributed to women's typically lower occupational and educational status (Kohlberg & Kramer, 1969).

*Study 1.* The design of this study matched participants for high levels of education and professional occupation to examine the variables of age, gender, and type of dilemma. The adolescents and adults included eleven women and ten men. The racial composition (nineteen white and two minority) was not statistically random, as race was not a focal variable of the study.

*Study 2.* In this study first-year students were randomly selected from two prestigious northeastern medical schools to be interviewed as part of a longitudinal study of stress and adaptation in physicians.[1] The twenty-six men and thirteen women students represented the proportions of each gender in the class at large. The nineteen white and twenty minority students (Black, Hispanic, and Asian Americans) were selected to balance the sample's racial composition (the only sample in the present study with such a design). The students ranged from twenty-one to twenty-seven years of age.

*Study 3.* The ten female and ten male participants were randomly selected from a coeducational private school in a midwestern city. The nineteen white and one minority student ranged in age from fourteen to eighteen years.

See Table 2 for the distribution of subjects by sample in age and gender categories.

TABLE 2

*Gender and Age of Subjects by Study*
*(Moral Orientation Studies)*

|  | *15–22 years* | *23–34 years* | *35–77 years* |
|---|---|---|---|
| *Study 1* | | | |
| Women (N = 11) | 4 | 2 | 5 |
| Men (N = 10) | 4 | 1 | 5 |
| *Study 2* | | | |
| Women (N = 13) | 9 | 4 | 0 |
| Men (N = 26) | 12 | 14 | 0 |
| *Study 3* | | | |
| Women (N = 10) | 10 | 0 | 0 |
| Men (N = 10) | 10 | 0 | 0 |

**Research Interview**

All participants were asked the following series of questions about their personal experience of moral conflict and choice.

1. Have you ever been in a situation of moral conflict where you have had to make a decision but weren't sure what was the right thing to do?
2. Could you describe the situation?
3. What were the conflicts for you in that situation?
4. What did you do?
5. Do you think it was the right thing to do?
6. How do you know?

The interviewer asked questions to encourage the participants to clarify and elaborate their responses. For example, participants were asked what they meant by words like responsibility, obligation, moral, fair, selfish, and caring. The interviewers followed the participants' logic in presenting the moral problem, most commonly querying, "Anything else?"

The interviews were conducted individually, tape recorded, and later transcribed. The moral conflict questions were one segment of an interview which included questions about morality and identity (Gilligan *et al.*, 1982). The interviews lasted about two hours.

### Data Analysis

The real-life moral dilemmas were analyzed using Lyons' coding procedure.[2] The three coders trained by Lyons were blind to the gender, age, and race of the participants and achieved high levels of intercoder reliability (a range of 67-95 percent and a mean of 80 percent agreement across samples on randomly selected cases).

The Lyons procedure is a content analysis which identifies moral considerations. The unit of analysis is the consideration, defined as each idea the participant presents in discussing a moral problem. The units are designated in Table 1 with brackets. To reach an acceptable level of reliability in identifying considerations required extensive training; the coders in these studies were all trained by Lyons and achieved reliability at acceptable levels (Lyons, 1983). Typically, a real-life moral dilemma consists of seven considerations with a range of 4 to 17.[3] The coder classifies these considerations as either justice or care. The Lyons score indicates the predominant, most frequent mode of moral reasoning (justice or care). For the present analysis predominance has been redefined, such that a real-life moral dilemma consisting of only care or justice consider-ations is labeled Care Only or Justice Only (Table 3). A dilemma consist-ing of 75 percent or more care or justice considerations is labeled Care Focus or Justice Focus, respectively. A dilemma in which both orientations are present but neither orientation accounts for 75 percent of the codable considerations is placed in the Care-Justice category. Thus, dilemmas are described as focused only when more than 75 percent of the considerations fall into one mode.

### RESULTS

This article summarizes the real-life dilemma data from three studies with comparable designs, that is, samples with male and female subjects matched for high socioeconomic status. Frequencies and statistical tests are presented across samples.[4]

Looking at Table 3, two observations can be made. First, the majority of people represent both moral orientations: 69 percent (55 out of 80) compared to the 31 percent (25 out of 80) who use Care or Justice Only. Second, two-thirds of the dilemmas are in the Focus categories (Care Only, Care Focus, Justice Only, Justice Focus), while only one-third are in the Care-Justice category. The question addressed by Table 3 is do people tend to focus their discussion of a moral problem in one or the other orientation? Using a binomial model, if one assumes an equal probability of care and justice orientations in an account of a real-life moral dilemma ($p = 0.5$), then a random sampling of moral considerations (typically $N = 7$) over eighty trials (eighty participants' single dilemmas) would result in an expected binomial distribution. To test whether the distribution of scores fits the expected distribution, the $\chi^2$ goodness-of-fit test is applied. The observed distribution differs significantly from the expected, $\chi^2$ (4, $N = 80$) $= 133.8$, $p < 0.001$,[5] and provides supporting evidence for our contention that an individual's moral considerations are not random but tend to be focused in either the care or justice orientation.

TABLE 3

*Moral Orientation of Participants by Category*

|  | Care Only | Care Focus | Care–Justice | Justice Focus | Justice Only |
|---|---|---|---|---|---|
| Observed | 5 | 8 | 27 | 20 | 20 |
| Expected[*] | 0.64 | 4 | 70 | 4 | 0.64 |

*Note: For the typical case, the ratio of care to justice considerations is Care Only, 7:0; Care Focus, 6:1; Care–Justice, 5:2, 4:3, 3:4, 2:5; Justice Focus, 0:7; and Justice Only, 0:7. Since the range of consideration is 4–17, percentages are used to define comparable categories across cases.*

[*]*Expected values are based on binomial distribution for N = 7, p = 0.5.*

In Table 4, the relationship between moral orientation and gender can be examined. The test of statistical significance, $\chi^2$ (2, $N = 80$) = 18.33,

$p < 0.001$, demonstrates a relationship between moral orientation and gender such that both men and women present dilemmas in the Care-Justice category, but Care Focus is much more likely to occur in the moral dilemma of a woman, and Justice Focus more likely in the dilemma of a man. In fact, if one were to exclude women from a study of moral reasoning, Care Focus could easily be overlooked.[6]

TABLE 4

*Moral Orientation by Gender of Participants*

|  | *Care Focus* | *Care-Justice* | *Justice Focus* |
|---|---|---|---|
| Women | 12 | 12 | 10 |
| Men | 1 | 15 | 30 |

We did not test the relationship between moral orientation and age, because the majority of participants were adolescents and young adults, providing little age range. Furthermore, in the present analysis, age is confounded with sample (i.e., the young adults are the medical students), making interpretation difficult.[7]

The medical student data (Study 2) raised further questions of interpretation which bear on the issues addressed in this analysis. First, the dilemmas from the medical students when tested separately do not show the same relationship between gender and moral orientation, $\chi^2$ $(2, N = 39)$ = 4.36, n.s. However, consistent with the overall findings, the two Care Focus dilemmas were presented by women.

Examining the pattern of difference in the dilemmas, the Care Focus dilemmas were presented by one white and one minority woman. The relationship between moral orientation and race for both men and women is that the dilemmas presented by white students are more likely to fall in the Care-Justice category and dilemmas of minority students in the Justice Focus category (Fisher's Exact $p = 0.045$ for women and $p = 0.0082$ for men).

## DISCUSSION

The present exploration of moral orientation has demonstrated that
(1) concerns about justice and care are *both* represented in people's
thinking about real-life moral dilemmas, but people tend to focus on one
set of concerns and minimally represent the other; and (2) there is an
association between moral orientation and gender such that both men and
women use both orientations, but Care Focus dilemmas are more likely to
be presented by women and Justice Focus dilemmas by men.

Our findings indicate that the selection of an all-male sample for
theory and test construction in moral judgment research is inherently problematic. If women were eliminated from the present study, Care Focus
would virtually disappear. Furthermore, most of the dilemmas described
by women could be scored and analyzed for justice considerations without
reference to the considerations of care. Thus, the interpretive question
hinges on the understanding of the care perspective.

Our analysis of care and justice as distinct moral orientations that
address different moral concerns leads us to consider both perspectives
as constitutive of mature moral thinking. The tension between these
perspectives is suggested by the fact that detachment, which is the mark
of mature moral judgment in the justice perspective, becomes *the* moral
problem in the care perspective--the failure to attend to need. Conversely,
attention to the particular needs and circumstances of individuals, the mark
of mature moral judgment in the care perspective, becomes *the* moral
problem in the justice perspective--failure to treat others fairly, as equals.
Care Focus and Justice Focus reasoning suggest a tendency to lose sight
of one perspective in reaching moral decision. The fact that the focus
phenomenon was demonstrated by two-thirds of both men and women in
our study suggests that this liability is shared by both sexes. The virtual
absence of Care Focus dilemmas among men in these samples of advantaged
North Americans is the surprising finding of this research.

This finding provides an empirical explanation for the equation of
morality with justice in theories of moral development derived from all-male
research samples (Piaget, 1932/1965; Kohlberg, 1969, 1984). In addition,
the Care Focus dilemmas presented by women offer an explanation for the
fact that within a justice conception of morality, moral judgments of girls
and women have appeared anomalous and difficult to interpret; Piaget cites

this as the reason for studying boys. Furthermore, finding Care Focus mainly among women indicates why the analysis of women's moral thinking elucidated the care perspective as a distinct moral orientation (Gilligan, 1977) and why the considerations of care noted in dilemmas presented by men did not seem fully elaborated (Gilligan & Murphy, 1979). The evidence of orientation focus as an observable characteristic of moral judgment does not justify the conclusion that focus is a desirable attribute of moral decision. However, careful attention to women's articulation of care concerns suggests a different conception of the moral domain and a different way of analyzing the moral judgments of both men and women.

The category Care-Justice in our findings raises important questions that merit investigation in future research. Dilemmas in this "bifocal" category were equally likely among men and women in our study, but it is possible that interviews involving more dilemmas and further questioning might reveal the focus phenomenon to be more common and eliminate the bi-focal category. But it is also possible that such studies might find and elucidate further an ability to sustain two moral perspectives--an ability which according to the present data seems equally characteristic of women and men.

If people know both moral perspectives, as our theory and data suggest, researchers can cue perceptions in one or the other direction by the dilemmas they present, by the questions they raise, or by their failure to ask questions. The context of the research study as well as the interview itself must be considered for its influence on the likelihood of eliciting care or justice reasoning. In the case of the medical student data (Study 2), the findings raise just such contextual questions. In this large-scale study of stress and adaptation which included extensive standard, evaluative inventories as well as the clinical interview, is it possible that the first-year medical students might have been reluctant to admit uncertainty? A large number could not or would not describe a situation in which they were not sure what the right thing to do was. Also, is it possible that the focus on justice represents efforts by the students to align themselves with the perceived values of the institution they are entering? The focus on justice by minority students is of particular interest since it counters the suggestion that a care orientation is the perspective of subordinates or people of lower social power and status.

Evidence that moral orientation organizes moral judgment as well as the discovery of the focus phenomenon has led us to make the following changes in our research procedures which we offer as suggestions for other researchers:

1. That interviewers proceed on the assumption that people can adopt both a justice and a care perspective and that they encourage participants to generate different perspectives on a moral problem ("Is there another way to think about this problem?") and to examine the relationship between them.

2. That interviewers seek to determine the conception of justice and the conception of care that organizes the moral thinking in the discussion of a particular dilemma. Kohlberg's stages describe the development of justice reasoning. We have described different ways women think about care and traced changes over time in care reasoning. Our work offers guides to thinking about development and the nature of transitions in two perspectives.

Evidence of two moral perspectives suggests that the choice of moral standpoint, whether implicit or explicit, may indicate a preferred way of seeing. If so, the implications of such a preference need to be explored. Orientation preference may be a dimension of identity or self-definition, especially when moral decision becomes more reflective or "post-conventional" and the choice of moral principle becomes correspondingly more self-conscious. Interviewers should attend to where the self stands with respect to the two moral orientations. In our present research we have included the question, "What is at stake for you in the conflict?" to encourage subjects to reveal where they see themselves in the dilemmas they describe and how they align themselves with different perspectives on the problem.

The promise of our approach to moral development in terms of moral orientation lies in its potential to transform debate over cultural and sex differences in moral reasoning into serious questions about moral perspectives that are open to empirical study. If moral maturity consists of the ability to sustain concerns about justice and care, and if the focus phenomenon indicates a tendency to lose sight of one set of concerns, then the encounter with orientation difference can tend to offset errors in moral perception.

## NOTES

1. Nineteen medical students could not (two would not) describe a situation of moral conflict and were not, therefore, included in the present study. This unprecedented high number may reflect the pressures on first-year medical students in a context which discourages the uncertainty of not knowing what is the right thing to do. Generalizations about physicians from this specific study would be unwarranted, however, as several physicians who participated in Study 1 provided both care and justice perspectives on their experiences of conflict and choice. (See also Chapter 12.)

2. Lyons' coding sheet (1983) specifies five categories that establish whether the consideration is assigned to justice or care. In the present study most of the considerations coded fit categories 2 and 3 under justice and care. When we ran our analysis using only these categories, some subjects were lost due to an insufficient number of considerations, but the direction of the findings reported in the results section remained. This is significant because categories 2 and 3 under justice and care best capture the distinction between justice and care: concern with fulfilling obligations, duty, or commitments; maintaining standards or principles of fairness (justice); concern with maintaining or restoring relationships, or with responding to the weal and woe of others (care). Lyons' categories 1, 4, and 5 under justice and care are consistent with her focus on the perspective taken toward others. In addition, they are suggestive of different stages or levels of justice and care reasoning as defined by Kohlberg (1984) and by Gilligan (1977, 1982). Yet categories 1, 4, and 5 can readily be confused with a conception of justice and care as bipolar opposites of a single dimension of moral reasoning where justice is egoistic and uncaring, and caring is altruistic and unjust. Since these categories were rarely evident in the current data, these questions, although important for other researchers to consider, are only marginally relevant to the present discussion.

3. A minimum of four considerations was required for the present analysis. When only four considerations were present, in all but one case, the four considerations were in one orientation. This provides additional support for the interpretation of justice and care as distinct orientations.

4. The statistical comparison of samples on moral orientation is not significant ($\chi^2$ (4, N = 80) = 9.21, n.s.). The medical student sample does show fewer Care Focus and more Justice Focus than the other two samples. Parallel tests have been performed for each sample, and discrepancies from the overall pattern were reported and discussed.

5. The distribution was compared to theoretical distributions for N = 4 and N = 10, p = 0.5, and the difference remained highly significant.

6. Though Care Focus dilemmas are raised by women, it is important to emphasize that the focus phenomenon in two moral orientations is replicated in an all-female sample of students in a private girls' high school. The moral dilemmas of these forty-eight adolescent girls are distributed as follows: Care Focus, twenty-two; Care-Justice, seventeen; and Justice Focus, nine. This distribution differs significantly from the expected binomial distribution as well ($\chi^2$ (2, N = 48) = 154.4, p < 0.001).

7. The test for relationship between moral orientation and age (grouping fifteen to twenty-two-year-olds as Adolescents and twenty-three to seventy-seven-year-olds as Adults) is not significant, $\chi^2$ (2, N = 78) = 1.93, n.s.

# 5

## THINGS SO FINELY HUMAN:
## MORAL SENSIBILITIES AT RISK IN ADOLESCENCE

**Betty Bardige**

Dear Teacher:

I am a survivor of a concentration camp. My eyes saw
what no man should witness: Gas chambers built by learned
engineers. Infants killed by trained nurses. Women and babies
shot and burned by high school and college graduates.

So, I am suspicious of education. My request is: Help your
students become human. Your efforts must never produce learned
monsters, skilled psychopaths, educated Eichmanns. Reading,
writing, and arithmetic are important only if they serve to make
our children more human.

--Author unknown; in Haim Ginnott,
*Teacher and Child*

*Facing History and Ourselves: Holocaust and Human Behavior* is
a course designed for adolescents that answers this survivor's challenge.
Students' responses to this course reveal the existence and emergence of
profoundly moral sensibilities. Yet these responses illustrate how certain
moral sensibilities are at risk. As adolescents develop new reasoning
abilities, they gain new capacities for understanding and helping as well
as new capacities for hurting, degrading, and turning away.

This article will illuminate how certain cognitive advances in the
transition from concrete to formal thinking jeopardize some moral sensibilities while potentially enlarging others. This process is traced in journals
kept by young adolescents as they studied the Holocaust. Three devel-

opmental levels of thinking found in a previous study of these journals (Bardige, 1983) are described. The present study identifies a particular response to violence found almost exclusively in the journals of girls whose entries were coded as exhibiting some thinking at the lowest of these developmental levels. It reveals the moral strength of this response through contrast with similar, developmentally more sophisticated responses, and examines transformations of this response in one student's journal as well as in a class discussion. The article, thus, illustrates ways in which education can sustain or erode moral sensibilities across a developmental transition that educators frequently encourage.

In pointing to moral sensibilities that may become muted as language becomes more abstract, I do not intend to deny the potential for abstract thinking to also expand moral awareness and inform moral judgment. Similarly, the use of categories derived from cognitive developmental theory should not be read as simply an attempt to rank the moral adequacy of students' responses. This article points out the moral strengths (as well as limitations) of moral language which has been called simplistic, naive, or "low stage."

This article challenges two different views of moral development that are prevalent in both psychological and popular literature: the image of the wise child who sees and speaks the truth until he or she is corrupted by civilization or education, and the image of a ladder comprised of a progression of moral stages leading finally, to the use of universal ethical principles. These oppositely charted developmental courses intersect in adolescence, when, in both views, the discovery of evil undermines previous loyalties and beliefs.

In exploring this intersection--through the writings of young adolescents who are confronting evil--the larger study (Bardige, 1983) on which this article is based demonstrated how adolescents' moral intensity can be engaged by a Holocaust course which raises moral issues in their minds and takes their moral questions seriously. Bringing together emotional/ empathetic responses and reflective thinking, this kind of education may sustain moral sensibilities that are "at risk" as formal reasoning develops, even as it expands moral awareness.

*Facing History* provided the context in which the phenomenon of moral sensibilities at risk was observed. There is no attempt to evaluate this course here.  Rather, the aim is to provide an understanding of how early adolescents' cognitive and moral discoveries can lead them to lose sight of or doubt important childhood sensibilities.  This understanding can inform educational efforts.

## DESIGN OF THE STUDY

The study began as an attempt to observe the effects of a course that would stimulate moral thinking and moral development in adolescence.  The course, *Facing History and Ourselves* (Strom & Parsons, 1982), is an eight to ten-week unit that challenges adolescents to explore their own moral options and responsibilities.  It presents material on the Holocaust and also the Armenian genocide, in a context that highlights the choices that people made and encourages students to "face history and themselves."  This course was designed by Margot Stern Strom and William Parsons, two Brookline, Massachusetts teachers.  Strom and Parsons felt that it was important for their eighth-grade students to know about the Holocaust.  They also believed that thinking about these periods of history could lead students to new understandings of themselves and increased moral commitment.

*Facing History* has been cited twice by the U.S. Department of Education as an outstanding and effective program (Far West Laboratory for Educational Research and Development, 1981, 1986), based on studies by Lieberman (1978, 1986[1]) of its role in promoting development in interpersonal perspective taking.

Extensive descriptive and anecdotal data collected by the project (Strom, 1977;[2] Strom & Parsons, 1983; Johnson & Strom, 1985) reveal that students and teachers see the course as raising vital moral questions and enlarging their moral thinking.  Students from many different settings testify that the course was a high point in their education (Whittier, 1981;[3] Intersection Associates, 1986[4]).

In their rationale for the course, Strom and Parsons (1982, p. 13) quote Hannah Arendt (1972).  "Could the activity of thinking, as such . . . be among the conditions that make men abstain from evil doing or even actually conditions them against it?"  Strom and Parsons go on to say, "If we are to meet our present problems in human and creative ways, it is most urgent that we face history and ourselves."

Teachers of *Facing History* in many different settings report that their students "hunger" for material that makes them think in the way Arendt proposes. Despite the reservations of many who would "protect" young adolescents from the awful truths of the Holocaust, eighth graders say they are ready to face it, and their teachers agree (Colt, Paine, & Connelly, 1981).

One requirement of *Facing History* is that each student keep a journal. Students are asked to write a response to each class, giving personal feelings, observations, opinions, and questions about what was seen or discussed and its significance. Thus, the journal provides a space and a structure for "facing history" and "facing one's self."

The journal is also a personal channel of communication between the student and the teacher. Students share their reactions to the class and their struggles with painful material. They ask questions that are difficult to voice in class and request emotional and intellectual support. A teacher's response can stimulate and complicate students' thinking, support their struggle, and honor their caring and their developing ideals.

The journals analyzed for this study came primarily from two eighth-grade classes taught in suburban public schools. The first class consisted of eight boys and eight girls and was taught in 1978. The second class, taught in 1979, contained sixteen girls and nine boys; however, three of the boys had sufficient difficulty with writing that they were unable to keep journals. Five additional boys' journals were obtained from a combined seventh and eighth-grade class at another suburban school.

The original intent of the study had been to elaborate Piagetian development categories and to follow the transition from one to the next in students' understandings of psychology, epistemology, history, and morality. This focus assumed that, as a developmental curriculum, *Facing History* would foster "development." The intention was to describe students' thinking in a way that would be helpful in understanding how they were interpreting the course material, in recognizing their questions, in appreciating their moral responses, and in documenting their expanding awareness. The descriptive categories are called "developmental" because they grew out of an attempt to bring a Piagetian interpretive framework to the journal data. No independent developmental assessments were used.

A pilot study by the author (1981) provided a foundation for the cognitive-developmental analysis of students' journals. Building on the work of Inhelder and Piaget (1958), Kohlberg (1981), Selman (1980), and Kegan (1982), journal responses to three films that are central to the course were analyzed in terms of complexity of perspective-taking. This analysis provided a basis for constructing integrated developmental descriptions that explain the understandings of epistemology, psychology, and history; the sense of morality; and questions that are expressed in students' journals. In constructing these ideal types, the various domains were assumed to be "structures d'ensemble," with ideas about history and morality grounded in understandings of epistemology and psychology.

## DEVELOPMENTAL ANALYSIS OF JOURNAL ENTRIES

Students' responses reflected three ways of seeing the material, analogous to Piaget's stages of concrete operational, emerging formal operational, and fully formal operational thinking. Some entries took what was presented at face value, recounting salient details without analysis, inferring motives, feelings, and character traits directly from actions without considering alternative possibilities, and taking accounts literally. These characterizations were one-dimensional and often evaluative; changes were portrayed as having single causes. This way of thinking, which would in Piagetian terms be called concrete, can also be called *face value thinking*. In other entries students drew composite pictures, putting pieces together into a whole story that would include "both sides," and looking below the surface to understand the thinking and motivations of the people involved. This way of thinking, which has many of the characteristics of Piaget's stage of early formal thinking, can be called *composite picture thinking*. Other responses revealed that students were using multiple lenses, considering situations from several points of view and recognizing that what people see is affected not only by where they stand but also by the language and values through which they filter their perceptions. This way of thinking reveals capacities that Piaget associates with fully formal thinking and can be called *multiple lens thinking*. Two modes of thinking (face value and composite picture, or composite picture and multiple lens) were often represented in a single student's journal, sometimes in the same entry.

As the developmental analysis of journals progressed, it became clear that most students' thinking was changing during the course. Some of the changes seemed to be developmental shifts--students whose writing had been characterized at one level began using statements revealing character-istics of the next level; students whose thinking in one domain had seemed to lag behind their thinking in other domains developed insights consonant with their "more advanced" thinking. However, the most striking changes, and those reported most often by students in their own assessments of what they had learned, were of a different nature. Rather than showing cognitive advance or restructuring, they reflected what one student called "a sort of enmoralment," an enhancement of moral awareness and a new commitment to moral action.

> Now I shudder whenever I hear . . . [a] prejudiced statement. That's what this course did for me.

> I think more carefully about the decisions I make. That each one be the best morally.

> I don't get as depressed as I used to . . . when I do get depressed it's usually over someone else's troubles.

> I've learned that, besides all the bad, there is a lot of good in the world.

Students report becoming more sensitive, more reflective, and less hasty in their judgments. They find that they are more aware of others' problems and of the consequences of their own actions or inaction. Many become attuned to the evils in their world--prejudice, deception, lack of care, and violence. Many also learn to recognize the good; they express appreciation of what they have been given and see what they can contrib-ute. Their *Facing History* journals capture the kind of response Terrence Des Pres (1976[5]) observed when he taught young people about the Holo-caust.

> And for all their shock and depression and yes, also their tears, what emerges finally are things so finely human, things so clearly good and life-enhancing, that the danger we run and the damage we share in meditation on the Holo-caust seem not too high a price to pay.

As students reflected in their journals on material that engaged their empathy and moral outrage or that challenged their theories about history and human nature and their sense of themselves as moral, as they saw the cost of avoiding issues or keeping silent and the possibilities for making a difference, the "finely human" aspects of their thinking were revealed and strengthened. New descriptions of moral thinking were needed to encompass these finely human aspects.

These descriptions departed from the work of structural developmental theorists (Piaget, 1932/1965; Kohlberg, 1976; Loevinger, 1976; Damon, 1977; Eisenberg-Berg, 1979; Selman, 1980; Kegan, 1982) by breaking the link that their theories posit between cognitive and moral adequacy. The moral strengths evident in the journals of young adolescents who were facing history and themselves were not reflected in the theoretical descriptions of moral thinking that corresponded to their cognitive levels and thus, this incongruity lead to a shift in the focus of the research.

**Face Value Morality**

The limitations of existing frameworks were clearest at the concrete operational level. The profoundly moral sense of justice and concern for others expressed in journal entries that were identified as face value responses is not reflected in structural developmental characterizations of this stage. Kohlberg's "stage of instrumental purpose and exchange" (1981), Kegan's "imperial self" (1982), and Loevinger's "self-protective ego" or "opportunistic stage" (1976) all portray a more self-centered individual than these students' journals reveal. In reacting to things that they see as clearly and obviously wrong, these students reveal a profound sense of morality that may not be exhibited when they are asked to solve hypothetical dilemmas or to complete sentences.

The moral strengths and altruistic potentials of face value thinking are evident in Angela's journal. Her first entry is a response to "Harrison Bergeron," Kurt Vonnegut's satiric account of a society which handicaps those with special talent so that all can be equal. The teacher used this story to raise issues about the relationship of the individual and society, but Angela took it literally.

> When we were reading that story I felt kind of angry. I wanted to get revenge on Diana [the Handicapper General] for having people have handicaps on themselves. I got a mental picture of everybody who had to wear those beepers [to prevent thinking] walking around with ear plugs with batteries in them and an antenna on each one. The ballerinas with weights on their feet, I picture them having heavy balls of iron chained to their feet, like people in the old prisons.

Angela's comments highlight the physical pains and tangible losses of the victims. She is outraged that people were hurt and hampered for no good reason. She wants revenge on the person she sees as the cause of others' suffering.

Angela's morality, like that expressed by others who take accounts at face value, demands fairness. You must not hurt "without giving them a chance" or "for no good reason." However, it is fair to hurt those who have hurt or are about to hurt others. Life is supposed to be fair, rewarding the good and punishing the bad.

This formulation incorporates the "concrete reciprocality" that characterizes Kohlberg's Stage 2. However, Kohlberg's description of this stage emphasizes self-interest: right action "instrumentally satisfies the self's needs and occasionally others'" (1969, p. 379). In the journals, however, one can often see the altruistic potentials and moral power of concrete reciprocity. Angela wrote:

> I was really touched by the film we saw today. It was really sad and disappointing. It was disappointing to think that human beings could treat other human beings that way. You could almost call the Germans of that time animals, anyway. And the people who wouldn't take those kids in for a while and give them food, they were mean, too. The children could have worked for them for a day for the food and lodging.

Angela proposes a fair exchange--work for food and lodging. Not looking at the fears or beliefs of those who turn away from a request for help, she sees them as "mean" because they will not even make a fair deal. Thus, although Angela recognizes self-interest as legitimate by not requiring people to help others for free, she expects people to be nice to each other and to help those in need.

Students who take accounts at face value respond with indignation, anger, and even hatred to those who grossly overstep the natural bounds of self-interest. They are seen as "insane" or as "greedy" and "power hungry." Similarly, those who take the film *Joseph Schultz* at face value consistently applaud the actions of this German soldier who was shot by his unit because he refused to shoot unarmed men. They see his action as "brave," "great," and "a good thing to do."

The "finely human" potentials of students who responded at face value were evident in their journals. They readily empathized with those who were hurt and found it painful to learn what others had suffered. "I was struck deep down by this. It hurt to hear what suffering those people went through." These students reacted to much of the course with outrage and puzzlement: "How could the rest of the world let this go on? It's disgusting!"

Their concern for others sometimes led them to stereotype groups portrayed as victimizers, but they tended to see prejudice against an individual as unfair. These students could become so angry at the small and large injustices they saw that they wanted to stop them immediately (even violently) or take revenge. When they saw another's suffering they wanted to help "because we should do something for those people." Often the immediacy of their perceptions, the passionate clarity of their judgments, the intensity of their involvement, and their eagerness to "do something" were striking.

## Composite Picture Morality

Composite pictures treat accounts as parts of larger wholes. Students read between the lines, search for underlying motives and explanations, try to "see both sides," and conjoin different and sometimes conflicting parts to arrive at the "whole truth." People are seen as mixtures of good and bad "sides" and of different capacities. Their "real personality" can be inferred from the pattern of their actions; however, it may be dominated, at least temporarily, by various kinds of "pressure to go against your real self." Thus, actions can only be understood in context, considering how the person perceived the situation, the pressures he faced, and his psychological as well as physical needs.

Students no longer assume that they can put themselves easily in others' places; however, they can build on their own experiences to empathize with others. "I fasted for Oxfam [an international hunger relief organization] last year and after one day I was about to die. Imagine how it must feel not eating for weeks." They can be simultaneously critical and supportive. "I would be paranoid too but I would still try to keep an open [unprejudiced] mind."

Their search for the whole truth is often coupled with a faith in human nature that leads them to be generous in their judgments. They want to hear all sides, "learn the minds" of the people involved, find and appeal to the good in individuals and societies. "It makes me glad to know that all the Turks weren't bad people."

Students who draw composite pictures present a morality that demands recognition of people and consideration of their perspectives. People are expected to try to put themselves in others' shoes, to realize that "people are people," and to look at both sides. "All I could think about was these important people being . . . killed just because of what they believed." These students can also realize how difficult it is, in many real situations, to do what you know you should. Life presents a series of moral tests; it is not always easy to "stand up for your beliefs," but you feel "small" when you don't.

### Multiple Lens Morality

Multiple lens users can construct systems in which the whole is more than the sum of the parts. They distinguish between knowing something superficially, and feeling, assimilating, and accepting facts that may have wider implications. They recognize that people filter their perceptions through lenses of language, preconception, emotion, and values; what appears negative to one person in one situation may be positive in other circumstances. They see individuals embedded in a society, retaining both their individuality and their common humanity. "Before it never really penetrated into my head that these Nazis were human."

Students who understand in this way can create a morality of personal integrity that values "individuality" and "rational" decisionmaking. They are upset by mass actions and social practices that restrict independent thinking. Recognizing how easy it is to evade responsibility, they try to be honest with themselves. "I think I understand my prejudices and am no longer afraid to admit I have them. This is not a justification but a start." "That really scared me about myself. I tried to relate it to school, to find specific instances where I denied responsibility for an action I performed." Morality, for these students, is a way of life that requires continued awareness and responsibility. "We are so caught up in our own lives. Even when I have free time, I rarely sit back and reflect . . . We have to change the road we're on."

## MORAL SENSIBILITIES AT RISK

Each moral vision or perspective has strengths as well as limitations. One can appreciate the passionate clarity of a face value judgment, the generosity of a composite picture judgment that looks for the good side, and the integrity of a multiple lens judgment that recognizes that actions that satisfy one's conscience may not be truly helpful. One can see the lasting importance of the protection of innocent victims, of following your conscience and upholding your values under pressure, and of continuous awareness, reflection, and responsibility.

### Responsive Face Value Language

The identification of distinct strengths in each vision of morality led us to look again at the powerful moral responses of some students whose thinking had seemed developmentally immature by comparison to that of their classmates. Angela was one of four girls whose journals represented discrepant data that raised questions about the potential cost of cognitive development. These students repeatedly responded to violence with language that coupled their own outrage, sadness, or disgust with uncomprehending shock (or a statement that the perpetrator must be insane or inhuman implying that he or she is so abnormal as to be outside of humanity) and a call for action to stop the violence. They were likely, especially near the beginning of the course, to assert that they would themselves take the "right" action of stopping, averting, or not participating in violence.

> Today we saw the movie *Obedience* [a documentary of Stanley Milgrim's classic experiments]. It was awful before I knew it was fake I thought that the person who ran the experiment was really bad to do that because people could have breakdowns from it so you shouldn't ever do that and if you know anyone who is doing it stop them because it's not right! If I was in that position I wouldn't do it at all no matter what would happen to me at all because I know it's wrong!

Another student wrote:

> People are so mean . . . I can't believe or understand . . . if I was alive then I wouldn't even want to be part of it [anti-Semitism] . . . I would tell them to stop and if they didn't I would leave.

This language calls attention to the central moral truth of the situation-- the fact that hurt is being inflicted and to the pressing need to stop it. It captures the impulse to respond both emotionally and actively.  It allows no excuses for torture and murder.

The importance of these elements is underscored in Lamb's analysis[6] of how violence can be explained away.  Lamb points out that:

> When we turn to ask why an individual inflicts such pain on another . . .
> when we focus on the victimizers . . . images of the pain, of the real hurt, of
> bruises, of blood, of broken bones become hazy . . . evil can be so readily
> reconciled with what we know is good . . . sympathy is too quickly turned into
> a release from responsibility . . . In their desire to account for social context
> and for the interaction between persons, [theorists of human behavior] describe
> acts without agents, harm without guilt.

The responses of students who do not think in terms of social context can focus our attention on the real hurt and guilt and responsibility.  In one of these girls' journals, the pain of witnessing violence and the expectation that people should stop the violence were dominant themes--expressed more than a dozen times.  The sense of shock that others expressed in conjunction with these themes was less apparent; however, they called Hitler "insane" and thought that allowing genocide to happen was "sick."

> I think it's cruel and sick to let that happen.  It makes me feel sad for the
> kids and upset that this was allowed to happen.  It also scared me that this
> could happen.  I think if it starts again we should stop it fast, and if this is
> what's happening in Iran I think we should stop it.

"'I did no more than you let me do' means Hitler did no more than the people let him do.  They could have stopped the killing *any time* but a lot of people didn't know and others were probably just so brainwashed . . ." However, she stops herself in mid-thought, resisting the implication that there is an excuse for non-response.  ". . . nobody had to let Hitler do it. A lot of people encouraged him and gave him new ideas.  I thought maybe someone should have tried to stop him . . . Why not die while trying to help the situation they were in?"

Another entry shows how much she expects of herself and others. "What happens to people who helped makes me sad and helpless because I wasn't there to help and only a few others were brave enough to really help and not just talk."

A reexamination of all the journals revealed that this language was also used by other girls who took accounts at face value or who also drew some composite pictures.

> Today we saw a movie called the *Warsaw Ghetto*. Some parts were really
> disgusting. I can't understand how the Nazis just took control of all the Jews
> and nothing happened. I wonder how people went along with it. *How come*
> *they couldn't realize what they were doing was bad?* [emphasis in journal]
> It was awful what the people in the Ghetto went through. It gives me the
> creeps thinking about it.

> Today we saw a film called *Obedience.* I could not believe that some people
> would just keep going even if the people getting the pain asked them to stop.
> One man made me mad--the one that kept going. I don't know what I would
> do because I am not under those conditions. But I say that I would *slug* the
> man conducting the experiment.

One boy, who used a mixture of face value and composite picture
thinking, used language that coupled empathy, shock, and an assertion that
he would take action.

> I think if I was that person I would have done it because why should you kill
> someone who has not done a thing to you and kill them because they are not
> German or your race and also how can you have the mind to actually murder
> someone. And I would have laid my life down too because if those people
> have to suffer by getting a bullet through them and having to wait for awhile
> is horror because those people must of been thinking how it must feel to die
> by getting shot in the head or the stomach.

Only one of the students who did not use any face value thinking
used language that coupled emotion, shock, and action. This girl, who
could draw composite pictures and see with multiple lenses, used this kind
of language on two occasions. "It was awful. Those were people and other
people did that to them. How? No matter what kind of teaching they had,
training or whatever. Didn't they ever stop and think that the people in
the Warsaw Ghetto were people? And why didn't anybody do anything?"

Responses that express emotion or moral outrage and shock and that
call for action to stop the violence were found, with one exception, only in
girls' journals. They were found, with one exception, only in the journals
of students who took the course at face value or who also drew some composite pictures. All but one of the girls whose journals contained at least
some face value thinking used this language. Because it contains a direct
response to the evidence of violence, taken at face value, the language that
couples empathy, shock, and a call for personal action to stop the violence
can be called *responsive face value language.*

In order to assess the objectivity of the judgment that face value thinking was present or absent, ten journals were randomly selected from the sample and the first several entries were given to a second reader. Intercoder

TABLE 1

Association of Responsive Face Value Language Use with Gender

|  | Responsive Face Value Language Present | Responsive Face Value Language Absent |
|---|---|---|
| Girls | 8 | 16 |
| Boys | 1 | 18 |

$\chi^2 = 5.03, p < 0.025.$

TABLE 2

Association of Responsive Face Value Language Use with Use of Face Value Thinking

|  | Responsive Face Value Language Present | Responsive Face Value Language Absent |
|---|---|---|
| Some face value thinking | 8 | 6 |
| No face value thinking | 1 | 28 |

Note: Although this table suggests a very strong relationship between the use of language and the use of face value thinking, a statistical comparison would be inappropriate. The identification and assessment of these two ways of writing was not entirely independent. The language was embedded in the journals and its logic contributed to the definition of face value thinking.

agreement was 90 percent on whether or not face value thinking was present (Cohen's Kappa = 0.78).

These same ten journals were then used to assess the reliability with which responsive face value language could be identified. Perfect (100 percent) inter-coder agreement on the presence of responsive face value language was achieved between the author and a third coder who was unfamiliar with the developmental analysis (Cohen's Kappa = 1.00).

The finding of gender difference is striking but not surprising. Gilligan's work (1982) leads us to expect that language that highlights hurt and that expresses a need to respond or intervene would be used more frequently by girls. Gilligan characterizes the form of moral thinking that predominates among girls and women as the "response" (or care) orientation. Moral problems arise when relationships are threatened or when someone is being hurt or excluded; they are resolved by seeking an inclusive solution that protects each person's welfare or maintains the relationship; the solution is evaluated in terms of its actual consequences. Dilemmas typically focus not on whether to act but on how to act in a way that would be helpful or minimize hurt.

The shock that girls who take accounts at face value express when people deliberately hurt "for no good reason" and when they fail to respond or intervene seems to represent a coming together of a morality that expects care and response and a psychology that directly links motives and actions. Only those who are "mean" or who "don't care as long as it isn't happening to them" can fail to respond to a cry for help.

It should be pointed out here that in most of the examples cited in this article, the care language that called attention to hurt and expects response is integrated with justice language like "fair," "no right," and "revenge." This integrated category was identified by Janie Ward in her 1986 study of inner city high school students' discussions of real-life violence. (See Chapter 9.) In this study, the girls' face value responses are not distinguished solely by the presence of care ideas or by the absence of justice ideas, but by the way in which these themes are organized. While they used language of justice to express moral outrage, their concern remained focused on a perceived lack of care.

Is the use and "loss" of this directly responsive language primarily a phenomenon of girls' development, or do boys who take accounts at face value show a similar strength that may be jeopardized by the development of abstract thinking? Journals are not a good measure for answering this question, as boys who are face value thinkers tend not to use them well. Girls who responded to the course with face value thinking wrote more, and more reflectively, than boys who showed similar thinking. Girls, from an early age, practice tuning into and sharing feelings in their imaginary play. Boys are more likely to focus on actions and plans (Wolf, Rygh, & Alt-

shuler, 1984). It may be that, among students who took accounts at face
value, the assignment to record personal thoughts and feelings in a journal
was more meaningful for girls than for boys.

Still, like girls who took accounts at face value, boys who thought in
this way tended to record graphic details. They turned moral outrage into
personal anger and urged that offenders be stopped directly. They also
expressed sadness. Yet the care language that calls attention to hurt as the
moral problem is missing from these boys' responses.

> Today in class we saw a movie called *Obedience* . . . If I was under the switches
> and I heard the screams I would stop under any circumstances . . . if he keeps
> on urging me I would punch him on the face cause that's a human body. I can't
> imagine [understand] the people's reaction. The point [the teacher] made dur-
> ing class I thought about it when someone you hated was there and I was a Jew
> and the guy in the seat was a German and people cheering me on to give him
> more volts. I would do it cause of what the Germans did to the Jews. I want
> revenge.

### Developmental Transformations of Responsive Face Value Language: Cross-Sectional Data

What happens to this directly responsive language as students develop
facility in drawing composite pictures and then in looking with multiple
lenses? Do students still respond emotionally? Are they shocked by delib-
erate and seemingly pointless hurt, torture, and genocide? Do they call for
action to stop what they see as hurtful or wrong?

Yes. Most of the journals of both boys and girls who draw composite
pictures or use multiple lenses show personal distress, profound concern,
incredulity, and a desire to "do something" or to become the kind of person
who will avoid and protest what he or she sees as evil or take action to help
its victims. However, the language and the linkages are different. Comparing the responses of students who did not take course materials at face value
with those of students who showed some face value thinking highlights
losses as well as gains, continuities, and rediscoveries.

Whereas face value thinkers describe movies and stories as "sad" and
"awful," students who draw composite pictures or use multiple lenses are
more likely to locate emotions within themselves. Many find that they are
most upset when they allow themselves to think about what they have seen.
"It pains me to think that people would have the gall and selfishness . . .
to . . . wipe out a whole race." Students who can think about thinking are

disturbed by ideas as well as by events. "I got upset watching this and
even more upset thinking about it."

Students can also focus on their own emotions and be pleased by their
capacity for emotional response. However, this inward-turning is sometimes criticized by multiple lens users. "To shed tears for, pity, or avoid
the film will not change anything." "All we did [by discussing questions
like 'Did they have hope?'] was take a rather narrow psychological joy
trip." These adolescent critics are acutely aware of the ways in which their
feelings can be manipulated. This can lead them to doubt the authenticity
of an account or response and to distance themselves from realities that
are painful to think about which they know they cannot change. At the
same time, it can also lead to a search for an adequate response.

This kind of distancing is seen by Kohlberg (1981) as a developmental advance, for it allows people to give the same weight to the claims
of strangers as to those of people they care about. The flip side of this
is evident in the *Facing History* journals of multiple lens users. These
students recognize that emotional response may be a prerequisite for action.
"Some issues make me fight with all my heart while others don't."

One girl who could use multiple lenses described how she made herself watch the films in a way that overcame her usual tendency to distance
herself. Like Angela, this girl reifies and enhances the images presented to
her, making the harm vivid. She indicates that she is reacting to friends
who think she cares less than they do. Although she presents her response
as new, it may be that she is drawing on a capacity that was more available at an earlier point in her development.

> [A friend] told me that since I didn't show everybody how I felt I was not
> responding and sharing with the rest of the class . . . I think for once the
> enormity . . . finally hit me. I've read books and I saw *The Holocaust*. I've
> even seen real live people who . . . are past caring what happens to them.
> But it never really sank in. When I was watching *The Warsaw Ghetto*, I
> imagined all these people who had families and little problems of life. Just
> being killed. I imagined what it would be like to have an innocent peaceful
> life disrupted like that. After realizing all that I couldn't . . . shake it off
> (or pretend to) like I usually do.

The inability to understand how or why any sane person could participate in mass killing is a common response to learning about the Holocaust. However, for students who do not take what they see at face value,
"How could people do it?" and "Why didn't anyone stop them?" are real

questions. These questions lose some of their force as protests as they
open the way to a more complicated view of human nature which acknowledges that ordinary people can be extraordinarily cruel. "How could any normal man go along with the Nazi persecution? Very simply it seems--they
were ordered."

The observation that people can be forced or "brainwashed" or peer-
pressured to "go against their real self" and the recognition that "both sides"
of the story must be taken into account help composite picture drawers to
explain some of the horrors they see. Multiple lens users are further able
to see how people can deceive themselves. "The real picture at the end
really disturbed me. The pictures were so disgusting they made me look
away. I guess that's what happened, people just looked away and didn't
face it."

Yet sometimes no explanation will suffice for the horrible realities
that students see. Their expressions of outrage and shock sound like face
value responses, but they are not followed by a call for action. Instead,
there is often a recognition that resistance is a less likely response than
tacit acceptance of reluctant complicity. "Those people were not human.
They could not have been. What they did only the lowest, most barbaric
animal could do." "It was like watching the Holocaust happen. I couldn't
believe it; they did it just because they were told to. Those men could
have been dead! . . . It was absolutely horrible watching it because it
meant that nothing bad had changed. If Hitler were in power now people
would do what he told them."

Another contrast is that while face value thinkers tend to call for
personal action to stop violence, composite picture and multiple lens users
are more likely to call for governmental or collective action, although they
hold individuals (both victimizers and silent bystanders) responsible.

> I felt bad because . . . my country did nothing. It makes me wonder about
> civilization. You can't tell me people didn't know what they did.

> The people who did this I feel are sub-human. How could they do this to
> a race? Why couldn't it have been made an international crime before
> because it would have saved a lot of people from this at the time.

The certainty about "what I would do" is eroded both by cognitive
development and by the course *Facing History*. Many students learn
from materials like *Obedience* and from their discussions of history and

human behavior that "I don't know what I'd do because I'm not in those circumstances." Often, as they recognize themselves in others who jumped to conclusions or who blindly followed orders or were too "brainwashed" or frightened to question and act, they learn to face their own limitations. Yet several note how, having faced history and themselves, they and their classmates are less likely to be bystanders. "Before I was a 'watcher,' now I'm a 'doer.'"

### Developmental Transformation of Responsive Face Value Language

Tracing changes in one student's journal over time, we can see what happens to her involvement and need for action as she moves away from face value responses and draws composite pictures. In early entries, Susan expressed uncomplicated condemnation of anyone who was portrayed as a victimizer. For example, she wrote of the hunters in *Love to Kill*, "Those people must be mental!"

Susan's response to a reading about an exercise in which a teacher's attempt to simulate totalitarianism with his class is a clear voicing of a responsive face value perspective--and contains the seeds of its undoing.

> We are doing a mind control thing. I think it is wicked. I would never do it. I would tell the teacher to screw. I can't believe that almost grown adults could do that. That people could be so blind as to not see what is happening to them. If the man could have done this for evil, if you start thinking almost anyone could do this and they could take over the world. It's scary to think there's something that big in me.

Other entries in Susan's journal show a close connection between moral outrage and action. "Putting fourteen-year old boys on the front! The man should be shot! And to think the same thing is going on in Cambodia. Can you get me Senator Kennedy's address so I can write to him about it?"

Susan was very concerned going into this unit because she doesn't "like gross things or blood." Yet she wanted to find out "why Hitler did the mass killings, because knowing that will make it easier to take, I hope." She takes comfort in her answer--that "Hitler was wacky;" this makes the Holocaust a fluke perpetuated by an inhuman monster rather than something humans have done and have to face. As she collected new information she reiterated her thesis. Eventually, though, she "change[d her] mind about him [Hitler]" as she began to look below the surface of actions and to learn that evil things can be done by people who are neither evil nor insane. "Now I kinda feel sorry for him; he was such a sick man." Thus, Hitler becomes a man, sick but still human. Susan's change of mind is followed by entries that show new concern for her classmates and a new willingness and ability to look at things from different points of view. At the same time, she became "ill with sadness" when watching *Warsaw Ghetto*, echoing an earlier face value entry. "All those brains dying, those pumping red hearts stopping--it simply aches me to think of it."

Susan was so upset by the film that she left the room, crying uncontrollably. As she reflected on this experience in her journal and later in a class discussion, she stated that she hates to cry and rarely does so in public. The film, and the true story it told, compelled her to respond. Where once she might have assumed that those of her classmates who didn't show emotions didn't have any, she now worried about how boys, who "aren't supposed to cry," could deal with their pain.

Susan's last entry shows the gains, losses, and continuities in her moral sensibilities. "[Joseph Schultz] thought that killing a person was wrong no matter what you do after. I don't know how I would feel or what I would do, but I think I might kill them if I were brainwashed; but now in my state of mind, I think I might break down crying--but don't know. He made one of the hardest choices in life and I think he made it right."

She has gained a more complicated vision that allows her to see the real difficulties of moral choices, and a new willingness to face her own limitations. Her earlier screams of protest at killing have changed to crying as she agonizes over a difficult decision. She retains her sympathy for the oppressed, empathizes with the decisionmaker, and takes a moral stand.

### Developmental Transformation of Responsive Face Value Language: A Class Discussion

By chance, the author observed a class discussion of *Joseph Schultz* in which the face value perspective was initially represented but then was apparently lost as the complexities of the situation were explored. This discussion took place in a combined seventh/eighth grade classroom in a public school. The teacher, who was clearly adept at fostering critical thinking, controlled the discussion. She would ask a question, then call on a student or a series of students to respond. She would have a brief discussion with each respondent, summarizing and reacting to the statement, rephrasing it in more abstract language, and relating it to what others had said. She would also add discrepant perspectives of her own or ones she had heard in other classes. This resulted in a teacher-focused discussion that built on the students' ideas, followed their questions, and continually pushed their thinking. For example, one student (responding with face value thinking) stated that if all the soldiers had refused to shoot, "the captain wouldn't have had enough bullets to shoot all of them." This was paraphrased by her teacher as raising the possibility of "collective action," which the class then discussed.

All of the girls and a few of the boys actively contributed to the discussion. They were eager to speak; some at times found it hard to wait for their turns. They elaborated their ideas, incorporated new possibilities, played with alternate interpretations, and asked questions.

Toward the end of this wide-ranging discussion, one boy who had not been speaking much said he felt Schultz had thrown his life away because he had not saved anyone with his death. The class discussed the impact of Schultz's act on his fellow soldiers (who were ordered to shoot him and did); they focused on the idea that, having shot a friend, the soldiers may now find it easier, rather than harder, to kill. The difficulty of Schultz's predicament was well represented by the students. Schultz was seen as an individual whose conscience led him to go against his society and who stood up for what he knew was right. At the same time, his act was represented as a foolish form of resistance that saved lives neither immediately nor in the long run. Earlier, students had suggested other ways in which Schultz might have been able to effectively resist. Some of these ways had been critiqued as unrealistic by other students.

Three perceptions commonly expressed in face value journal responses to *Joseph Schultz* got lost in this discussion: (a) the image of Schultz as a brave hero who would not kill innocent people, even to save his own life; (b) the reality that Schultz was a *victim* and that his comrades shot him; and (c) the fact that others could have made the same choice. These visions are captured in the following journal entry:

> I thought he was incredibly brave. I'm a little ashamed to say it, but I don't think I could have given up my own life like he did. When he was getting ready to walk towards the blindfolded people he didn't even look scared, he just had a look of pride on his face. I was mad when the soldiers shot him.

I think they should have all dropped their guns. Those people were innocent and unarmed, there was no reason to shoot them.

This discussion focuses attention on both the promise and the risk of "higher stage" thinking. When we see a situation from both sides (composite picture), we can appreciate the difficult predicament of the unwilling or "brainwashed" victimizer; we can also absolve him of responsibility. When we look with multiple lenses, we can distinguish a solution that is truly helpful from a "noble" but futile or ultimately destructive gesture. However, we can also rationalize non-involvement by convincing ourselves that nothing will work.

This tension was captured by an eighth-grade girl whose journal showed her development of multiple lens thinking. A visitor from Oxfam had come to tell her class about the genocide that was going on in Cambodia. This student wrote in her journal: "A comment . . . was really good: 'a big difference between Cambodia and the Holocaust is we can do something about Cambodia.' Well we should do something about it. We could sent money to Oxfam, but $23 is not going to make a lot of difference in saving human lives. Maybe I am unconsciously trying not to 'get involved.' But, I honestly don't think $23 is worth sending."

She could hold on to the reality that demanded a response at the same time that she recognized the difficulty of responding adequately. She was able to face herself, to see how easy it would be "not to get involved," and how important it was to "do something."

## EDUCATIONAL IMPLICATIONS

A "more powerful" framework, in the Piagetian sense, can also be a more dangerous one. The ability to see both sides can bring a new understanding of others and, therefore, an enhanced ability to take their needs into consideration. Yet it can also allow a concern for the rights or welfare of the victimizer to obscure the experience of the victim and the reality that the two sides are not equal. The use of multiple lenses can bring a new assumption of responsibility. But on the other hand, this ability can, as several multiple lens users pointed out in their journals, be used to rationalize inaction, evade decisions, or shrewdly manipulate others into complacency in the face of evil.

The survivor whose message begins this chapter reminds us that
formal education was a necessary but not sufficient condition for the Nazi
Holocaust. Physicians who must have been able to use multiple lenses
poisoned healthy children; this was considered a "medical matter." Arendt
(1963) tells us that the perpetrators of the Holocaust acted, for the most
part, not out of fear or passion or even self-interest, but out of loyalty to
their organizations, in conformity with prevailing norms, or as builders of
a state whose ideology demanded totalitarian control, "language rules"
(euphemisms), and eventually genocide. She demonstrates how education
enabled people to overcome their moral impulses.

> And just as the law in civilized countries assumes that the voice of conscience
> tells everybody "Thou shalt not kill," even though man's natural desires and
> inclinations may at times be murderous, so the law of Hitler's land demanded
> that the voice of conscience tell everybody: "Thou shalt kill," although the
> organizers of the massacres knew full well that murder is against the normal
> desires and inclinations of most people. Evil in the Third Reich had lost the
> quality by which most people recognize it--the quality of temptation. Many
> Germans and many Nazis, probably an overwhelming majority of them, must
> have been tempted *not* to murder, *not* to rob, *not* to let their neighbors go off
> to their doom (for that the Jews were transported to their doom they knew, of
> course, even though many of them may not have known the gruesome details),
> and not to become accomplices in all these crimes by benefiting from them.
> But, God knows, they had learned how to resist temptation. (Arendt, 1963,
> p. 150)

If we are to meet the challenge of educating in ways that help our
children and adolescents become more human, then we must attend to and
build on the "finely human" aspects of their thinking. As we help them to
see and understand the realities, complexities, and laws of the world, we
must also help them to hang on to their moral sensitivities and impulses.

In her novel *To Kill a Mockingbird,* Harper Lee (1960) illustrates
how a white child's moral "instincts" make him unable to watch the brutal
cross-examination of an innocent black man. When the boy runs from the
courtroom, sick to his stomach and in tears, he is comforted by a man who
has no use for the community's bigotry, and so lives apart and pretends to
be an alcoholic. Through this man's eyes, we see how the child's growth
and education are likely to dull his moral sensitivity. "Things haven't caught
up with that one's instinct yet. Let him get a little older and he won't get
sick and cry. Maybe things'll strike him as being--not quite right, say, but
he won't cry, not when he gets a few years on him."

The *Facing History* project continues to develop educational materials and methods that sustain children's visions as well as their tears, as it helps them to think about the things in their world that are "not quite right." Perhaps students educated in this way will grow up to cry out when they see pain or injustice, and to find ways to help the victims.

## NOTES

1. Lieberman, M. "Final Evaluation Report of the First Year (1977–78), Facing History and Ourselves:  Holocaust and Human Behavior." In "Annual Project Report to the Massachusetts Department of Education," submitted by M. S. Strom (1978); also in M. Lieberman, "Evaluation Report #78680D to the Joint Dissemination Review Panel" (1986).  These documents are available at Facing History and Ourselves Resource Center, Brookline, Mass.

2. Strom, M. S.  "Excerpts from the End of the Year Student Evaluations for 8th Grade Social Studies," Brookline Public Schools (1977).  Available at Facing History Resource Center.

3. Whittier, D.  *Kennard House Seniors* (1981).  Videotape available at Facing History Resource Center.

4. Intersection Associates.  *A Visit with Facing History* (1986).  Videotape available at Facing History Resource Center.

5. Des Pres, T.  "Lessons of the Holocaust."  *New York Times* (April 27, 1976).

6. Lamb, S.  "Harm Without Guilt:  A Critique of the General Systems Theory Analysis of Violence in the Family."  Unpublished paper, Harvard Graduate School of Education (1984).

## ACKNOWLEDGMENTS

I am deeply grateful to Margot Stern Strom and William S. Parsons, the developers of "Facing History and Ourselves:  Holocaust and Human Behavior," for helping me to see the potential of young adolescents and of curriculum.  I owe a special debt to Barbara Perry and Joyce Rakowski for their sensitive teaching of the course, and especially to their students who so generously shared their remarkable journals.

# 6

## THE ORIGINS OF MORALITY IN EARLY CHILDHOOD RELATIONSHIPS

Carol Gilligan and Grant Wiggins

This article was prompted by an observation made while listening to the discussion at the conference "The Origins of Morality in Early Childhood" (Harvard University, 1984). When psychologists traced morality to the child's discovery of the idea of justice, girls and women were seen to have less sense of justice than boys and men. This deficit in moral reasoning was explained in part by women's preoccupation with relationships and feelings (Freud, 1925/1961; Piaget, 1932/1965; Kohlberg & Kramer, 1969). Now, as the focus of psychologists' attention shifts to moral emotions or sentiments (Kagan, 1984), sex differences seem to have disappeared. Empathy and concern about feelings, once seen as the source of limitation in women's moral reasoning, are now viewed as the essence of morality but no longer associated particularly with women. The question is: What has changed?

Recent reports of research finding no evidence of sex differences in empathy or moral reasoning (Eisenberg & Lennon, 1983; Kohlberg, 1984; Walker, 1984) are presented as a sign of progress, both in research methods and in social justice. Such findings of no sex differences may appear to dissolve the difficult conceptual problems that findings of sex differences pose. But the inference that there are *no* sex differences in moral development is problematic on both empirical and theoretical grounds. Empirically, sociologists point to striking sex differences in both incidence and forms of antisocial behavior, manifest at the extreme in the statistics on violent crime (Wolfgang, 1966; Iskrant & Joliet, 1968; Kutash *et al.*, 1978). Naturalistic observers like parents and teachers as well as psychological researchers are struck by sex differences in aggression among children as well as in the patterns of their social interaction and play (Maccoby & Jacklin, 1974; Lever, 1976, 1978; Maccoby, 1985). On a theoretical level, cognitive developmental psychologists such as Piaget and Kohlberg explain moral development in childhood as mainly a function of peer group interaction; yet differences similar to those which Piaget described continue to mark the games that boys and girls play as well as the forms of conflict resolution that govern the same-sex peer groups of middle childhood. Theorists in the psychoanalytic tradition explain moral development in terms of family attachments and identifications; yet the gender asymmetry which Freud (1914, 1931) encountered as an obstacle to any neat parallelism between male and female development still characterizes family relationships. Women for the most part continue to assume primary responsibility for the care and nurturance of young children and as a result, the pattern of childhood attachments and identifications and the pattern of adult moral or "prosocial" behavior typically differ for males and females.

Psychologists have shied away from these observations for a variety of reasons including the dangers of stereotyping, the intimations of biological determinism, and the fact that in discussions of sex differences there is no disinterested position. In addition, recent claims that there are no sex differences in moral development may reflect a change in the way psychologists are studying morality. Attention has tended to shift away from the problems of relationship that preoccupied Freud in his analysis of family conflicts or Piaget in his study of children's games and toward problems in moral logic or moral feelings *per se.* Since both males and females demonstrate the human capacity to think rationally and to feel compassion, it is no surprise that researchers measuring morality in these terms find no sex differences in their data. Yet stereotypes of males as aggressive and females as nurturant, however distorting and limited, have some empirical basis. The overwhelmingly male composition of the prison population and the extent to which women care for young children cannot readily be dismissed as irrelevant to theories of morality or excluded from accounts of moral development. If there are no sex differences in empathy or moral reasoning, why are there sex differences in moral and immoral behavior? Either there is a problem in the way that empathy and moral reasoning are being measured or the role of empathy and cognition in moral development has been overstated. The question is how to incorporate sociological facts and general observations of what would appear to be relevant differences in morality between the sexes into a coherent conception of morality and a plausible account of moral development. To do this, we claim, it is necessary to revise the theoretical frame.

We begin with the issue of perspective, because it affects what observations are made in studying morality as well as how they are assessed. A major constraint on previous discussions of sex differences in morality has been the assumption of a single moral standpoint, defined as *the* moral perspective, which renders it impossible to talk about sex differences except in terms of invidious comparison. Cast in these terms, discussions of sex differences are marked by signs of unease, suggesting a discomfort in speaking and yet also the necessity for speaking about what has been seen. Freud, introducing his statement that women have less sense of justice than men, begins with a rhetorical gesture ("I cannot evade the notion though I hesitate to give it expression") and then aligns himself with "critics of every epoch" (1925/1961, p. 257) as if to fortify himself. Piaget disarmingly disavows any privileged position in describing female moral deficiency, claiming that "the most superficial observation is sufficient to show that in the main the legal sense is far less developed in little girls than in boys" (1932/1965, p. 77). Kohlberg, writing with Kramer (1969), describes the third of his six stages of moral development as "functional" for housewives and mothers but hurries to explain that if women, like men, were to obtain higher status jobs and more education, they too would advance to higher stages of moral development.

Immediately one senses the predicament of the observer who has no neutral position from which to comment on sex differences, and, therefore, no way to avoid the alternatives of moral arrogance and moral self-abnegation which Nietzsche described as quintessentially masculine and feminine stances. The virtue of the sex difference question in discussions of moral development lies precisely in the fact that it renders the issue of perspective inescapable. To ask, from what perspective are sex differences being considered, leads readily into the question: From what perspective is morality being defined? It is this question that we wish to consider in tracing the origins of morality to relationships in early childhood.

## TWO MORAL PERSPECTIVES/TWO DIMENSIONS OF RELATIONSHIP

Apart from our relationships with other people, as Piaget (1932/ 1965) observed, there would be no moral necessity. This observation is central to our position that a perspective on relationships underlies any conception of morality. Recent research on infancy provides compelling demonstrations that the foundations of morality are present early in child development--in the infant's responsiveness to the feelings of others and the young child's appreciation of standards (Kagan, 1984; Stern, 1985). But to explain the nature of moral feelings and standards, it is necessary to consider how these capacities become organized and thus, to consider the infant's experience of relationships with other people. We locate the origins of morality in the young child's awareness of self in relation to others and we identify two dimensions of early childhood relationships that shape this awareness in different ways. One is the dimension of inequality, reflected in the child's awareness of being smaller and less capable than adults and older children, of being a baby in relation to a standard of human being. This dimension of relationship has been stressed by theorists of moral development in both the cognitive and psychoanalytic traditions and is reflected by the emphasis placed on the child's feelings of helplessness and powerlessness in relation to others, feelings tied to the fact of being dependent on others who are more powerful. Focusing on the constraint of the young child's situation, psychologists have defined morality as justice and aligned development with the child's progress toward a position of equality and independence.

But the young child also experiences attachment, and the dynamics of attachment relationships create a very different awareness of self--as capable of having an effect on others, as able to move others and be moved by them. Characteristically, young children come to love the people who care for them, desiring to be near them, wanting to know them, being able to recognize them, and being sad when they leave. In the context of attachment, the child discovers the patterns of human interaction and

observes the ways in which people care for and hurt one another. Like
the experience of inequality, although in different ways, the experience of
attachment profoundly affects the child's understanding of human feelings
and how people should act toward one another. The moral implications
of attachment relationships have generally been overlooked in theories of
moral development, in part because the passivity of early childhood love
has been stressed, rather than the child's activity in creating and sustaining
connections with others, and in part because the emergence of self awareness during this time has been tied to separation and detachment. Yet the
experience of attachment generates a perspective on relationships that
underlies the conception of morality as love.

Thus, the different dynamics of early childhood inequality and attachment lay the groundwork for two moral visions--one of justice and one of
care. The growing child's experience of inequality and of attachment, sometimes but not always convergent, grounds a distinction between the dimensions of inequality/equality and attachment/detachment which characterize
all forms of human relationships. Although the nature of the attachment
between child and parent varies across individual and cultural settings and
although inequality can be heightened or muted by familial and societal
arrangements, all people are born into a situation of inequality and no child
survives in the absence of adult connection. Since everyone is vulnerable
both to oppression and to abandonment, two stories about morality recur in
human experience.

Children know both stories and test them in a variety of ways. American children appeal to justice in the face of unequal power by claiming, "It
is not fair" or "You have no right." They assess the strength of care by
stating, "You do not care" or "I do not love you anymore." In this, children
discover the efficacy of moral standards, the extent to which justice offers
protection to the unequal in the face of oppression and the extent to which
care protects attachment against threats of abandonment or detachment.
The lessons learned about justice and care in early childhood relationships
generate expectations which are confirmed or modified in later childhood
and adolescence. Two moral injunctions--not to treat others unfairly and
not to turn away from others in need--define two lines of moral development, providing different standards for assessing moral judgments and
moral behavior and pointing to changes in the understanding of what

fairness means and what constitutes care. By tracing moral development across two intersecting dimensions of relationship, it is possible to differentiate transformations that pertain to equality from transformations that pertain to attachment and to consider the interplay between problems of inequality and problems of detachment. Observations of sex differences in moral understanding and moral behavior reflect a tendency for these problems to be differentially salient or differently organized in male and female development.

The sex difference question, when framed in this way, does not carry the implication that one sex is morally superior, nor does it imply that moral behavior is biologically determined. Instead, it draws attention to two perspectives on morality. To the extent that biological sex, the psychology of gender, and the cultural norms and values that define masculine and feminine behavior affect the experience of equality and attachment, these factors presumably will influence moral development.

For example, the experience of attachment in early childhood may attenuate the experience of inequality by empowering the child in relation to the parent, who otherwise seems unmovable and all-powerful. If girls identify with their mothers, to whom they are attached and with whom they remain in closer physical proximity, the experience of inequality may be less overwhelming and the sense of efficacy gained by creating connections with others may be more central to the organization of their self-concept and self-esteem. By adolescence, girls may be less attentive to the consequences of unequal relationships and more apt to focus their attention on the nature or the strength of connection, especially when norms of feminine behavior impede strivings toward equality. If boys are more strongly attached to their mothers but identify with their fathers and do not see beyond their father's authority and physical power, then the experience of inequality and the desire to overcome that status may become more salient in the organization of self-concept and separation or independence more crucial for self-esteem. If recurrent childhood experiences of inequality are less mitigated by experiences of attachment in boys' development, compounded by social inequality in adolescence and a high cultural valuation of male dominance, feelings of powerlessness may become heightened and the potential for violence may correspondingly increase.

These schematic observations are intended to suggest the ways in which experiences of inequality and experiences of attachment can interact with one another, leading one dimension of relationship to overshadow the other or to color its meaning. We have indicated how girls may tend to lose sight of the problems that arise from inequality and how boys may tend to lose sight of the problems that arise from detachment. Yet the tension between these two moral perspectives may best illuminate the psychology of moral development, by drawing attention to conflicts in relationships that give rise to genuine moral dilemmas.

When seen in terms of *either* justice or care, the following problems *appear* to have right, if difficult, answers. Seen from *both* perspectives, their ethical ambiguity appears. With this shift one comes to a different understanding of the child who is uncertain over whether to adhere to standards of fairness or help another child on a test, or the adolescent who is torn between loyalty to particular relationships and loyalty to ideals of equality and freedom, or the adult who wonders in allocating resources whether it is better to respond to the perception of need or to follow principles of justice. Like the dilemma posed by Sartre (1948) about whether a young man should join the resistance or stay with his mother, or the dilemma of mothers who wonder whether to join the resistance or stay with their children, these conflicts can be seen as paradigmatic human moral problems--problems that arise when the demands of equality and the demands of attachment clash.

The metaphor that illuminates our discussion of moral development is, therefore, the ambiguous figure, illustrating how the same scene can be organized in at least two different ways and how one way of seeing can lead another to disappear. We will begin with a summary of research on moral orientation to present evidence that the two perspectives we have described are manifest in the ways people define and resolve moral problems. We then will turn to the question of moral feelings and indicate how the different perspectives on relationship color the meaning of compassion and organize the moral emotions of shame and guilt, love and sorrow. Finally, we will offer an overview of moral development and the relational life of the child. Drawing on insights we have gained from rereading Piaget and from Bowlby's work on loss and detachment, we arrive at the position that moral emotions, like moral judgments, are not primary data but are effects of relationships. The egocentric fallacy is to assume that strong feelings and clear principles are self-generated or *sui generis*. Our argument is that strong feelings and clear principles are dependent on "authentic" relationships. Because relationships vary in nature, the conditions that affect relationships and the moral psychologies generated by different forms of relationships become central empirical questions and theoretical concerns. In this article, we will focus our attention on two dimensions of relationships and suggest their implications for the development of moral reasoning and moral feelings.

## EVIDENCE OF TWO PERSPECTIVES IN MORAL REASONING

Evidence that the two moral orientations we have described structure people's thinking about the nature and resolution of moral conflicts comes from studies of the ways people describe moral conflicts they have faced. Analysis of such descriptions indicates that people tend to raise considerations of justice and of care in recounting experiences of moral conflict and choice. In a sample of eighty educationally advantaged adolescents and adults, fifty-five people (69 percent) introduced both justice and care considerations (see Chapter 4). Two-thirds of the people studied (fifty-seven out of eighty, or 67 percent), however, focused their attention on either justice or care concerns so that of the considerations they raised, 75 percent or more were framed in the terms of one or the other orientation. This "focus phenomenon" was manifest equally by males and females among the high school, college, and medical students, and the adult professionals who were studied. But the direction of focus revealed a difference between the sexes. For example, care focus in moral reasoning, although by no means characteristic of all women, was almost exclusively a female phenomenon in this educationally advantaged North American sample. Of the thirty-one men who demonstrated focus, thirty focused on justice. Of the twenty-two women, ten focused on justice and twelve on care.

The clearest demonstration of moral orientation appears in a study designed and conducted by Johnston (see Chapter 3) who, adapting Aesop's fables, developed a standard method for assessing spontaneous moral orientation and orientation preference. In essence, this research suggests that people understand two logics of moral problem solving and that the analytically distinguishable orientations of justice and care prompt different ways of perceiving and resolving conflicts. The research findings are consistent with our analysis of human relationships and moral development, indicating that eleven-year-old children as well as adolescents and adults orient toward the moral values of both justice and care and are capable of shifting orientations in considering conflicts in relationships.

Langdale (1983) studied moral orientation in judgments of hypothetical dilemmas and reported an interaction between spontaneous moral orientation (as reflected by self-generated "real-life" moral conflicts) and the orientation characteristics of hypothetical moral problems. The validity of the justice-care distinction in the coding procedure developed by Lyons (Coding Manual, 1982) is indicated by Langdale's finding that Kohlberg's justice reasoning dilemmas elicited the highest frequency of justice considerations from both males and females in a life cycle sample of 144 people. Langdale found sex differences in moral orientation across four different dilemmas, with women consistently raising more care considerations than men, even in resolving the justice-focused Heinz problem.

It should be emphasized, however, that at this point we suspend any claim as to the generality of these findings. It clearly will be necessary to examine the vicissitudes of these two orientations among both men and women embedded in different socioeconomic, educational, and cultural contexts as well as across a wider range of moral problems.

## THE IMPLICATIONS OF MORAL ORIENTATION
## FOR THE STUDY OF MORAL EMOTIONS

The two perspectives we have designated as a "justice orientation" and a "care orientation" imply a shift in the conception of what is relevant to the moral domain. According to this thesis, the two orientations would not only entail different notions of "morality" manifest in different forms of moral reasoning but also different conceptions of the emotions and the relations of the emotions with morality. Certain activities that are treated dismissively from one perspective may be elevated from a different perspective. For example, forms of human relationship that, from the perspective of a justice orientation, may be relegated to the status of residues of an outgrown developmental stage may, from a care orientation, be viewed as significant and even central. This shift in world view is key to our representation of the moral significance of attachment relationships, seen not as residues of early childhood need but as central to the development of what in the past was called "moral sensibility." Detachment, which is highly valued as the mark of mature moral judgment in the justice framework becomes in the care framework a sign of moral danger, a loss of connection with others. The sharp subject-object distinction that is considered essential to development in most psychological theories, thus, is called into question. A more fluid conception of self in relation to others is tied to the growth of the affective imagination, namely, the ability to enter into and understand through taking on and experiencing the feelings of others.

In the traditional literature, governed by a predominant justice orientation, shame and guilt have been seen as the paradigmatic moral feelings. Hoffman (1976) has taken the lead in criticizing this view and emphasizes the need not only to consider empathy, sympathy, and altruistic motives in conceptualizing morality and moral development but also to pay attention to evidence of empathy, sympathy, and altruism in early childhood. Blum (1980) in his philosophical study of *Friendship, Altruism and Morality* argues for the moral significance of human connection and personal care and contrasts two modes of responding to others that resemble our contrast between justice and care.

Our conception of the care orientation as grounded in attachments leads us to consider love and sorrow as moral emotions as well as other feelings which are closely linked to attachment and to fears of alienation and isolation. Moral outrage can be provoked not only by oppression and injustice but also by abandonment or loss of attachment or the failure of others to respond. In a study of high school girls, moral passion marked their descriptions of situations in which someone did not listen, recalling Simone Weil's and Iris Murdoch's definition of attention as a moral act. It is important to emphasize that in our conception love does not imply fusion or transcendence. Instead, love is tied to the activities of relationship and premised, like attachment, on the responsiveness of human connection, the ability of people to engage with one another in such a way that the needs and feelings of the other come to be experienced and taken on as *part of* the self. As experiences of inequality and attachment organize moral reasoning, generating a preoccupation with justice and care, so, too, these experiences structure feelings of shame, guilt, love, and sorrow.

Shame and guilt, love and sorrow can be traced to experiences of inequality and attachment in that shame and guilt imply falling below a standard while love and sorrow imply connection. In the individual person, however, these feelings, like the experiences themselves, intermingle. Guilt may be engendered by the inability to reciprocate love; shame as well as sorrow may be provoked by a loss of attachment or by inattention; and sorrow as well as shame and guilt can accompany the experience of oppression or injustice. These feelings define moral experience and clarify moral violation; yet the power of moral feelings coexists with the recognition that such feelings can be interpreted differently in different contexts.

These problems of interpretation are illustrated clearly by the discussion of the word "compassion" in Milan Kundera's novel, *The Unbearable Lightness of Being* (1984). The discussion of compassion begins with the observation that, "All languages that derive from Latin form the word 'compassion' by combining the prefix meaning 'with' (*com*) with the root meaning 'suffering' (Late Latin, *passio*)." In other languages, such as Czech, Swedish, and German, the word is translated by a similar prefix combined with a root meaning "feeling" (pp. 19-20). The significance of this etymological distinction is that the meaning of compassion changes from sympathy to love as the relationship implied changes from one of inequality to one of attachment. This shift in meaning, drawn out in the following passage, is key to our thinking about the nature of moral feelings and the role of emotion or sentiment in moral development:

> In languages that derive from Latin, "compassion" means: we cannot look on cooly as others suffer; or, we sympathize with those who suffer. Another word with approximately the same meaning, "pity" (French *pitié*; Italian *pietà*, etc.), connotes a certain condescension towards the sufferer. "To take pity on a woman" means that we are better off than she, that we stoop to her level, lower ourselves.
>   That is why the word "compassion" generally inspires suspicion; it designates what is considered an inferior, second-rate sentiment that has little to do with love. To love someone out of compassion means not really to love.
>   In languages that form the word "compassion" not from the root "suffering" but from the root "feeling," the word is used in approximately the same way, but . . . The secret strength of its etymology floods the word with another light and gives it a broader meaning: to have compassion (co-feeling) means not only to be able to live with the other's misfortune but also to feel with him any emotion--joy, anxiety, happiness, pain. This kind of compassion . . . therefore signifies the maximal capacity of affective imagination, the art of emotional telepathy. In the hierarchy of sentiments, then, it is supreme. (Kundera, 1984, p. 20)

In its English usage, compassion means sympathy, and the tinge of suspicion Kundera's narrator describes extends across the entire discussion of altruism and prosocial awareness, conveying an uncertainty over whether altruistic emotions are really self-interested and whether they are welcomed by the recipient. It is only when compassion means co-feeling that its moral qualities are clear. No longer does one remain distant in the presence of another's feelings, and the opposition between egoism and altruism disappears. Yet the idea of co-feeling goes against prevailing assumptions about the nature of the self and its relation to others, since co-feeling implies neither clear self-other boundaries nor a merging or fusion between self and other. Considered on a theoretical level, co-feeling, however morally desirable, would seem to be psychologically impossible. Yet the contrast between sympathy and co-feeling occasionally appears in empirical studies, often in conjunction with observations of sex differences in empathy or prosocial awareness. To consider the meaning of co-feeling and its possible significance in moral development, it is necessary first to distinguish more closely between different forms of moral emotions and different ways of knowing others.

Hoffman (1976) suggests that one can feel another's feelings only to the extent that the other's feelings are similar to one's own. Kagan's view of morality as grounded in emotions assumes "a family of feelings, each of which has a prototypic core" (1984, p. 169). Although feelings are felt by the individual, the suggestion of a family of feelings mediated by standards of feeling to which everyone is assumed to have access leaves open the question of how this access is gained. Our interest in co-feeling lies in the implication that such feeling develops through the experience of relationships which render *others'* feelings accessible. The distinction between co-feeling and empathy is that empathy implies an identity of feelings--that self and other feel the same, while co-feeling implies that one can experience feelings that are different from one's own. Co-feeling, then, depends on the ability to *participate* in another's feelings (in their terms), signifying an attitude of engagement rather than an attitude of judgment or observation. To feel with another any emotion means in essence to be *with* that person, rather than to stand apart and look *at* the other, feeling sympathy *for* her or him. For example, when a child suffers, one may feel the child's suffering as part of one's own, or one may observe that the child is suffering and feel concern for the child.

The moral emotions of shame and guilt convey a distance between self and other; to feel ashamed in the eyes of others or guilty for one's wishes or actions toward others is to feel lower than them or perhaps more powerful in the sense of being capable of doing them harm. When one feels ashamed or guilty in one's own eyes, the implication of inequality remains but is structured in terms of self-regard. One has fallen beneath one's standards or failed to live up to one's aspirations, as the terms superego and ego ideal imply.

To see love and sorrow as moral emotions--as feelings that affect the ability to care for oneself and for others and inform the understanding of how one should act or what actions constitute care--is to see experiences of attachment and detachment as relevant to moral development. With this shift, there is a change in the assumptions usually made about relationships in discussions of morality. For example, the reason love does not connote condescension is not because it implies equality but because it signifies connection. Through co-feeling, self and other, whether equal or unequal, become connected or interdependent. Difference in this context may stimulate interest or signify the potential for an expansion of experience or for detachment and misunderstanding, but it does not imply that one is higher or lower than the other. Conversely, co-feeling does not imply an absence of difference or an identity of feelings or a failure to distinguish between self and other. Instead, co-feeling implies an awareness of oneself as capable of knowing and living with the feelings of others, as able to affect others and to be affected by them. With this shift in the conception of self in relation to others, moral questions change.

No longer does moral inquiry turn on the question of how to live with inequality--that is, how to act *as if* self and other were, in fact, equal or how to impose a rule of equality based on a principle of equal respect. Instead, moral inquiry deals with questions of relationship pertaining to problems of inclusion and exclusion--how to live in connection with oneself and with others, how to avoid detachment or resist the temptation to turn away from need. The games children play and their friendship patterns reveal their engagement with these questions. Children's experiments in inclusion and exclusion, seen most darkly in clique formation and ostracism, lead to some of the more painful experiences of childhood and adult life. But they also prepare people--within the context of relationship--for the difficult questions about inclusion and exclusion which arise throughout life. The costs of detachment and the conditions for attachment or connection are, thus, lessons that can be learned through experience.

The role of feelings in knowledge about attachment and detachment raises the question of how knowledge of feelings is gained and expanded. The infant, responding empathically to the feelings of others, demonstrates co-feeling in its most inchoate form. As the child develops, different experiences of human connection--with parents, siblings, friends, teachers, etc.--may deepen and widen the experience of feelings, expanding the child's vocabulary of feelings and increasing his or her interest in knowing how people feel. The aesthetic sensibilities of children which are evident in their drawings and stories demonstrate their ability to enter into the feelings of others and to imagine affectively how others feel.

For example, it is the child's and parent's responsiveness to each other that gives life to the relationship between them, imbuing it with the pleasure that comes from responsive engagement and creating an interplay of feelings that leads the child to wonder at the adult and the adult to delight in the child. Through the attachment or connection they create between them, child and parent come to know one another's feelings and in this way discover how to comfort as well as how to hurt one another. When the responsiveness between parent and child decreases and their inequality comes to the fore, the child may feel ashamed or guilty in the eyes of the parent, and the parent, at best, looks on the child with sympathy and feels compassion for his or her distress.

This distance between self and other has been celebrated as the mark of the subject-object distinction, the birth of subject-object relations. But it also carries with it the danger of objectification, the ability to treat others as objects and to feel no connection with them. The sense that safety and insight are gained through detachment is countered by the recognition that in the absence of co-feeling one cannot know what others are feeling, and therefore, one may live in egocentric ignorance, dangerously prone to rationalization.

Two descriptions of knowledge, thus, underlie two ways of thinking about morality. One is the conception of knowledge as arising through the correspondence between mind and pure form, so that moral knowledge becomes the reflective equilibrium between the self and moral principles. One can then take the role of the other or assume Rawls' original position or play Kohlberg's game of moral musical chairs--all without specifically knowing anything about the other but simply by following the laws of perspective and putting oneself in his or her position (Kohlberg, 1982). The other conception is of knowledge as gained through human connection, a conception conveyed in the Biblical passage: "And Adam knew Eve." The young child's feelings of shame and guilt, love and sorrow, signify the presence of both forms of knowledge and point to their origins in the relationships of early childhood.

In studies of empathy, sympathy, and prosocial behavior such as help- ing, sharing, and caring the distinction between compassion in the sense of sympathy, and compassion in the sense of co-feeling is generally not made, or if made, associated with the presence or absence of self-other boundaries. These studies often focus on children's response to distress and equate development with the child's ability to see the distress as belonging to the other and to "own" his or her own feelings. Thus, Hoffman distinguishes between the infant's empathic responsiveness and the child's sympathetic distress and sees in this contrast a developmental progression that reflects the emergence of self-awareness and the growth of cognitive capacities.

Hoffman (1977) notes, however, in a survey of the literature on sex differences in empathy, that one of the few instances of clear sex differ- ence is the finding that girls and boys are equally able to identify and understand the feelings of others but that girls tend to *experience* the other's feelings. In analyzing children's narratives Wolf, Rygh, and Alt- shuler (1984) have observed that girls and boys of similar age have the same repertoire of feelings but tend to "string" feelings together differently in composing narrative sequences. The most compelling example of sex differences that suggests the distinction between co-feeling and sympathy arose as a fortuitous observation in a study of reflective thinking and prosocial awareness in early adolescence. The findings of this study, con- ducted by Bardige (see Chapter 5), suggest a tension between co-feeling and formal operational thinking in a context where this tension raises questions about the nature of moral development.

Bardige (1983) analyzed the journals kept by forty-three suburban eighth graders who were taking the course, *Facing History and Ourselves: Holocaust and Human Behavior.* Bardige set out to trace the growth of logical thinking in early adolescence by analyzing students' ability to understand complex historical events. In conducting her analysis, however, she noticed that four girls whose journals showed signs of concrete operational thinking repeatedly responded to films and stories portraying violence with language that coupled sadness, horror, or distress with shock and a call for action to stop the violence. Reexamining the journals, Bardige found that this pattern appeared in the journals of eight of the twenty-four girls in the study and one of the nineteen boys. She called the pattern "responsive face-value language" to denote the tendency of these students to take evidence of violence at face value and respond directly.

The limitations of "face-value thinking" were clear and the naivete of its good intentions apparent; yet the immediacy of perception, the passionate clarity of judgment, the intensity of involvement, and the eagerness to "do something" were striking--particularly in light of the observation that those students whose reasoning was more sophisticated (they sought to see the other side of the story or were capable of seeing through multiple lenses) did not respond to the perception of violence with the same moral intensity. In one sense, the face-value responses called attention to "the central moral truth of the situation--the fact that violence was being inflicted and the need to stop it." The strength of responsive face-value language, thus, lies in the fact that "it captures the impulse to respond both emotionally and actively. It allows no excuses for torture and murder" (Bardige, this volume).

The fact that this response was associated with evidence of what are generally taken to be lower levels of cognitive, moral, and ego development lead Bardige to reconsider her analysis of the journals and to question wheth er moral sensibilities are at risk in adolescence. All the students showed personal distress, profound concern, incredulity, and a desire to "do something" in response to the violence they witnessed, but the language they used and the linkages they made were different. Contrasting the "passionate clarity of a 'face-value judgment' [with] the generosity of a 'composite-picture judgment' that looks for the good side, and the integrity of a 'multiple lens judgment' that recognizes that actions that satisfy one's conscience may not be truly helpful," Bardige saw a pattern of gains and losses.

Kant had argued similarly. The moral insights implicit in the ideas and behavior of the common man may well be muted or lost, he noted, in the moral philosopher's ability to "confuse his judgment with a mass of alien considerations and cause it to swerve from the straight path" (1785/1948, pp. 22-23). Piaget saw the onset of formal operations in adolescence as carrying with it a danger of the most pervasive egocentrism and thus, characterized adolescence as "the metaphysical age par excellence" (1940/1967, p. 64). Bardige, too, considered the ways in which a more powerful cognitive framework can be more dangerous:

> The ability to see both sides can bring a new understanding of others and therefore, an enhanced ability to take their needs into consideration. It can also allow a concern for the rights and welfare of the victimizer to obscure the experience of the victim and the reality that the two sides are not equal. The use of multiple lenses can bring a new assumption of responsibility. This ability can also, as several multiple-lens users pointed out in their journals, be used to rationalize inaction, evade decisions, or shrewdly manipulate others into complacency in the face of evil. (Bardige, see Chapter 5)

Most striking in the responses of the students who took evidence of violence at face value was the direct expression of feeling in response to the perception of hurt. The expressions of sadness or disgust, coupled with statements of uncomprehending shock, became the ground on which these students felt called to take action. In the absence of face-value thinking, the evidence of co-feeling disappeared from the journals. The more sophisticated thinkers were more likely to locate emotion within themselves and to express sympathy for the victims. Some were suspicious of emotional responses, recognizing how feelings can be manipulated; others spoke of their efforts to overcome their tendency to distance themselves.

Kagan has speculated that "Perhaps each of us is persuaded of the moral rightness of an idea by two different, incommensurate processes. One is based on feelings; the other, on logical consistency with a few deep premises." He goes on to observe that "when a standard derives its strength from either foundation, we find it difficult to be disloyal to its directives. When it enjoys the support of both, as it does for torture and unprovoked murder, its binding force is maximal" (1984, p. 124). Our analysis of justice and care as two moral logics and of sympathy and love as two meanings of compassion corroborates Kagan's distinction but suggests further that both feelings and premises characterize moral voice and moral orientation. The focus phenomenon in our studies, where subjects tend to view moral problems largely in terms of justice or care, suggests a dynamic tension between these two perspectives, in that the adoption of one tends to obscure the other. Consequently, problems that arise when moral development is assessed from a single perspective may seem elusive.

The nature of sex differences in moral reasoning is clarified by the fact that care focus appears in our data primarily in the moral judgment of girls and women and by the fact that Bardige found face-value responses to violence primarily in girls' moral thinking. Thus, what appears as dispassion within a justice framework appears as detachment from a care perspective: the ability to stand back and look at others as if one's feelings were disconnected from their feelings and one was not affected by what happens to them. This ability to see relationships in two ways or to tell a story from two different angles underlies what may well be among the most searing experiences of moral dilemma, creating an irreducible sense of ethical ambiguity and also perhaps a temptation to eliminate one version or one perspective and, thus, make the incongruity disappear.

## IMPLICATIONS FOR THEORIES OF MORAL DEVELOPMENT

In the final section of this paper, we will consider the implications of our data for describing the moral development of the child. Our metaphor of the ambiguous figure calls attention to the persistent danger that lies in the loss of perspective. It follows from our analysis of justice and care as two moral perspectives that either perspective can represent the concerns of the other within its own terms. Within a justice framework, care becomes a matter of special obligations or supererogatory duties. Within a care framework, justice becomes a matter of including the self as well as others within the compass of care. Yet this effort to construct one orientation in terms of the other, like attempts to cast the two orientations as opposites so that caring is unjust and justice uncaring, misses the reorganization of relationship that occurs with the shift in perspective. To argue whether morality is *really* a matter of justice or of care is like arguing whether the ambiguous rabbit-duck figure is really a rabbit or a duck.

The care ethic cannot be reduced to a "personal" aspect of morality conceived as justice, as Kohlberg and others have argued.[1] To do so not only fails to see that care can be "principled"--governed by standards of authentic relationship--but also overlooks those dilemmas that arise from conflicts between perspectives or from blind spots within one point of view. For example, moral psychology, looking at development from the perspective of the thinking or feeling self, construed as a detached ego attaining its freedom, cannot account for the classic errors of moral blindness or rationalization. Similarly, a moral psychology that represents development only as progress toward equality and mutual respect runs the risk of confusing detachment with objectivity, so that relationships end up serving heteronomous and reified moral norms.

Our relationship-focused perspective on morality leads us to see experiences of equality and attachment as critical to the growth of moral understanding. Looking at the dynamics of development, we pay particular attention to the interweaving of these two dimensions of relationship and, thus, to conflicts between concerns about justice and concerns about care. When the child's search for equality--the effort to become stronger and more competent, like the adult--comes into tension with the child's search for attachment--the effort to create and sustain authentic relationships--the experience of moral dilemma may be most intense and the potential for moral development may as a result be heightened. Early childhood and adolescence would appear to be such times, since biological growth, new psychological capacities, and new worlds of social experience combine to change the terms of both equality and attachment. Relationships consequently must be renegotiated along both dimensions. To see early childhood and adolescence as periods of heightened vulnerability, when relationships undergo rapid transformation, is to see the moral problems that younger children and adolescents are likely to encounter. The implication that detachment constitutes a solution to such problems in either period is, in our view, the major blind spot in current theories of self and moral development.

In this light, we come back to Piaget's insights about the moral wisdom and generosity of the eleven-year-old child and consider, in addition, Bowlby's work on the ways children rationalize disordered attachments. Piaget's question--"How is it that democratic practice is so developed in the game of marbles played by boys of eleven and thirteen whereas it is so unfamiliar to the adult in many spheres of life?"--has never been answered, beyond Piaget's reflection that the eleven-year-old is the "sovereign" in the childhood world (1932/1965, p. 76). This question continues to challenge the assumption of incremental progress contained in stage theories of moral development.[2] Piaget's observation of the eleven-year-old boy's "insights into the ideal or spirit of the game which cannot be formulated in terms of rules" (1932/1965, p. 386) corresponds to our observation of similar insights among girls of eleven into "the spirit of the relationship" which also cannot be fully articulated at this age. In light of the sex differences we have noted in moral reasoning and moral emotions, the question as to whether insights about games and relationships, equality and attachment, are held in common by children of both sexes may better be phrased as a question of whether boys and girls tend to organize such insights differently in relation to one another. Adolescence becomes a critical time in moral development because the childhood organization of equality and attachment no longer fits the experience of the teenager. Thus, the wisdom of the eleven-year-old about the rules of the game and the nature of relationships, rather than being solidified and progressively expanded in adolescence, is in danger.

Puberty moves the sovereign eleven-year-old into an insecure position between the attachments of childhood and of adulthood, where the child's early assumptions about care and about justice are often radically upset. Formal thinking opens up the world of powerful moral ideals and hypothetical arguments, but puberty also opens up the world of reproductive sexuality and mystifying attachments. The potential for alienated rationalizing and for detached feelings is, therefore, heightened in the difficult social world of the teenager, especially in the presence of systematic injustice or rationalized indifference on the part of adults. Inhelder and Piaget offer vivid descriptions of the seduction of metaphysics in adolescence, and they see the adolescent's egocentrism as "messianic," liable to produce private fantasies that even the thinker himself or herself later might find to be "pathological megalomania" (1958, p. 344). The critical variable for moral development in adolescence may be the development of genuine intellectual and emotional attachments which would counter the potential for such egocentrism. But the question arises: Is Piaget's picture a necessary one? Or are alienation and rationalization a response to inadequately formed or thought through attachments? In this light, we look at Piaget's own example of the eleven-year-old he identifies as Camp.

Camp, contrary to Piaget's intentions, illustrates how care can override justice, but the example is inadequately explained--in part to sustain Piaget's contention that "equality and solidarity go hand in hand":

[Interviewer:]  *What do you think about cheating?*

For those who can't learn, they ought to be allowed to have a little look, but for those who can learn, it isn't fair.

*A child copied his friend's sum. Was it fair?*

He ought not to have copied. But if he was not clever, it was more or less alright for him to do it. (Piaget, 1932/1965, p. 289)

Surprisingly, Piaget observes, "This last attitude seems to be rather the exception among the children we examined. But no doubt many others thought the same without having the courage to say so." Piaget solves the problem posed by his example by claiming that it illustrates the conflict between solidarity among children and adult authority. He then discusses the Kantian question of whether one should lie to avoid betrayal. But the egalitarian justice that Piaget sees as developing with age among children in correlation with the idea of solidarity does not address the issues of attachment and detachment which the example contains. Nor are these issues articulated by Camp.

Camp illustrates compassion in the sense of sympathy rather than co-feeling, distancing himself from the less clever child whom he thinks it "alright" to help. Thus, he implies that one only modifies justice for those in a lower position. But the attachment implications of such dilemmas are often articulated explicitly by girls of this age, who speak of the costs to themselves of turning away from the perceived needs of others--the memory of the unheeded cry for help as well as the danger of "losing all your friends."

Adolescent girls' resistance to detachment has generally been interpreted as a failure of separation which occurs at the expense of their intellectual and moral growth. Viewed instead from the standpoint of the costs of detachment, it seems to contain a different moral insight whose application is not limited to the private sphere. A high school philosophy student, discussing the dilemma posed by Sartre about whether a young man should join the resistance or stay with his mother, illustrates both the coherence of an attachment-based care logic and the contrast with justice reasoning.

> If I were the boy, I think that I would have chosen to stay with the mother. I do not know if that would be best, but it is a more immediate and good solution. Are there no other men to be loyal to the state, when he is the only one whom his mother's existence depends on? I feel strongly toward directing actions toward the good of individuals. If everyone did so, logically, these actions would be for the good of everyone.

The response to the mother is grounded not only in the immediacy and reality of her need but also in the logic which argues that, were the norms guiding care in particular relationships realized in a general way (i.e., universalizing the norm of attention to each idiosyncratic relationship), such conflict might be unnecessary. Seeing differences between people as opportunities for creative solutions that are responsive to everyone's need, this adolescent illustrates how the logic of the ethic of care and its preference for inclusive solutions is designed to avoid turning moral dilemmas into binary choice, win-lose situations. Yet the inclusive or creative solution does not fit the standard of equality from the justice perspective. If she were to adopt a role-taking stance (of the justice perspective) and put herself in the other person's position, she would assume that he would have similar needs or duties (vis-à-vis mothers) when, in fact, that might not be the case. Thus, detachment, impartiality, and "ideal role taking" may obscure the possibility of the win-win solution that she imagines.

But there is another point to be made. Co-feeling characterizes her approach to solving the dilemma in that she "lives with," rather than reconstructing in her own terms, the mother's need. In this sense co-feeling underlies respect for the feelings of others and removes the presumption of deciding for others whether or not their needs are "real." It is in this way that the shift from inequality to attachment changes the organization of thinking about the relationship between self and others and makes possible compassion in the sense of love.

Another high school student, discussing Kohlberg's Heinz dilemma, sees a problem in detachment, not only in the dilemma itself--the unresponsiveness of the druggist to Heinz and his wife--but also in the implications of what is generally taken to be its right answer, the statement that life takes priority over law and property. Although she is able logically to justify the rightness of Heinz's stealing on these grounds, she finds a problem in saying that a person should steal a drug to save the life of a stranger when she knows that in her own city people are dying because they cannot afford medication. She sees how the "right answer" is right but she also sees it as morally problematic, as raising the question of what it means to divorce moral judgment from action. In addition, she questions whether stealing would constitute a good solution to problems of unfair distribution.

The current debates about the child's capacity for altruistic feelings and motives have not addressed a crucial point: If such feelings are natural and present in early childhood (and Piaget as well as Kant and Rawls regard them as so--necessary, if insufficient), their loss or harmful transformation must be the *result* of certain kinds of experience. Thus, we ask: What experiences might be present in the lives of those who lose these sensibilities? Do some children never lose them, and if so, what form has their experience taken?

Piaget suggested that knowledge of the good is acquired after knowledge of pure duty, but he never indicated how that knowledge is attained (1932/1965, pp. 73, 106, 350). Kohlberg claimed that his sixth stage integrates caring and justice, but he never described how caring develops or how one knows what constitutes care (1984, pp. 349-358). What if knowledge of the good is not acquired after knowledge of pure duty but is possessed in embryo form at a far earlier developmental point, such as in the case of the girls whom Piaget fails to understand (who do not sanction hitting back as an appropriate response to blows received and who more quickly shed egocentrism in the experience of cooperation)? Or what if this knowledge is also possessed by eleven-year-old marble shooters and exam takers? What if the upbringing and moral experience of the girls and the insights of eleven-year-old boys, as reflected in Piaget's own data, point to a different kind of complex, idiosyncratic moral development, dependent on the fate of attachments?

Perhaps the relational experience of girls, both their connection with their mothers and their friendships throughout childhood, mitigate against detachment and its attendant egocentrism, keeping both their relational nature and their moral knowledge intact, if unsystematic. The extent to which school age girls acquire a factual knowledge of human feelings and can explain and predict complex patterns of interaction within a family or school classroom has never been addressed in its significance for moral understanding. Perhaps the quiet uncertainty of so many adolescent girls reflects their conflicting feelings, the multiplicity of perspectives and possible judgments based on a non-egocentric knowledge of how others feel.

Piaget's work contains the seeds of this argument, but they have been lost in the language and focus on justice considerations and in an overly cognitive reading of his work by Piagetians. Piaget's notion that autonomy develops in peer interaction, often in spite of the parents, merely highlights the essential role of relationships in moral development (1932/1965, pp. 190-193, 319). The morality based on a self-evident good, a morality of intention and co-feeling, depends not only on the experience of genuine cooperation but also on the experience of genuine attachment. The loss of the natural moral emotions, thus, seems less a loss than a repressive transformation where ego developmental needs formed in detachment adapt moral feelings to personal aims. Thus, norms and rules become reified as "self-chosen principles," removed from the relational contexts which give them life and meaning.

If the persistent error in care reasoning is vacillation and lack of clear judgment resulting from a tendency to include all possible ways of seeing, the persistent danger in justice reasoning is moral arrogance, the irrational faith in the infallibility of judgments from principles rigidly applied to a situation. It follows then that development need not entail moral "progress"; if attachment is a primary datum, moral wisdom may exist early in the life of the child and be lost in the evolution of relationships. Moral immaturity may consist not in an absence of general moral knowledge but in an absence of the attachments necessary for making moral notions moral insights. The experienced and negotiated relations of the child, particularly in early childhood and adolescence, may provide critical data about both the promise of moral wisdom and the danger of losing moral insight. The question then becomes not how do moral "selves" develop, but what might be the developmental moments in relationships which both promote and threaten moral progress.

Our perspective on moral development as occurring through the transformation of attachment, as well as through the child's progress toward equality, highlights the value of Bowlby's work on loss and detachment and suggests further avenues of study. The vulnerable child, due to the physical or psychological loss of the parents' intimacy, experiences a "disordered mourning" resulting in either "compulsive care giving" or "independence of affective ties." Many of the victims of loss of intimacy are subject to *intermittent* discontinuities in parental affection and profound mixed messages from parents about their love for the child. How will the child respond to such mixed messages? Bowlby suggests several possible outcomes to this dilemma:

> One is that the child adheres to his own viewpoint even at the risk of breaking with his parent(s). That is far from easy . . . A second and opposite outcome is complete compliance with the parent's version at the cost of disowning his own . . . A third and perhaps common outcome is an uneasy compromise whereby the child oscillates uneasily between them. (Bowlby, 1973, vol. II, p. 318)

In this most common outcome, the child oscillates between "two incompatible pairs of models, each pair consisting of a model of his parents and a complementary one of himself." Bowlby observes that while misattribution of the source of anxieties by the child characterizes many rationalizations, the theories which document this phenomenon offer little evidence that the child's fears are not, in fact, justified. Bowlby argues that fear of loss of attachment underlies, quite understandably and realistically, many children's rationalizations: They either fear the loss of love or fail to grasp how their "loving parents" can seem so unloving in reality.

The unsuccessfully developed adult might then be highly intelligent but detached and egocentric, prone to unwitting rationalization. The rationalizer calls forth a "rational" solution to an irrational problem and thus, the confusing feelings and images generated by inauthentic relationships are resolved through detachment, often viewed mistakenly as the necessary origins of healthy autonomy. Egocentric detachment is, therefore, an avoidable result of a certain kind of morally alienating experience, not a paradigm case of development. Thus, we reverse Piaget's argument, adopted by most Piagetians and consonant with most psychoanalytic accounts of the child's situation. Piaget claims:

> The individual, *left to himself, remains* egocentric . . . The individual begins
> by understanding and feeling everything through the medium of himself . . .
> It is only through contact with the judgments of others that this anomie will
> gradually yield. (Piaget, 1932/1965, p. 400, emphasis added)

Left to himself or herself, we claim, the individual *becomes* egocentric; able
only to feel and understand through the medium of himself or herself, he
or she loses contact with the feelings of others and thus, must rely on egocentric judgments. In this way, anomie grows.

Acknowledging the universal ground of moral problems in the often
divergent aims of equality and attachment requires moral psychology to
make major changes in its concepts and methodology. Once we recognize
that there are (at least two) different moral orientations, not only the
locus of our data but our conception of "development," "stage," "self-in-
relationship," and "moral maturity" must change to encompass different
moral languages and the attendant problems of translation. If moral development begins in and proceeds through relationships, the child's cognitive
and affective development must be seen not as final causes but also as
dynamic effects of the child's relational life. If egoism is not a given, if
co-feeling is not an impossibility, if the aims of equality and attachment
diverge as well as converge, moral psychology must make room for a range
of moral experience dependent on particular kinds of relationships as well
as on cognitive and emotional maturation and on the particular societal and
cultural context. Thus, the domain of morality becomes more appropriately
complex. Moral development does not entail the disappearance of moral
dilemmas, and the attempt to chart development from one moral perspective
only ensures the continuation of a fruitless debate about rabbits and ducks.

We began with a question about the disappearance of the issue of sex
differences in the discussion of moral development. In the course of this
article we have suggested how that discussion might be transformed into a
more general dialogue between two moral voices whose deep resonance in
human experience suggests their origins in early childhood. In Virginia
Woolf's novel *Jacob's Room*, the narrator comments: "Either we are men
or we are women. Either we are cold or we are sentimental. Either we are
young, or growing old . . . Such is the manner of our seeing. Such are the
conditions of our love" (1922, p. 72). In this article we have suggested
that men and women may have a tendency to see from different standpoints
or, put differently, to lose sight of different perspectives. Our view of

morality as originating in early childhood relationships makes it possible to explain how as men and women we can become both cold and sentimental when genuine attachments fail.  It also calls attention to the fact that we are all destined to be unequal when young and to strive toward moral equality as we grow older.  While it is true that either we are men or we are women and certain experiences may accrue more readily to one or the other sex, it is also true that the capacity for love and the appreciation of justice is not limited to either sex.

For a variety of reasons, girls and women presently speak more readily about the costs of detachment, although men in various ways have highlighted these costs across time.  Perhaps at this moment in history, as psychology turns its attention to the human capacity for empathy and compassion, we will think more deeply about the ability to respond to feelings in someone who is otherwise a stranger and through that response, experience the co-feeling that renders her or him less strange.  Valuing that capacity, we may choose to turn our attention to the women who have been most closely involved with the much studied infants and young children as well as to the increasing involvement of men.  In this way we may alter our manner of seeing and observe how the infant's empathy contains the seeds of co-feeling and ask how the ability to live with the feelings of others can be nourished and sustained.  Then, attending to problems of inequality, especially as encountered by adolescents, we may also attend to the transformations of attachment when we consider the fate of early childhood relationships and chart the course of moral development.

# NOTES

1. Kohlberg (1984) criticizes Gilligan's account of metaethics to argue that the ethic of care is "not well adapted to resolve justice problems, problems which require principles to resolve conflicting claims among persons, all of whom in some sense should be cared for." There is, thus, in his view, no "moral point of view" from which to tackle problems of care and responsibility separate from issues and norms of "justice" (pp. 231-232). But the "morality of care" represents not merely the sphere of "personal decision-making," as he puts it, but an alternative point of view from which to map the moral domain and reveal "the laws of perspective" (in Piaget's phrase) which describe a relationally grounded view of morality.

2. In fact, we should remember that Piaget argued that moral development could not be understood in stage-theory terms precisely because autonomy was continually at risk in every new relationship of constraint (1932/1965, p. 86)--thus, dependent on the social circumstances facing the growing child, the adolescent, and the adult. Furthermore, Piaget also noted the problems in confounding moral development with intellectual development, observing that "an intelligent scamp would perhaps give better answers [to questions about moral conduct] than a slow-witted but really good-hearted little boy" (p. 116). See also Kagan (1984, Chapter 4).

# PART II

# Implications:
## Defining an Approach to
## Adolescent and Adult Development

# EXIT-VOICE DILEMMAS IN ADOLESCENT DEVELOPMENT

## Carol Gilligan

In *Exit, Voice and Loyalty: Responses to Decline in Firms, Organizations, and States* (1970), Albert Hirschman contrasts two modes of response to decline in social organizations--the options of exit and voice. Exit, central to the operation of the classical market economy, is exemplified by the customer who, dissatisfied with the product of company A, switches to the product of company B. In comparison to this neat and impersonal mechanism that operates "by courtesy of the Invisible Hand," voice--the attempt to change rather than escape from an objectionable situation--is messy, cumbersome, and direct. "Graduated all the way from faint grumbling to violent protest," voice is political action par excellence, carrying with it the potential for "heartbreak" by substituting the personal and public articulation of critical opinions for the private, secret vote. Introducing exit and voice as the two principal actors in his drama of societal health, Hirschman puts forth a theory of loyalty to explain the conditions for their optimal collaboration. Loyalty, he maintains, the seemingly irrational commitment of "the member who cares," activates voice by holding exit at bay, while sustaining in the implication of disloyalty the possibility of exit as the option of last resort.

To the economist's view of the individual as motivated by the desire for profit and to the political theorist's view of the individual as seeking power in social organizations, Hirschman adds a new dimension--an image of the individual as motivated by loyalty or attachment to stem decline and promote recuperation.  Demonstrating the power of attachment to influence action and shift the parameters of choice, Hirschman illustrates across a wide range of situations how the presence of loyalty holds exit and voice in tension and, thus, changes the meaning of both leaving and speaking.  The psychological acuity of Hirschman's analysis of exit and voice is matched by the transformation implied by bringing the psychology of attachment to the center of developmental consideration.

In honoring Hirschman's contribution I wish to illuminate the psychological dimensions of his conception by extending it to the seemingly remote domain of adolescent development.  Here it is possible to see not only the interplay of exit and voice that Hirschman describes but also the dilemmas posed by loyalty at a time of intense transition in human life.  The central themes of Hirschman's work--the importance of values and ideas in the developmental process, the connection between passions and interests, the reflection on historical periods of development--will be addressed here in the context of the life cycle.  But following Hirschman's example of trespass, I will suggest that the analysis of loyalty in family relationships speaks across disciplinary boundaries to the problems of interdependence that face contemporary civilization.

Hirschman's focus on loyalty is in part a correction to the more popular view of the exit option as uniquely powerful in effecting change.  In challenging this view, he underscores the problems of attachment which arise in modern societies--problems which have taken on an added intensity and urgency in an age of nuclear threat.  This threat which signals the possibility for an irredeemable failure of care also calls attention to the limits of exit as a solution to conflicts in social relationships.  Yet "the preference for the neatness of exit over the messiness and heartbreak of voice" (p. 107), which Hirschman finds in classical economics as well as in the American tradition, extends through the study of human development, emerging most clearly in the psychology of adolescence.  This paradigm of problem solving, based on an assumption of independence and competition, obscures the reality of interdependence and masks the possibilities for cooperation.  Thus, the need to reassess the interpretive schemes on which we rely, the need to correct a "defensive representation of the real world" (p. 2) in which our actions take place, extends across the realm of economics to the psychological domain, calling attention to shared assumptions about the nature of development and the process of change.

This parallel is forcefully evoked by the easy transfer of the characters from Hirschman's drama to the adolescent scene where puberty signals the decline of the childhood world of relations, and exit and voice enter as modes of response and recuperation. The growth to full stature at puberty releases the child from dependence on parents for protection and heightens the possibility of exit as a solution to conflicts in family relationships. At the same time the sexual maturation of puberty--the intensification of sexual feelings and the advent of reproductive capability--impels departure from the family, given the incest taboo. The heightened availability of and impetus toward exit in adolescence, however, may also stimulate the development of voice--a development enhanced by the cognitive changes of puberty, the growth of reflective thinking, and the discovery of the subjective self. Seeing the possibility of leaving, the adolescent may become freer in speaking, more willing to assert perspectives and voice opinions that diverge from accepted family truths. But if the transformations of puberty heighten the potential for both exit and voice, the experience of adolescence also changes the meaning of leaving and speaking by creating dilemmas of loyalty and rendering choice itself more self-conscious and reflective.

Adolescents, striving to integrate a new image of self and new experiences of relationship, struggle to span the discontinuity of puberty and renegotiate a series of social connections. This effort at renegotiation engages the adolescent voice in the process of identity formation and moral growth. But this development of voice depends on the presence of loyalty for its continuation. Hirschman, pointing out that the availability of the exit option tends "to atrophy the development of the art of voice" (1970, p. 43), but also noting that the threat of exit can strengthen the voice's effective use, observes that the decision of whether to exit will often be made in light of the prospects for the efficacy of voice. Development in adolescence, thus, hinges on loyalty between adolescents and adults, and the challenges to society, families, and schools is how to engage that loyalty and how to educate the voice of the future generation.

In the life cycle the adolescent is the truth teller, like the fool in the Renaissance play,[1] exposing hypocrisy and revealing truths about human relationships. These truths pertain to justice and care, the moral coordinates of human connection, heightened for adolescents who stand between the innocence of childhood and the responsibility of adulthood. Looking back on the childhood experiences of inequality and attachment, feeling again the powerlessness and vulnerability which these experiences initially evoked, adolescents identify with the child and construct a world that offers protection. This ideal or utopian vision, laid out along the coordinates of justice and care, depicts a world where self and other will be treated as of equal worth, where, despite differences in power, things will be fair; a world where everyone will be included, where no one will be left alone or hurt. In the ability to construct this ideal moral vision lies the potential for nihilism and despair as well as the possibility for societal renewal which adolescence symbolizes and represents. Given the engagement of the adolescent's passion for morality and truth with the realities of social justice and care, adolescents are the group whose problems of development most closely mirror society's problems with regeneration.

In analyzing these problems I will distinguish two moral voices that define two intersecting lines of development--one arising from the child's experience of inequality, one from the child's experience of attachment. Although the experiences of inequality and attachment initially are concurrent in the relationship of parent and child, they point to different dimensions of relationship--the dimension of inequality/equality and of attachment/detachment. The moral visions of justice and care reflect these different dimensions of relationships and the injunctions to which the experiences of inequality and attachment give rise. But these experiences also inform different ways of experiencing and defining self in relation to others and lend different meanings to separation. These different conceptions of self and morality (Gilligan, 1982, chap. 2) have been obscured by current stage theories of psychological development that present a single linear representation, fusing inequality with attachment and linking development to separation. But the problems in this portrayal are clarified by observing how the axis of development shifts when dependence, which connotes the experience of connection, is contrasted with isolation rather than opposed to independence.

To trace this shift and consider its implications for the understanding of progress and growth, I will begin with theories of identity and moral development that focus on the dimension of inequality/equality, noting that these theories have been derived primarily or exclusively from research on males.[2] Then I will turn to research on females to focus the dimension of attachment/detachment and delineate a different conception of morality and self. Although these two dimensions of relationship may be differentially salient in the thinking of women and men, both inequality and attachment are embedded in the cycle of life, universal in human experience because inherent in the relation of parent and child. By representing both dimensions of relationships, it becomes possible to see how they combine to create dilemmas of loyalty in adolescence and to discern how different conceptions of loyalty give rise to different modalities of exit and voice.

## CURRENT THEORIES OF ADOLESCENT DEVELOPMENT

The theories that currently provide the conceptual underpinning for the description of adolescent development trace a progression toward equality and autonomy in the conception of morality and self. All of these theories follow William James (1902/1961) in distinguishing the once from the twice-born self and tie that distinction to the contrast between conventional and reflective moral thought. This approach differentiates youth who adopt the conventions of their childhood society as their own, defining themselves more by ascription than choice, from youth who reject societal conventions by questioning the norms and values that provide their justification. The distinction between two roads to maturity and the clear implication that the second leads far beyond the first appears in Erikson's division between the "technocrats" or "compact majority" and the "neo-humanists" (1968, pp. 31-39). The same contrast appears in Kohlberg's division of moral development into preconventional, conventional, and principled thought (Kohlberg, 1981).

This dual or tripartite division of identity formation and moral growth generates a description of adolescent development that centers on two major separations--the first from parental authority and the second from the authority of societal conventions. In this context, loyalty, the virtue of fidelity that Erikson (1964) cites as the strength of adolescence, takes on an ideological cast, denoting a shift in the locus of authority from persons to principles--a move toward abstraction that justifies separation and renders "the self" autonomous.  Key to this vision of self as separate and constant is the promise of equality built into the cycle of life, the promise of development that in time the child will become the adult.

Tracing development as a move from inequality to equality, adolescence is marked by a series of power confrontations, by the renegotiation of authority relationships.  To emerge victorious the adolescent must overcome the constraint of parental authority through a process of "detachment" described by Freud as "one of the most significant, but also one of the most painful, psychical accomplishments of the pubertal period . . . a process that alone makes possible the opposition, which is so important for the progress of civilization, between the new generation and the old" (Freud, 1905/1963).  This equation of progress with detachment and opposition leads problems in adolescence to be cast as problems of exit or separation.  Observing that, as "at every stage in the course of development through which all human beings ought by rights to pass, a certain number are held back; so there are some who have never got over their parents' authority and have withdrawn their affection from them either very incompletely or not at all," Freud concludes that this failure of development in adolescence is one that occurs mostly in girls (p. 227).

Thus, exit, in resolving the childhood drama of inequality, symbolized for Freud by the Oedipal dilemma, becomes emblematic of adolescent growth.  Yet the option of exit, as Hirschman observes, leaves a problem of loyalty in its wake, a problem which if not addressed can lead to the decline of care and commitment in social relationships (p. 112).  In this light, adolescent girls who demonstrate a reluctance to exit may articulate a different voice--a voice which speaks of loyalty to persons and identifies detachment as morally problematic.  To represent this perspective on loyalty changes the depiction of adolescent growth by delineating a mode of development that relies not on detachment but on a change in the form of attachment--a change that must be negotiated by voice.

Yet the preference for the neatness of exit over the messiness and heartbreak of voice, the focus on inequality rather than attachment in human relations, and the reliance on male experience in building the model of human growth have combined to silence the female voice.  This silence contributes to the problems observed in adolescent girls, particularly if these problems are seen to reflect a failure of engagement rather than a failure of separation. But this silence and the implicit disparagement of female experience also creates problems in the account of human development--a failure to trace the growth of attachment and the capacity for care and loyalty in relationships.

The omission of female experience from the literature on adolescent development was noted by Bruno Bettelheim in 1965, and the significance of this omission was underlined by Joseph Adelson who edited the *Handbook of Adolescent Psychology*, published in 1980. Adelson had asked a leading scholar to write a chapter for the handbook on female adolescent development, but after surveying the literature she concluded that there was not enough good material to warrant a separate chapter. In their chapter on psychodynamics, Adelson and Doehrman observe that "to read the psychological literature on adolescence has, until very recently, meant reading about the psychodynamics of the male youngster writ large" (1980, p. 114). They end their chapter by noting that "the inattention to girls and to the processes of feminine development in adolescence has meant undue attention to such problems as impulse control, rebelliousness, super-ego struggles, ideology and achievement, along with a corresponding neglect of such issues as intimacy, nurturance, and affiliation" (p. 114). They found particularly troubling the fact that current biases in the literature reinforce each other, with the result that "the separate, though interacting emphases on pathology, on the more ideologized, least conformist social strata, and on males has produced a psychodynamic theory of adolescence that is both one-sided and distorted" (p. 115).

In girls' accounts of their experience in the adolescent years, problems of attachment and detachment emerge as a central concern. Because girls-- the group left out in the critical theory-building studies of adolescent psychology--have repeatedly been described as having problems in adolescence with separation, the experience of girls may best inform an expanded theory of adolescent development.

## THE MISSING LINE OF ADOLESCENT DEVELOPMENT

In adolescence the renegotiation of attachment centers on the inclusion of sexuality and inclusion of perspective in relationships--each introducing a new level of complication and depth to human connection. Conflicts of attachment that arise at this time are exemplified by the problems that girls describe when they perceive the inclusion of themselves (their views and their wishes) as hurting their parents, whereas including their parents implies excluding themselves. The revival of the Oedipal triangular conflict which psychoanalysts describe demonstrates how such problems tend to be recast by girls as a drama of inclusion and exclusion rather than of dominance and subordination. If the "Oedipal wish" is conceived as a desire to be included in the parents' relationship--to be a "member of the wedding" in Carson McCullers' phrase--then the Oedipal threat in the adolescent years is that of exclusion, experienced as endangering one's connection with others.

But adolescents, gaining the power to form family relationships on their own, confront the implications of excluding their parents as they remember their own experience of having been excluded by them. Construed as an issue of justice, this exclusion seems eminently fair, a matter of simple reciprocity. Construed as an issue of care, it seems, instead, morally problematic, given the association of exclusion with hurt. In resisting detachment and criticizing exclusion, adolescent girls hold to the view that change can be negotiated through voice and that voice is the way to sustain attachment across the leavings of adolescence.

Adolescents, aware of new dimensions of human connection, experiment in a variety of ways as they seek to discover what constitutes attachment and how problems in relationships can be solved. Girls in particular, given their interest in relationships and their attention to the ways in which connection between people can be formed and maintained, observe that relationships in which voice is silenced are not relationships in any meaningful sense. This understanding that voice has to be expressed in relationship to solve rather than escape the dilemmas of adolescence, calls attention not only to the limitations of exit but also to the problems that arise when voice is silenced. In sum, adolescent girls who resist exit may be holding on to the position that solutions to dilemmas of attachment in adolescence must be forged by voice and that exit alone is no solution but an admission of defeat. Thus, their resistance may signify a refusal to leave before they can speak.

Hirschman, describing how the high price of exit and the presence of loyalty in family relationships encourages the option of voice, also indicates that resort to voice will be undertaken in a conflict situation when the outcome is visualized as either possible victory or possible accord. But adolescents in their conflicts with their parents cannot readily visualize victory, nor can they visualize full accord, for given the closeness of the relationships, a meeting of minds may suggest a meeting of bodies which is precluded by the incest taboo. Therefore, exit must be part of the solution, and some accommodation must be found, some mixture of leaving and speaking which typically may occur in different proportions for boys and girls.

The focus on leaving in the psychology of adolescence, manifest by measuring development by signs of separation, may be an accurate rendition of male experience, at least within certain cultures, since the more explosive potential of tensions between adolescent sons and parents highlights the opposition between dependence and independence which renders exit appealing. In contrast, the propensity toward staying, noted as the "problem" in female development, may reflect the different nature of the attachment between daughters and parents and the greater salience for girls of the opposition between dependence and isolation. In this way the two opposites of the word dependence--isolation and independence--catch the shift in the valence of relationships that occurs when connection with others is experienced as an impediment to autonomy and when it is experienced as a protection against isolation. This essential ambivalence of human connection creates an ongoing ethical tension that rises sharply in adolescence and leads to exit-voice problems.

The ways in which adolescents consider decisions about staying and leaving, silence and speaking, illustrate the interplay of exit, voice, and loyalty that Hirschman describes. But the dilemmas of adolescence become more intense when they involve conflicts of loyalty, especially when attachment to persons vies with adherence to principles. Psychological theorists typically have given priority to principles as the anchor of personal integrity and focused their attention on the necessity and the justification for leaving. But in doing so, they have tended to overlook the costs of detachment--its consequences both to personal integrity and to societal functioning. Since adolescent girls tend to resist detachment and highlight its costs to others and themselves, we may learn about ways of solving problems through voice within the context of ongoing relationships by observing the way that they struggle with conflicts of loyalty and exit-voice decisions.

In a series of studies (conducted by the Center for the Study of Gender, Education, and Human Development), concerns about detachment have emerged saliently in girls' and women's moral thinking, pointing to an ethic of care that enjoins responsibility and responsiveness in relationships. In a study of high school girls, these concerns were so insistent and focused so specifically on problems of speaking and listening that it seemed important to inquire directly about situations in which voice failed: we sought to explore empirically the conceptual distinction between problems of inequality and problems of detachment.[3] Thus, two questions were added to the interview schedule in the second year of the study--one pertaining to incidents of unfairness and one to incidents of not listening. Asked to describe a situation in which someone was not being listened to, girls spoke about a wide variety of problems that ranged across the divide between interpersonal and international relations. "The Nicaraguan people," one girl explained, "are not being listened to by President Reagan." Asked how she knew, she said that Mr. Reagan, in explaining his own position, did not respond to the issues raised by the Nicaraguans and, thus, appeared to discount their view of their situation. The absence of response, as it indicated not listening, was acutely observed by girls in a wide range of settings and interpreted as a sign of not caring. The willingness to test the extent of detachment, to ascertain whether not listening signified a transitory distraction or a more deeply rooted indifference, appeared critical to decisions girls made about silence and speaking.

The same moral outrage and passion that infused girls' descriptions of not listening was also apparent in their accounts of unfairness. Yet, over the high school years, concerns about listening tended increasingly to temper judgments about fairness, reflecting a growing awareness of differences in perspective and problems in communication. The amount of energy devoted to solving these problems, the intensity of the search for ways to make connection and achieve understanding, led girls to express immense frustration in situations where voice failed. When others did not listen and seemed not to care, they spoke of "coming up against a wall." This image of wall had as its counterpart the search for an opening through which one could speak. The nature of this search, together with the intensity of its frustration, are conveyed in the following girl's description of an attempt to reestablish communication with her mother without abandoning her own perspective:

> I called my mother up and said, "Why can't I talk to you anymore?" And I ended up crying and hanging up on her because she wouldn't listen to me . . . She had her own opinion about what was truth and what was reality, and she gave me no opening . . . And, you know, I kept saying, "Well, you hurt me." And she said, "No, I didn't." And I said, "Well, why am I hurt?" you know. And she is just denying my feelings as if they didn't exist and as if I had no right to feel them, even though they were . . . I guess until she calls me up or writes me a letter saying I want to talk instead of saying, well, this and this happened, and I don't understand what is going on with you, and I don't understand why you are denying the truth . . . until she says, I want to talk, I can't, I just can't.

Simone Weil, in a beautifully evocative and paradoxical statement, defines morality as the silence in which one can hear the unheard voices (1977, p. 316). This rendering of morality in terms of attention and perception is central to Iris Murdoch's vision (1970) and appears as well in Hannah Arendt's question as to whether the activity of thinking as such, "the habit of examining whatever happens to come to pass or to attract attention, regardless of results and specific content," can be considered a moral act (1972, p. 5). The visions of these women philosophers illuminate the activities of care that high school girls describe, their equation of care with the willingness "to be there," "to listen," "to talk to," and "to understand." In girls' narratives about conflict and choice, these activities of care take on a moral dimension, and the willingness and the ability to care become a source of empowerment and a standard of self-evaluation. Detachment, then, signifies not only caring in the sense of choosing to stand apart but also not being able to care, given that in the absence of connection one would not know how to respond. Thus, girls' portrayal of care reveals its cognitive as well as affective dimensions, its foundation in the ability to perceive people in their own terms and to respond to need. As this knowledge generates the power not only to help but also to hurt, the uses of this power become a measure of responsibility in relationships.

In adolescence when both wanting and knowing take on new meanings, given the intensity of sexual feelings and the discovery of subjectivity, conflicts of responsibility assume new dimensions of complexity. The experience of coming into a relationship with oneself and the increasing assumption of responsibility for taking care of oneself are premised in this context not on detachment from others but on a change in the form of connection with others. These changes in the experience of connection, both with others and with oneself, set the parameters of the moral conflicts that girls describe when responsibility to themselves conflicts with responsibility to others. Seeking to perceive and respond to their own as well as to others' feelings and thoughts, girls ask if they can be responsive to themselves without losing connection with others and whether they can respond to others without abandoning themselves.

This search for an inclusive solution to dilemmas of conflicting loyalties vies with the tendency toward exclusion expressed in the moral opposition between "selfish" and "selfless" choice--an opposition where selfishness connotes the exclusion of others and selflessness the exclusion of self. This opposition appears repeatedly in the moral judgments of adolescent girls and women, in part because the conventional norms of feminine virtue, which hold up selflessness as a moral ideal, conflict with an understanding of relationships derived from experiences of connection. Since the exclusion of self as well as of others dissolves the fabric of connection, both exclusions create problems in relationships, diminishing the capacity for care and reducing one's efficacy as a moral agent.

The bias toward voice in girls' moral thinking contains this recognition and directs attention toward the ways that attachments can be transformed and sustained. "There is not a wall between us," one adolescent explains in describing her relationship with her parents, "but there is a sort of strain or a sieve." This metaphor of connection continuing through a barrier to complete attachment conveys a solution that avoids detachment while recognizing the need for distance that arises in adolescence. The following examples further illustrate the mixture of exit and voice in adolescent girls' thinking about relationships, indicating the value they place on loyalty or continuing attachment. In addition, these examples suggest how attachments can be sustained across separation and how relationships can expand without detachment.

> I have been very close to my parents mentally . . . We have a very strong relationship, but yet it is not a physical thing that you can see . . . In my family we are more independent of each other, but yet we have this strong love.

> All the boyfriends that I have ever really cared about, they are still with me . . . in mind, not in body, because we are separated by miles. But they will

always be with me. Any relationship that I have ever had has been important to me. Otherwise I wouldn't have had it.

Such evocations of the mind-body problem of adolescence convey a view of continuing connection as consonant with autonomy and growth. Within this vision, dependence and independence are not opposed but are seen instead to commingle, as exemplified by the following description of a relationship between close friends:

> I would say we depend on each other in a way that we are both independent, and I would say that we are very independent, but as far as our friendship goes, we are dependent on each other because we know that both of us realize that whenever we need something, the other person will always be there.

In this way, the capacity to care for others and to receive care from them becomes a part of rather than antithetical to self-definition.

Defined in this context of relationships, identity is formed through the gaining of voice or perspective, and self is known through the experience of engagement with different voices or points of view. Over the high school years, girls display an increasing recognition that attachment does not imply agreement and that differences constitute the life of relationships rather than a threat to their continuation. The ability to act on this recognition generates a more empirical approach to conflict resolution, an approach which often leads to the discovery of creative solutions to disputes. Hirschman describes how the willingness to trade off the certainty of exit for the uncertainty of improvement via voice can spur the "creativity-requiring course of action" from which people would otherwise recoil. Thus, he explains how loyalty performs "a function similar to the underestimate of the prospective task's difficulties" (p. 80). The observation of girls' persistence in seeking solutions to problems of connection, even in the face of seemingly insurmountable obstacles, extends this point and indicates further how attachment to persons rather than adherence to principles may enhance the possibility for arriving at creative forms of conflict resolution.

Yet the vulnerability of voice to exclusion underscores how easily this process can fail when a wish for victory or domination defeats efforts at reaching accord. "If people are thinking on two different planes," one girl explains, then "you can't understand." Asked whether people on different planes can communicate, she describes how voice depends on relationship while exit can be executed in isolation.

> Well, they can try, maybe they can . . . if they were both trying to com-
> municate. But if one person is trying to block the other out totally, that
> person is going to win and not hear a thing that the other person is saying.
> If that is what they are trying to do, then they will accomplish their
> objective: to totally disregard the other person.

This vulnerability of voice to detachment and indifference becomes a major problem for girls in adolescence, especially when they recognize a difference between their own perspectives and commonly held points of view. Given a relational construction of loyalty, the drama of exit and voice may shift to the tension between silence and speaking, where silence signifies exit and voice implies conflict and change in relationships. Then development hinges on the contrast between loyalty and blind faith, since loyalty implies the willingness to risk disloyalty by including the voice of the self in relationship. This effort to bring the subjectively known self into connection with others signifies an attempt to change the form of connection and relies on a process of communication, not only to discover the truth about others but also to reveal the truth about oneself.

"If I could only let my mother know the list (that I had grown inside me . . . of over two hundred things that I had to tell my mother so that she would know the true things about me and to stop the pain in my throat), she--and the world--would become more like me, and I would never be alone again" (Kingston, 1976, pp. 197-198). So the heroine of Maxine Hong Kingston's autobiographical novel, *The Woman Warrior*, defines the parameters of adolescent development in terms of the contrast between silence and voice. The silence that surrounds the discovery of the secret, subjectively known self protects its integrity in the face of disconfirmation but at the expense of isolation. In contrast, voice--the attempt to change rather than escape from an objectionable situation-- contains the potential for transformation by bringing the self into con- nection with others.

In adolescence, the problem of exclusion hinges on the contrast be- tween selfish and selfless behavior. This is juxtaposed against a wish for inclusion, a wish that depends upon voice. In recent years the exit option has become increasingly popular as a solution to conflicts in human relationships, as the high incidence of divorce attests. The meaning of such leaving, although commonly interpreted as a move toward separation and independence, is, however, more complex. For example, the more

unencumbered access to exit from marriage can spur the exercise of voice
in marriage, which in turn can lead to the discovery of the truth about
attachment. The distinction between true and false connection, between
relationships where voice is engaged and relationships where voice is
silenced, often becomes critical to exit decisions both for women considering divorce and for adolescent girls. Given the tendency for girls
and women to define loyalty as attachment to persons, exit constitutes
an alternative to silence in situations where voice has failed. Thus, the
recognition of the costs of detachment, not only from others but also
from oneself, becomes key to girls' development in adolescence since it
encourages voice while sustaining exit as the option of last resort.

The wish to be able to disagree, to be different without losing connection with others, leads outward in girls' experience from family relationships to relationships with the world. The adolescent girl who seeks to
affirm the truths about herself by joining these truths with her mother's
experience aspires through this connection to validate her own perceptions,
to see herself as part of the world rather than as all alone. But the difficulty for girls in feeling connected both to their mothers and to the world
is compounded in a world where "human" often means male.

Consequently, the problem of attachment in adolescent development is
inseparable from the problem of interpretation, since the ability to establish
connection with others hinges on the ability to render one's story coherent.
Given the failure of interpretive schemes to reflect female experience and
given the distortion of this experience in common understandings of care
and attachment, development for girls in adolescence hinges not only on
their willingness to risk disagreement with others but also on the courage
to challenge two equations: the equation of human with male and the
equation of care with self-sacrifice. Together these equations create a self-
perpetuating system that sustains a limited conception of human development and a problematic representation of human relationships.

By attending to female voices and including these voices in the psychological schemes through which we have come to know ourselves, we
arrive at a correction of currently defective modes of interpretation. As
the understanding of morality expands to include both justice and care, as
identity loses its Platonic cast and the experience of attachment to others
becomes part of the definition of self, as relationships are imagined not

only as hierarchies of inequality but also as webs of protection, the representation of psychological development shifts from a progression toward separation to a chronicle of expanding connection.

## ADOLESCENT DEVELOPMENT IN THE CONTEMPORARY CONTEXT

The student protest movements of the late 1960s focused on the consequences of social inequality and held up against existing unfairness the ideals of justice and rights. But these movements contained as a countercultural theme a challenge to the existing state of relationships, articulated by the generation of "flower children" that included a large female representation. With the disillusionment of the 1970s, these movements for change degenerated into privatism and retreat, as concerns with both justice and care focused increasingly on the self. Yet concomitant changes on the world scene, such as the growing awareness of global pollution and the escalation of the nuclear threat, have underlined the illusory nature of the exit solution and drawn attention to the reality of interdependence. The need to develop the art of voice, then, becomes a pressing agenda for education. The popularity of psychotherapy may reveal the extent to which voice has been neglected in a society that has come increasingly to rely on exit solutions and to prefer neat, impersonal, and often secret forms of communication.

As the youth of both sexes currently oscillate between moral nihilism and moral indignation, given the impending potential for an irretrievable failure of care on the part of the older generation, the relativism that has diluted the engagement between adolescents and adults may give way to a recognition of the moral challenges which they commonly face: the challenges of fairness--that coming generations be allowed their chance to reach maturity; the challenge of care--that the cycle of violence be replaced by an ecology of care[4] that sustains the attachments necessary to life.

When Erikson (1965) pointed to adolescence as the time in the life cycle when the intersection of life history and history becomes most acute, he called attention to the relationship between the problems of society and the crises of youth. In this light the current increase of problems among adolescent girls, including the startling rise of eating disorders among the high school and college population (Crisp *et al.*, 1976; Bruch, 1978), may reveal a society that is having problems with survival and regeneration. The anorexic girl, described in literature as not wishing to grow up, may more accurately be seen as dramatizing the life-threatening split between female and adult (Steiner-Adair, 1984). This tragic choice dramatizes the extent to which care and dependence have been doubly disparaged by their association with women and children rather than seen as part of the human condition. To heal the division between adult and female, thus, requires a revisioning of both images, and this revision retrieves the line that has been missing from the description of human development.

The unleashed power of the atom, Einstein warned, has changed everything except the way we think, implying that a change in thinking is necessary for survival in a nuclear age. Our indebtedness to Hirschman is that he charts the direction for a change in thinking that also carries with it the implication of a change of heart. By describing modes of conflict resolution that do not entail detachment or exclusion, he aligns the process of change with the presence of loyalty or strong attachment. Thus, he offers an alternative to the either/or, win/lose framework for conflict resolution, which has become, in this nuclear age, a most dangerous game. In this article I have tried to extend the optimism of Hirschman's conception by demonstrating the potential for care and attachment that inheres in the structure of the human life cycle. By describing development around a central and ongoing ethical tension between problems of inequality and problems of detachment, I have called attention to dilemmas of loyalty as moments when attachment is at stake. The importance at present of expanding attachment across the barriers of what Erikson called "sub-speciation" brings problems of loyalty to the center of our public life. As the contemporary reality of global interdependence impels the search for new maps of development, the exploration of attachment may provide the psychological grounding for new visions of progress and growth.[5]

# NOTES

1. For this analogy I am grateful to Jamie Bidwell, a student at the Harvard Graduate School of Education.

2. Kohlberg's six stages of moral development were defined on the basis of his longitudinal research on seventy-two white American males, originally age ten to sixteen (Kohlberg, 1958, 1984). Erikson has drawn almost exclusively on the lives of men in tracing the crisis of identity and the cycle of life (Erikson, 1950, 1958, 1968, 1976). Note also Offer (1969) and Offer and Offer (1975).

3. The study was jointly undertaken by the GEHD Study Center and the Emma Willard School for Girls in Troy, N. Y. The study was designed to address the relationship between girls' development and secondary education.

4. For the phrase "the ecology of care," I am grateful to Scott McVay and Valerie Peed of the Geraldine R. Dodge Foundation, Morristown, N. J.

5. I am grateful to Daphne de Marnette for her careful reading of an earlier draft of this paper and her excellent suggestions.

# 8

## MORAL CONCERNS AND CONSIDERATIONS OF URBAN YOUTH

Betty Bardige, Janie Victoria Ward, Carol Gilligan, Jill McLean Taylor, and Gina Cohen

> Although there was always generosity in the Negro neigh-
> borhood, it was indulged on pain of sacrifice. Whatever was
> given by Black people to other Blacks was most probably needed
> as desperately by the donor as by the receiver. A fact which
> made the giving or receiving a rich exchange.
>
> --Maya Angelou, *I Know Why the Caged Bird Sings*

Theories of moral development (e.g., Kohlberg, 1969; Loevinger, 1976; Gilligan, 1982) have been generated initially from samples that were largely white and middle or upper-middle class. Like the omission of women from theory-building samples, this oversight creates a potential tunnel vision through the exclusion of important perspectives. If moral concepts are learned through life experience and the reflection on one's own observations, then one's moral development should be influenced by whether one grows up in a poor, middle-income, or wealthy neighborhood. Both the experience of growing up in "poverty amidst affluence"--denied resources and opportunities that others take for granted--and the oppor- tunity to observe and participate in the kinds of "rich exchange" that Maya Angelou describes, should color moral thinking. In order to correct for this class bias in our own work, the researchers from the Center for the Study of Gender, Education and Human Development (GEHD) extended the investigation of adolescent moral and identity development into three low-income Boston neighborhoods.

The investigation of the moral thinking of early and mid-adolescents in these neighborhoods was concerned with how to listen to and represent their experiences of moral conflict, moral decision making, unfairness, and not being heard (indifference). We expected not only that young adolescents would have had such experiences but that some of them would have experienced injustice, lack of attention, carelessness, and difficult choices more intensely than adolescents in more protected settings. Thus, interviewees were asked to tell stories from their own lives. They were asked, "Can you tell me about a time when something happened that you thought was unfair?" and "Can you tell me about a situation where someone wasn't being listened to?" Follow-up questions attempted to clarify the sequence of events, the situational and relational context, the interviewee's thoughts, action, consideration of alternative actions, moral perspective, and the meanings (in this particular narrative) of any moral terms that were used.

The following questions framed the study:

1. Would the themes of care and justice identified in earlier studies (Gilligan, 1982) be reflected in the moral thinking of these adolescents? That is, would these adolescents talk in terms of "justice," citing standards, laws, obligations, and principles as maintaining or restoring fair relationships and guiding conflict resolution? Would they also speak in "care" terms, representing attention to others' particular needs and perspectives, avoidance of hurt, and maintenance of attachments as moral goals? Would these moral ideas be represented in their self descriptions, as well as in their discussions of moral violation and moral conflict?

2. Would these concepts of justice and care illuminate the adolescents' moral thinking, bringing forward its logic and insights?

3. Would the voices of these urban teens contribute new language or new representations to the understanding of care and justice?

4. When asked to describe a difficult moral decision, would these adolescents describe situations and conflicts similar to those described by
   more privileged adolescents?

5. Would the gender differences in use of moral language that we had
   seen in more privileged samples (see Chapter 4) be apparent in this
   group?

## METHOD

The study was carried out in collaboration with Boys and Girls
Clubs in three low-income neighborhoods of Boston. These clubs are
long-standing community agencies, providing after-school daycare,
recreation, counseling, and tutoring for the neighborhoods' children and
adolescents.

Each of the neighborhoods has a particular identity. South Boston is
best known for its historic Irish Catholic population and for the community's fervent and angry protest against the 1975 Boston public school
court-ordered, desegregation plan. It had a median annual family income
of about $15,000 at the time the interviews were conducted (1985).
Predominantly white Charlestown and predominantly Black and Hispanic
Roxbury are considered transitional communities, with urban "gentrification"
quickly eroding the historic identities of these older, previously working
class Boston neighborhoods. Charlestown's median family income was
about $17,000; Roxbury's, about $10,000 at the time of the study.[1]

Engaging in a collaborative effort with the clubs of South Boston,
Charlestown, and Roxbury was essential, as the staffs had intimate knowledge of the communities they served. They shared their knowledge of the
unique identities of these communities, of the effects of change such as
urban decline which has led to high levels of street crime in most areas,
court-ordered busing which has forced large numbers of middle class whites
and blacks out of the public school systems and created increasing numbers
of transfers into neighboring parochial schools, and gentrification which has
increased competition for the few units of low-income housing available.
Club staff also contributed questions to the interview, helped refine the
language of proposed questions that they felt would be misheard, and

assisted in finding children and adolescents who were willing to be
interviewed.

The sample consisted of twenty-seven younger girls (ages ten to
twelve), eighteen older girls (ages fourteen to sixteen), twenty-eight
younger boys, and nineteen older boys. Because interviews were voluntary,
it is likely that this sample is not representative of club attendees. In
addition, adolescents who come to the clubs during the after-school hours
in which our interviews were conducted are themselves a select population
within their neighborhoods. Many of the children and adolescents told us
that they come to the clubs after school in order to be with their friends;
however, a number of those we interviewed had been hired by the clubs
(or were volunteering) as coaches or supervisors of younger children.
Nevertheless, the sample of ninety-two was large and diverse enough for an
exploration of moral perspectives among teenagers living in of low-income
urban settings.

Each participant was interviewed individually for approximately one
hour by an interviewer trained in clinical research methods. The purposes
and procedures of the study were explained, confidentiality was assured, and
consent was elicited. The interview questions dealt with reasons for coming
to the club, identity, moral conflict and decision making, experiences of unfairness and not being listened to, and future plans and aspirations. Because pilot interviews indicated that it might be difficult for some preteens
to generate an example of a difficult decision involving moral conflict, the
younger adolescents were not asked for such examples. However, other
parts of the interview provided opportunities to explore their moral constructs, conflicts, and decisions.

Because this study was more exploratory than hypothesis testing,
transcribed interviews were first analyzed according to content categories
derived from the data. A sample of sixteen interviews was randomly
selected to include two boys and two girls from each race and age group.
This sample was used to determine coding categories for responses to each
question. These content categories were then used to code the entire sample. Additions were made when a response did not fit the established
categories.

The moral decisions described by the thirty-seven older adolescents
were also analyzed using a more sophisticated technique. Each dilemma was

read four times by the same researcher: first, for an understanding of the sequence of events and the situational and relational context in which it occurred; second, for an understanding of the narrator's moral conflict, as indicated by his or her answer to the question, "What was the conflict for you?", by his or her spontaneous use of moral language, and by his or her statements about wants and beliefs; third, for an understanding of the concepts of justice that were used in discussing possible solutions and evaluating actions; and fourth, for the concepts of care that were used in discussing possible solutions and evaluating actions. When one perspective (justice or care) was missing, the researcher sought a plausible explanation for its absence.[2]

## FINDINGS

### Moral Themes and Moral Identity

Developmental studies over the past two decades concur in the observation that adolescence is a time of heightened moral awareness and moral concern (Kohlberg & Gilligan, 1971; Gilligan, 1982). The inclusion of the voices of urban youth in this study is particularly interesting because of the social inequities which so often diminish their chances for economic parity. It is possible that this lack of equality could lead to indifference and despair. It is also possible that inner city adolescents have special insights based on their perceived experiences of injustice, indifference, or failure to care. Not surprisingly, virtually every child and adolescent in the study was able to describe a situation in which something happened that was unfair and one in which someone was not listened to. These interview questions evoked moral passions and reflections on what could have been done differently. In most, but not all cases recounted, the interviewee was the victim of the unfairness or "not listening."

Another finding was that in this group morality was an important aspect of identity. Moral concerns emerged repeatedly across the range of questions exploring identity: how do you see yourself, how do you see yourself as having changed, how do you imagine your life in the future, what kind of things do you do that make you feel good about yourself, who would you like to be like someday, and what will you need to do to see yourself and your life as successful?

More than three-quarters of the interviewees spontaneously mentioned moral considerations in response to at least one of our identity questions. Moral considerations included descriptions of oneself as helpful, sharing, liking to care for little kids, not prejudiced, caring about others, trying to make people feel good, being a sensitive and patient listener, being careful not to say things that hurt other people's feelings, being a peacemaker, avoiding fights, staying out of trouble, being obedient and/or helpful to parents, and being a "good" or "decent" kid. These judgments of oneself as moral convey feelings of self-esteem.

Positive self representations would be expected in this kind of interview data, since people tend to present themselves to others in positive terms. However, in this sample the rarity of negative self-descriptions was in notable contrast to studies of low-income youth at risk for school dropout and early pregnancy due to low self-esteem (e.g., Dryfoos, 1983; Ladner, 1985).

Many of the interviewees offered moral activities in response to the question, "What kinds of things do you do that make you feel good about yourself?" Examples included: helping others acknowledge when they have been wrong, caring for a sick grandmother, staying out of trouble, and playing with a child who seemed left out. Several children and adolescents expressed concern about social problems--for example, poor people, those who are handicapped, the Ethiopians, crime and drugs in their neighborhoods, hunger, and homelessness--as part of their identity discussions. A young boy who said he felt good about himself when he succeeded at sports said in the next breath that he felt sad for handicapped children who couldn't play. A girl described giving money to poor people as an activity that made her feel good about herself. Several respondents imagined future jobs that would enable them to address social problems or help others. Also, respondents wanted to copy people who modeled helpfulness, caring, and adherence to moral standards--for example, one adolescent said, "John Kennedy, the way he wanted to change a lot of things," and another stated, "everyone at the club, they understood people. I want to be an understanding person, too."

**Moral Logic**

Other parts of the interview examined the children's and adolescents' sense of morality in more depth, asking for examples of unfairness, of not listening, and of decisions involving moral conflict. These provided windows into the realities of these young people's lives and illuminated the concepts of morality they use to judge themselves and others.

This study suggests the limitations of using concepts derived from structural developmental measures (e.g., Kohlberg, 1969; Loevinger, 1976; Rest, 1979) as the sole way of representing the thinking of members of an inner city population. Several boys' discussions of choices they faced revealed a sense of morality that could be misrepresented or missed entirely by these measures. These boys used language that could readily be assigned to developmental stages; however, a careful reading of other parts of their discussion casts doubt on the classical structural-developmental interpretation of these codable statements.

The primary concern for these boys in their discussions of moral conflicts appeared to be a purely selfish one--staying out of trouble. This concern is seen as representing a low stage in major theories of moral and ego development (Piaget, 1965; Kohlberg, 1969, 1984; Loevinger, 1976; Damon, 1977; Selman, 1980; Kegan, 1982). It is portrayed as typical of young children whose "egocentrism" causes them to equate right and wrong with the rewards and punishments of an all powerful adult. In later childhood, according to these theories, a new moral sense emerges, one that recognizes the need for reciprocity, yet is still grounded in self-interest, equating what is right with "what meets my needs" and occasionally those of others.

Either of these formulations is considered problematic in adolescence and adulthood; both have been found to be associated with delinquency and psychopathology as well as with low social class (Laufer & Day, 1983; Snarey, Kohlberg, & Noam, 1983; Kohlberg, 1984). Using these prevailing theories, we could easily dismiss as morally deficient the adolescent whose sense of justice seems limited to the avoidance of getting caught. Yet in reading the responses of some of the older boys, we were struck by the illogic of this inference.

One of these boys describes a situation in which his friends wanted him to go back to someone's house after a dance but he did not go because his mother wanted him home by a certain time. His concern was "getting in trouble with my mother, and I didn't care what they said." However, when asked if he thought that he had done the right thing, he articulates a sense of morality that governs his self judgments. His moral concern is with not hurting his mother and not being selfish. "My mother would have been worried about me all night if I stayed out . . . She wouldn't get any sleep because my sister used to do it to her. She didn't get any sleep all night . . . It would be pretty bad if I kept her up like that, you know, just thinking about myself and not thinking about her . . . Why should I just go off and not worry about her and just think about myself?"

This line of reasoning recasts the classic "low stage" assessment of this boy's response to another query. Asked to define a moral problem, he says, "Doing something that's wrong and knowing it's wrong and doing it . . . You get in trouble for it if it's wrong and if you don't, it's right." In this statement he seems to be defining morality in terms of consequences to himself, without any internal standards that can be maintained in the absence of an authority figure to mete out rewards and punishments. Hearing only the concern with avoiding punishment, the traditional researcher may well suspend further questioning, assuming a match was made with a codable low-level classification. Yet when the researcher recognizes the boy's understanding that his actions can hurt his mother, his moral strengths are more readily seen. He expresses a concern for not hurting others that is central to a care orientation. His awareness of what will hurt is based on his own observations. He does not need to imagine how he would feel in his mother's place (which would earn him a higher score on both Piaget's and Kohlberg's stages of moral development), because *he knows* from experience how *she* will feel.

A second boy presents a more complex dilemma. He had "hooked school" with a friend and was considering hooking again. His lack of concern with breaking the school's rules or with being unfair to his teacher and classmates was striking. It would be easy to read his interview as showing no sense of justice or an inconsistent sense of morality, since, although he knew it was wrong to hook, he was considering hooking the next day. His only concern seemed to be with not getting caught.

Looking at this boy's discussion of getting caught with a care lens, we can see a morality that is grounded in his observations of family life and relationships. "If I got caught my mother would have been mad with my father and everything, and they would have got upset and got a headache." He goes on to tell how his mother would have to miss work if she were called into the school. Again, one can see that the problem with getting into trouble is that, in a very specific and tangible way, it makes trouble for his mother.

Do external rules have no hold on this young man, beyond the possibility that he and others will suffer if he is caught? Does he have no internal standards? His interview does not contain the information to answer these questions; however, he does offer an explanation as to why he is not invested in the rules of his school. His sister had missed the equivalent of several months of classes and "the school never cared enough to call my mother." Given his experience and his belief that what he missed held no educational value for him, one would not expect him to represent his dilemma as involving a responsibility or obligation to attend school.

## Moral Language

This study emphasizes the importance of listening for the natural moral language that these adolescents use and recognizing that it may be inconsistent with a public moral language that they also know. For example, a twelve-year-old girl, describing the difference between "good guys" and "bad guys," defines the terms of her moral world. "Bad guys" do things she disapproves of--"swearing, smoking, stealing, cheating" and being disrespectful of the elderly. "Good guys" do not violate these conventional prohibitions; however, they also know "what's wrong and what's right and when to do right, and they know when it's necessary to do wrong." Thus, a public moral language is counterposed to necessity; a good person is one who can judge when it is necessary to override the rules.

Asked for an example, the girl goes on to describe a time when she was told not to leave her house because she was being punished. A neighbor who had cut herself badly called needing bandages. "She needed my help so much, I helped her in any way I could. I knew that I was the only one who could help her, so I had to help her." The moral language of necessity is heard clearly. The words "had to," "need," and "absolutely necessary" are repeated throughout her discussion of this incident.

Focusing only on her ideas of right and wrong, one might hear a simplistic notion of absolute rules, without a consideration of motivation. Piaget calls this "heteronomous morality" and sees it as a primitive conception. Similarly, Kohlberg ties this conception to "pre-conventional" morality. The girl's inability to anticipate her mother's approval would be seen in Selman's theory as a low level of interpersonal perspective taking. Yet the girl's insistence that "I did the right thing," and her belief that her actions would have been right even had her mother not agreed, suggests a more "autonomous" sense of morality.

The moral sophistication of this twelve-year-old becomes more apparent when she is seen as using two moral languages--a conventional language of right and wrong and a language of necessity. Her moral, evaluating self actively mediates between these two conceptions. She sees herself as moral because she knows how to judge which concept should prevail; her decisions are guided by her belief that help must be provided when it is needed. "You can't just stand there, and watch the woman . . . die."

A sixteen-year-old girl uses similar language in describing her response to a child who appeared injured from falling off his bike. "He was shaking and he looked scared. I couldn't walk away, even if I wanted to." She helped him up, checked for cuts and bruises, and asked if he was okay. "He didn't want to talk. But I don't blame him. I wouldn't want some stranger trying to take care of me." At first, this seems like a contradiction. Why did she help if she didn't think the boy would want her assistance?

This teenager has psychological insights that are not expressed by the twelve-year-old; she realizes that what she has to offer may not be wanted, yet she retains the younger girl's sense of necessity. For the twelve-year-old, just as her mother's commands became secondary to her neighbor's need for bandages, so the teenager's sense of pride was secondary if the boy was really injured. Until she knew the child was all right, the teenager "couldn't walk away"; she had to provide whatever help was needed.

## Types of Moral Conflicts

In developing descriptions, theories, and measures that can represent these insights, it is necessary to keep in mind the context in which such

lessons are learned and applied. The conflicts described by the adolescents
in this study are similar in form to those described by more privileged
teens. We heard dilemmas of peer pressure, when friends encourage one
to do things that one has been taught are wrong. We heard dilemmas of
conflicting loyalty, when one feels pulled between different friends or
groups of friends. We heard about problems with school authorities,
decisions about which parent to live with or spend time with, and difficult
choices about school and activities. Most of the peer pressure dilemmas
described by the urban adolescents involved drinking, drugs, curfew, or
skipping school, all of which are similar to dilemmas reported in studies of
more advantaged adolescents. Three out of the nineteen older boys in this
study described dilemmas involving serious crimes. In contrast, only one
such instance was described in a related study (carried out by the GEHD
Center) of 100 male and female adolescents at a selective private school.[3]
While there was little difference between the types of dilemmas experienced
by upper-middle class teens and the teens in this study, the same conflict
may have different repercussions for the two groups. The "wrong decisions" of inner city youth are much more likely to have lifelong negative
impacts. Several of the adolescents mentioned a concern about the courts
and with getting "a record." Their stories remind us that adolescents' natural impulsivity can have far greater consequences for those who do not
have resources and connections than for those who do.

If life chances can be spoiled by a misstep on the road to success,
they can also be stunted when roads are not taken. In a previous study
(undertaken by the GEHD Center at a private girls' school), a middle class
high school girl discussed the dilemma she faced when her mother asked
her to stay home in order to help care for younger siblings rather than to
go away to boarding school. An inner city teenager was also asked to stay
home to care for siblings, but her mother, who could not afford daycare for
the two younger children, had asked her to forego school entirely. Such
stories poignantly illustrate how human resources must fill in where
material resources do not exist. These stories drive home the need for
researchers of moral and social development to consider socioeconomic
context.

In general, the children and adolescents who were interviewed
expressed an understanding of both justice and care concerns. A sense of

morality governed their lives.  Inner city youths, however, face particular difficulties as they try to maintain their moral sensibilities and act in moral ways within a social context that is all too often violent, uncaring, and unjust.  This struggle is highlighted by an eleven-year-old boy who spoke in his interview of his frequent desire to strike back when provoked, but he avoided fighting, since it was against his religion and his father's teachings.  After the formal interview had been completed, he was asked what the experience of being interviewed had been like for him.  He told the interviewer that he had been nervous about giving "wrong" answers; he had been particularly careful not to recommend fighting as a solution to conflict.  It was clear to the interviewer that this boy was aware of a conflict between what he wanted to say and what he felt he should say.  Furthermore, his conflict in the interview situation paralleled his real-life conflict:  wanting to fight or take action but believing he should restrain himself.  Such decisions are frequently difficult for urban teens, as they find their principles tested.

### Gender Differences

Gender differences observed in adolescents' discussions of moral dilemmas were similar to those observed in our earlier studies.  Almost all of the boys (nine of eleven) whose dilemmas involved friends, described peer pressure dilemmas, situations in which they felt pressure to do something they did not believe was right.  Most of the girls (six of ten) whose dilemmas involved friends focused on loyalty issues.  They felt pulled between two people or groups who were making claims on their time and commitment.  For example, one girl was faced with a dilemma of deciding what school to attend.  She and her best friend had both been accepted at the same private school.  Her friend would be going, but for the interviewee and her family a selective public school seemed a better choice.  Her problem was that "I didn't want to make it feel to my very best friend that I was leaving her because I didn't like her any more or something."  At the same time there was the conflicting pull of her family's financial needs and her mother's desire for her children to stay in the same school system.  Mostly though, it was her own sense of what would be better for her--which school she would feel more comfortable in, which would provide better preparation for the college she had already chosen, and what she could "handle" academically and socially--that dissuaded her from her friend's school.

The girl's belief that it is morally necessary to consider her own needs is grounded in her awareness of individual differences. "You have to decide what's best for you and what's best for somebody else. I mean, you can't go around, well, doing something because it's good for somebody else . . . I guess you can't wear anybody else's shoes." There is no expectation on her part that her friend should come to the more academically demanding school which she has chosen ("She said she didn't think she could handle [my school] but she can handle [her school]") and no claim that her friend has put her in an unfair position. Instead, the interviewee takes great effort to construct an inclusive solution. "We talked about it a lot every morning before school. Then at the end of the year, we finally accepted that we weren't going to be seeing each other every day of the year any more." "I still see her. I see her like once a week. I call her up even if I don't see her."

Girls were more likely than boys to describe dilemmas that continued over time, rather than describing one-time or repeated incidents. In addition, they were more likely to describe staying with a problem and with the people involved, while the boys were more likely to talk about leaving. Exceptions to the peer pressure/loyalty difference fit this pattern as well. For example, one boy's friendship dilemma raised issues of loyalty rather than peer pressure--when two of his friends were fighting he decided to walk away rather than take sides. In contrast, a girl with a similar loyalty dilemma repeatedly tried to defuse the conflict and keep her friends from escalating arguments into fights.

Two of the three girls who described peer pressure dilemmas voiced their disagreement in a way that allowed them to stay with the friends whose actions they saw as wrong. One girl went to all her friends' parties and drank Sprite rather than liquor. In the other dilemma, rather than simply saying "no" when asked to "hook" school, the interviewee convinced her friend not to hook. The only boy who presented an ongoing dilemma that involved an inclusive solution spoke of his problem in maintaining a relationship with both of his divorced parents. These findings are similar to those discussed in Chapter 7.

## CONCLUSIONS

This study of moral thinking among Boston youth in low-income neighborhoods reveals the centrality of moral concerns to adolescents in their self descriptions, decision making, and social understanding. Both sexes were able to articulate both care and justice moral concepts and give examples of situations where these ethics were violated. Furthermore, reading the interviews for both justice and care thinking clarified the logic of their moral reasoning. In several cases responses that would have been coded as developmentally delayed and amoral had they been seen only in terms of justice were shown to reflect complex social observations and strong moral commitments when analyzed from a care perspective.

The natural moral language of these urban adolescents includes words and concepts used by their more privileged counterparts. Some teenagers also use a language of necessity, a unique rendering of the care perspective not heard as clearly in settings where "giving and receiving" are easier, and perhaps, therefore, a less "rich exchange."

The types of dilemmas offered by the teens in this study are similar to those offered in our other studies by teens attending private school. However, the repercussions that many of the inner city teens feared from wrong decisions were more serious and long-lasting than those envisioned by the more privileged teens.

Patterns of gender difference in the framing and resolution of moral problems observed in this study were similar to those found in our previous studies. For both boys and girls, peer relationships were the most common social context for the dilemmas offered. Girls tended to focus on issues of loyalty, care, and responsiveness--staying with friends whose actions they disapproved of or with whom they disagreed, while at the same time seeking relationships and situations in which they could "be themselves," develop their potential, and express their opinions without feeling "weird" or out of place. Boys tended to cast their dilemmas in terms of peer pressure, seeking to do the "right" thing, yet concerned about losing friends or losing face.

Finally, the moral insights and commitments of these youths, many of whom play vital roles in their communities by teaching and helping younger children, provide an important corrective to theories that find correlations between "moral development" and social class. Social class certainly influences moral development; it is a salient component of the context in which moral development takes place. However, seeing low socioeconomic status as merely retarding the development of universal moral constructs can lead one to misrepresent both the experience and the knowledge of low-income adolescents.

## NOTES

1. *Boston Sunday Globe.* "Poverty Amidst Affluence:  The Bostonians the Boom Left Behind" (December 13, 1985).

2. This approach to reading interviews of moral conflict and choice has since been formalized.  The study reported here was conducted while this methodology was under construction.  Collective reading of some of the inner-city interviews helped to define and refine the coding methodology.

3. Gilligan, C., Johnston, D. K., & Miller, B.  *Moral Voice, Adolescent Development, and Secondary Education: A Study at the Green River School.* GEHD Center Monograph #3, 1987.

## ACKNOWLEDGMENTS

We are grateful to the Rockefeller Foundation for their support and encouragement of this project.  We would like to thank the administrators, staff, and the boys and girls who are members of the three clubs for their collaboration and participation.

# 9

## URBAN ADOLESCENTS' CONCEPTIONS OF VIOLENCE

Janie Victoria Ward

### INTRODUCTION

Violence is a daily reality that affects the lives of many urban youth. The victimization rate of residents in inner cities, twice that of suburban areas, has led many experts to call teen violence a deadly and insidious public health hazard, particularly in black and low-income communities. According to Department of Justice statistics (1983), homicide is the second leading cause of death among both black and white youth between the ages of fifteen and twenty-four. Among black males between the ages of fifteen and thirty-four, murder is the leading cause of death. Ninety-five percent of the blacks who perish in this way are killed by other blacks, often by other black youths. Nationwide, guns are used in over seventy percent of these murders.

Serious consideration of morality in American culture can no longer overlook two disturbing observations. First, that it is senseless to discuss morality without looking more closely at the issue of violent behavior, and second, that we can no longer discuss violence without immediately acknowledging sex differences in this frightening social phenomenon. Males are more often both the primary victims and the perpetrators of violence. Women, however, are increasingly the indirect victims of violence, for behind the male homicide statistics is a mother who has lost a son, a wife who has lost a husband, or a little girl who has lost her father.

Disturbing as well is the fact that many educators and psychologists are observing more violent behavior in young women today, as increasingly, females, like their male counterparts, are turning to aggression as a means of conflict resolution. Furthermore, while violence against women within the family unit is well recognized and documented, researchers are discovering that violence against younger women may be increasing within intimate relationships outside the immediate family. This abuse against adolescent women in dating situations appears disturbingly similar to abuse patterns found in many marriages (Roscoe & Callahan, 1985).

Across the nation, large urban schools have long presented a challenge to educators. Such institutions often experience problems of student alienation, overt racial and ethnic prejudice, and high rates of interpersonal violence. The city of Boston is well known for its incidents of racial tension, which include the violence that surrounded the controversial court-ordered desegregation of its public school system in the 1970s. By 1983 the racial breakdown for students in the Boston schools was 49 percent black, 18 percent other non-white (primarily Hispanic and Asian), and 33 percent white. Despite the fact that the violent response to busing has abated throughout the city, neighborhood rivalries continue to shift from community settings to the schools, and Boston public school officials still see violence as a very serious concern.

In 1983 the Boston Safe Schools Commission Report cited that weapons were found on school grounds in at least four of Boston's seventeen high schools (including the school in which this study took place). Not only did 50 percent of the students who were interviewed for the Commission's report indicate that their peers were carrying weapons, but 28 percent admitted having carried weapons themselves. In the 1984-85 school year, officials reported that nearly 300 suspensions were issued for weapons possession.

Whether in or out of school, teenagers are more than twice as likely as adults to be the victims of rape, robbery, and assault. For example, according to Bureau of Justice statistics, 60 of every 1,000 teens versus 27 of every 1,000 adults were victims of violent crimes between 1982 and 1984. Much of the violent crime that plagues urban areas is perpetrated by young people, usually preying on one another, and increasingly, teens are likely to be acquainted with both perpetrators and victims of violence.

In contrast to the many studies that focus on teens who commit violence, this research focuses on the ways in which violent behavior is judged and explained by adolescents who have *not* been adjudicated delinquent or engaged in criminal behavior, but who must live in the midst of frequently occurring incidents of violence. Social scientists have developed many ways to define the problem of violence, used many instruments to measure its rate, and offered many theories to assess and propose treatment for both its perpetrators and its victims. Yet there are few, if any, theories of how ordinary, everyday residents of American cities make sense of the violence surrounding them. In particular, little data exist on the thinking of normal teens about violence in their lives and environments.

Adolescents growing up in our large urban communities have too often been seen as the throwaways of our society. They are summarily dismissed as poorly educated, low-skilled members of a growing, permanent underclass. On psychological tests these teens often score at the lowest levels--from intelligence testing to social development to moral reasoning. Consequently, their opinions are not given much weight, nor are they generally sought. This research seeks to redress this omission. It presents data from a group of urban adolescents in a large public high school who reflect upon their own real-life experiences with violence, a topic which is central to their lives and a central concern to society-at-large.

## METHODOLOGY

### The Setting

In 1983 Central High School (a pseudonym), with a population of nearly 2,000 teenagers, had one of the highest rates of violence among the Boston public schools. The Alternative Program (also a pseudonym) was created in the school administration's attempt to restructure the large, impersonal, and unsafe environment. The Alternative Program has a smaller student body, involving less than 200 students in grades ten through twelve. The students include teens with a wide range of academic abilities. School faculty, in designing and implementing the goals and objectives of the Alternative Program, stress that its uniqueness lies in its willingness to provide a community-like, caring environment for its racially and linguistically mixed student body.

As a requirement of the Alternative Program, all students must take part in a year-long course that grapples with moral issues raised by current events. Apartheid in South Africa, the violence in Central America, the preservation of the environment, and racism and prejudice are a few of the topics that the teens have explored in this course. As this research project was about to begin, the Alternative Program introduced an eight-week unit entitled *Facing History and Ourselves: Holocaust and Human Behavior* (Strom & Parsons, 1982; see Chapter 5) as a component of the larger year-long social events course. Educators who have used this curriculum have noted success with students who were considered to be alienated, hard to reach, or violence prone.

*Facing History and Ourselves: Holocaust and Human Behavior* addresses both history and human behavior. The intention of the course is to bring the terrible events of this catastrophic tragedy in modern history out into the open where they can be examined. They hope that engaging the adolescents in reflective questioning about themselves and the social and moral world in which they live will ultimately reduce psychological and physical violence in our schools, homes, and communities.

The curriculum attempts to create a climate within the classroom which enables students to draw upon and examine their own experiences, behaviors, and prejudices. Students are encouraged to imagine alternative responses to violence which will help prevent it in the future. Teachers assist students in developing a sense of confidence in their own moral voices as they are shared, listened to, and reflected upon within the classroom. This chapter reports on how a group of urban teenagers think about real-life violence, prejudice, moral choice, and decision making.

## Subjects

In January 1985, thirty-seven adolescents drawn from a tenth-grade class that was about to take the *Facing History* course were interviewed. Later, an additional fourteen students were interviewed as well. All but eight of the students were interviewed twice. At the end of the two interviewing periods, a total of seventeen males and thirty-four females (N = 51) had been asked a battery of questions. Specific demographic information was not collected on each individual subject; however, the Alternative Program population is primarily black, white, and Hispanic,

with a small number of Asian students.  The majority of the teens participating in this program are from low to moderate-income Boston families.
Some of the children are recipients of federal aid, such as Aid to Families
of Dependent Children (AFDC), and/or are living in public housing.
A smaller percentage of students are from Boston's middle-class
families.


**Conceptual Framework**

In previous research, concepts of justice and care as points of moral
orientation (as explicated by Kohlberg, 1969, 1976, 1981; Gilligan, 1977,
1982; Lyons, 1983; Johnston, 1985) helped us understand the logic that
the students brought to their judgments of events.  This study applies the
concept of different moral orientations to descriptions of real-life violent
events.

Even before the first round of interviewing was complete, the initial
research assumptions were confirmed.  Urban adolescents do, in fact, use
moral language in their explanations and justifications of violence, and they
are willing and able to make thoughtful judgments of those who participate
in violent acts.  As expected, it was apparent that this group of urban teens
had already experienced a great deal of violence in their lives and possibly
due to this fact, had already created their own theories of why such violence occurs.

Generally, students used moral language in response to our questions
regarding violence.  Judgments usually follow the use of moral language
--words or phrases which are of a prescriptive nature, suggesting an underlying belief about the way things should or should not be.  This language
uses words such as should/shouldn't, ought to/not supposed to, fair/unfair,
and hurt, and it usually signals that a moral judgment is forthcoming.  Moral judgments typically included the judgment of fault and blame, the justification of actions as right or good as well as their supporting explanations.  To understand the logic behind the students' determination of who
is right or wrong and why, it is necessary to locate and follow the moral
language, since the language gives meaning to the students' underlying
belief system.

**Procedures**

*Data Collection*

The violence questions were included in a larger interview protocol which asked the students open-ended questions about moral conflict, choice, self-perception and change, and unfairness. Students were asked, "Tell me about a violent situation, or a situation in which someone was being hurt." Following the description of the violent event, the students were asked, "Why do you think this happened?" and following their reply, "Do you think the people involved were right or wrong in what they did?"

*Data Analysis*

Data analysis for this study was begun by first looking closely at the responses to the violence questions. Nearly all of the teens could readily recall a personal episode involving violence. Indeed, there were many students who, in addition to their responses to the violence inquiry, also recalled violent episodes when being questioned about personal moral conflict, situations of unfairness, and times in which they made a decision not to speak up. In answer to these other questions, this small group of urban adolescents (N = 51) made reference to violence over 125 times. Since the questions asked in the other sections of the interview were different from those asked in the violence section, not all of these extra violent episodes were usable. Many lacked moral judgments or did not include complete enough descriptions of the violence to be coded by the criteria developed to code the solicited descriptions of violence. After careful scrutiny, a total of ninety-three violent events was determined to be codable for this analysis.

The author developed (Ward, 1986) a coding procedure which traces how the interviewee was involved in a violent event, what he/she was thinking about, and who, if anyone, he/she was judging. In addition, the coding system provides empirically derived categories of moral judgments and considerations used by the adolescents. For a statement containing moral language to be coded, it had to fit two criteria. First, it had to be of a prescriptive nature. Second, there had to have been enough reasons stated to offer an explanation or supporting evidence for the moral judgment.

Once the moral judgments were identified, they were coded for the orientational logic which they represented. Data analysis was begun by searching for the conventional hallmarks of justice and care. The data did not fit neatly into only these two categories. Some of the statements combined considerations of justice as well as considerations of care. These formulations were categorized as "both." In other narratives, moral themes of justice and care were interwoven in such a way that discrete "justice" and "care" ideas could not be pulled apart without destroying the meaning of the moral judgments. These were coded as "integrated." Thus, the coding system was not created *a priori*, nor was it derived from searching for "buzz words" which might capture a notion of justice or caring. Instead, the categories represent distinct ideas that recurred in the data and seemed to refine the concepts of moral orientation as operationalized in moral judgments.

## Overview of the Coding Categories

*Justice.* Justice as a moral orientation has fairness as its moral objective. Statements were coded as operating from a justice logic when a moral judgment was made because a particular violent action was seen as a violation of personal rights, rules, or standards of behavior.

*Care.* The care logic proceeds from the assumption that people are interconnected. Statements were coded as operating from a care logic when the central concern of the subject was to call attention to hurt, pain, or suffering (both psychological and physical) as intrinsically wrong and/or morally problematic.

*Both.* In addition to the categories of justice, care, or uncodable, two additional sets of responses were offered in the students' judgments of real-life violent events. These were coded as "both" and "integrated." To meet the criteria for the category of "both," each moral statement(s) had to be complete enough to be considered a codable articulation of a care concern *and* a codable articulation of a justice concern, as defined by the criteria stated above.

*Integrated.* The "integrated" category is unique in that there are two criteria to meet in order to qualify for inclusion. Both justice and care considerations and judgments must occur together in the same statement; however, unlike the "both" category, which codes justice and care statements separately, an integrated statement cannot easily be separated into its component parts, because the two concepts sound as if they are either *interwoven* or could be heard as *either* care or justice. There may be elements of justice in a care consideration, elements of care in a justice consideration. When this occurred, the statements that contained interwoven justice and care logic were coded as integrated. A second condition for being coded as integrated was the idea of setting limits on violence. This is elaborated in a following section, "Integrated Moral Operant Concepts."

*None.* Sometimes a student chose to discuss an event in a manner in which moral judgments were not present. If the teen offered neither justice nor care considerations or judgments in response to interview questions, or if the violent event described expressed no moral judgments, it was coded as "none."

*Uncodable.* In this final category are statements that include a moral judgment, but that were generally unaccompanied by the necessary moral considerations to be coded as justice, care, or integrated. Usually these statements, while moral in nature, do not offer enough information to be reliably coded.

Following the initial classification, the operant concepts of justice, care, and integrated were identified. Thirty of the student interviews were coded by two raters. Using the operant concepts as the coding criteria, interrater reliability of 83 percent was obtained.

What does it mean that individuals have access to (at least) two moral orientations, though they may prefer to organize their reasoning around one? Consider the following discussion of the same basic event as seen from two different perspectives of moral orientation.

Two students, speaking to two different interviewers, witnessed and described a similar episode. In both stories an argument turned violent and soon weapons were fired. In one incident, the argument was between some teenagers who were known to the young man telling the story. In the other event, there was a group of unknown men (about ten) who were attacking one another on a street near the home of the young woman who was interviewed. Both students were close enough to the situation to witness at least part of the event. The students were asked why this event occurred and who, if anyone, was at fault. Listen to the two different moral judgments brought to the situations.

1. You shouldn't interfere [in those types of violent situations]. 'Cause what's it going to prove? 'Cause if two kids are fighting, people shouldn't interfere because they can get hurt themselves. People were wrong in what they did, 'cause the thing with the gun could have hurt somebody, could have even killed them. Little kids are around there. He could have shot one of them. It was a shotgun. [male]

2. I think they were wrong because they shouldn't be doing that in the first place--fighting. Especially when there are a lot of kids around, a lot of little kids and they see that and they think, I should do it too--it's fun. It's a bad example and they're supposed to be adults and they are supposed to know what is right or wrong, and not to do that stuff. [female]

The young man focuses on the harm that could come in a situation where someone is wildly firing a shotgun. He suggests that not only might the person who is being fired upon get injured, but also well-meaning individuals who feel compelled to intervene are placed at risk as well. He calls attention to the potential danger to bystanders witnessing the event, and he is particularly incensed that innocent children were being placed in danger. The idea of people getting hurt or the idea of accidentally or intentionally harming others is central to this young man's moral condemnation of the event.

The young woman observing a very similar event organizes her concerns around issues of justice. Like her male counterpart, she too condemns the violence itself. Although she also focused on the innocent bystanders who were watching the event, particularly the neighborhood children, her concern has more to do with the example that the violent participants may set for the children witnessing the incident. Impressionable children watching the excitement of the fight may find the situation "fun" and may choose to imitate this behavior in the future. The violent adults were behaving irresponsibly, not living up to the standards of moral conduct expected of them.

What do we make of this? Two events, more similar than different, yet two urban teens respond to two different sets of moral concerns. The first student formulates a judgment against the man with the gun as wrong because of the potential harm he could cause to innocent bystanders. His comments were coded as operating from a care logic. The young woman condemns the immature behavior and the poor example that the adults were setting for their children. Her statements were coded as operating from a justice logic. Clearly, both students offer valid and important insights arising from thoughtful observations of human behavior. Faced with evidence of two distinct ways of conceptualizing a problem, the educator, rather than attempting to determine which moral formulation is better or more developmentally mature, might, instead, acknowledge each adolescents' insights. This approach allows us to see the strengths as well as the limitations inherent in the thinking of both students. Both justice and care thinking provide a foundation upon which educators can build as they attempt to nurture and sustain moral reflectiveness and responsibility.

## FINDINGS

### Nature of Violence

Overwhelmingly, the violent events reported in this study were embedded in a narrative of human relationships that had gone awry. Students described an astonishing array of violent episodes ranging from face slapping to three separate incidents of murder. Generally, the violence involved physical attacks against another person (e.g., beatings, muggings, use of weapons, rape, assault and battery). Occasionally students chose to relate an event which involved psychological attack or pain (e.g., neglect, verbal abuse, intensive arguments, "brainwashing") and when this occurred, the student made it clear to the interviewer that in their opinion this action was a form of violence.

### Location

In nearly every setting in which these urban adolescents interact, violent acts occur. Of the ninety-three codable incidents, the violence occurred in these four generalized locations: (1) neighborhood/community: outside of the home, usually on the streets in either the student's neighborhood or one nearby (N = 54); (2) family: includes the immediate family, parents, siblings, grandparents, aunts and uncles, and violence occurring within intimate boyfriend/girlfriend relationships (N = 19); (3) school: includes areas either inside or outside of the school classrooms, hallways, bathrooms, sports facilities, and school buses (N = 10); and (4) other: includes violence cited from the media (TV programs and film presentations, events presented in TV and radio newscasts, newspapers, and periodicals) or information mentioned in class (N = 10).

## Moral Operant Concepts

The term moral operant concept is defined as the ideas, beliefs, or principles that are used to organize a moral orientation. The idea here is that the content of the moral consideration is organized into a structure upon which judgments are made. Examples are offered to illustrate the various moral beliefs which organize moral judgments.

## Justice Operant Concepts

For a moral judgment to be coded as operating from the justice orientation, statements had to include one or more of the following ideas:

### Justice Logic Requirements

1. Violation of a person's rights
2. Violation of standards of behavior
3. Violation of a rule or sets of rules or a principle or law; includes unequal application of a rule or law
4. Violations of fairness
   a. taking advantage of unequal power
   b. undeserved punishment
5. Violation of the "Golden Rule"; doing something to others that one would not want done to oneself

Justice logic could justify or support violence under the following conditions:

6. Rectifying or avenging a situation of unfairness, violation of rights, or violation of standards, rules, laws, or principles

Justice as a moral orientation has fairness as its moral objective. Three major beliefs highlight the explanations of the students who judged violence from the justice perspective. First, that violence is often justifiable when it is used to rectify or to avenge a previous injustice, such as being treated unfairly. Second, violence often erupts after someone has been forced to suffer undeserved punishment. And last, that when people step outside of the boundaries of standard behavior, violence, while condemnable, often follows.

The following young woman illustrates the first viewpoint. She begins by describing a disagreement which she had with another female student that subsequently turned into a fight. The student insisted that she did not want to physically fight with the girl, yet she was bullied and called offensive names on the school bus in front of her friends. Eventually she fought back. "She pushes me and that was it," she says, explaining her actions in this way,

> . . . like if I had done something to her personally, I could see it. I could see her not liking me or something. But I hadn't done anything to her . . . I wasn't going to stand there. I felt I was in the right, because she was the one to initiate the fight, but when she did, I just happened to finish it. I think she was in the wrong and she knew it. She had to know that.

For this student, violence could be used in retaliation to a situation that was unfair from the start. Fairness and equity, the essence of the justice perspective, form the basis for justification. It is interesting to note that 40 percent of the judgments determined to be operating from a justice orientation (out of a total of twenty-five) indicated that the violence was justifiable, and most of these statements centered around the notion of rectification.

The most frequent explanations given for justice reasoning involve avenging unfairness or violations of standards, rules, and principles. A focus on undeserved punishment was the second most frequently cited concern of the students whose interviews were coded as justice. The following statement exemplifies the comments which were most often heard from the students in this category. Complained one young man, "They (the attackers) shouldn't have taken it out on him, because it wasn't his fault."

Sometimes breaking a rule was what was seen as precipitating the violent event, and the violating action was what the student considered in judging who was right or wrong or responsible for the violence. For one young man, stepping outside of established norms of behavior was the reason why a divorced mother living in his apartment complex had been assaulted. She was accosted by an intoxicated guest who refused to leave her home once a party she was hosting had ended.

> It was 4:00 A.M. After everyone went home, he came back, screaming to be let in. So they started fighting, arguing. So the lady must have done

something to the guy, so the fight soon ended up outside. My whole family woke up 'cause of the noise . . . I was looking out the window. The guy was smacking and punching the lady. She was calling for someone to call the cops. [Interviewer: *Were the people right or wrong in what they did?*] It's her. She's a divorced lady with three kids. All she has to do is keep her kids and do certain family stuff every night. Like stay with the kids, watch TV. But no, that lady likes to drink, invites friends over, puts on loud music all night. What kind of mother is that, especially for them kids? The best thing for her to do is just stay home. She doesn't have a husband, but she had kids. She wouldn't mind just staying around with the kids, playing games, having fun. But not the way she was carrying things.

Listening closely to this young man's explanation, it is possible to hear him organizing his opinions about his neighbor's behavior around what appears to be a set of internally sanctioned rules regarding role behavior: Women who are unmarried should do this; mothers who are unmarried shouldn't do the other, and so on. Those who transgress are held responsible, are blamed, and they may even be punished. This is not to say that the interviewee is advocating violence as a means of punishing his neighbor for her wrongful behavior; there is nothing here to support that notion. But what is suggested is that the single mother has violated an unspoken yet conventional norm of role behavior, and this has led to the violence against her. From this logic, one might assume that all this unmarried woman must do to prevent violence being directed against her in the future is to "act right."

Before leaving this category, it is important to note one last operant concept of retributive justice, since it encompasses a perspective shared by many of the teens interviewed. The situation described involved the fatal beating of a Chinese man by two drunk white men in the streets of Boston several years ago. According to the interviewee, the attackers were found not guilty in court, and this infuriated the Chinese community. Angrily, the student determined, "If they hit (killed) him, they should be put in jail or even executed." This viewpoint, the eye-for-an-eye philosophy, is commonly espoused in our culture, and it is the foundation upon which proponents of capital punishment stand. In this research sample, there were three codable events in which murder was involved, and in all three interviews, a similarly violent death was proposed for the identified murderer.

**Care Operant Concepts**

For a judgment to be coded as operating from the care orientation, one or more of the following ideas has to be expressed:

*Care Logic Requirements*

1. Attention called to hurt, pain, or suffering (both physical and psychological)
2. Hurt, pain, or suffering seen as morally problematic
3. Someone in need turned away from, not attended to, or not listened to
4. Someone in need allowed to suffer unnecessarily
5. Violence seen as wrong because it prevents understanding by cutting off dialogue
6. Violence seen as wrong because it is unnecessary since it could have been avoided through dialogue
7. Attention to the effect of harm to the victim as well as harm that came to others from seeing the victim harmed
8. Attention called to a history of a lack of care or lack of care determined to be morally wrong

Care logic could support violence under the following conditions:

9. Violence seen as intrinsically wrong because people get hurt but violence seen as sometimes necessary
   a. Belief that people involved saw no choice; violence was the only way they could protect themselves and others who may have been endangered
   b. Violence was an understandable response by persons who had suffered a history of lack of care or abuse

In this sample many of the adolescents interviewed organized their thoughts around the notion that the violence described caused someone to suffer and that this hurt, pain, or suffering (both psychological and physical) is intrinsically wrong and/or morally problematic. While violence itself most often implies hurt, pain, and suffering, there were some students who formulated their moral judgments exclusively around these concerns, and they were coded as care. When students articulate a care logic, they seem to be much slower to accept the violence described and much more uncomfortable with its occurrence. In fact, the most common insight of the care perspective is that violence is unnecessary and through dialogue, it can usually be prevented. Based upon a belief in the interconnectedness of interpersonal relationships, students who use care logic exclusively express deep concern when others are allowed to suffer needlessly. Finally, some students call attention to the idea that suffering often affects more people than just the person to whom the violent behavior is directed. They may also express dismay as they consider the harm that violence causes to others who witness the event or who may be secondarily involved.

Here are some examples of what the care orientation sounds like when it speaks about violence that is witnessed. "Two of my friends was fighting. We was in the (school) hall one morning and my friend had this radio." Thus begins a story offered by a young male student. Before the fight, he explains, he and his friends anticipated trouble and asked the boy who was being abrasive toward his other friend to go home. "'Cause we know how this guy was." A fight broke out over the radio's volume level.

> [ *Why did this happen?* ] 'Cause the guy (who got beat up) wouldn't listen. The other guy was older and he looked . . . kind of drunk. They was both wrong. He was wrong for just fighting in the first place, and he was wrong for not listening to us. If he woulda listened and just went outside . . . that would have been prevented.

In contrast to the adolescents for whom justice concerns were central, most of the fourteen teens who were coded as care, focused on the prevention of the violent act instead of the reasons why violence was deemed justifiable. Violence was perceived as wrong because it was seen as unnecessary, since it could have been avoided through dialogue and its companion, listening. The notion of talking as a move toward mediating violence was seen as the key to preventing a violent event. The judgment was made against the violence, or those who committed it, because it was deemed unnecessary and preventable.

Incidences of psychological pain were described with the same degree of anger and moral outrage as the episodes of street crime which were more frequently heard. An event recalled by a young man offers a chilling example of how the care logic can judge as morally problematic those actions which would cause or allow someone to suffer unnecessarily. The young man's father, who had converted to another religion, kept telling his son that his aunt who was ill was dying "because she wasn't (a particular religion) and that this is God's way of getting her back," because she didn't like him (the father).

> So to me it was like he was trying to persuade me not to like my [aunt], and for me to realize that she was going to die. Even though it wasn't . . . a sense of him hitting or anything like that. It was a violent act on him . . . to do to me. Because I think he was feeling violence or anger towards someone else and he was letting it out on me. [ *Why?* ] Because he told me, he knew I was going to tell someone and that way they would really know how he felt. And he did tell me not to tell anyone. So to me that was . . . kind of abuse because he asked me specifically not to tell anyone. My father was dead wrong. And I'll always feel that way because, why would you tell someone something like that? . . . persuading me not to like my [aunt]?

These stories, particularly those in which moral outrage is expressed in family interactions, seem especially jolting since the victim and the victimizer often have a history of an intimate relationship. Unlike the isolated, anonymous attack from an unknown assailant, the people who are hurt and the people who do the hurting often must, to some degree, maintain a relationship. Sometimes these relationships are destroyed by the advent of violence, but other times they are not. Both kinds of situations were represented in this study. How interpersonal violence transforms an existing relationship is a fascinating finding and will be discussed toward the end of this article.

Finally, the care perspective tends to be concerned not only with those directly injured by a violent event, but turns our attention to the effect upon those who may witness the harm. In this violent story, a young female student witnessed an event that took place in her community.

> Out in front of my house one time somebody got shot. I guess that they were fighting or something and the guy shot the other one. [I was scared] just thinking that someone got shot on my street and the guy could still be around and shoot someone else. I thought it was wrong because you shouldn't go shooting people right there on the street in front of houses. 'Cause then everybody would see it and everybody would get scared.

It appears that a primary concern here is in maintaining attachment and in acting on behalf of another when needed. Similar to the example offered earlier, this young woman draws attention to the idea that all of the residents of a neighborhood can be affected by the harm and fear that comes to one person. This is an important concept, since feeling connected to the plight of one's neighbors might, for some, compel them to help others in need.

## Both Justice and Care Moral Operant Concepts

Initially it was thought that there would be only the categories of justice and care or uncodable. However, in assessing the moral logic used by teens in this sample, it became clear that many students were building upon both justice and care concerns. When ideas were incorporated from a second orientation, this additive approach led to a more complex understanding of motives and behavior. Two additional categories of responses were offered in the students' judgments of real-life violent events. The two categories in which justice and care concerns were used *in combination* were coded as "both" and "integrated." To meet the criteria for the category of both, each moral statement had to be complete enough to be considered a codable articulation of a care concern *and* a codable articulation of a justice concern as defined by the criteria listed above. The category of integrated will be explained later. These categories of moral response represent a refinement of previous work on moral orientation. While Johnston's (1985) work indicates that people know and are able to use both moral orientations, empirical evidence was needed to determine if people could sustain both orientations simultaneously in discussions of real-life events. The adolescents in this study indicate that this can be done. Furthermore, the both formulations can often express particular insights about the nature of morality and violence that are not as clearly articulated when only one orientation is used. Take for example this student who transforms a common dilemma of adolescent peer pressure into a more complex story, a conflict between whether to risk standing alone on principle or avoid risking the fear and vulnerability of such a stand.

> There's a lot of situations where you see kids get beat up. In school you see a lot of kids getting picked on, and get smacks in the head or something like that [teasing and harassment]. I don't like that at all. It makes my stomach turn. [ *Why do people do that?*] Maybe one person's not as smart, or they're different looking. They come from a different town, they talk different. [There's discrimination against] anyone who's just not in the right clique, so to speak. The way they want them. Spiked hair kids aren't allowed by the black and Spanish kids.

This student goes on to explain that many students are afraid to speak up for what they like or want.

> Because they're afraid they may hurt someone's feelings or they might get rejected. Because a lot of people, that's what happens. They say, "I don't

like this," and they say, "Well, then I don't like you--leave!" I think people should have a freedom of choice and not have to worry about getting picked on because of what they like or what they stand for.

In this interesting display of simultaneously sustaining two moral orientations, the student clearly speaks of a violation of individual rights (justice logic). She sees freedom of choice as superseding the need to conform to majority norms of dress and behavior. This is typical of the issues raised frequently by teenagers, often involving conflicts over peer pressure. Rather than this being a simple issue of conformity to peer pressure, we have a greater, more complicated problem highlighted by the use of both justice and care concerns.

The interviewee recognizes how stands taken by individuals against group conformity can be perilous, jeopardizing friendships and closing off options for intergroup understanding. The interviewer asked, "Why is it important for people to feel they are liked?" She responds, "Maybe a sense of security. They go, oh yeah, somebody likes me. I'm not alone in this world. I'm not going to get stepped on, and things like that."

This student expresses her concerns about inclusion and attachment, both hallmarks of the care perspective. Fitting in, she senses, prevents one from standing alone, vulnerable to attack. She is equally sensitized to issues of fairness and concerns of self expression. Her conflict expresses a central struggle of adolescence between justice concerns on the one hand (be yourself) and care concerns on the other (stay in connection). The threat of violence for some closes doors and subverts the process of reaching a balance between the competing needs of identity and attachment during the adolescent years.

In this next event the care logic is used to justify and support the violence described because the people involved saw no other way to protect themselves and others near them from harm. The latter is an important point that the both category focuses upon, for it expands the category of care significantly, and it offers a unique perspective on family violence.

I can remember when my mother and father had their first fight. I was twelve . . . my parents were divorced. My mother went out. My father kept calling and asking where my mother was. He came over and my mother had told us not to open up the door. He told me to open up the door and I opened it. He came in and went through my mother's stuff. My mother got home. We were upstairs and all of a sudden we heard fighting. There were some punches thrown on both sides. [Dad] got scratched and stuff like that, and they hit each other. I think he came out a lot worse than she did. But I think he realized that it was time to stay cool. I think she was pushed to the point, not that she could have killed him--they just had a fight--but she released all her emotion and stuff that happened in the past. [ *Who was right and wrong?*] On my mother's behalf, she was right. 'Cause I guess she was tired of it. And she had to show him she couldn't, she didn't want it to happen anymore. [My father was wrong] because first of all . . . he made me go against my mother's rules. I was living under my mother. I think it was wrong for him to ask, threaten me to open the door. Also he invaded my mother's property. I think that was wrong on his behalf.

As noted earlier, almost half of the students whose responses were coded as justice found violent behavior a justifiable means of rectifying unfairness. Of the fourteen students who were coded as exclusively care, none found violence justifiable in any way. It was not until a care consideration was accompanied by a justice consideration that the care logic was used to justify hurting another person. But care calls for an injunction *against* hurt, and even in justifying the violence, hurting another is still seen as intrinsically wrong. The fact that the young woman described her mother as unwilling or unable to take any more abuse, coupled with the announcement that this incident was their first physical fight, suggests that the violence had escalated, perhaps from psychological to physical assault. The introduction of justice considerations, including the right for a mother and her children to be safe in their own home, may have allowed the daughter to understand that hitting back was the only way left for her mother to protect herself and her children who would be endangered as well. Therefore, the inclusion of justice considerations within an existing injunction against hurting others (care logic) is seen as justifying violence when it was felt that people had reached their limit and there was no other choice.

In family situations, often students mentioned being upset by having witnessed fights between their parents, or, for some, by being victims of the violence themselves. In several cases adolescents related the story of the mother who took a stand to stop the pain and suffering. One student said, "It was shocking because I had never saw my mother get like that, and we had to call the police and stuff like that. And in a way I felt pretty good because finally she got a chance to show him that she wasn't afraid of him."

It is not surprising that the teens focus on the violence of men against women as much as they do. This confirms much of the research findings of those who study family violence (see Gelles, 1980; Straus *et al.*, 1980). It is striking, however, that these teens chose to discuss events in which women were empowered. The statement above suggests that the young girl's assessment of her mother's retaliatory violence as being good has, in some sense, helped the girl break through the terror that her family had repeatedly experienced.

### Integrated Moral Operant Concepts

The group of integrated responses sheds new light on moral perspective, because it enables the researcher to record more subtle nuances of moral reasoning than previously possible. Since an integrated statement involves integrally interwoven themes of justice and care, it reflects a wide-ranging and complex moral perspective. A second condition for being coded as integrated is when a statement(s) suggests the idea of setting limits on violence--when this specifically arises from reasoning that combines both justice and care considerations. The violence (or psychological aggression) may have been considered justifiable for various reasons, or it may have been renounced, but in either case the statement must include the notion that the aggression should have been contained in some way. Statements were coded as integrated if they met either one or both of the above conditions--justice and care interwoven or a limitation of violence.

Take for instance this young male student's recollection of an incident several years back when he and his mother were mugged as they were coming home from grocery shopping. The student takes the opportunity to comment upon street crime.

> What we have in Boston is criminal crime, the way our record is now, it's terrible. Rapes and thieves and murderers--it's crazy. It's stupid--people who mug ninety-year-old ladies. They're wrong because what people that [sic] steal from other people? It's psycho too. They go after a bank and little old ladies and rob their purse. Of course a ninety-year-old lady can't do nothing at night. Because she's totally unarmed and what's she thinking? Of course she's scared, someone walks in and just steals her purse. You just can't do that . . . we can't do that to them. It makes you wonder. You say to yourself, what if that's my grandmother? So the first thing that would ever come to my mind is saying, that looks like my grandmother. I'd just be out there, and I'd do anything I can do to help. Families--you've gotta care about them, and I don't know if anybody will care. [*Even if you knew you'd get hurt, is it worth it?*] Yeah, I think so. Who cares if the cops come by and say you're a hero? Who cares? At least you show you care and respect other people and you help them. That's what a good citizen does.

This student was coded as integrated because of the form in which his ideas were presented. First, there is a clear articulation of care. He expresses deep concern for the pain and suffering that victims might endure, particularly the elderly. His moral outrage results from the sense of connection that he apparently feels with his own family and which enables him to feel empathic connection with other older adults. Even if a victim is unknown to him, he is able to imagine the person as being like someone he knows and could care about, and thus, he is able to imagine taking action. Interwoven in this formulation of why to care for and assist those in need is a justice consideration--respect for others because that is what a good citizen does. Justice perspectives such as social membership and duty, and respect and protection of the rights of others are prominent concerns in this young man's statement. While both justice and care considerations are evident, it is the care logic that seems in this case to be more dominant.

A number of statements included the second idea associated with the integrated category--containment of violence. Some students had a very specific perspective toward violence, one which considers violence to be acceptable up to a point, but because of this, it must be kept under control. It is felt that there is a limit to how much pain one can inflict upon another, even when necessity dictates. This is quite different from care logic which claims that hurting another is in itself morally problematic. Often hurting another person is seen as unavoidable, and thus, the injunction not to hurt must be modified. Or, as is more often the case, hurting someone a little might be tolerable or might even represent fair play, but there is a certain point at which the hurt becomes morally wrong. For example, in the mind of the teen who believes that in roughhousing between boys, a certain amount of physical pain is expected and accepted, there is a presumed balance about the amount of hurt the two can inflict upon each other. If one of these boys escalates the pain by pushing the other into a nearby bonfire (as occurred in this case), it is seen as cruel, unfair, and uncaring ("it hurts too much"). Such behavior tips the balance that regulates physical aggression. Thus, students explain that a certain level of acceptable aggression between individuals is both tolerable and fair. However, it must be modified by a code of limitation, set in place to obviate the possibility of irreparable danger and harm.

## DISCUSSION

In highlighting the kinds of thinking that accompany and help organize the moral logic of the adolescents interviewed, this chapter illuminates
different sets of moral concerns and the strengths of these perspectives.
However, it is in examining both the social context in which these teens
live, and the moral knowledge that they have gained, that we truly come
to comprehend the meaning of violence in their lives. The urban teens
interviewed were not found in an homogeneous pocket of the community.
Due to busing in the metropolitan area of Boston, students in each school
are often from a variety of city neighborhoods and represent a variety of
different ethnic and racial backgrounds. Presumably, family socialization
patterns vary as well. Thus, it is easy to point out the differences that
exist in this adolescent population, yet, it is the similarities that stand out
in this study on violence. With very few exceptions, stories of personal
experiences of violence came forth with frightening ease, and no neighborhood, racial group, sex, or income level was spared.

Two major sets of findings focus on the location of acts of violence
in the lives of urban teens and the moral orientations used to make sense
of these situations. Neighborhood and family violence accounted for almost
three-fourths of the violence recounted. In over half of the ninety-three
violent events described, urban adolescents spoke of an incident that occurred in their neighborhoods. It is clear that these teens are witness to
or are involved in a great deal of violence, which occurs in all of their
communities. For many urban teens, the threat of violence is a daily
reality, and actual events of violence a common occurrence. This finding
supports many of the reports of high levels of street crime and violence
found throughout urban areas in this country.

A related finding involved the frequent use of justice reasoning in
connection with neighborhood violence. Often, in cases of violence
occurring in the neighborhood (as opposed to school or home), the relationship between the student and the other people involved was unclear
or was relatively remote. Students may have been more likely to rely on
rules alone to determine what was right and wrong when the victims and
victimizers were unknown, or when they saw themselves as uninvolved
witnesses. Whatever the explanation, justice reasoning was nearly always
present in descriptions of neighborhood violence.

Finally, the context of neighborhood violence is more fully understood when the unique perspective on violence found in the integrated category is considered. Specifically, the notion of setting limits on violence is an intriguing one, although not new. From the justice perspective, such limitation is expressed in "an eye for an eye"; from the care perspective it is manifest in the injunction to "turn the other cheek" or to walk away. Yet, within the integrated reasoning mode, the call for setting limits on violence is different, and it raises the importance of determining whether the interwoven justice and care concerns are a different form of moral thinking. Further research may shed light on these distinctions.

Given the level of aggression urban residents face, particularly urban adolescents who spend significant time on the streets, it is evident that these conditions require particular kinds of coping behavior and attitudes. Many comments were made by teenagers about the increasing number of weapons used to resolve conflicts on the streets and in the home. Students complained on the one hand that guns were readily available, but on the other hand they mentioned the need to have protection of their own, saying they could not know who is armed and who will use a weapon in an argument or dispute.

The students who highlight the problem of weapon availability and advocate the use of physical aggression (such as fist fighting) as an alternative may sound as though they are condoning the violence that they see in their lives. However, these teens do not seem to be espousing the values of a subculture of violence. Rather, they clearly express moral outrage and anger at the aggression they witness. It is the availability and abundance of weapons that in many ways forces the response of violence as a necessary defense. The moral stance articulated by the students who decry the use of weapons, calls for limit setting to militate against the potential social mayhem that can result. The ease with which guns can be obtained, coupled with a fear that convinces many youth of the need to protect themselves, may be forging a new code of street "sense" and street justice. The appearance of the integrated justice and care judgment which acknowledges but sets limits on violence may be related to this emerging phenomenon.

Just as it was rare that a neighborhood violent event was described without justice considerations, it was rare for a violent event in the family to be described without care considerations. The stories of family violence, or violence that occurred in premarital intimate relationships, were the second most frequently described type of violent events that the adolescents experienced. Again, incidents were not limited to any specific racial or ethnic group. These painful and distressing stories draw our attention to the complex moral formulations that the adolescent must employ to make sense of and come to terms with the pain which loved ones inflict upon one another.

The following event demonstrates this common dilemma. One young woman was witness to many separate battering instances, always involving her father striking her mother. When asked who was right or wrong, the student was clear in her indictment of her father's behavior: he was wrong for the pain he caused. Finally, the student says, her mother couldn't take the abuse any longer, and she fought back against her husband's injustice. In justifying her mother's behavior, she explains that in her eyes it was violent but not really abusive.

> My mother never really abused my father or anything, like stabbing him or shooting him . . . He was so unreasonable. He didn't ever talk about anything . . . He started talking to her and he would go and grab her arm, rip her clothes off her. My brother would get in the middle. My father was a preacher. Two married people are not supposed to get divorced or something like that. It's in the Bible somewhere. It being that we was his children and my mother didn't want them getting divorced. She really didn't want to divorce him. She wanted him to understand. I guess it was hard for him. I guess he was slow. He's now accepting the fact that it's time for her to live her life. He can't run her life. It was making the whole family miserable. Neither one of them was right in the situation, but I think my mother was more right than he was. Being that she was my mother, I'd think she was right. He was right in some ways. It's hard to take sides in a family.

Indeed, it must be very difficult to even feel that one needs to take sides in a family dispute. Often there is validity to the concerns of both competing sides. There are many in this society who condemn divorce on religious grounds. Staying married in respect to the laws of the church is a clear justice formulation. But there is another idea embodied in this young woman's feeling that her family should stay together. "We was his children" is a statement which can be understood from both a justice and a care perspective. A father has a right to stay with his children, but also, family members should stay together out of a sense of attachment and connection to one another. Both interpretations seem equally valid. "She didn't want to divorce him. She wanted him to understand," might, from the daughter's perspective, be articulating the belief that rather than wanting to hurt her husband, her mother wanted him to understand her position so that the hurting between the two could be brought to an end. This story exemplifies the attempt to maintain intimate relationships despite situations of family violence.

This young woman, and the story that she told about her mother's response to violence, was not an isolated case. Many of the adolescents who discussed family violence identified with an empowered mother in a similar fashion. In fact, most of the cases of family violence were stories recalling when the mother finally stood up for herself.

When the caretaker becomes disempowered through long-term family violence, the literature suggests that her children also come to respond with a sense of futility and powerlessness in the face of violence. If mom is silent, she is sending a message to her children that what is happening isn't really violence or isn't really hurt, or that one is powerless to bring it to an end. The message heard by her children may be that violence is a normal part of family life and that this is how families show one another attention or love. Or, if the violence is known to the child and the pain is not denied or covered up, the mother who continues to sustain abuse may communicate to her child, "I'm sorry. I can't protect you or myself. Life is tough kid. You're on your own." A non-protesting, abused mother often tacitly communicates that the violence against her and her children is acceptable or unpreventable, that it is a norm of living. Yet children and adolescents who witness this abuse may have a fundamental moral sense that such behavior is not right.

The phenomenon of teens choosing to discuss events in which their mother was empowered stands out in the data. Teenagers attach importance to times when a mother declares violence against herself as unjust and uncaring, and the moral outrage of these adolescents is an important contribution to the literature on the effects of family violence. In this sample, students who were able to understand and articulate both justice and care concerns in such situations appeared to recognize that it was both wrong and futile for mom to retaliate blow by blow yet equally wrong for her to constantly turn the other cheek. Instead of the futility and powerlessness predicted by many researchers of child abuse, the data from this study suggest that these children who had witnessed the hurt, also witnessed and identified with their mothers' empowerment and were ultimately relieved by her efforts to end the hurt.

## CONCLUSION

In this study, urban adolescents' understanding of the violence that surrounds them has been identified and elaborated. Students were found to use moral language in their explanations and justifications of violence, and they make sophisticated and thoughtful judgments about those who participate in violent events. Central to the task of illuminating these understandings of violence were concepts of justice and care as moral orientations. These organize the structures upon which judgments are made. A bimodal representation was found to be too limiting to capture the complexity of moral considerations used by some adolescents. Thus, it was necessary to create an expanded analytical framework with coding categories of justice and care, and combined categories of both and integrated. These categories, empirically derived from the real-life stories of violence and moral conflict in the lives of urban adolescents, represent an analytic distinction not made in previous data analysis. They may ultimately offer valuable insights and perspectives that can lead educators, psychologists, and others to help reduce the impact and consequences of violent behavior.

## ACKNOWLEDGMENTS

I am grateful to the faculty, staff, and students of the Boston public schools, the creators of the "Facing History and Ourselves: Holocaust and Human Behavior" curriculum, the Adolescent Project interviewers, the Edmonds–Cheng Fellowship, and the Mailman Family Foundation for their support.

# 10

## IN WHOSE TERMS: A NEW PERSPECTIVE ON SELF, ROLE, AND RELATIONSHIP

Jane Attanucci

## INTRODUCTION

At the turn of the century Baldwin, Hall, James, and Dewey began the tradition of studying self in empirical psychology. Not long afterward Mead initiated his analysis of self and the role-taking process. Role theory, as chronicled by Sarbin (1954), came to equate the self with social role, the socially determined "me" in Mead's terms. Role theory, by focusing on social roles, loses sight of the self as the first-person perspective on social experience. As Mead forewarned, "the self is essentially a social process going on with these two distinguishable phases, I and me. If it did not have these two phases, there could not be conscious responsibility, and there would be nothing novel in experience" (Mead, 1934, p. 178).

Roles, as the sociocultural rules which direct interpersonal behavior, are learned in the process of socialization and are a necessary source of social knowledge. By taking the role of the other (Mead's language), a person perceives the responses of others to one's own actions and perceives oneself from the other's point of view. Viewed from the standpoint of traditional role theory, relationships are essentially reciprocal roles--interactions between people based on shared expectations, learned in a common societal context.

One also has, however, perceptions of oneself and behavior from one's own personal point of view. These subjective perceptions or experiences of self often agree with objective perceptions or social role expectations. Congruity between self and role, often termed adaptation contributes to personal and social stability.  On the other hand, incongruity between self and role creates conflict.

The incongruity between self and role, between "I and me," can be expected, particularly at this time in American society when the roles of parent, spouse, and worker for both men and women are undergoing dramatic changes.  Within the context of changing cultural values, roles, as shared expectations, are redefined by individuals faced with new conflicts and new choices.  Thus, these two phases of self generate new opportunities for novelty (i.e., change) and conscious responsibility, as described by Mead.  In this article both phases of self--personal and role--constitute an individual's understanding of self in relation to others.

The central question of this article, "in whose terms," arises from this incongruity between self and role, between first-person and third-person perspectives on self in relationship.  This analysis assumes, as do all major theoretical traditions in psychology,[1] that the experiences of self emerges through interpersonal relationships.  Both self and other can be viewed objectively, in terms of social purposes and roles, and subjectively, in the person's own terms.

## THE CASE OF MOTHERING

Theoretical approaches to the self make the assumption that self emerges through interaction with others.  While psychology extols the mother-infant relationship as the foundation of the infant's growing sense of self, theoretical approaches describe the infant as an individual cared for, disregarding the relationship with the parent who provides care.  Given the critical importance attributed to the mother-infant relationship, the lack of an empirically derived description of maternal self and mothering, that is informed by the experience of adult women as mothers, is a serious and glaring omission.

How is it that psychology has failed to provide an adequate description of maternal self, from the point of view of the mother, particularly in the light of the essential part her role is assigned in the models of healthy child development?  It is, in fact, the equation of the mother with her role as enhancer of the child's growing sense of self which creates this blind spot.

Balint (1939) eloquently describes this preponderant tendency to objectify the mother, to see her only in instrumental role terms.

> Most men (and women)--even when otherwise quite normal and capable of an "adult," altruistic form of love which acknowledges the interests of the partner--retain towards their own mother this naive egotistic attitude throughout their lives. For all of us it remains self-evident that the interests of mother and child are identical, and it is the generally acknowledged measure of the goodness or badness of the mother how far she really feels this identity of interests. (p. 97)

Not only do most men and women maintain this perception of mothers, but many women who are mothers hold this perception of themselves. They experience themselves only through their roles as promoters of their children's (as well as their husband's and others') well-being.

It is this idealized equation of the mother's interests and the child's interests which hinders adult men and women, psychological theorists, and even mothers themselves from recognizing and articulating the mother's own terms. Within this framework the good mother responds to the child's needs and demands in the child's terms and is, thereby, rendered selfless. The bad mother takes into consideration her own needs and is, thereby, perceived as selfish.

Thus, a question arises, "in whose terms," that is, from whose perspective are the women's self-description statements being made? This question guides the following analysis of the clinical interview material drawn from a sample of American mothers. This research seeks to represent the adult woman's perspective on herself and mothering. Self for women is not solely the internal organization of qualities and dispositions but the interpersonal reality of ongoing relationships. Self in relation to others is the central focus of this study.

## BACKGROUND: EARLIER RESEARCH

The unexpected findings of an earlier study (Attanucci, 1982) raised questions which are also addressed. That study focused on Gilligan's question, "How would you describe yourself to yourself?" asked as a part of the interview. Gilligan identified two modes of self description: the connected self and the separate self. The connected self description

naturally includes other people as part of the self. Self description in
this mode is characterized by an understanding of relationships as the
interdependence of people and by a concern for the good of others in their
own terms. The separate self description more formally includes other
people as part of the self. Self description in this separate mode is characterized by a view of relationships as reciprocal roles of obligation and
commitment between people and a concern for considering others objectively and fairly as one would like to be considered oneself. These two
ways of describing the self in relation to others are presented by both males
and females across the life cycle (Lyons, 1981). However, females show a
greater propensity for defining themselves in connected terms, and males
show a greater tendency to use separate terms when describing themselves
in relation to others.

Gilligan's work offers empirical support for Chodorow's contention
that "feminine personality seems to define itself in relation and connection
to other people more than masculine personality does" (1974, p. 44).
Chodorow claims that the mother as a woman and feminine personality
experiences and treats her infant sons and daughters differently. The
mother, thereby, socializes infant daughters toward connection and dependency and infant sons toward separation and autonomy.

The findings of the earlier study (Attanucci, 1982) contradict an
expectation informed by Chodorow's theory and Gilligan's empirical
observations that mothers, as women, would define themselves predominantly in connection with others. The mothers described themselves not
only in Lyons' connected mode but also in the separate mode traditionally
attributed to men. Six mothers used connected mode, nine used separate
mode, and only one used both modes of self description.

Drawn from men's and women's responses to the describe yourself
question, Lyons' conceptualization (which was used for coding the mothers'
responses) of connected and separate self adhere to traditional sex-role
stereotypes. Lyons distinguishes connected and separate modes by asking,
what is the perspective toward others? Connected self is responsive to
others in their own terms, a definition synonymous with the feminine role
of selflessness. Separate self is related to others through the duties and
obligations of reciprocal roles, a self distanced and autonomous in the

contractual manner of traditional male roles. Lyons' concept inadvertently equates self and role. It lacks a perspective on self.

It is the interaction of the perspective on self and the perspective on others which creates the analytic framework for the study. Both self and other can be viewed objectively, in terms of social purposes and roles, and subjectively, in the person's own terms. The combinations of perspective on self and other establish the positions presented in Table 1. The following examples from the interviews elaborate the scheme.

1. Self "for other," other "for self": relationship mediated by reciprocal roles defined by standards of society. Self and role are undifferentiated.

   When self description reveals an understanding of self and other in reciprocal roles, the self and the other are described from a perspective outside the interpersonal relationship. For example, "I think I am a fairly successful mother. I think I am fairly confident. But I have to say that I have this matter that I see as, it sounds like too idealized, but he really is a wonderful, wonderful father and it really makes the job of being a mother very different." The woman describes mutually beneficial roles but does not distinguish herself or her husband as individuals.

2. Self "for others," other in other's own terms: self maintains role instrumental to the well-being of other, other has personal terms.

   Self description in this category characterizes the traditional feminine role of self subordinated to other (to the extreme denigration of the self in some cases). For example, "The important things are with the kids and my husband. Other than that, I don't know what I can say. Without them I have nothing, I think. I have always wanted to have children and now I have them and I do everything for them I can."

3. Self in self's terms, other "for self": self asserts personal needs, other is instrumental to self.

   Self-description in this category is both self-assured and self-protective. Others seem to be instrumental to the person's own sense of self rather than persons in their own right. For example, "So I think I am strict but loving and trying to provide some structure for them. I think I am fairly imaginative, and the kind of things we do are fun and interesting, and a lot of the things we do I remember having done as a child and having enjoyed and now I recognize their benefit." The relationship is described through the woman's own experience. She mothers as she was mothered, without articulating the child's perspective.

4. Self in own terms, other in their own terms: self and other each in their own personal terms, including the relationship as their own.

Self description in this category represents the honest recognition of self and other in their own terms, achieved through the shift Gilligan (1977) describes as the transition from goodness to truth. Self description reveals an understanding of self and other in a relationship that requires dialogue between the two for mutual consideration of each other's terms. For example, "*I like* to be with my kids, to try to

TABLE 1

*"In Whose Terms"--A Perspective on Self and Others*

|  | | PERSPECTIVES ON SELF | |
|  | | Role Terms | Own Terms |
| --- | --- | --- | --- |
| | | 2<br>*Selfless* | 4<br>*Mutual* |
| *Own Terms* | | Self "for other"<br>Other in other's own terms | Self in own terms<br>Other in other's own terms |
| PERSPECTIVE<br>ON OTHERS | | | |
| | | 1<br>*Reciprocal* | 3<br>*Selfish* |
| *Role Terms* | | Self "for other"<br>Other "for self" | Self in self's terms<br>Other "for self" |

fit time, you know, quality time in with them--things *they like* to do"
(author's emphasis).

The incongruity between the experience of self and the demands of
role generates the movement from an understanding of self and other
through roles to an understanding of self and other beyond roles. Gilligan
(1977) purports that the critical transition for adult women is the transition
from a conventional feminine role in which "goodness" is self-sacrifice,
toward a truthful acknowledgment of oneself as deserving of the consideration one grants others. This transition emerges from a growing awareness of the deception inherent in the feminine role of selflessness and the
destruction to self and other which that deception breeds. Women, having
achieved this transition from goodness to truth, in fact, do not become
indifferent individuals, a trait women fear; rather, they acknowledge their
interdependence as caring individuals, including themselves in the circle of
those for whom they care.

The four-category scheme represents this as a transition from conventional feminine role (category 2) to an inclusion of self (category
4). This orientation or transition for women might be characterized as
a recognition of the "feminine mystique" (Friedan, 1963). This scheme
can also trace another path of realization and movement out of the "feminist mystique." Some women describe themselves in terms of the role of
autonomous selfhood (category 3) in a way that undervalues relationships with others. Their developmental task is an acknowledgment of
others in their own terms and the reality of interdependence in relationship (category 4).

Many of the women in this sample experience a painful disparity between self and the roles of wife and mother, inevitable when they assume
the traditional feminine role of selfless caregiving. In contrast, the women
who expressed the greatest personal satisfaction and contentment in their
relationships described a perspective on themselves and their relationships
beyond role expectations. Roles are, by definition, generalized terms that
have limited usefulness for individuals in particular circumstances. These
women seem to be informed by role expectations but not dominated by
them.

## METHOD

While seeking a method for eliciting the maternal sense of self, it became clear that methodology has been a persistent problem in the empirical approaches to the self. Traditionally, work on the self incorporates the theoretical perspectives of psychoanalytic, social, and developmental psychology, and utilizes psychological testing methods. Under the powerful, positivistic influence of behaviorism since the 1920s, insights from theory were filtered through experimentally controlled, standard research settings to yield null findings. Wylie (1974), who has done the most extensive and thoughtful review of self-concept research, summarizes the situation in her most recent volume.

> It is fascinating that hundreds of thousands of research hours have been devoted to studying self-concept variables, especially overall self-regard, and that both lay persons and professional individuals from many disciplines evidently continue to be impressed with the importance of the topic despite numerous resounding failures to obtain support for some of their most strongly held hypotheses. (p. 685)

Wylie cites lack of evidence for a relationship between overall self-regard and such hypothesized antecedent variables as age, sex, socioeconomic level, or use of psychotherapy. She concludes that the study of the self has been approached "too simplistically" and has failed theoretically and methodologically.

Given Wylie's evaluation, Bromley (1977) suggests a radical shift from traditional approaches to a more fruitful way of thinking about the nature of the self. He suggests that the study of self description in ordinary language is, using Freud's image, the "royal road" to understanding the self. The present study of naturally occurring self descriptions focuses on the woman's view of herself and, thus, subordinates the relevant theoretical perspectives to the individual's perspective. Rather than fitting empirical data to theory, the goal is for theory and data to interact continually with the data becoming the ground from which theoretical insights can develop and empirical investigations proceed (see also Glaser & Strauss, 1967; Bakan, 1969; Gutmann, 1969; Schatzman & Strauss, 1973; Mishler, 1979).

This open-ended, unstructured approach is obviously limited by the willingness of women to disclose information about themselves to researchers. Furthermore, there are no guarantees that it will represent the full gamut of "ways of describing the self." However, the observation of self description which occurs in the course of a wide-ranging discussion provides valuable and presently unavailable information about what women tend to say about themselves in a clinical interview. It is in attending to this "accessible surface" that LeVine argues one can "return to the empathic stance of clinical psychoanalysis-- ' listening to the patient' --but with the recognition that empathic listening in another culture is impossible without knowledge of the culture-specific meanings and contexts through which feelings are expressed" (LeVine, 1982). This research aims to describe some of these culture-specific meanings of self and motherhood revealed by the women in the semi-clinical interviews. Approached as a person-centered ethnography, the research question "in whose terms" examines the women's perspective on self and other as coordinates for understanding maternal self and role.

## Participants

The twenty women in the present group were participants in the Comparative Human Infancy Project. They comprise the American sample of this longitudinal, multicultural study of parenthood and child development. The women (ranging in age from twenty-seven to thirty-eight years) reside with their husbands and children in the Greater Boston area. They were recruited through local pediatricians when their infants (second, third, or fourth-born to insure comparability with infants in the other samples) were either four or ten months of age. Involvement in the Comparative Human Infancy Project was a serious commitment of time for a rigorous schedule of home observations and interviews. The infants were ten and sixteen months old at the time of this last interview. One woman requested that the behavioral observations be discontinued; however, she agreed to be interviewed at the end of the study and is included here.

Ten cases were randomly selected to be coded by two independent judges. The percent of agreement ranged from 79 to 90 percent for the assignment of self descriptive statements to the categories outlined in the introduction.

## RESULTS

A total of 269 statements of self description were drawn from the interview transcripts for the twenty women in the sample. The average number of statements was 13.4 (mean) with a range from 5 to 20. The distribution of the statements across the coding categories for all subjects is presented in Tables 2 and 3. The largest number of statements fall into the specific relationship categories: self in relation to children (89), self in relation to husband (87), and self in relation to own mother (59). In general, categories 2 and 3 hold the greater proportion of statements.

In order to summarize the information (four dimensions of self in relation to others) and to minimize the loss of information at the same time, a cluster analysis was performed. The cluster analysis, by considering the profile of four dimensions of self, creates a single variable. The raw data for this analysis were vectors of sixteen scores for each subject to represent the presence (1) or absence (0) of statements in each of the four categories (1-4) for each relationship [husband, children, own mother, and (general) others]. In cluster analysis the comparison and grouping of scores is based on the sixteen scores simultaneously. In the present study, Ward's Minimum Variance Method was applied. It begins with each subject as a cluster and produces a hierarchical tree structure building from each subject as a separate unit to the top where the sample is one cluster.

For the purpose of this study, three clusters are examined. The subjects are divided between the three clusters with N's of 6, 9, and 5. It is readily apparent from an examination of the raw data matrix (rearranged by cluster membership) that the distinguishing characteristic between the clusters is the presence of category 1 statements (cluster 1), of category 2 and 3 statements (cluster 2), and of category 4 statements (cluster 3).

The results of the cluster analysis support a typology of maternal self description that can be depicted in three distinct manners. Cluster 1 is distinguished by self description in the idealized terms of reciprocal roles. Cluster 2 is characterized by the conflict between self and other. (The central dilemma--"in whose terms" will the self be defined?--will be elaborated later in the chapter.) Cluster 3 features a perspective on self and other based on dialogue and mutual recognition of terms, a perspective that tends to promote vital connection.

This finding supports the visual inspection which suggested that the women in cluster 1 tend to describe themselves in reciprocal roles, particularly in relation to their husbands. The women in cluster 2 describe themselves with category 2 and 3 statements conflicted between "for others"

TABLE 2

*Perspectives on Self in Relation to Others:*
*Number of Responses by Category*

| | Category | | | | |
|---|---|---|---|---|---|
| | *1* | *2* | *3* | *4* | *Total* |
| Self in relation to husband | 13 | 17 | 41 | 16 | 87 |
| Self in relation to children | 3 | 32 | 38 | 16 | 89 |
| Self in relation to own mother | 5 | 28 | 25 | 1 | 59 |
| Self in relation to (general) others | 0 | 15 | 17 | 2 | 34 |

TABLE 3

*Perspectives on Self in Relation to Others:*
*Number of Subjects with Statements in Each Category*[*]

| | Category | | | | |
|---|---|---|---|---|---|
| | *1* | *2* | *3* | *4* | *Total* |
| Self in relation to husband | 5 | 8 | 12 | 7 | 20 |
| Self in relation to children | 3 | 16 | 13 | 6 | 20 |
| Self in relation to own mother | 3 | 16 | 16 | 1 | 20 |
| Self in relation to (general) others | 0 | 6 | 6 | 2 | 9 |

[*]*Note that all women had statements in more than one category. Therefore, the columns are not additive.*

and "for self." The women in cluster 3 reveal a perspective which encompasses both self and other.

## RELATIONSHIP BETWEEN SELF DESCRIPTION VARIABLES AND LYONS' SCORES

The responses of the present sample of women to the question, "How would you describe yourself to yourself?" were coded using Lyons' coding scheme and reported in an earlier paper.[2]  The present self description variables are drawn from the entire interview protocol and are coded in the manner described in the introduction (see also Attanucci, 1984, for a detailed description of the coding).  The interrelationship between the two sets of scores is presented in Table 4.

TABLE 4

*Relationship of Cluster Membership to Lyons' Scores
("How Would You Describe Yourself to Yourself?")*

|  |  | Lyons' Scores | |
| --- | --- | --- | --- |
|  |  | Connected Self | Separate Self |
|  | 1 | 0 | 4 |
| Cluster Membership | 2 | 1 | 5 |
|  | 3 | 5 | 0 |

$\chi^2 = 11.52$, d.f. $= 2$, $p = 0.003$.

Consistent with Lyons' category definition, the cluster 1 women who use reciprocal role statements were also coded in the separate self category. The cluster 2 women who use both "for others" (category 2) and "for self" (category 3) statements were more often coded as separate self in the Lyons' scheme.  Finally, the cluster 3 women who reveal the perspective inclusive of their own and others' terms were coded connected self in Lyons' coding scheme.  Though there is this relationship between Lyons' categories and the clusters, Lyons' scheme fails to capture the conflict for women with role demands to be both "for self" and "for others." The present analysis represents this conflict and the dynamics of self in relation to others that are not included in Lyons' static trait dichotomy of connected and separate self.

## DISCUSSION

This study demonstrates that the different ways women who are mothers describe themselves can be reliably identified and fitted to a new model of explanation. It confirms the need to examine the perspective on self in interaction with the perspective on others in order to understand the dynamics of maternal self and role and the transition to perspective beyond role. Expressed only in the connected and separate modes of Lyons' scheme (Attanucci, 1982), maternal self-conception was framed in the dichotomy of traditional deficiency models. Women either described a connected self, responsive to others, which qualified them as good mothers and "selfless" adults, or they described a separate self, related through roles, which made questionable their capacity for connection as mothers but aligned them more closely with a "male," autonomous identity. This new conceptualization, as elaborated and validated by the present findings, contributes a method for exploring the mothers' self-descriptions in their own terms in the context of the relationships which are central to their lives.

The discussion will be organized around the following questions:

1. How do the women describe themselves in relation to their husbands as fathers?
2. How do the women describe themselves in relation to their children?
3. How do the women describe themselves in relation to their own mother?
4. How do the dimensions of self description, as outlined above, relate to each other?

### How Do the Women Describe Themselves in Relation to Their Husbands as Fathers?

The present evidence contradicts Gutmann's (1975) model of reciprocal sex roles between men and women during the parenting years. He argues for a necessary link between roles and personality traits. That is, mothers stay home to provide emotional security and are, therefore, passive

and dependent, while fathers go off to provide for physical security and
are, therefore, aggressive and independent.  Though the mothers in the
present sample devote most of their time to child care and their husbands
are the principal breadwinners, they do not describe themselves solely in
the terms of the traditional feminine role of passivity and dependency.

While some of the women do make statements which describe a marital relationship of reciprocal roles (category 1), none of the women use
these terms exclusively.  All of the women reveal some tension between
the experience of self and their role as wife.  This experience of incon-
gruence is evident in the predominance of statements in categories 2 and
3 for self in relation to husband.  Categories 2 and 3 are prototypes of
traditional feminine and masculine roles respectively.  Category 2 is characterized by a subordination of self to the needs, demands, and goals of
others.  Conversely, category 3 subordinates the other to the self in the
self's terms.  The diagonal positions of these two categories in the coding
scheme represents the inherent imbalance between these two positions.
Their apparent reciprocity and complementarity in the idealized role relations between men and women are challenged by the experiences of these
women.  Viewed from within, the subordination of self to others and the
subordination of others to self are the poles of conflict, seemingly contradictory and incompatible.

Though they represent contradictory views of the marital relationship,
these two ways of describing self in relation to husband are both typically
present in the women's interviews.  Furthermore, it is an acknowledgment
of this imbalance and a recognition of the trade-offs which mark the
transition beyond role.  The women who reveal a perspective inclusive
of self and other (category 4) have not resolved all conflicts with their
husbands, but they have achieved a new understanding of them.  This
transition beyond role, rather than being an individual developmental
achievement, is the product of the actual relationship between the woman
and her husband.  It is unlikely that a woman could maintain this perspective without a similar shift in her husband's understanding of their
relationship.

While the diagonal positions of categories 2 and 3 can depict the poles
of conflict in traditional sex roles, they also represent two fundamentally
different ways of seeing self in relation to others.  Each way of viewing

relationships has its characteristic blind spot. In category 2, there is a danger of losing sight of the self. In category 3, there is a danger of losing sight of the other. It is the women who describe themselves in relation to their husbands solely in one or the other of these ways who appear to be at the greatest risk.

Though this study did not include formal measures for evaluating the mental health of the women, it seems evident upon reading the interview material that some of the women were seriously depressed at that time. In fact, those women who used solely category 2 or category 3 statements to describe their relations with their husbands appeared most depressed. (See Chapter 11 for further evidence of the relationship between role terms and depression.)

### How Do the Women Describe Themselves in Relation to Their Children?

Based on the frequency of statements across categories describing self in relation to children, use of category 1 statements (reciprocal roles) is extremely rare. Such statements as this seldom occur: "When I feel good, the kids feel good and when I'm upset, they're upset--that's natural." Their absence in this nonclinical sample lends support to the psychoanalytic notion that complete identification of needs between mother and child is a sign of maladjustment.

Typically, the women describe the conflict in mothering to be the competing urges to comfort or to correct the child. One woman expressed the conflict this way:

> I love my children with an intensity that I couldn't have imagined possible. If there was--anything I could do, if there was any pain I could take from them, or anything like that, I most certainly would. (category 2)

> Yeah, I think I tend to expect too much of my children sometimes. It is really hard. You want so badly to be doing everything right and I guess, the saying, children will be children . . . it is real hard being a parent--that's all. It's real hard being a parent and you want to do right and you want your children to do right. (category 3)

The resolution of this conflict between responsiveness to the child and responsibility for the child's education can be seen in the following remark:

> I think it's important to be honest with my children, to let them make mistakes
> and feel disappointment and to see that I am ambivalent about things and I
> make mistakes, too. (category 4)

This characteristic allusion to honesty confirms Gilligan's initial observation (1977) that the transition from conventional to postconventional
understandings is the transition from goodness to truth. The women who
use category 4 statements describe themselves as mothers in terms beyond
the conventional definitions of good mothers and bad mothers. They see
themselves in a human relationship of mutual nurturance and benefit,
interwoven with their own strengths and weaknesses.

> I think I'm a pretty good mother. Hah, hah. I think I have, you know,
> naturally my faults. I lose . . . I have a lot of patience but I lose my
> patience a lot . . . I wish I had more time, to do more things, you know,
> take them more places, because that way, they let me spend time with them.
> (category 4)

It is apparent throughout the interviews that women see their relationships with their children in a qualitatively different light than their relationships with their husbands, mothers, or other adults. Recognizing the
temporary inequality (Miller, 1976) of the parent-child relationship, the
mothers portray the delicate balance of accepting the responsibility for
their children's welfare and granting the children responsibility for themselves as they grow in maturity. The conflict for the mothers often re-
volves around considering the child's terms as the child expresses them
and considering her own perspective, informed by careful observation and
thought concerning the best interests of the child. The mature perspective
acknowledges the greater responsibility of the parent and the enormous
importance of nurturing the child's growth toward eventually assuming
personal responsibility.

### How Do the Women Describe Themselves in Relation to Their Own Mothers?

At this point an important distinction between Chodorow's conception
of feminine personality and the nature of the present research must be made.
Chodorow illuminates earliest personality development and the unconscious
formation in the pre-Oedipal period of gender identity which is the result
of being mothered by a woman. She does not describe the conscious sense
of self and the conscious process of learning about how to be a woman,

which is the material available in the present interviews. Though gender
identity remains an intrapsychic constant--that is, an unchanging identification of self as male or female--the conscious understandings and
expressions of self change with experience. Therefore, the self descriptions
in relation to their own mothers from the present cases are not evidence of
the unconscious gender identification to the mother which Chodorow describes. This sample of women reveals a variety of conscious commonalities
and differences with their own mothers as well as a variety of actual relationships with their mothers in the present. One woman describes the conscious identification process with her mother as follows:

> I can describe a sort of series of events that made me decide not to be like
> my mother. I always adored my mother, thought she was a marvelous person,
> nearly sacrificing her life for her children, just putting her life on the shelf
> . . . But when my sister and I were old enough so that we weren't a care
> anymore, I saw that my mother is a victim. A professional victim, and she
> perpetuates it. And then I looked at myself and saw how she perpetuated it
> in me, and that as a teenager I was afraid to do everything, always overly
> cautious, I was just afraid to do anything . . . Slowly, little by little . . . And
> the funniest thing, when I went into the hospital to have my second child, my
> first child stayed with my mother, and when he came back, suddenly every
> time I turned around, he was afraid of something. He suddenly couldn't do
> anything that we knew he could do. And so since then I have been working
> on not being a victim. But it's also very difficult when you decide to do that.
> At first, the first stage was not to be like my mother, but when you're push-
> ing against that goal, it is not your own goal really. It is against someone
> else's, which would say that she was ruling me anyway.

This woman's story of identification is representative of how the women
described themselves in relation to their own mothers. Some women made
more statements describing their similarities and some made more describing their differences, but the descriptions centered around their role identification with their mothers. Their self description in relation to their
own mothers clustered in categories 2 and 3, with negligible variance.
There are two explanations for the uniformity of pattern of this category
of self description.

First, it should not have been surprising to find the self description
focused on role identification rather than the actual relationship because
the interview questions were framed so tightly around this issue: "Describe
your mother; how are you similar to your mother, and how are you different?" The question on how the woman sees herself in relation to her
own mother must include more in-depth exploration of the adult mother-
daughter relationship, specifically seeking expressions of "in whose terms"

the women construe the relationship, if we are to get beyond the role identification.

Second, when the women do describe their present relationships with their mothers beyond similarities and differences, they are describing just that, an ongoing relationship between two people. While the adult daughters may be willing to let go of their idealized role perceptions of their mothers, it is not clear that the mothers are ready to shed their idealized role images of themselves. Identification is an interpersonal process embedded in the context of a relationship. Therefore, in order to progress beyond role identification to a personal identification and have a relationship of honest and mutual terms (which would be described in category 4 terms: self in self's terms and others in their own terms), both mother and daughter would need to share a perspective beyond conventional role definitions.

It is part of the role specifications for a mother to set a good example. Friedman (1980) states:

> In addition to their maternal, nurturing roles, one major task that mothers have is to hold down a legacy of womanhood--to teach it, cultivate and nurture it, and especially to share it and be an example of it. This message from mother to daughter is about what it is to be female. (p. 90)

However, when a mother aspires to setting an example of selfless servitude to husband and children, then the legacy is a lie; selflessness is anathema to personhood and relationship. Though the evidence is sketchy on the nature of the relationship between the sample women and their mothers, when the women describe an unfulfilling and difficult relationship with their own mothers, the issue is frequently dishonesty. Conversely, when the women cherish their present relationship with their mothers, the bond is characterized by mutual honesty. For example, one woman said:

> I have just discovered recently that all the time my mother was having seven children, she would sneak out after we were in bed and go to the dog track and I never knew that, and here I am, like, and I think that is the way she kept her sanity, do you know what I mean, her release . . . And I am starting to enjoy her sense of fun and escape and realizing it is alright to want to, you know. And the one thing she keeps telling me all the time is, nobody is going to give you a medal for doing that. Don't overextend yourself like I have, because I keep finding myself doing, overextending myself just as much as she did. And I guess she's sorry that I've done it, too. Just trying to be everything to everyone all the time, you can't do that.

The lives of the women in this sample, as they were portrayed in the semi-clinical interviews, confirmed the observation by Cohler and Grunebaum (1981) that the mother-daughter relationship is of central importance across the life cycle.

> Throughout life, people continue to remain attached to or depend both on their own parents and on their offspring to a far greater extent than has been considered "ideal" by many psychological theorists. On the other hand, as this book shows, many adult women may not have become fully differentiated as psychologically separate from their own mothers. This statement sounds at first pejorative--a most unfortunate conclusion for two men to make--particularly since we have tried to avoid making any judgment regarding the significance for adjustment of this flexible differentiation that characterizes the mode of relationship between women and their relatives. Clearly, it is time to reexamine traditional views of the supposed ideal mode of adult interpersonal relationships and to recognize the degree of interdependence that is far more characteristic of adult relationships than the "autonomy" described by theorists such as Goldfarb. (pp. 334-335)

The women describe a relationship with their own mothers which characterizes interdependence far more closely than autonomy. Those who are disappointed in their present relationship with their own mothers express a desire for a more honest and caring relationship.

### How Do the Dimensions of Self Description Relate to Each Other?

Rather than assuming that the self in relation to others would be consistent across relationships, it was expected that consistencies and inconsistencies would be revealing. In all but one case, there was a remarkably high correlation between how the women portrayed themselves in relation to their husbands and in relation to their children. Typically, the pattern of category usage in relation to the husband coincided with the category usage in relation to the children.

The only woman in the sample who was not born and reared in this country describes herself firmly in a role which orients her in one way toward her husband (category 3, self in self's terms and other in role terms), and in the opposite way toward her children (category 2, self instrumental to others, others in their own terms). She does not reveal the personal conflict over her roles as wife and mother which the American women express. One example from her interview was her response to the describe yourself to yourself question:

> The important things are with the kids and my husband. Other than that, I don't know what I can say. Without them, I don't know. I have always wanted to have children and now I have them and I do everything for them that I can. I might as well. My husband, he's actually the one that works, so naturally I have to kind of make sure he's happy, the best way I can. It doesn't always work, but most times it does.

The woman reiterates this theme in the following passage, where she expresses the importance of her husband's instrumental role.

> Sometimes I say to myself (laughing), God, if I have another life, I will stay single. No, I wouldn't. Not really. Only when I get mad. Oh, I don't know. I have the children for one thing; they are most important. I have my own home which I probably wouldn't have if I wasn't married. I don't know--it just means everything to me.

She reveals her personal resistance to changing American values in her goals for her daughters:

> I don't want the girls involved in that women's lib stuff, but like, I don't know. Things like they say a lot of people finding themselves, even when they are married and have two children, all of a sudden they discover they don't know who they are and all this. Well, I totally disagree with that. It seems like they are confused as to what their role in life is. Hopefully they will know what their role in life is before they make a mistake, before they marry . . . It doesn't have to be a home and family, but they know what they want, they know who they are and what they want and do their best to get that and keep it when they have it and not do anything to destroy it. I think if it's home, then let them stay home and take care of the children.

The divergent data presented by this woman from a different country emphasizes the importance of the cultural context to an understanding of maternal self and role. Her difference brings attention to the need for research on the dynamics of self and role in cultures where the status of women is not undergoing dramatic changes as it is in American society.

Returning to the question which begins this section, how are the dimensions of self description related to each other, we find the profile of self description in relation to husband, children, own mother, and (general) others is summarized by the cluster analysis. The dimensions of self in relation to husband, and self in relation to children contribute most to determining cluster membership. As was noted earlier, the interview questions limited the opportunity for exploring the mother-daughter relationship in greater depth.

The results of the cluster analysis support a typology of maternal self description that can be depicted in three distinct phases. Cluster 1 is distinguished by self description in the idealized terms of reciprocal roles.

Cluster 2 is characterized by the conflict between self and other, the dilemma of "in whose terms" the self will be defined. Cluster 3 features a perspective on self and other based on dialogue and mutual recognition of terms, a perspective that insures vital connection. These phases, by definition, comprise a developmental progression of increasing personal awareness and responsibility for the self in relation to others. While this directional assumption awaits further tests, the empirical patterns in this study suggest a developmental line.

Given the naturalistic rather than psychometric orientation of this study, the cluster analysis is based upon similar patterns of presence and absence of statements across categories rather than on the predominance of statements in specific categories. Thus, it is important to emphasize that while cluster 1 evidences more use of category 1, none of the women used exclusively reciprocal role statements to describe themselves. This fact supports the present claim that role is inadequate to encompass identity, and that the tension between self and role is a common experience for all of the women in the study.

Just as reciprocal role statements fail to fully represent feminine identity, the presence of statements in category 4, self and other in their own terms, does not preclude description of self in relation to others in categories 2 and 3. It is rare, however, for a woman to use both categories 1 and 4.[3] The perspective on self and other achieved by those women in cluster 3, as evidenced by the category 4 statements, does not insulate them from the conflicts between doing "for others" and doing "for self." It does, however, allow them to see the problem of denying their own terms or ignoring the other's terms. Their perspective affords them the opportunity for communication and choice. As such, this perspective on self and other is not a solution to dilemmas of relationships but a more adequate strategy for maintaining relationships.

## SUMMARY

Thinking? She would not have said so. She was trying to catch hold of something or lay it bare so that she could look and define; for some time now she had been "trying on" ideas like so many dresses off a rack. She was letting words and phrases as worn as nursery rhymes slide around her tongue: for towards the crucial experiences custom allots certain attitudes, and they are pretty stereotyped. "Ah yes, first love! . . . Growing up is bound to be painful! . . . My first child, you know . . . But I was in love! . . . Marriage is

a compromise . . . I am not as young as I once was." Of course, the choice
of one rather than another of these time-honoured phrases has seldom to do
with a personal feeling, but more likely your social setting, or the people you
are with on an occasion. You have to deduce a person's real feelings about
a thing by a smile she does not know is on her face, by the way bitterness
tightens muscles at a mouth's corner, or the way air is allowed to flow from
the lungs after: "I wouldn't like to be a child again!" Such power do these
phrases have, all issued for use as it might be by a particularly efficient
advertising campaign, that it is probable many people go on repeating "Youth
is the best time of your life" or "Love is a woman's whole existence" until
they actually catch sight of themselves in a mirror while they are saying
something of the kind, or are quick enough to catch the reaction in a friend's
face.

--Doris Lessing, *The Summer Before the Dark*

While, in fact, the observer, the researcher or clinician, can only infer
a person's real feelings, there is merit to considering the forms of natural
language which shape our social construction of motherhood and self. This
study contributes a new framework for understanding maternal self and role
through an empirical methodology that addresses the question, "in whose
terms" are a woman's self descriptive statements being made? This new
conceptualization of relational self incorporates the person's perspective on
self and other and can be reliably identified in transcriptions of clinical
interviews. Rather than creating a psychological measurement of personality or self, the method provides a map of how women experience themselves and others in their daily lives.

This study demonstrates a method for examining the women's self
descriptive statements in their own terms and in the context of their most
central relationships. While some women describe relationships of reciprocal
roles, none of the women use those terms solely to describe themselves.
Role is inadequate to encompass feminine identity, and the tension between
self and role is a common experience for the women. The women who
portray themselves exclusively in the other's terms (category 2) or in the
self's terms (category 3) reveal signs of depression and raise questions for
future research. Some of the women describe self and other from a stance
of mutual inclusion and consideration. From this perspective the women
are able to see the problem of denying their own terms or ignoring the
other's terms.

The results of this study illuminate both personal and institutional
understandings of self and motherhood. Men and women, as fathers and
mothers, theorists, researchers, doctors, teachers, and therapists might well

reconsider "in whose terms" they understand self and mothering. In that regard, borrowing from Kluckhohn and Murray (1948, p. 35), the following dictum provides a fitting summary:

Every mother is in certain respects:
- a. like all other mothers
- b. like some other mothers
- c. like no other mother

Traditional perspectives on mothers, represented by item a., consider solely their universal characteristics and functions. This stance objectifies the women who are mothers, recognizing them only in terms of their instrumental value to others. American psychology has unwittingly embraced item a., failing to acknowledge potential group differences in item b. and the individual differences of item c. This study highlights the influence of historical and cultural contexts on the experience of self and mothering, simultaneously acknowledging the individual expressions of subjective experience. The study demonstrates the need for considering self and role in the context of specific interpersonal relationships and in the woman's own terms. Clearly the universal, historical-cultural, and individual are all necessary perspectives for understanding self and mothering.

# NOTES

1. Developmental, psychoanalytic, and social psychology describe the self as forming in relation to others. As recent critiques by self–in–relation theorists (Miller, 1976; Chodorow, 1978; Gilligan, 1982) suggest, the importance of this initial relational context is diminished in approaches which espouse the developmental goal of independence and separation. The present approach emphasizes the ongoing interpersonal nature of self. "In whose terms," as a theoretical construct, is relevant to both male and female experiences of self; any sex differences in findings would depend upon sex role expectations in the social context under study and the perceptions of the research participants.

2. Attanucci, J. "How Would You Describe Yourself to Yourself: Mothers of Infants Reply." Unpublished qualifying paper, Harvard Graduate School of Education (1982).

3. Only one woman who uses category 4 statements also uses category 1. She describes herself as simply the same as her own mother. It is difficult to determine whether she might have differentiated her response with more interviewer queries.

# ACKNOWLEDGMENTS

I would like to thank Kay Johnston for her work on intercoder reliability. I would also like to thank the Spencer Foundation and the Hoffman Foundation for research support during the years I conducted this study.

## 11

## CULTURAL SCRIPTS FOR MOTHERING

Ann Willard

> No job is more important than raising a child in the first three
> years of life.
>
> > --Burton White, *The First Three Years*

> If you have someone you're counting on to do the job, your
> expectations don't change just because a child has entered the
> picture.
>
> > --Ron Greene, senior advisor for human relations
> > training for Alcoa (quoted in the *Wall Street
> > Journal,* September 19, 1984)

The quotations above represent two current viewpoints about employment and mothering. Conflicting views of what women "ought" to do per-
meate the media, the child development literature, and the emerging literature on adult development. These views are embodied in "cultural scripts"
for motherhood, messages from the culture about the "right way" to be a
mother.

Women, upon becoming mothers, are subject to numerous voices, each
representing a different point of view--that of the child, as represented by
a substantial literature, and that of friends, relatives, and often the institutions or businesses that employ women. Women are, thus, informed about
what is good for the company, what is good for the baby, even, to some
extent, what is good for the marriage.

Increasingly, there is a literature telling women what is "good for them." Studies have focused on whether or not it is good for mothers to work, and women have been advised that work is good for their mental health. Recently, some professional women have discovered the satisfaction of spending more time with their children and they advise women that it is better for them to stay at home (Fallows, 1985). Such global advice cannot take into account the situation of individual mothers who need, in fact, to make these decisions for themselves. This article outlines a process that women have found helpful in making decisions about employment and mothering. Rather than seeking a rule that women should follow, it examines ways of making decisions, which take into consideration the complexity of women's lives and choices.

This study presents the viewpoint of women who are mothers of young children and who face often difficult decisions about motherhood and employment outside the home. In the midst of the many and conflicting voices which tell women what they should be doing as mothers, this study listens for the voice of the mother herself. For some women, their own voice is clear and strong as they make decisions about their lives and their mothering. For others, the cultural scripts, and the many voices which convey them, drown out the woman's own voice, leaving her vulnerable to the conflicts which are inherent in our culture's mixed messages about how to mother.

Cross-cultural evidence indicates that there is tremendous variation in the way work and mothering are organized. Cultures provide a script or a rather specific cultural set of ideas about how events should take place so that members of that culture can be guided through major life events and changes. Though there is never one-to-one correspondence between individual behavior and cultural prescriptions for how and what should take place, the script functions as a map for people in a culture, helping to guide their choices. A script works well when clear cultural expectations are supported by social structures that make it possible for people to carry out their roles in accord with the culture's expectations. When the script is not supported by appropriate social structures, it cannot serve as a useful guide. In a period of rapid social change, there may be a shared belief that following certain scripts continues to be possible and desirable, even though the script has come to contain inherent contradictions.

Japanese and Swedish cultures, for example, present women with very different scripts about how to carry out their roles as mothers, but the two cultures are similar in that they present women with a clear, non-conflictual script of how to deal with employment and mothering, and they provide social structures which support women in carrying out these roles. In Sweden, for example, the general availability of daycare means that the existence of a cultural script that calls for employment on the part of mothers is supported by provision of the means for carrying out the role. Japanese mothers have a very different script to follow in that they are expected to be responsible for not only nurturing their children but also for actively supporting their education. The existence of highly structured learning activities that demand the participation of the mothers --such as Suzuki violin lessons and preparations for children's school examinations--provide the vehicles through which mothers can meet those cultural expectations. Although conforming to such dominant cultural scripts can present problems for individual women whose interests are not compatible with these roles, the existence of a single dominant script and of social structures that support the script leave most women able to fulfill role expectations without experiencing a great deal of conflict.

American culture, in contrast, offers several scripts to women who become mothers. This range of choice can offer opportunities for personal development, but at the same time, the existence of more than one script can pose a dilemma or even a crisis, especially when the scripts are in conflict with one another or are not tied to the realities of women's lives because supportive social structures have not been developed. While many mothers are in the work force, structural supports for employed mothers, such as daycare, flexible work schedules, and adequate maternity and paternity leaves, are only beginning to be developed.

The cultural scripts for mothering in this culture are, increasingly, divergent from new realities of the lives of women who mother. A woman is left with three alternatives in this situation. First, she can try to follow a culturally prescribed script such as the traditional script that calls for the role of selfless wife and mother. Or she can try to follow the newer "superwoman" script that focuses on development of the self in the workplace in addition to being an ideal mother. The third possibility is to try to create ways of mothering that respond, not to a script, but to the reality of one's own family and situation.  In order to follow this course, a woman must be able to define her "own terms" in the decision.

## SCRIPT 1: SELFLESS WIFE AND MOTHER

There are volumes written on mothering.  A virtual flood of literature has focused on mothers and their infants, and developmental psychologists from Bruner to Mahler have emphasized the early years as a time of tremendous importance in a child's development.  In this literature on mother-child interaction, however, the mother appears as a shadowy figure.  Beside the vivid, detailed descriptions of the developing infant is a woman who encourages or discourages the child's development, who smiles approvingly, offers a toy, appreciates or fails to recognize that her child's fingerpainting with the orange juice is a scientific exploration.

The reader of the literature on child development sees a picture of an unidimensional mother figure who appears to exist only in relation to her child.  Turning to the literature on women's experience of motherhood, one would expect to find a representation of a multifaceted individual who has, among other relationships, this singularly important relationship with her child.  Instead, the literature that looks most directly at women as mothers confuses the woman herself with her role as mother, and our sense of the maternal self disappears.  There is, in fact, little study of the mother's self because the maternal role, generally, has been seen to be self*less* (Atta-nucci, 1982; see Chapter 10).  By this definition, it was only a bad, selfish mother who had a self to be studied.

Various schools of thought within psychology have contributed to this notion in different ways.  The child development literature, concentrating on how the child can optimally develop, views other members of the child's environment only as instrumental to the child.  The mother's self in this body of work is invisible.  Other researchers recognized that the mother did, in fact, exist as an individual, and they designed studies intended to describe her experience.  Traditionally, the study of women's experience of first-time mothering has followed women through the transition to motherhood and measured their adaptation to their new role.  Since the cultural definition of motherhood remained relatively static for a number of years, researchers measuring adaptation seldom stopped to ask the question, "Adaptation to what?"

The focus on adaptation to the role of mother led to an emphasis on looking at intrapsychic variables to explain the variation that was found on such measures of adaptation as depression and self-esteem. Inevitably, when women appeared poorly adapted, the tendency was to see what was wrong with *them* rather than question the conditions of the role to which they were adapting. As long as the emphasis was on adaptation, the distinction between self and role was blurred.

Early studies of women's experience of motherhood came out of the psychoanalytic tradition and were influenced by assumptions that came with that theory and that period. One of the earliest writers to look directly at women's experience of mothering through a psychoanalytic lens was Deutsch (1945). She describes pregnancy as a time of extreme introversion during which psychic energies are diverted from the outside world. "With this step," she states, "the polarity between individual existence and service to the species changes its balance in favor of the latter" (p. 138). Given this belief, it is no wonder that she found that "the psychologic difficulty that stands in the way of direct realization of motherhood can have various causes; their most frequent common denominator [is] woman's fear of losing her personality in favor of the child" (p. 47). This tradition is important not only because in describing motherhood through its own lens, it prescribed a correct way to be a mother, but because it has had a powerful and lasting influence on the way that more recent empirical studies of motherhood have been framed.

## SCRIPT 2: IMAGES OF SUPERWOMAN

An alternative that has been presented to the selfless mother script has been the "superwoman" script. The predominant characteristic of the superwoman has been her success in the workplace and her ability to "do it all." The superwoman is seen as making decisions by asking the question, "What is best for me?" In some cases this is really a narrower question that means, "What is best for my career?" "Me" is narrowly defined and, in fact, may simply be instrumental to different others than those whom the selfless mothers serve. This woman may serve the needs of the workplace rather than the needs of her family.

For example, Harragan, a business consultant and author of the book, *Games Mother Never Taught You*, sympathizes with companies that are losing experienced and productive female employees for any amount of time. "I hear stories of women who become pregnant and don't feel very well and so don't work very hard. Then they go off on maternity leave for weeks or even months. That can be hard for the organization." Harragan says she recommends that women not take the fully allowable leave time. "The really ambitious, committed women get back between two weeks to one month" (*Wall Street Journal*, September 19, 1984). Such advice assumes that what is good for the company is good for a woman's career and, thus, is best for her.

While some women succeed in following the superwoman script for a number of years, the advent of motherhood introduces a complication. In order to continue to be successful as superwoman, the same commitment to the workplace that would get a woman back to work within "two weeks to one month" also needs to be made to the baby.

A number of researchers and psychologists, having seen the risks that women experienced in trying to follow the "selfless woman" script, have seen work as the answer for women. Baruch and Barnett (1983), on completion of a large study of mid-life women, advise that, "The best 'preventive medicine' for women against depression is fostering their sense of mastery. The confident, autonomous woman is likely to be less vulnerable to depression" (p. 22). The authors point out that because their findings are based on mid-life women, only 20 percent of their sample have a child under the age of seven. And they caution the reader that "If we had interviewed them at an earlier time, perhaps those with full-time careers would have shown a greater sense of role strain" (p. 149).

Since the cohort of women for whom the superwoman script has been an important formative influence is still rather young, there is less data to turn to in understanding the risks of that position. Baruch and Barnett, for example, found that the major regret of their sample of mid-life women was that they had not taken their work more seriously. The cohort they interviewed had only a few women who had put themselves at risk of making work too central. It is important here to take seriously Giele's (1982) caution that "past negative experiences of middle-aged and older women do not automatically reveal an obverse set of positive developmental steps that each young woman should try in the future" (p. 121).

## AN ALTERNATIVE FRAMEWORK

In order to understand the reality of women in their multiple roles, it will be necessary to turn our focus away from those cultural scripts that are increasingly unconnected to the realities of women's lives and turn toward the experience of women themselves as they make decisions about their lives in relation to cultural expectations and realities. Recognizing that people's lives are "permeated with cultural meanings . . . the focus of interest becomes how people make sense of their lives with ideas drawn from their cultural environment, what kind of order they find there, and how they are affected by conclusions they draw from their culturally-guided introspection" (Levine, 1982, p. 290). As Gilligan (1982) has pointed out, "The meaning of mid-life events for a woman is contextual in the sense that it arises from the interaction between structures of her thought and the realities of her life."

Gilligan has recognized a general developmental progression in the way that women think about moral choices in their lives. She found that, within the context of an ethic of care, women move through a progression of (1) orientation to individual survival, (2) understanding of goodness as self-sacrifice, (3) a move from goodness to truth. It is in the move away from an understanding of goodness as self-sacrifice that women find their own voice and begin to define their own terms.

Attanucci has elaborated the concept of "own terms" in the lives of women who are mothers (see Chapter 10). Her work develops the understanding that thinking in one's own terms involves defining one's terms in the context of caring both for others and for oneself. My study is an application of that concept to a situation of choice and possible conflict in women's lives. It asks the question, "in whose terms" do mothers make decisions about employment and mothering? This conception calls into question the notions of self and development that are implicit in the motherhood scripts described above, which place care of self and care of others in opposition.

Mothering, which brings with it the necessity to make choices that involve the well-being of oneself and others, provides an opportunity to redefine one's understanding of the place of the self in such decisions. The activity of mothering is a particularly interesting place to look at women's thinking about such choices, because cultural definitions of self as autonomous and separate often lead people to encounter the choices in the experience of mothering as being associated with self *or* other.  Because mothering presents women with an opportunity to experience care of others as self-enhancing, it highlights the possibility of finding ways to think about self *and* other.  Care of self and care of others need not be seen as opposing choices.

The focus of this chapter is on women's thinking about combining motherhood with employment outside the home.  This focus was chosen because such issues come up so frequently when women are asked about what choices stand out for them as mothers.  In addition, because employment holds a central place in each of the cultural scripts for mothering, it points out the importance of reaching new understandings about the relationship of maternal self and maternal role as defined by cultural scripts for mothering.  While the ideal mother is supposed to place home above outside work, the superwoman is expected to add total commitment to mothering to total commitment to her job, an obvious contradiction in terms.

## THE STUDY

This study is based on two in-depth interviews with twenty women, all residents of the greater Boston area.  All of the participants in the study were white, college-educated, middle class, married women who were first-time mothers.  They were interviewed around the end of their first year of mothering.  This period was chosen because the women had been mothers long enough to reflect on their experience of the transition to motherhood and the changes it had brought to their lives.  There had been time to adjust to some of the demands of motherhood.  The infants were becoming mobile and assertive.  The employed women had returned from maternity leave and, for the most part, had been back in the work force for a period of time.

The average age of the children at the time of the first interview was just under fourteen months, with a range of nine to eighteen months.  A number of the women spontaneously commented that the end of the first year had seemed to be a kind of marker for them, causing them to reflect on their mothering and to evaluate the way their mothering fit in to the other parts of their lives.

The sample was recruited to consist of women who had been in school or employed full-time outside their homes before they became mothers. It was divided so that there were three groups: one was employed full-time, one part-time, and one was at home full-time at the time of the interviews.

In order to have a sample of women who had been in the work force long enough to have some identity as "workers," it was necessary to recruit a sample that is somewhat older than the average first-time mother in our culture. The average age of the women in this sample was 31.4 years, with a range of 26 to 35 years. The respondents were interviewed twice, with each interview lasting between an hour and a half and two hours. The time lapse between interviews allowed both interviewer and respondent time to reflect on the responses. Often the women elaborated on their first week's responses at the second meeting.

The rest of the interview was modeled on the semi-structured clinical interview. The semi-structured clinical interview has been particularly valuable in formative research on adult development, where the goal is to obtain the respondent's perspective on his or her life. This was of paramount importance in this research, as reviews of the literature made it very clear that women's own perspective on the experience of mothering is glaringly absent. Since this study was designed to explore the ways women think about decisions in their lives and, in particular, the way they think about themselves in those decisions, an interview which allowed the researcher to look at the women's own construction of their experience was needed. This part of the interview focused on questions about choice, self-concept, and change. Women were asked specifically about employment-related decisions and their responses were probed. Because higher depression has been seen as accompanying the transition to motherhood, the Center of Epidemiological Studies depression scale (CES-D) was administered at the end of the second interview.

The narratives in which women described their decisions about employment were analyzed in order to determine whether "own terms" and "not own terms" could be reliably coded in a decision-making process and to allow the testing of three hypotheses. The first hypothesis is derived from the selfless mother script. The work of Deutsch, for example, suggests that women give up their own personality in favor of that of the

child when they become mothers. This implies that it is in responding to
the child that women's voices are lost.

The second hypothesis is derived from the superwoman script, which
places a woman in the professional work world as a way of reinforcing her
sense of self. The third hypothesis suggests that women who use "own
terms" thinking to make the employment decision would be less vulnerable to depression than women who rely on the current cultural scripts for
mothering. Before turning to the coding, I will present four of the women
and their thinking about decisions regarding whether and how much to
work.

## BECKY

In Becky's thinking about her decision to stay at home full-time,
she measured herself against the superwoman cultural norms that she feels
dominate the media but which conflict with her husband's belief that mothers should be at home with their children. In response to the question,
"Looking back over the year since Heather was born, what are the choices
that stand out for you?" Becky said,

> Deciding to stay with Heather more, be with her more than the average woman
> today. I think we measure ourselves against the norm, against other people a
> lot, especially with this issue. There's always a talk show about daycare . . .
> It's come up every time I answer but it's the one thing I've fought with myself
> about.

Asked if she considered any other ways of doing it, Becky continued:

> I felt I wasn't being a supermother and that's the only kind of mother there is
> these days . . . I had the TV on and it made me feel meaningless. What would
> eat away at me was that I didn't have any more choices. We had decided this
> was what I had to do. I felt this was what I had to do, that I didn't have any
> control. I didn't have money, didn't have choices. I really fought with myself
> about it . . . I had to finally say, "I'm tired, this is enough for me."

As she tried to resolve the conflict between the superwoman script that she
felt dominates the culture and the script that her husband believed was
right for her to follow, she adopted the terms of his script. He had pointed out that not only did he think it was right for her to be with Heather,
but also that they would be worse off financially if she had an outside job
at this point. This left Becky with some unresolved contradictions. When
asked who she thought about in making the decision to stay at home, she
explained:

My husband is pretty conservative. He believes I should be home with Heather
. . . and I do too. You're fighting yourself also with what's in vogue, with
what's expected in society and want to be as contemporary as possible. But I've
resolved that and it's fine, just fine. Sometimes I'd say I don't care about the
money. Dan saw it in a practical, logical way, but I felt for my own peace of
mind I needed to work, so perhaps I felt he wasn't thinking of me, only of the
practical view, and sometimes I'd think he's not even thinking of Heather. All
he cares about is the money. But he did have Heather in mind so she was
thought of and perhaps he could see so to be convincing about that.

## MONICA

The outlines of Monica's days and the ways she spent her time were
very similar to Becky's. The way Monica thought about the decision to
spend her time that way, however, was quite different from Becky's. Asked
to describe her decision to stay at home full-time, leaving a responsible and
challenging job, she replied:

It wasn't a hard decision at all. We thought it was real important for one of us
to be here. Bill's job is not suited, nor is he . . . Bill makes enough money.
I look at that as a luxury these days. I didn't want to miss a day of Tim's
growing up, and I felt career and work would be there. I viewed this as a
precious time for my child and myself. I wanted to be able to put energy into
this and not be split. I didn't feel comfortable with the idea of a day-care
center. I wanted to be with him, I wanted to raise him, I wanted to get to
know him. I feel now that my relationship with him is so solid.

Monica's clarity about the fact that it is her own desire to care for
her child helps her acknowledge the benefits of her decision, both for her
child and for herself. Though she also recognizes that there are difficulties
that come with her decision, she is not experiencing conflict about the difficulties she faces.

## HELEN

Helen described her decision to take a full-time job that she didn't
really want when her child was three months old. In response to the question, "Looking back over the year since Sally was born, what are the choices
that stand out for you?" she said:

Getting called back to work, to a job I didn't really want, to me was a very big
point. I felt I would have to put in that year to get back to the school system I
wanted. It's an unfortunate thing that women have to do that, to prove they're
serious about work. If I had stayed home I would have not looked serious to
them about my work.

Knowing that her career was very important to her, and also recognizing that her family needed the income, she decided to take a calculated risk, recognizing the trade-offs. She described the considerations in the following way:

> The superintendent (from my old job) had recommended me and I really wanted to show them I was a person they'd want back. I was thinking of my career. I saw it as a way of proving myself. I took it as a calculated risk. If I'd stayed home they might have wondered if I was the kind of person they wanted. We needed the money with the expenses of my husband's dissertation, and his job is not full-time. And fortunately, I found someone I really liked and who really liked Sally. For Sally it worked out fine. I had a terrible year because I hated the job. Coming home to Sally was always the light at the end of the tunnel.

## PAT

Pat had one of the longest working days of anyone in the sample. She was an attorney and estimated that she worked about fifty hours a week. Pat found that her work really took off at the time her son was born and demanded many more hours from her than she originally had bargained for. Asked to think of a situation during the previous year where she didn't know what was the right thing to do, Pat responded: "There's plenty of those. Actually the most classic one is the one I've been describing" (how many hours to devote to her work and how to set up good child care). She described the conflicts in that situation for her:

> In many ways it's a conflict of my growing up in the 50s, and later the influence of the 70s, and that typical conflict I'm sure you're looking at between the pulls of career and the pulls of being a mother and the responsibilities of each . . . Another conflict is the selfish me versus the giving me . . . we're talking about, you know, my career versus his life. I don't want to be selfish, but on the other hand, I'm being selfish . . .

Asked at this point to explain what she meant by "selfish," she responded:

> When I've always been number one, having to look at someone else as number one. And I'm not doing such a great job I might add. There's this whole . . . you're supposed to feel all this giving and oh, I'm a mother and ergo, you know, my child comes first and I can float down this little path and it's a bunch of bull.

Asked how she evaluated the decision to continue to work and whether she now felt it was the right one, Pat replied:

> Yes. It's the only decision . . . There's a lot of reasons . . . that have to do with self-image also as to why I chose . . . I guess it's the right decision,

even though I feel guilty. Is all this stuff worth more than his well-being?
. . . I'm putting all these things ahead of him, and he's my son and mother's
aren't supposed to do that. You know, mothers are supposed to put their,
especially their nine-month-old, babies first. Then, once kids get older, that's
when you go back and do that. There's this feeling, you know, that even
though a lot of women are working, there aren't that many working with little
tiny babies. And there aren't that many working the amount of hours and the
amount of stress and energy that I have to put into the job which, you know
. . . there's a limited amount of energy, . . . he's not going to get what I
spend. It's the guilt over, I mean, it's the same selfish-ness that I'm putting
myself or all womankind ahead of him.

Because there is not a single, clear cultural script for mothering in this
culture, women's conceptions of cultural norms varied within the sample.
Becky sees herself as out of the mainstream because she is not employed
and spends a great deal of time with her child. Pat, on the other hand,
worries that her pattern of working away from her home for many hours a
week is not in accord with cultural standards, as exemplified in her statement, "there's this feeling that, you know, even though a lot of women are
working, there aren't that many working with little tiny babies."

In the descriptions of decisions about employment, it was possible to
see the women's orientation toward the judgment of others. In some of the
dilemmas the women's investment in what others thought and their wish
to please others overshadowed, or even prevented, them from finding and
hearing their own voices as they thought about the decisions they faced.
These women, struggling to see the self in others' definitions and in others'
expectations, were characterized by an inability to hear the self's own voice
in the self's own terms. For other women, the awareness of others' views
was accompanied by the woman's awareness of her own needs and desires
and by a willingness and ability to hear and be guided by her own voice.

## THE CODING

In order to be able to code systematically for whether or not women
made the decision about employment in "their own terms," a coding system
was developed to examine this aspect of women's thinking. It asks the
question, "Is the decision ultimately made in a way that allows the woman
to include her voice (own terms), or is her voice drowned out so that the
decision cannot include the woman's own terms?"

A critical distinction in this coding system is made between women's
vulnerability to allowing themselves to be judged in others' terms and

women's needs to respond to and care for others. Traditionally, in this culture women have been at risk of losing their own voices in the process of
being submerged in caring for others in the other's own terms, a risk of
following the selfless mother script. In this time of cultural change, however, other voices are also defining women. In a culture where self has
been equated with autonomy, women are also at risk of not hearing and
responding to the voice which emphasizes their own need to be in relationships and to care for others. It is this part of a woman's terms that may
be lost in attempts to follow a superwoman script.

### Deciding in One's Own Terms

The women who made the employment decision by listening to their
own voices and including their own terms were characterized by either one
or a combination of the following:

1. The entire decision was described in a voice which the coder could see
   was clearly the woman's own. The use of the first person was most
   prominent, as was the use of active verbs (I want, it's my choice, I
   see myself, I know). The presence of the woman's own voice by no
   means excluded her awareness of the needs and desires of others.
   Others' needs were considered along with the needs of the self, neither voice drowning out the other. For example, looking back at
   Monica's decision to stay at home full-time to care for her son, this
   kind of clarity could be heard: "I wanted to be with him, I wanted to
   raise him, I wanted to get to know him."

2. In the woman's description of the decision-making process, the coder
   could see that the process was one in which she discovered her own
   terms. The respondent was able to seek an inclusive solution, recognizing the terms of connection to others as well as her own individual
   needs. Connection does not mean subordination of one's own terms
   to others, but an engagement with the other that seeks to find an accommodation of the terms of both. The solution sought is an inclusive
   solution.

   With Helen's decision to take the job so that she would not have
   to sacrifice her career, she was able to contribute to the financial sup-

port of the family and, with good daycare, she could still be assured that her child was happy and well cared for. She took the needs of all three of the family members into account. Though there were other things that they have given up for the time being (time to see friends, reading novels, and maintaining as clean a home as they were used to doing), this decision was made as the best way to care for everyone in an inclusive way, without the sense that someone had been sacrificed.

## Deciding in Others' Terms

The women who did not make the decision in their own voice were characterized by one or more of the following:

1. A nonreflective quality in which other people's terms were accepted and acted upon. The description was characterized by language in the third person ("He says I could," "You have to be," "You just get used to it"), by language of obligation, guilt, and judgment ("Mothers are supposed to," "You're supposed to feel"), and by the use of passive verbs.

2. Hints of the woman's own voice entering into the decision were drowned out by external voices or lost because she herself could not identity her own voice. For example, in listening to Becky, one can hear her sense of what society in general expects mothers to do. "I felt I wasn't being a supermother and that's the only kind of mother there is these days." Equally strong was her husband's voice and his beliefs about the maternal role. "He believes I should be home with Heather." Her own voice, concerned about the fact that she felt she "didn't have any choices" was silenced. as she "had to finally say, ' I'm tired, this is enough for me.' "

3. There was frequently an unconscious denial of the constraints that limited the woman's choices. This denial of the limitations within which she was operating led to internal contradictions within the decision. For example, Becky's statement that "it's fine, just fine" was belied by concerns that she was "fighting with herself" over this decision, that she "felt she didn't have any choices."

## FINDINGS

In this sample of twenty women, twelve were coded as having made the decision about outside employment primarily in their own terms. Eight made the decision predominantly in others' terms. "Own terms" or "not own terms" decisions were coded at 80% reliability. In response to the first hypothesis, it was found that most women were not, in fact, likely to lose their own terms in responding to the needs of their infant. All the mothers who were coded as making the decision about employment in their own terms did consider the needs of the infant in an integral way.

In order to address the second hypothesis, a second part of the coding system was developed to determine what other voices the women considered in making their decision. In the inner dialogue about whether or not to work outside the home, mothers of infants consider the perspectives of a number of other people. Other voices can either drown out the voice of the self or they can inform it. The second part of the coding process asked the coder to look for the presence or absence of any of the following voices in the woman's thinking: (1) self in relation to child, (2) self in relation to husband, (3) self in relation to work, (4) self in relation to own mother, (5) self in relation to authorities on childrearing, (6) self in relation to society and to others in general.

For all of the women in this sample the decision about employment clearly involved the needs both of adults and of the baby. The women described listening to the voice of some adult in the decision-making process, and 90 percent of the sample described thinking about the self in relation to the child. It was not considerations of the baby's needs that led the women to lose their own voice in the decision but the voice of other adults, very often adults who were not directly involved in the decision. Of the eight cases where the decision was not made in the woman's own terms, it was the voices of society, husband, and childrearing experts that defined the terms of the decision. Thus, it was not a woman's perceived needs of her infant that drowned out her own voice in the decision but the voices of others. The others were either directly described by women as "they" or as "society," expressing the terms of a cultural script, or they came through the voice of an important person in the woman's life, as in "my husband thinks I should be home with the baby"--also a cultural script.

Spearman correlations were used in order to see whether there was a correlation between having made the decision about employment in one's own terms and measures of well-being. The women who made the decision in their own terms had lower depression scores on the CES-D ($\rho$ = 0.4, p < 0.05). Thus, it appears that making the decision about outside employment and mothering in one's own terms can provide some protection against depression.

## DISCUSSION

Women who have made the decision about employment and mothering in their own terms describe a mode of thinking that no longer fits into either script. While cultural scripts for mothering see the self of the mother and the self of the child as competing forces, women who are able to make the decision in their own terms recognize their own need to care for the child as aligned with the child's need for care. In this framework the question changes from, "Who do I put first, the child or me?" to "How can I best care for this child and for myself?"

Current cultural scripts for mothering offer definitions of the self that ask the mother to either "give up" the self or sacrifice care of the child in order to develop the self. Since these are the terms of choice which our culture presents to women, it is not surprising that women who try to make choices within that framework appear to be more vulnerable to depression. In fact, the terms of the superwoman script for mothering demand that a woman add self-sacrifice to self-fulfillment. Unless women come to think in their own terms, they are left vulnerable to increasing distance between a self-ideal which embodies conflicting understandings of self, and the reality which they experience. When the distance between self-concept and self-ideal is great, depression is a likely outcome.

Making decisions in her own terms does not eliminate conflict or dilemmas from the woman's relationship with her child; her own needs can still be at odds with those around her. Because the activity of caring in the relationship with an infant is by definition unequal, and the child's needs for care are immediate and compelling, the challenge for the women in this group is to balance the needs of the self with the needs of the child in a way that does not deny the legitimacy of either. This way of thinking offers a framework within which to consider decisions; it does not offer solutions.

While the role-defined way of caring offers an automatic rule to rely upon in resolving conflicts that arise between the needs of the child and the self--the needs of the child always come first--the cost of this ready formula for conflict resolution is that the legitimacy of the self in the relationship is lost. Alternatively, women who do not follow a script by subordinating the self, experience the legitimacy of the self in the relationship and have access to a process for resolving the inevitable conflicts that exist in a relationship between two legitimate selves. Conflicts that arise need to be resolved by attention to both the needs of the self and others, requiring that a woman resist easy answers and live with the ambiguity of judging the rightness of her own response without reference to a ready-made rule.

The power of the cultural scripts for mothering was such that for some women, the scripts dictated not only the way women should care for others, but the way they should care for themselves. Caught in a contradiction that saw care of self as separate, several women described going to dance classes or taking lessons that they hated and were not good at. For one woman these activities were described as "what you're supposed to do to take care of yourself." Real pleasure came into her voice as she described walks that she and her friends took with their children, but these were not seen in her framework as a way of caring for both herself and her child.

The equating of care and selflessness, and the dichotomy which that equation creates between care of self and care of others leaves some women without a forum within which to resolve conflicts between their desires and a role-defined definition of the "right" way to care. The women who experienced the most conflict about the employment decision talked about the way mothers were "supposed to feel." Pat could not get away from seeing herself as "selfish" for working because she has absorbed the role-defined idea of care: "You're supposed to feel all this giving and oh, I'm a mother and ergo, you know, my child comes first and I can float down this little path . . ." She goes on to describe herself as experiencing constant conflict between the "selfish me and the giving me . . . we're talking about, you know, my career versus her life."

Women who were clear about their own terms--those who had made their employment decision in terms of their own and their families' needs rather than by trying to meet the demands of a script--were able to work out a variety of arrangements for mothering that worked for them and their families. In fact, this study found that women who could recognize their own terms were less depressed even when they had limited choices. A woman who could hear her own voice was less at the mercy of cultural prescriptions about how she ought to think and act and was better able to make choices within the constraints of her particular life situation. Given the difficult choices that many women now need to make, these research findings have far-reaching implications and offer hope for innovative solutions to difficult but common problems experienced by many women and families.

## ACKNOWLEDGMENTS

Thank you to Norman, Mara, and Christopher, and to my parents, Mary and Bernard Kinsella. Thank you also to the women who gave generously of their time and shared thoughtful reflection on their experience of mothering.

# 12

## THE VULNERABLE AND INVULNERABLE PHYSICIAN

Carol Gilligan and Susan Pollak

> The essence of being human is that one does not seek
> perfection, that one is sometimes willing to commit sins for the
> sake of loyalty, that one does not push asceticism to the point
> where it makes friendly intercourse impossible, and that one is
> prepared in the end to be defeated and broken up by life, which
> is the inevitable price of fastening one's love on other human
> individuals.
>
> --Orwell, *On Gandhi*

The practice of medicine ideally combines scientific knowledge and
technical skill with intimate personal care. Medicine differs from other high-
status professions in joining the exercise of power with intimate care, just
as it differs from other care-giving occupations in its exalted social status.
For the physician, this conjunction creates two distinct vulnerabilities--the
danger that intimacy will cloud objectivity and over-come professional re-
straint, and the danger that perfection of knowledge and skill will distance
the doctor from human relationships. Although the dangers of intimacy are
well marked in ethical codes and professional texts, the dangers of isolation
remain comparatively uncharted in medical practice and education.

The association of danger with intimacy has a long history in the
Western tradition and appeared in our previous research (Pollak & Gilligan,
1982) to be salient in the fantasies of men. Eighty-eight men and fifty
women in a psychology course on motivation were asked to write imaginative stories in response to pictures on the Thematic Apperception Test

(TAT). The observation of violence in men's stories about intimacy led to a comparative analysis of men's and women's fears pertaining to achievement and affiliation. This analysis revealed that the men in the class projected more danger into situations of close, personal affiliation than into achievement situations. They associated danger with intimacy, expressing a fear of being caught in a smothering relationship or humiliated by rejection or deceit. In contrast, the women in the class saw more danger in impersonal achievement than in personal affiliation and connected danger with the isolation that they associated with competitive success. These contrasting perceptions of safety and danger in attachment and separation led to the identification of fear of intimacy as the corollary to fear of success.

In American medicine ideals of heroic achievement increasingly have overshadowed the value of nurturance and close personal affiliation. Technological advances have repeatedly been gained at the expense of the doctor-patient relationship. This split in medicine parallels a division in the psychological literature on motivation where the needs for power and achievement are counterposed to the need for affiliation. This antagonism generates an illusion that is particularly dangerous for the physician--the image that safety lies in success, and invulnerability can be gained through separation.

While wishes for power, achievement, and affiliation can all be engaged by the practice of medicine, such wishes may have different meanings in the lives of women and men. McClelland (1975), observing differences between men's and women's fantasies of power, concluded that women orient more toward relationships of interdependence while men tend to organize relationships in a hierarchical mode. In their fantasies men tend to associate power with domination, linking assertion to aggression. In contrast, women tend to join power with nurturance, connecting assertion with affiliation--the ability to make and sustain relationships (see also Miller, 1976, 1982). These differences in the way power is imagined by women and men parallel differences observed in conceptions of morality and self (Gilligan, 1977). Specifically, a morality of justice and rights that protects separation contrasts with a morality of care and responsibility that sustains connection, and these two moralities imply different ways of experiencing and understanding power, achievement, and affiliation. A greater tendency for women to focus attention on problems of connection underlies many of the gender differences found in research on identity and moral de-velopment (Gilligan, 1982).

The current study examines how men and women envision the com-ponents of medical practice by asking whether they perceive power and achievement as in conflict with affiliation, or whether they see intimacy and nurturance as consonant with power and success. In our previous study we interpreted the presence of violence in fantasy as indicative of the places where people see danger. In this study, we again use the imag-ery of violence as particularly revealing of people's fears, but extend our analysis to focus on the relationship between achievement and affiliation by analyzing themes of success and failure, intimacy and isolation, both in TAT stories and in interview data.

## METHOD

### Subjects

The main subjects of this study were 236 first-year medical students, 168 men and 68 women enrolled in the medical schools of Harvard Uni-versity and Tufts University. The study itself was part of a longitudinal study of stress and adaptation in physicians (Nadelson, Notman, & Preven, 1983; Notman, Salt, & Nadelson, 1984). During the first week of medical school incoming students were given a series of psychological tests to evalu-ate stress, depression, and so on. Also included was the TAT. In addition, a randomly selected sample of eighty first-year and third-year medical stu-dents was interviewed. All first-year students received the TAT.

### Procedure

The TAT was administered according to the standard group admin-istration format, with the exception that the pictures were included in the test booklet, and the test was not strictly timed. As a result, more time was available for censorship of fantasy and story editing. The pictures chosen for this test were used previously by McClelland (1975) to meas-ure achievement, affiliation, and power motivation. Four pictures appeared in each test booklet; the first three were the same for all of the students, while the fourth picture differed for each half of the group. Gender dis-tribution on this picture was the same.

Four of the five pictures are used in this analysis because they provide suggestions of achievement and affiliation.  One picture is of a man
sitting alone at his desk in a high-rise office building with a picture of his
wife and children on the desk (TAT 1).  The other three pictures show
people together--a couple sitting on a bench by a river (TAT 2), two
women working in a lab (TAT 3), and a man and a woman on a trapeze
(TAT 4).  The man is hanging by his knees and holding the woman's
wrists.  TAT 4 is the only picture where people touch.  TAT 5, a picture
of a ship's captain, was dropped from the study because it measures power
motivation.

The following questions appeared after each picture to serve as guide-
lines for the stories:  What is happening?  Who are the people?  What has
led to this situation?  What has happened in the past?  What is being
thought?  What is wanted?  By whom?  The students were informed that
there were no "right" or "wrong" answers and were instructed to make their
stories "interesting and dramatic."

**The Interview**

The interview was conducted individually and followed the "Méthode
Clinique" developed by Piaget (1932/1965).  The questions included those
designed by Gilligan *et al.* (1982) to assess self-definition and moral judgment.  There were also questions pertaining specifically to stresses encountered in medical treatment and to ideals of medicine and student aspirations.  The interview data were analyzed for recurrent themes of achievement, intimacy, isolation, and death.

**Data Analysis:  TAT**

A simple present-absent scoring system was used for violent imagery,
conceived as imagery that represents a threat to the integrity of the self.
Whenever people wrote about death, suicide, homicide, rape, kidnapping,
physical assault, or fatal disease, the story was scored as "violent."  In the
first analysis, the presence or absence of violence was tabulated for men
and women on each of the four pictures.  In a second independent analysis,
we coded the content of the violent stories in order to determine if danger
was associated with intimacy, isolation, failure, or success.  The following
definitions were established:  *Fear of intimacy*--violence tied to entrapment,

rejection, or betrayal in an intimate relationship. *Fear of isolation*--death or violence was linked to being set apart, left alone, or abandoned. The mention of being orphaned was also coded as fear of isolation. *Fear of success*--violence associated with competitive success. This category contained two subcategories: the effects of success on the men in the pictures and the effects of success on the women in the pictures. *Fear of failure* --violence or death tied to failure in an achievement situation, ranging from failing grades or a failed experiment to an inability to save a dying person or cure a fatal disease.

Death or violence, to be scored, had to be an active component of the story. It was not scored when used in an implied or descriptive manner. An example of an item not scored is the following: "Sally, whose parents passed away when she was young, had just married Jack, a handsome and accomplished acrobat."

## RESULTS

The results summarized in Table 1 show that the men in this sample wrote more violent stories than did the women. Out of a total of 168 men, 45, or 26.7 percent, wrote at least one story that portrayed violent events. For the women, out of a total of 68, 9, or 13 percent, wrote stories that described violent incidents, $\chi^2 (1) = 5.06$, $p < 0.025$.

The distribution of violent imagery across the four pictures reflects the fact that, due to the experimental design, only half of the sample wrote

TABLE 1

*Incidents of Violence in Stories Written by Males and Females*

|  | Violence | No Violence |
|---|---|---|
| Males (N = 168) | 45 (27%) | 123 (73%) |
| Females (N = 68) | 9 (13%) | 59 (87%) |

*Note:* $\chi^2 (1) = 5.06$, $p < 0.025$.

stories to TAT 4. Therefore, the numerical base for the percentage on that card is different. The analysis of the distribution indicates that 17.5 percent of the men (14) saw violence in TAT 4; 13.6 percent (23) projected violent events into TAT 3; 7.1 percent (12) saw violent events happening in TAT 2; and 5.3 percent (9) perceived violence in TAT 1. In contrast, 9.7 percent (4) of the women saw violence in TAT 4, 5.8 percent (4) saw violence in TAT 1; and 1.4 percent (1) perceived violence in TAT 2. No woman projected violence into TAT 3.

Table 2, the content analysis of the TAT stories, shows that the men associated danger with intimacy. Fifteen, or 33 percent, of the men who wrote violent stories connected violence with entrapment, betrayal, or deceit in an intimate relationship. Fourteen men, or 31 percent, wrote stories in which violence was connected with success. This category has two components: fear of success for the women in the pictures, and fear of success for the men. Nine men, or 20 percent, wrote stories in which success for women led to violence. Five men, or 11 percent, connected disaster with men's success, following the pattern of enhancement (success) leading to deprivation described by McClelland (1975) and May (1980). Six men, or 13 percent, of those who wrote violent stories, linked danger with failure; ten men, or 22 percent, saw danger in other situations. No man connected danger with isolation.

TABLE 2

*Content Analysis of Stories Containing Violence:*
*Violence Associated with Intimacy, Isolation, Success, and Failure*

|  | Intimacy | Isolation | Success | Failure | Other |
|---|---|---|---|---|---|
| Males (N = 45) | 15 (33%) | 0 (0%) | 14 (31%) | 6 (13%) | 10 (23%) |
| Females (N = 9) | 0 (0%) | 4 (44%) | 1 (11%) | 1 (11%) | 3 (33%) |

Note: $\chi^2$ (5) = 24.15, p < 0.001.
   Success for women: 9 (20%).
   Success for men: 5 (11%).

In contrast, four of the nine women who wrote violent stories, or 44 percent, connected violence with isolation, associating danger with abandonment or separation. One woman (11%) associated danger with success, and one woman with failure. Three women (33%) perceived danger in other situations. No woman linked danger with intimacy.

## DISCUSSION

The results of this study--the contrasting images of success and failure, intimacy, and isolation in the medical students' TAT stories and interview data--suggest two ways of perceiving and understanding relationships. In this sample, these ways are differentially associated with gender. From the perspective evident more frequently, although not exclusively, in the responses of the men, relationships appeared potentially dangerous. From the perspective taken more frequently, although not exclusively, by the women in the sample, relationships appeared safe. These two perspectives toward relationships have significance both for psychological theories of human development and for medical practice and education.

The need for a change in the perspective toward relationships with respect to understanding psychological development is underscored by the work of John Bowlby, who built on the work of Renee Spitz. Spitz had observed that infants, when isolated from human attachment, often become dispirited and die. Bowlby (1969, 1973, 1980) traced the development of children's capacity to love and linked that capacity to their ability to survive separation and loss without detachment. In Bowlby's view, detachment from others signified a *pathogenic* response to separation, a defense whose cost was extreme. Observing such detachment both in adults and children, Bowlby saw a death of the spirit. Thus, intimacy, which from one perspective carries with it a danger of infection or contamination, from another perspective appears as the condition for psychic health.

For the physician, these two perspectives on intimacy are both heightened. The danger of infection is literal, given the doctor's contact with life-threatening diseases. The danger of isolation is increased by the structure of medical training and practice. Both of these dangers are dramatized in the plays of Chekhov, in which doctors frequently appear. For Chekhov, himself a physician, the doctor's risk of infection on the one hand, and of isolation on the other, illuminates a central dilemma of the human condition. In our sample of medical students, the representation of this dilemma tended to vary by gender; women focused more frequently than men on the dangers of isolation, while men tended to consider more saliently the risks of connection. In discussing this contrast and its implications for medical education, we begin with Chekhov as a reminder of the universality of the dilemma we portray and also as a way of calling attention to the fact that the differences we describe, although best illustrated in our data by comparisons between males and females, are not gender specific. In this sample of contemporary medical students, however, they are gender related.

The tension between fear of intimacy and fear of isolation haunts the doctors in Chekhov's plays. They struggle in the face of defeat to remain connected to life, and they describe the temptation to avoid suffering by becoming invulnerable to pain, the temptation to numb their feelings with drink or distance themselves from human relationships. In the plays, this search for invulnerability creates the greatest vulnerability of all. Chebutykin, the doctor in "Three Sisters," detaches himself from suffering and pain as he speaks about a patient's death:

> They think I can treat anything just because I'm a doctor, but I know positively nothing at all . . . Last Wednesday I attended a woman at Zasyp. She died, and it's all my fault that she did die. Yes . . . I used to know a thing or two twenty–five years ago, but now I don't remember anything. Not a thing. Perhaps I'm not a man at all, but I just imagine that I've got hands and feet and a head. Perhaps I don't exist at all, and I only imagine that I'm walking about eating and sleeping. (Weeps.) Oh, if only I could stop existing. (1964, p. 229)

At the end of the play, Chebutykin announces another death, telling the three sisters that his friend the baron has been killed in a duel. As the sisters begin to weep, asking about the death of his friend, he turns away, asking what difference it makes.

> I'm tired . . . Let them cry for a bit . . . Tararaboom di–ay, I'm sitting on a tomb–di–ay . . . What difference does it make? (Reads the paper.) What does it matter? Nothing matters! (p. 330)

In contrast, Astrov, the doctor in "Uncle Vanya," also tempted to distance himself from suffering, pain, and defeat, describes instead how his feelings "woke up."

In ten years I have become a different man. And what is the reason? I am overworked, nurse . . . I haven't grown stupider, my brains, thank God, are in the right place, but my feelings somehow have grown numb. There's nothing I want, nothing I need, nobody to love . . . I was hard at it all day, never sat down, didn't have a bite to eat and when I came home, they wouldn't let me rest, they brought in a railroad switchman; I put him on the table to perform an operation and then he ups and dies on me under the chloroform. And just when I didn't need any feelings, my feelings woke up, my conscience was stricken, as if I had killed him deliberately . . . I sat down, closed my eyes-- like this--and I thought; those who will live one or two hundred years after us, and those we blaze the trail for now, will they remember us with a kind word? (1964, p. 188)

These Chekhovian doctors point to different conceptions of physician vulnerability: one is rooted in the fear that intimacy will erode objectivity; the other in the fear that the practice of medicine will distance the doctor from human relationships. The characters of Astrov and Chebutykin illustrate this contrast and frame our discussion of medical students' fears of intimacy and isolation.

Variations on two "vulnerabilities"--the fear that intimacy will compromise professional practice and the fear that isolation will diminish the doctor's capacity for relationships--ran through virtually all the interviews with third-year medical school students. The TAT stories of first-year students, thus, can be seen to foreshadow conflicts that preoccupy doctors in training, conflicts around issues of vulnerability, intimacy, isolation, and the costs of failure and success.

Among our sample of medical students, the approach to these issues appeared to vary somewhat by gender. In this study, both men and women projected violence most often into TAT 4, the picture of the acrobats on the trapeze which explicitly joins achievement with connection (to succeed the acrobats must hold on). Violent stories written in response to the other three pictures, however, showed a greater tendency for the men in this sample to associate danger with intimacy and for the women to associate danger with isolation, the same tendency we found in our previous research (Pollak & Gilligan, 1982, 1983, 1985).

**The TAT Stories**

The stories which entering medical students wrote about the picture of the man alone at work suggest some of the ways they imagine professional success. Violent stories written by the men in response to this picture link high achievement with disaster, replicating the pattern McClelland and May have identified as characteristic of male fantasies, a sequence they call "enhancement followed by deprivation." This pattern is exemplified by the following story:

> This architect recently designed a multimillion dollar hotel which was constructed as a secluded resort in the Rocky Mountains. At the grand opening of the resort which was acclaimed to be an architectural triumph were wealthy and distinguished people. Arsonists set fire to the kitchen in an insurance fraud attempt, but the fire spread uncontrolled killing forty-seven people. The architect's family was killed. He is now designing a church.

The non-violent stories men wrote about this picture depict success as being in conflict with close personal relationships. Although not eventuating in disaster, success was associated with problems in personal relationships. A common theme was that a man's success would lead to divorce or marital strain, with achievement resulting in increasing separation from family relationships.

Women medical students wrote stories about this picture that revealed different concerns. Themes of loss, abandonment, and isolation predominated. The following violent story written by a woman illustrates how problems of disconnection (loss, death, and isolation) are seen as interfering with achievement and success. Rather than achievement leading to personal disaster, as in the men's tales, problems in relationship, for the women, compromise the ability to work.

> Jim is a mechanical engineer. He is married and has two young children. His wife was recently diagnosed with breast cancer, and the prognosis is not very good. Recently Jim has had trouble concentrating on his work and finds himself looking at his family photo. Luckily, his superiors are quite understanding and are trying to put as little pressure on him as possible. When Jim looks at the picture he feels many things: he realizes how important his wife is and how much love for his children he feels. He realizes how much he depends on his wife. He feels a panicky sick feeling in his stomach at the thought of her death. He is trying to be optimistic about her therapy.

Conflicts portrayed between love and work appeared in descriptions of entrapment and betrayal in the stories male students wrote about TAT 2, the picture of the couple on the bench. For example, in the following story about fatal disease, the narrator describes how he begins to detach himself from his girlfriend and her dying mother in order to start his medical career.

> This situation could be my girlfriend and I talking about her difficulties with
> her family situation. Her mother is dying and the entire family has to move
> from a farm in Vermont to Florida. Her mother has probably a year or two to
> live but has just had heart failure and may die at any time. I've listened and
> sympathized with her feelings although I'm not that helpful because I have to
> leave soon to go to medical school. The situation resolves itself as both she
> and I admit that we have careers to pursue but that we will keep in contact.

Men's non-violent stories about the couple suggest fears that intimacy will interfere with their professional aspirations. Like Chebutykin in "The Three Sisters," these contemporary medical students describe ways of maintaining distance from others in order not to be affected by their suffering.

Only one woman projected violence into the scene of the couple on the bench. In contrast to men's stories about conflict between personal connection and professional achievement, women medical students often wrote unabashedly romantic stories about love and marriage. Some saw a rendez-vous in Paris on the banks of the Seine, some wrote of blissful relationships between couples who lived "happily ever after." In the single violent story written by a female, a woman is stabbed by a mugger but then is comforted by her lover as she recovers in a hospital bed.

The difference between the stories written by these men and women medical students is most marked in response to the picture of the two women in the lab. Stories written by men portray conflicts between success in scientific work and the feelings aroused by personal relationships. The following story illustrates a recurrent theme: A woman's commitment to her career and interest in her work is associated with problems in family relationships.

> The woman in front of the test tubes tirelessly continues her experimentation
> in biochemistry. She is moved by the wish to discover even one clue to the
> puzzle she has been facing. Excluded from her range of thought are the
> problems at home--the loss of her husband's faculty appointment, the trouble
> she is having with her teenage son, etc. This is a world she has "successfully"
> kept separate from the business at hand, or so she thinks. The woman behind
> her watches her without yet being noticed. She has sensed that her colleague
> may be in pain, but remains silent. The lab is a poor place for people to
> speak and feel. This has disturbed her from the start of her voyage into sci-
> ence. And she has persuaded others to reveal more of themselves while still
> wearing the scientific garb. But this one seems impenetrable. So steadily she
> works. So quietly she pursues. Where is her life? Where are her feelings
> and promises? And how can she and others be invited to be themselves and
> not so rigidly divide their personal selves from their professional ones? The
> observer will move in softly, speaking first of herself and then patiently
> inquiring of her too-preoccupied neighbor.

The story suggests that success for women is dangerous to men and that
the lab--"a poor place for people to speak and feel"--is dangerous for
women.  The split between working and speaking or feeling appears in
other stories as well, which also stresses the consequences of this division
for women--an increasing isolation and the curtailment of their capacity for
nurturing relationships.  In one story the scientific work leaves the women
"strangely isolated from each other"; in another story the problem is seemingly solved by the older woman who has "no apparent concerns for social
life and home ties."  Her protege, the younger woman, marries another
scientist who "shares her disposition," but they do not have children despite
"a nagging suspicion that she cannot go through life without the stimulation
others seem to enjoy in social areas . . . She deals with this by immersing
herself in work."

In other stories written by men, the women in the labs are described
as "ex-nuns," or portrayed as having lost all vestiges of compassion or
concern in their struggle for success.

> The woman performing the experiment is a post-doc, and she is incredibly
> nervous.  The other woman is a bitchy, tenured professor who has no sym-
> pathy for women in science and is extra hard on them.  She has obtained her
> position only through years of toil and against the considerable resistance of
> her male co-workers.  But now it seems that other women can achieve this
> goal without having to pay the price that she had to pay.  She is compelled
> by this apparent injustice to make things tough for this girl.
>     The experiment is extremely trivial and the post-doc will make a lot
> of errors.  She will keep hoping that the prof will turn out to be a secretly
> sympathetic stoneface, but she is really a terrible bitch.  She will write the
> post-doc terrible letters of recommendation.  The prof never does experiments
> herself because she has a keep-clean fetish.

This split between achievement and nurturance is sometimes associated
with violence in the men's tales.  The following story illustrating this association ends with a "mysterious" and fatal disaster:

> This scene shows Jane Nathanson, an eminent chemist of the late 1800's, and
> her assistant Eva Hanfmann.  Both are intently involved in their work and
> have made great sacrifices in other areas.  Neither has married, and both spend
> fourteen-hour days in the lab.  Jane is on the brink of a breakthrough that
> could lead to the development of molecular biology.  Looking back now we
> know that she failed, as she and the laboratory were destroyed by a mysterious
> explosion.

In contrast to the twenty-three men whose stories about the two
women in the lab contained murder, death, suicide, gun fights, and sabo-
tage, no woman medical student projected violence into this scene.  Women

wrote stories in which the relationships between the women were not only safe but were also the key to the women's success. Friendship between the women mediated their loneliness and tempered the possibility of defeat. The following story illustrates this potential in relationships and exemplifies women's portrayal of the affinity between professional achievement and human connection:

> Ms. Gibson was known among the students as the "terror." She was reputed to fail over half of the medical students who took her course. It was Michelle's first day in the lab and she was having some trouble pipetting the solution. Suddenly, she became aware of the piercing eyes of Ms. Gibson. In her confusion she dropped her pipette which shattered into a thousand fragments, spraying Ms. Gibson's spotless white lab coat with the bright red eosin stain. Michelle began to apologize, shaking in anticipation of the consequences. To her incredulous surprise, Ms. Gibson smiled and said, "It takes everyone some time to learn to use the equipment. I'll get something to clean up the mess while you continue to experiment." This was the beginning of a life-long friendship between Michelle and Ms. Gibson.

Given these contrasting perceptions of social reality among the men and women medical students we studied, and given that until recently, medicine has been a male-dominated field, women's stories often sound naive, even to the women themselves. Yet women's perceptions of professional achievement and personal connection as essentially interdependent draws attention to a theme displayed on TAT 4, the picture of the acrobats on the trapeze. This was the picture to which the medical students most often wrote violent stories. When written by men, the violent stories contained a theme of mysterious accident and inexplicable cause--that is, the violence appeared unpredictable and disconnected from preceding events. The following story illustrates this theme:

> When their arms grasp each other they both feel an electricity running through their bones. They are the best husband-wife team of acrobats in the world. They love the circus more than anything else except for each other. Married for seven years they have suffered through the problems that circus people inevitably meet. Together they handled most of them, were hurt by others. It was the most beautiful years of their lives. Below them looking up is their only child. A six-year-old in the circus can feel respect, for he has seen what most adults never see in a life time. And he is about to see the most terrifying spectacle of his short life.
>   It is the last stunt in the act and the most dangerous. All the circus advertisements called the townspeople to see the Great Harrambe team laugh in the face of death. She made a perfect jump into his strong arms and the electricity flowed once more. But thousandths of a second later for inexplicable reasons the grip broke and the woman he loved soared to the ground--without a sound. He reached out. He could grab her. He must.

> He would.  Like two fallen birds they were hurled to the ground by the
> mysterious force Gravity.  Together.

In contrast, the violence in stories written by women is explained.
Women's explanations for the violence they portray pertain to dangers of
detachment.  In addition, women often link violence with a demonstration
of how affiliation and achievement can safely converge.  The following
story shows how violence on the trapeze is prevented and links the prevention of violence to increased closeness rather than to separation or detachment.  Failure and aging change relationships but the "silently shared
knowledge of how difficult this is . . . adds a new dimension to (their)
relationship."

> This father and daughter team is part of a family acrobatic group who are
> natives of Eastern Europe but travel with a second-rate circus through
> Western Europe.  This girl has performed with her family since she was five
> but has become the star of the troupe in the last couple of years.  She has
> always been very close to her father and loves and respects him deeply.  She
> is concerned that his strength and agility are beginning to fade although he
> seems unaware of it.  She wishes she could discuss it with him but she knows
> that he has yet to face the fact that his performing career is nearly over.  Even-
> tually he begins to drop her in practice and the family decides that her older
> brother should act as her catcher while the father becomes her full-time coach.
> The silently shared knowledge of how difficult this is for her father adds a
> new dimension to her relationship with him.

Even in violent stories written by women, the healing power of human
connection and the possibility of transforming relationships are predominant
themes.  In one story, a woman orphaned in childhood is taken in and nur-
tured by a family of clowns.  She grows up to marry their son who also
becomes her partner on the trapeze.

Instead of linking intimacy with danger, these women's stories demonstrate how intimacy can assuage loss and separation.  Danger lies in severing relationships, which creates a hidden wound, an inner detachment.  As
mending relationships becomes part of the narrative, violence appears both
inexplicable and preventable.

### The Interviews

While the TAT provides evidence of the unconscious fantasies, hopes,
and fears of students beginning their medical training, interviews with the
third-year medical students suggest their conscious struggles with their med-

ical education.  In these interviews, women's voices speak most forcefully about resistance to detachment, the refusal to be numbed by the stresses of medical practice, which Astrov articulates in Chekhov's play.

Mary describes a philosophy of the doctor-patient relationship that she recalls was inculcated on the very first day of medical school, a philosophy that centers on maintaining distance.

> As soon as we entered medical school, we had crossed the divide, and I guess it just relates to the larger issue of establishing distance, how much of a distancing process between the doctor and patient is taught from the first day and how throughout medical education one is encouraged to think of themselves as different and distinct from the patient.  Always calling the person who sought help "The Patient," that is a reflection of that philosophy.

To Mary, the image of "the doctor" as superhuman implies that the doctor should not resent demands made by the patient.  Yet she questions how she can "do it all," how she can achieve a responsiveness to her own needs and desires and also to the needs of others for care.  Mary's understanding of care and responsiveness in the doctor-patient relationship implies a doctor who is

> . . . competent and responsible, doing all the right things for my patients, and then equally important, is being a wise doctor in terms of an understanding doctor and a doctor who can be leaned on, a doctor who provides just the right things emotionally for my patients.  A rested doctor.  A doctor with enough time to really be there for patients.  Not a stressed doctor.

To Mary, personal connection and professional achievement seem consonant and interdependent.  Yet, within the structure of medical training, affiliation may appear an impediment to success.

Janet elaborates on the danger of this split to both doctor and patient and points to this division as the basis of physician impairment.  Asked to describe herself, Janet speaks of this tension:

> A person with concerns.  A person who really wants to accomplish something, but not at the cost of being a totally isolated, alone character.  It is not worth it.  What good does it do to save the whole world if you lose your soul? What good does it do to be the best kind of doctor one can think of if you love no one?  And if you can have no one in your personal life that you care about and live for, what good is it?  You can't take patients home with you, you know.

Rendering these concerns more specific, two other women talk about their experiences with patients' deaths.  Sharon says she never gets used to it:

> Well, I think that you don't get used to it. I think every time it really hurts.
> Every patient that I had die has really hurt me in a sense. I find myself
> getting a little shaken by it. I don't think you really get used to it. You
> have to learn to care for your patients. But they can die on you and when
> they die, you can't let that keep you from helping other patients. So you just
> have to sort of keep going and realize that you have done the best that you
> could do, and that's not always good enough, and just go on from there.

Julia describes her sadness when a patient died and talks about how
hard it was "to be faced with that emptiness."

> Here he is dying, and like five seconds ago we were working so hard to keep
> him alive and now he is dead. And he has no clothes on and the nurses are
> pulling all his lines and doing all this stuff to him and I just remember seeing
> this little cold body and it was so sad. Everybody was leaving him and I like
> wanted to crawl into bed and put my arm around him or something like that it
> was so sad. Like now he had to be off and do all this stuff by himself, and
> that was hard and I cried, but my resident was pretty good . . . What if I was
> the intern and had to go to tell the little old Italian lady and I felt like I prob-
> ably wouldn't want to be crying, so I felt bad for crying . . . and you just
> start realizing that we don't do that much. It was the first time I felt there
> wasn't anything we could do. We had done everything we could do, there
> wasn't any more. He was going to sit there and die. That was real hard, to
> be faced with that emptiness. I saw how shallow, how really little we do for
> people.

In the face of death, the illusion of the omnipotent, superhuman doctor
falls away. Yet as a third-year medical student, Julia "felt bad for crying"
and wondered if she could do this as an intern. Would the display of her
emotions, she asks, cause the family to be more upset?

The women students in this study struggled explicitly to hold professional achievement and human connection together. The following
TAT trapeze story, written by Rachel, illustrates how achievement and
connection can, in fact, be in harmony. Yet Rachel dismisses her story as
"corny."

> It's amazing how much I have to trust this guy. Every evening we go through
> this act, every evening my life is in his hands--if you'll excuse the pun.
> Everyone said I would grow tired of circus life, tired of him. But neither has
> happened and I don't think it ever will. Harmony. The key to our work.
> The key to our marriage. We must work together on the ropes, because a
> movement out of synch might cost us our lives. And a loss of that harmony
> in the house would cost us a marriage. The circus is small, crowded and
> packed with tension. Through each other we dissolve the tension. (P.S. This
> is disgustingly corny. But what can I do? No one will ever read this diary
> anyway.)

Judging her voice as "corny" and, thus, better unheard, Rachel displays
her willingness to abandon her own perceptions in favor of the more prev-

alent view that people cannot dissolve the tension between high achievement and close personal connection. At the same time, Rachel's qualified articulation of a different perspective suggests that the division between nurturance and achievement, especially in a healing profession, may be of particular consequence for women. One indication at the extreme may be the far greater incidence of suicide among women physicians than among other women in the population. Given the differences observed in this sample between the fears expressed by women and men and the contrast between their perceptions of success and failure, each sex may be differentially affected by current practices in medical education. As medical schools seek to improve and humanize medical education, support and confirmation for women may bring a different perspective on what constitutes achievement, power, and affiliation. Women's perceptions about the healing power of relationships and their vigilance to the dangers of detachment may both explain greater stress among women doctors and may provide a new understanding of physician vulnerability and success.

Ironically, it is the invulnerable physician who appears to be the most vulnerable of all. Ibsen portrayed the view of the doctor as heroic in his capacity to stand alone. The character Dr. Stockman, the "enemy of the people," is ostracized by the people of the town for his refusal to conceal the pollution of the baths, the major source of the local revenue. He ends the play with the following definition of strength: "And the essence of it, you see, is that the strongest man in the world is the one who stands most alone" (1964, p. 386). In contrast, Dr. Rieux, the physician in Camus's novel *The Plague*, offers a vision of strength as tied not to the ability to stand alone but to the willingness to be infected by others and broken up by life.

> When I entered this profession, I did it "abstractly" so to speak; because I had a desire for it, because it meant a career like another, one that young men often aspire to. Perhaps, too, because it was particularly difficult for a workman's son, like myself. And then I had to see people die. Do you know that there are some who refuse to die? Have you ever heard a woman scream "Never!" with her last gasp! Well, I have. And then I saw that I could never get hardened to it. I was young then, and I was outraged by the whole scheme of things, or so I thought. Subsequently, I grew more modest. Only, I've never managed to get used to seeing people die. That's all I know.

The inclusion of women in psychological theory and research has brought about a change in the understanding of human motivation, given women's tendency to align achievement with close personal connection or affiliation. Similarly, the increasing number of women entering the medical profession prompts a rethinking of medical education. Like the canaries taken into mines to reveal the presence of unseen dangers, women medical students in their heightened sensitivity to detachment and isolation often reveal the places in medical training and practice where human connection has become dangerously thin. Women's concerns about connection, however, may also invoke the specter of disconnection, with the result that women may be reluctant to initiate conflict and change.

If women currently articulate a perspective which links achievement with attachment, women physicians may help to heal the breach in medicine between patient care and scientific success. For this reason the encouragement of women's voices and the validation of women's perceptions may contribute to the improvement of medical education. Since humanism in medicine depends on joining the heroism of cure with the vulnerability of care, reshaping the image of the physician to include women constitutes a powerful force for change.

# 13

## WOMEN LAWYERS: ARCHETYPE[†] AND ALTERNATIVES

Dana Jack and Rand Jack

### INTRODUCTION

Our work arises out of the conjunction of two events--recent findings
in developmental psychology which show that women and men often construct differing moral orientations, and the rapid increase of women entering the legal profession.  How does an individual lawyer's moral perspective
interact with the demands of professional role?  What is the relationship
between a lawyer's personal morality and the way that person practices
law, encounters conflicts in legal work, and adjusts to being an attorney?
As women enter the legal system, do they bring with them a moral orientation which is in tension with the presuppositions of that system?  Do the
institutions of law remold those who come with contrary ways of valuing
and thinking or does the tension persist?  What are the consequences of
this kind of tension, both for the individual attorney and for the legal
system?

These questions guided our study of moral choice and conflict in the
practice of law of thirty-six attorneys.  Eighteen women--all the women
practicing in a county in the northwest--were matched with eighteen male
lawyers on the basis of length and type of practice.  The lawyers were
interviewed in depth about their decision to practice law, their experience

---

[†]The word "archetype" is not used here in the Jungian sense but rather in its more
traditional meaning suggesting an original model after which others are patterned.

of law school, how legal practice affected their relationships, their experience of self, and their understanding of morality and justice. In addition, we asked them to describe moral dilemmas encountered in the practice of law as well as to respond to two hypothetical moral dilemmas designed to measure care and rights reasoning. In this article, part of the larger study, we consider only the women's perspective and describe the patterns of women's adjustment to the role of lawyer.

## THE RULES OF THE GAME: PREPARATION OF THE PLAYERS

When lawyers talk about their work, they commonly liken it to a game. People in other professions that affect people's lives--doctors, teachers, therapists, ministers, scientists--seldom use the term game to describe what they do. For attorneys, the metaphor is apt, in part, because law can be understood as a contest with rules, winners, and losers. If we take the metaphor seriously, what does it tell us about the nature of the contest, about qualifications to play, about training of the players, and about who owns the game?

In 1932 Swiss psychologist Jean Piaget observed that childhood games offer a window for understanding the moral development of children. He noted marked gender differences, especially in how children related to game rules. Boys stuck to the rules, resorting only to "legal elaborations," while girls emphasized harmony and invented new rules to suit their play. Of girls' attitude toward rules, Piaget wrote: "A rule is good so long as the game repays it" (1932/1965, p. 76). When faced with an argument over the rules, girls ended the game, starting over or finding something else to do; boys argued their way through the dispute with continual reference to "the rules of the game." Girls sought to preserve the relationships of the players, while the boys maintained the rules. Taking boys as the standard, Piaget judges girls as lacking. "The most superficial observation is sufficient to show that in the main the legal sense is far less developed in little girls than in boys" (p. 69).

In our culture boys play competitive games with clear rules and winners and losers. Boys learn to "depersonalize the attack," to compete against friends and cooperate with people they dislike. Team games teach boys emotional discipline--self-control rather than self-expression. Boys tend to practice adversarial relationships and organizational skills necessary to coordinate large groups.  In contrast, girls most often play cooperatively in pairs, with no explicit goal, no end point, no winners.  Competition is indirect, and taking turns produces comparisons rather than winners and losers.  Girls' games reinforce nurturant skills, expressions of personal feelings, cooperation rather than competition.  Girls *play* more than boys; boys *game* more than girls (Lever, 1976, p. 482).

Parents and coaches have told many generations of boys that sports build character, teach respect for rules, engender a sense of healthy competition, thus preparing them for life in a depersonalized, adversarial society.  Though they usually do not, mentors might add that these attributes all provide the first stage of pre-law training.  Until recently relatively few girls got this same message or this kind of childhood practice for skills useful in the lawyer game.

Early pre-law preparation takes place at home as well as on playing fields.  Intimate childhood relationships affect boys and girls differently.  Because they are of the same sex as their primary caretaker, girls form their sense of gender through identification with sameness.  For boys, establishment of masculine identity requires separation and differentiation from a female primary caretaker.  To affirm masculinity, young boys distance from and devalue "feminine" characteristics; to strengthen femininity, girls affirm their connectedness.  The similarity to their mothers gives girls a firm basis for empathetically experiencing as their own the needs and feelings of others.  On the other hand, gender development leads boys to value separateness, autonomy, objectivity.  The differing psychological tasks required for gender development lead to certain differing personality traits and moral perspectives in women and men.  "In any given society, feminine personality comes to define itself in relation and connection to other people more than masculine personality does" (see Chodorow, 1978; Gilligan, 1982; Miller, 1984).  Because of these different developmental paths and social contexts, women also develop distinct ways of knowing, valuing, and understanding (Belenky *et al.*, 1986).

From early childhood, then, our culture prepares females and males for different roles.  For boys, pre-law training begins almost from birth--in the home, on playing fields, in relation to peers.  For girls, these same influences instill different values, different ways of assimilating and responding to life's experiences.  Each gender receives its own gifts and its own ways of making sense out of life. Most boys gain a vision suited for a world of advocacy, stoic detachment, autonomy, and suspension of emotional judgment. Girls' development usually instills sensitivity to others' feelings, cooperation, involvement, and contextual understanding.

Such broad generalizations obviously admit many exceptions. Despite exceptions, these generalizations describe patterns in our society which have arisen out of particular cultural contexts and historical realities. In a culture of inequality, the danger is that sex differences such as these may be used to justify the relegation of women to secondary status. This danger is acute when the stereotypes are taken as normative rather than descriptive; that is, as the way things should be rather than simply as the way things have been.

Not only do girls play different kinds of games, but women learn that in law practice, feminine ways of participating are not welcome. If they want to play, it has to be by the men's rules. One of these rules, the requirement for emotional detachment, reinforces the attitude that law is a game to be played for its own sake. Furthermore, the adversarial nature of law makes it easy to maintain personal distance. "You win some and you lose some" (Fox, 1978). From an attorney's point of view, moral neutrality is easily reinterpreted to mean "it's just a game," even though the stakes are often high and lawyers get deeply invested in the contest. When taking part in a game, it is hard not to become preoccupied with winning, by whatever the prescribed rules. It is difficult to examine the premises behind the rules that govern the play, even if the rules are personally demeaning.

If the values learned by women at home and in play make them vulnerable in a predominantly male profession, one solution has been that some women have attempted to eradicate "feminine" characteristics. For example, a female partner in a larger firm advises, "Don't think of yourself, or allow anyone to think of you, as anything but a hard-driving, capable lawyer." In *The American Bar Association Journal*, "female" characteristics are simultaneously designated and demeaned, as women are counseled to "hide" those which disrupt the masculine culture. Current rules specify how women should think, talk, dress, and act.

> Dress and talk in a conservative and professional style. Avoid wrap-around skirts, casual shoes or hair color changes. Dress like a lawyer, in a conservative suit. Don't chew gum. When called "dear" or flirted with in business meetings or professional settings, respond only with entirely professional and

> business-like statements, so that all communications are place [sic] on and remain on a highly professional plane. (Strachan, 1984, p. 95)

Femininity here is associated with liability and with "silly" characteristics which detract from professionalism, which is equated with male behavior. Generally missing from the literature are positive feminine traits or an acknowledgment of the positive differences women may introduce to the attorney role.

The general social devaluation of femininity prepares women entering law to separate from the disliked characteristics of their sex and align with the culture, against the feminine attributes within themselves. Particularly in the legal profession, which prides itself on objectivity, professionalism, and combativeness, traditional feminine traits are unacceptable. For many women this results in an internal tension of "me/not me" when they define themselves as feminine yet try to negate within themselves the stereotypes which discount them in the legal world.

The possibility that women may place relationships over success at some point in their careers calls them into question in a male dominated profession. As one lawyer who had followed the traditional male path to success wrote:

> While most male lawyers are assumed to be serious and to be embarking on a lifelong career, females still are viewed as question marks who may quit and stay home to raise children. Each woman therefore must establish herself as a committed and competent professional and convince each judge and opposing counsel that she means business and is in the profession to stay. Top quality, hard work will do this. Work longer and harder on tough assignments. Don't shirk late hours or weekend projects. Don't go home to cook dinner--or if you do, don't tell anyone. Get the work done on time, and in the best possible manner. (Strachan, 1984, p. 94)

In other words, not only do women have to play by men's rules, they have to play longer and harder to earn the right to compete on equal terms. Family roles must be kept invisible, not to intrude on professional life. For women in law, rejecting a one-sided emphasis on professionalism in order tc affirm interrelatedness, cooperation, and involved concern carries the liability of being dismissed as a "question mark" within the profession. The safest way to success is emulation of males, even to the extent of learning to "speak louder and lower" and "actively becoming an intimidator" (M. Gilligan & Luchsinger, 1986).[1]

Ann, a public defender we interviewed, makes clear how important following the rules is for practicing law. "I have agreed to play by the rules of the game and the day that I cannot do that anymore I will have to quit being a lawyer." The rules she follows include not only professional ethics and procedural standards, but other, unwritten norms governing attitudes and behavior. In order to succeed, women may have to adopt the stereotypic image of the adversarial attorney, an image which excludes feminine characteristics.

As women experience a clash between their values and those of the legal game, they are beginning to express discomfort with what it takes to be a successful lawyer.[2] The conflict surfaced at Yale Law School in 1984 when a number of women and minority law students documented their "dissatisfaction and alienation" in an open letter to the law school community.[3] As our interviews might have predicted, they identify alienation as the opposite of feeling "connectedness, belonging, engagement . . ." Noting their success as law students, the women assert that "for many this success comes at a price--a price, paid gradually and often silently, of alienation and disillusionment." These students cited the "combative, monopolizing and self-promoting style of discussion" encouraged in the classroom as a source of alienation.

> The voice that troubles us is the monolithic, confident voice of "insiders" who see themselves as the norm and who have (often unconsciously) little tolerance for our interest in diversity and difference. This voice, tone, style is often defended as "the way lawyers speak" . . . to the extent that this *is* the way lawyers speak, *we* must conclude that we cannot be lawyers--or that we cannot be ourselves.

The students bring a perspective to the law which generates a compelling dilemma: forsake the law, or forsake the self. Because the adversarial structure of legal discourse precludes the voice of cooperation and interdependence, women and men with such an orientation risk alienation. They are the outsiders and theirs is the different voice. These women recognize that law school offers only one alternative of how to be a lawyer. If they want to practice law in different ways, they must invent those for themselves. With insight perhaps most possible before law school has fully done its work, the Yale women are saying that legal education has an obligation to help invent alternatives to a "combative" style and not simply to excommunicate those with a different perspective. (Yale Law School responded by securing a Rockefeller Foundation Grant for a two-year study on "Gender and Professional Socialization: Issues in Law and Legal Education." The goal is "To study whether, and if so how, the style, motivating values and content of legal education and the legal profession place insufficient emphasis on the perspective and values of women, thus leading to alienation and professional dissatisfaction on the part of women law students and lawyers.")

Both we and the Yale law students detail a set of problems which fall disproportionately on women. As the primary practitioners of care morality, women are the attorneys who most often experience the gap between personal morality and the role which they are supposed to play. What price do women pay for mimicking the male, and at present, the only officially sanctioned version of the lawyer role? Are there other alternatives compatible with remaining in the profession? Can care-oriented women reshape the role to make it compatible with their personal values? Is it possible to protect both relationships and rules, to be caring advocates?

The women we interviewed describe different patterns of adjustment to the practice of law. For the most part, all play by the rules of the game, but at the same time they acknowledge conflict and the need to modify professional expectations. We begin with the story of Jane, a woman who tried to deny her caring self in order to be a lawyer, as defined by men's rules. More than any other woman we interviewed, she accepted the male model and tried to mold herself to fit its dictates. She did this well and was rewarded with professional success. We use her story to illustrate both the pressures women face to copy male behavior, and the personal costs of doing so. This extreme solution Jane describes--changing the self to conform with what the system demands--produces the archetypal, successful woman lawyer. This adjustment, "emulating the male model," contrasts with two other kinds of adjustments women describe--trying to live up to the standards of both professional role and personal morality ("splitting the self") and shaping the role to fit their own values ("reshaping the role").

The conflicting demands of personal values and professional imperatives led most of the women attorneys with whom we talked to choose the stressful challenge of trying simultaneously to meet divergent standards: the justice or rights morality of the legal system *and* the care or response morality salient to women. The central problem for all these women is

what to do with their personal morality of care when they enter the practice
of law. The official solution, the one tried by Jane, is to minimize the
caring self--talk like a lawyer, think like a lawyer, act like a lawyer. The
other two types of adjustment attempt to maintain a care orientation while
taking on the characteristics of the lawyer role. Since care persists, women
pursuing either of these courses must decide how a caring self fits into the
life of a practicing lawyer.

## EMULATING THE MALE MODEL:
## DENIAL OF THE RELATIONAL SELF

At age thirty-six, Jane had practiced law in a small, well established
firm for six years. Hers was the most diverse practice of any woman in
town--personal injury, criminal law, business, and domestic relations. Jane
was a role model of today's successful, self-made woman. "I have women
who have called me almost on a daily basis, just to have contact with someone who is out in the world and surviving." Emphasizing how the law
"makes me feel important," she says that she derives a lot of satisfaction
from her work, "more than I thought possible."

Jane portrays herself as a dedicated, hard working professional who
subjugates personal concerns to role demands. She describes how "criminal
attorneys have a real tight spot . . . characterized by whether you would
represent the guilty person . . . who's atrocious and his crime's atrocious,
and he's psychotic on top of that." Though she recognizes the difficulty
that defending such a person presents for others,

> . . . it does not pose a problem for me. Of course you do. That's your job.
> You're an advocate. It's not your decision whether they're guilty--that's not
> the way it works. The jury over there makes the decision. It's your job to
> present the case and make sure that the person--if they have a defense--
> has an opportunity to present it. That's your job. You're not that person.
> There's no reason for you to feel badly about it.

Jane maintains distance by seeing herself as part of the legal system and by
following the rules. Turning to an actual case in which she defended a
man accused of raping and murdering an elderly woman, Jane takes the
position of a neutral partisan.

> The standard that I had in my own mind was, if the defendant was my broth-
> er, what would I be doing? Would I be doing more or would I be doing less,
> and that was the kind of standard. If it were me or if it were someone that
> I truly, truly cared about that was in his position, what would I be doing . . .

within the budget I had, how much work would I be doing? And I did it just like that. I shut down my private practice and did the case for several months. And that's what I would have done if it had been my brother sitting there. So that was sort of the standard. I would have done the same job if that person had been my own brother.

To describe the intensity of commitment to client, Jane compares it to loyalty of family relationships. It is as though her caring devotion to her brother became the standard for the lawyer's commitment to duty.

How did Jane become this ardent advocate? She describes law school as a turning point, as the replacement of one way of seeing with another.

I felt it happening in law school. I honestly felt it happening. I know people thought I was crazy, but I can remember first-year law school--I have this feeling when I was being forced to change my set and I can feel it. It's hard to describe but I felt it. And I remember saying to my friends, "They're fucking with your brain. Can't you feel it?" I could feel them changing my perspective on situations and yet I honestly think that happens. I don't think you ever look at situations the same after you go through three years of legal training. I'm not saying it's bad or anything like that. It's probably in many respects better . . .

Jane's response confirms that her previous ways of seeing and interpreting the world were not tolerated by her new environment. To opt for the norms of the legal system, she must deny her culturally formed, feminine ways of knowing and relating to the world.

This adjustment to law by suppressing her feminine self establishes a central motif in her practice--the subjugation of personal to professional life. To fulfill the role of the dedicated advocate, she describes how "there's a whole side of me that stays at home," which is her "affectionate side." In fact, professional life so overshadowed everything else that the affectionate side became nearly dormant. "I just denied everything in my life except work." The affectionate, feeling side is incompatible with "conducting myself in a professional manner" which she feels is essential for women in the practice of law.

Jane explores the roots of her decision to become a lawyer when she describes her desire to differentiate herself from a mother whom she saw as devalued.

Coming from my background, I was climbing, I was scratching, I was trying to get out of what I saw was going to be my destiny in terms of married with children, and a husband that got up and went to work every day, where cleaning the house was it. I was afraid of that. I made a decision at a young age I did not want a life like my mother's . . . I can remember thinking I don't

> want to live like my mother. My father, he goes places, he does things, he meets people, he goes to the office, he's an important person there, and I couldn't figure out what my mother was doing.

Choosing law, she rejects the dependence and unimportance she saw in her mother's life in favor of the self-reliance and excitement she perceived in her father's world. Jane adopts the culture's negative attitude toward her mother and turns that attitude toward what she identifies as the feminine aspects of herself. She associates femininity with an orientation to relationships, and relationships with vulnerability and dependence. "I joined the National Organization of Women in 1971--and that was my senior year in college--and I was definitely getting the impression that if you married and stayed home you were settling for less." Happiness appears linked with independence and success; unhappiness lies in fulfilling traditional roles. Her denial of traditional feminine attitudes fit perfectly with her decision to enter a profession which likewise negates feminine attributes. Jane accepted the image of the lawyer as independent and masculine, and tried to eliminate her need for intimate relationships, seen as conflicting with the demands of the profession.[4]

In addition to a childhood which taught her to devalue her mother, a second influence leading this woman to subordinate relationships to work was a marriage which ended in divorce while she was in law school. In her mind, the divorce confirmed her belief that close relationships and career are incompatible. "I took full responsibility for the divorce. I thought it was definitely my fault and I'd obviously chosen a career over marriage and family; therefore, I was not entitled to marriage and family." She thought that her husband could not "handle it because I was succeeding at this and therefore he wanted out." After the divorce Jane did not seek help to deal with her pain or to sort out her equation of the loss with the pursuit of her own career goals. Instead she denied her own healthy needs for relatedness and intimacy within which she could grow.

> Particularly after I went through my own divorce, I had decided for myself for various reasons that I did not need anything or anyone and I had never said, "I need you," to anyone in my life because I would not allow myself to need. I would not acknowledge dependency because I had to be in control.

In addition, her decision to suppress her relational self was supported by a professional environment which promised independence, success, and happiness if she could assume the traits of successful male lawyers.

Saying that she feels "okay" about elevating her professional life at the expense of her affectionate self, Jane notes that "if I had children it would become increasingly difficult to break out of that segment of myself or to have enough time." Her decision not to have children was not made simply on the basis of her own desires and needs but involved a choice between seemingly incompatible worlds. Assessing the demands of living out the lawyer role made the practical realities of simultaneously raising children seem impossible.

Equating marriage and children with "settling for less," she reiterates her decision not to have children unless she could have what men have--a "wife/servant" to take care of them.

> How would you feel if you had a partner who was going to take this extended leave of absence to have children or who was working part days because of their obligation for children or would have to cancel appointments because their child was sick? I don't have a wife to take care of those things. Those guys go down with their little brown bag and have lunch in the lunchroom. I don't have a wife to pack my lunch in the morning. I mean, they have this servant. I don't have that and it would be very difficult to maintain the level that I'm maintaining with children.

Jane recognizes that women in law are forced to accommodate their private lives to the public sphere, just as men have had to do. Yet, traditionally men have had a wife who took care of the private sphere--the world of children and family. She designates the private sphere as the appropriate domain of a "servant," clearly less valuable than the job of a lawyer which "makes me feel important."

While Jane describes the decision not to have children as "very difficult," she speculates that her solace in old age will come from feelings of "having helped somebody" in her lawyer role, rather than from relationships with her children.

> I figure when I'm an old lady sitting in a rest home and people are looking at pictures of their kids, I'll get out my folder of thank you notes. I have saved every thank you note that I have ever gotten. The first one I got was from a little old lady. It was a handmade note, had glue, sprinkle stuff on it. I mean, it was just incredible.

In this vision of the future, she ends up alone, imagining she will find her continuing connection to others through her contribution as a lawyer.

To flourish as an attorney, Jane subordinates relationships to achievement, love to work, femininity to professionalism. In her words, she feels that "I was sort of sacrificed in terms of creating options for women." She sacrifices a part of herself--her "affectionate" relational side--in the interest of achievement, to pave the way for other women. Her decisions are made to conform with a new feminine standard, which stresses the rewards of achievement. The competing standard she sees for women is exemplified in her mother's life--represented by subservience, self-sacrifice, dullness.

Though the conflict between her relational needs and her professional goals is evident, Jane manifested no outward ambivalence about being an attorney. It appeared that she had resolved the tension by leaving her relational needs out, by emulating the model of the successful lawyer. However, a year and a half after the first interview, we were surprised to hear that she was "taking an extended leave to develop the personal side of my life, which means separation for a time from the demands of practice." We reinterviewed her, and discovered why her adjustment to law had not worked. In her words:

> I am making room in my life for priorities other than work. Giving priorities to a relationship is something that I had never done, and so when I say my thinking has come full circle, it means coming back around to that. Because at some point in my life, earlier on I think, I did in fact give relationships priority.

Like the swing of a pendulum, a one-sided emphasis on profession is balanced by a corrective swing back toward a personal life which includes relationships. Jane appears to be picking up the pieces of a shattered "home world," a prior self cast aside in the socialization of law school and legal practice.

Talking about her unsatisfactory adaptation to the rules of the game, Jane describes how repressed relational needs haunted her with two images. One image was of

> . . . this cartoon image that really bothered me and what it was, was a woman who is about thirty-five years old, unmarried, without children, getting out of her BMW, complete with little tie, brief case, with money, going into a shrink's office and saying "I don't know why I am unhappy." You know, it is just so classic. I have accomplished these things and I don't know why I am unhappy.

The other picture was "of myself on the bench, unmarried, without children, as a dried up prune." These images of herself, with all the outward manifestations of success, depict isolation and sadness rather than the culturally promised independence and happiness. From these visions, she sees "the things that are missing, of course, are any kind of love and what we call a meaningful relationship, a growth situation with another individual, totally missing."

In her second interview Jane comments on her earlier adjustment to the lawyer role through denial of relational needs.

> It appears to me that the law is a real bastion of male dominance and so you adopt all those trappings. You see, my goal in life up until a year and a half ago, my goal in life was to be respected by my peers and the goal that motivated me through law school was I wanted to be taken seriously. See, my mother was someone who was never taken seriously. You assume education will achieve that for you so you pursue that route. You get into a profession, and for me I just denied everything in my life except work. I was a classic workaholic and it was just denial not of just feminine realities or needs, but of human needs. Because of the age that I was in, my confusion was that I thought it was feminine and I thought that's what I was denying, and then I would achieve success and pursue things, just as a male. All I had to do was deny the feminine, okay? Well, as I come along, I've decided that what I'm denying is not necessarily male or female but is human, and to be a whole person, you don't walk around denying need and love and nurturing and those kinds of relationship things. I just denied all that because I was intent on succeeding. That's what I did and it took a couple of major traumas for me to step back and look at it.

Jane correctly perceives that traditional roles have relegated women to non-achievement in a market economy. She began to associate femininity with relationships, and her relational needs with weakness and non-success. Femininity loomed as an obstacle to success in law. If she could deny that part of herself, "then I would achieve success and pursue things, just as a male." As she begins to examine what it means "to be a whole person," she reclaims the formerly denied aspects of herself, renaming them as human rather than feminine needs. Her goal of success also comes under the scrutiny of her broadened vision, which reveals her image of success as narrow and constricting to her development.

Rather than assuming there is something wrong with this woman for withdrawing from the practice of law, we should try to understand how the role of lawyer, as currently defined, pushed her into an untenable position. Perhaps there is something healthy in her inability to live out the image of the detached, competitive lawyer, for whom the law is a "jealous mistress" and admits of no competing demands on time or emotional energy. In her interviews, Jane points out her growing recognition of the emotional costs of gaining success through denial of self.

Society presents people with competing alternatives for adulthood--either achievement or relationships. Traditionally this problem was solved by division of responsibility within a marriage. Men achieved and women knit together the fabric of social relationships. Each gender was denied the rewards and benefits of the other's world. With changing social mores, this arrangement has broken down. Since feminine roles are still societally devalued, there is relatively little pressure on men to assume responsibilities in the private sphere or to emulate feminine attributes. On the other hand, the traditionally masculine domain of competitive achievement is increasingly held up as desirable to men and women alike. The result is that women are more and more told that to achieve adult social worth they must be professional *and* domestic, competitive *and* nurturing. Rather than seeing the public and private domains as interdependent and continuous, society teaches women and men alike to accommodate their private lives to the demands of the professional role. For women, this often translates into the experience of impossible demands from each sphere.

Jane's conflict raises a central question for women in the professions: How is it possible to have both love and work? The social context presents women with choices which seem mutually exclusive and limits the frameworks for thinking about their choices. Dichotomous thinking fails to apprehend a reality of paradox, contradiction, and change. However, not only are both sides of the choice between relationships and career valued, but increasingly for women, neither alone is sufficient for satisfaction or self-esteem. The students at Yale Law School and many of the women with whom we spoke seek social support and approval for new arrangements that will address the dilemma. Jane chose a career but was haunted by a need for relationships. She sees no way to be a lawyer without forfeiting relationships, and no way to have relationships without jeopardizing her career. For Jane, an integration of personal self and professional self may come from her plans to marry, take a leave, and then re-enter practice with a new equilibrium of work and relationships.

Jane's solution to dealing with the rules of the game is not suggested as every woman's solution. In her reexamination of how she fulfills the lawyer role, Jane replaces emulation of the societal model for lawyer success with self-awareness and self-realization. Emulation of a male model is replaced by self-reflective choice as the basis for her decision making, moral or otherwise. Jane's struggle to define herself or her purpose is not simplified by this change, but the solution to conflict becomes inner directed and authentic rather than dictated by external standards.

## SPLITTING THE SELF: A PROBLEM OF BACKGROUND, FOREGROUND, AND UNITY

Unlike Jane who emulated the male model and denied her relational self, most of the women with whom we spoke bring their care orientation into their professional role while at the same time playing by the male rules of the game. One strategy for trying to preserve a feminine way of seeing and relating while also practicing law requires dividing the self into two parts--the lawyer self and the caring self. At work, the lawyer self dominates the foreground and the caring self remains subdued. Outside of the office, positions are reversed. This allows the appropriate self to respond to each setting in a manner consistent with its training and values. By splitting the self in two, each part should have the opportunity to develop and remain proficient. Thus, the two parts of the self, each in its own compartment, should remain healthy and on call. At least this is the plan.

In fact, women attorneys told us of two related problems. At the office the relational, caring self did not readily remain neatly boxed and relegated to the background, but rather, as the first learned morality of these women, it insisted on a more prominent role. The second problem was that of disunity. While conceptually neat, division of the self can lead to tension instead of mental health. For these lawyers, compartmentalizing the personality and keeping care in the background is both stressful and often unsuccessful. Without integration, the result of a divided self is conflict and self-condemnation. At the same time, giving care full reign at work causes pain and threatens professionalism. Susan, a lawyer in private practice, sums up the situation: "You feel like emotions are a luxury that you can't afford. But sometimes you want to afford them, you know."

Describing her most difficult adjustment in practicing law, Susan talks of the necessity and the loss involved in dividing the self. In her comments we see that it is impossible to neatly divide the relational, caring self from the lawyer self. Psychological defenses that are developed to deal with the adversarial nature of law spill over to affect personal life.

> People are mean to you a lot. I hate it . . . a lot of times I'll have a bad day with a number of different people calling up and yelling at me about various things. And I try to put on a persona that makes it appear to them that it's water off a duck's back. And as I grow in the profession my skin gets thicker and it increasingly is water off a duck's back. In terms of doing the job and surviving emotionally, it's essential. I remember when I was first starting out after law school, it was my first phone call . . . and a secretary was really mean to me and I got off the phone and cried because she'd been mean to me. You know, very calmly walked to the door of my office, closed the door, sat down and cried, wiped my eyes and kept going. You can't do that every time somebody's mean to you. You know, you need to develop defenses so that those things go away. But as you do . . . that defense mechanism carries over into the part of me that's not a lawyer . . . Recently some of my partners' wives worked in the office and I was really struck by the difference between them and me . . . I was always rushed. They had time to talk about how they felt; I never did. That was really an experience for me because I realized that here we were, women who'd had similar backgrounds and yet, because of our experiences, had taken off in real different directions, and I really was the hard bitten career woman. At times it made me feel impatient with them because I had a job to do, damn it, and why were they so busy caring about how they felt. It made me envious of them too.

To survive emotionally, Susan must develop a thick skin; yet the thick skin negatively affects her personal life. "Being a lawyer makes you real good at things like arguing and cross-examining which are not especially positive elements to bring into a relationship." The comparison of her rushed, work self to other women's more feeling selves causes her to label herself a "hard bitten career woman" and to envy their freedom to feel.

Janet likewise attempts to reconcile a care orientation with the legal system by splitting her intuitive, feeling self from her rational, objective, lawyer self. She describes two different ways of knowing, one of which is valued by the law, while the other is devalued. Her most difficult adjustment practicing law is

> . . . being rational and intellectual a lot of the time. I mean, this has nothing to do with what's hard about being a lawyer; this is what's hard *for me* about being a lawyer . . . I'm just different now, my thought has, the emphasis on the intellectual and analytical has really changed me. I'm different, but I'm not lost to that; it's just harder to reach back for it . . . The legal system demands that you divorce emotion from reason in order to convince the reasoners, men, the judges, that you have a case . . . the vast majority--and I'm proud to be among them--choose to use analysis solely and leave emotion out, because you're unsure whether that will work or turn off the person listening to you.

Janet recognizes who owns the game and in whose language she must speak. Uncertain of its effect on those who may negatively judge it, she relegates her own voice to the background.

Janet requires retreat from the law's one-sided emphasis on rationality in order to rediscover personal unity.

> After law school and the bar exam I took myself up into the mountains for a week and I couldn't feel, I couldn't feel. And I'd always gone to the mountains backpacking to--it would take a couple of days--but I would get the feeling of being, of a unit, a part of a unity. And I couldn't feel that at all. All I could see was this sort of poster picture of beautiful scenery, and that wasn't much satisfaction. I couldn't feel. It took a long time, a week of sitting around, then being at a girlfriend's place on a lake, and sitting under the rocks and swimming all day and watching the sun go down, talking to the herons. You know, just dealing with nothing but physical sensations and animals . . . I had darkened out my brain somehow, I'm serious. It felt silly but it was that much of a number I did to myself. I had overextended--had just overemphasized the intellectual.

Analytic thinking in law requires objectivity, skepticism, and impersonal reasoning which effectively separates the knower from that which is known. This impersonal way of knowing temporarily alienates Janet's ability to feel. It also erodes her sense of identity as part of a larger context, part of the ecological web of life.

In a similar vein, Ann expresses the problem of bringing her whole self, including her compassion and empathy, into her practice. She experiences the hurt of the world and her own inability to prevent it.

> God, there was a day last week when just so much was happening--the full moon or something like that. There was just so much grief and misery and bizarre stuff that was happening. At the end of the day it was like, ohhh, stomach in a knot, you know, just wrought apart by it. I don't think you're thinking as clearly then and doing as good a job. I think I even told my last client of the day, "Well, we'll reschedule because I just can't hear any more."

Trying to reduce the pain, she "disassociates the emotional, intuitive self from the analytical, professional. I have a certain job to do here for my clients that has very little to do with who I am as a person." Yet the consequences of splitting herself in order to deal with conflict between the demands of role and personal orientation are risky.

> To be a full person you don't want to lose the emotional side of yourself. You would hope to be able to have in your personal life that emotional response that you aren't necessarily allowed in your practice. And you hope that your analytical, critical self just doesn't eat that all up because then you're left with a void. That's something I fight against, you know, and almost all the other women I know fight against also.

Ann recognizes the dangers of her analytical, critical self gaining ascendance and making emotional capacity a "void." She struggles to maintain a vital, feeling response while the lawyer role continually belittles emotions with requirements of professionalism, detachment, and neutrality.

> That is the struggle for me. I think some other people would say their big-gest struggle is time--finding enough hours in the day to do all the things they can't do at the office. But I'd say my number one problem is maintain-ing myself as a full person including emotions and such.

Aware of the danger of banishing feeling into the background, Ann tries to compensate for leaving "who I am as a person" out of legal work. "I have in my life tried to keep myself a full person so that outside of the office I have other things besides the law to do. I try to maintain real strong relationships so that I can keep developing myself as a person as well." For Ann, growth as a person takes place through relationships, while her development as a lawyer depends upon splitting off the "emo-tional, intuitive self" to do her job.

Ann continually experiences stress from carrying out role demands which conflict with her personal orientation and from her inability to re-spond to the human pain she witnesses as a lawyer. In part, this stress is born of living with competing world views. Psychologists tell us that peo-ple develop "structures of knowing" which allow them to "make meaning" of events and to commit themselves to certain courses of action (see Kegan, 1977, p. 99). Meaning making involves one's whole being and includes "an existential process of generating a new vision to which one can commit oneself" (Kegan, quoted in Sassen, 1980). When women take on the new vision taught by law school and yet retain their old ways of seeing, the new vision may not root deeply enough to become a "structure of knowing," a new way of making sense. They may effectively use the new vision as a tool, but it may not reach deeply enough into who they are to give mean-ing to their lives.

Ann and Janet are both uncertain about their commitment to a pro-fession which excludes their way of making meaning, which forces them to separate off a valued part of themselves. Janet daydreams about how she can express an aspect of her self which the law excludes and how she can develop a sense of balance.

> I spend a lot of time daydreaming now about what I want to do instead. And about whether I want to do this [law] and how I want to do it differently if I do law at all. And I write a lot of poetry. I'm going to send some of it out for publication. Because I want to balance it, you know, and bring that part of myself into more focus and more power.

Ann also despairs about the costs required to play the lawyer game.

> It's a constant questioning process, you know. Am I being true to myself if I proceed in this respect. If you cannot be true to yourself and proceed in that respect, maybe you should quit the game. Most of the whole lawyers I know are trying to quit. I think maybe I should quit too. I can't take this anymore, the conflict over yourself as a person and yourself as a lawyer, and at the point that one outweighs the other, it's time to leave.

She arrives at precisely the same dilemma as did the women at Yale Law School: forsake the self or forsake the law. A statement of the dilemma is not a sufficient stopping point. Because the choice is unfair and destructive to women and because law needs an infusion of care values, lawyers must push beyond the dilemma to find ways of integrating the fairness of justice and the responsibility of caring.

## RESHAPING THE ROLE:  CHANGING OWNERSHIP OF THE GAME

Several strongly care-oriented women reveal another strategy for adjusting to the lawyer role. Rather than emulate the stereotype of the successful lawyer or split the caring self from the lawyer self, these women shape the role to conform with their personal morality. Despite devaluation of feminine traits in the law, they assert themselves as women and integrate their care orientation into legal practice. Integration of care transforms the way the job is conceived and the meaning of a lawyer's responsibility. But again there are risks. This posture, like the one before, exposes an empathetic practitioner to an array of client demands and misery which at times may become unbearable. The stress of being a caring advocate is heightened, for care does not slip in the back door of the office as it does when the self is divided, but instead is manifest as part of how the job is done. This points to a second danger--an openly caring attorney may be seen as unprofessional and perhaps incompetent. As long as the rules of the game remain unchanged, care will appear marginal to the profession.

Carol designed a practice where the feminine self is a welcome partner. By intention, her work allows "exposure to people's basic and most personal problems . . . and trying to help them." Identifying her "feminist perspective," she describes herself as "interested in what women go through in their lives . . . and in helping them through a period of time

. . . giving them some insight into maybe why they are where they are economically, or why they're responding a certain way to something." She has structured her practice to conform to *her* values. "We sat down and talked about our philosophies and the kind of firm we wanted to have"--keeping clients informed, non-hierarchical office relationships, responsiveness to clients in need.

In order to deal with tension between the demands of her role and her morality, Carol limits the types of cases she will take. "What I've tried to do is just be honest with myself about what I feel comfortable doing within my own set of values, and I've excluded certain things because of that set of values. Therefore, I don't have to deal with them and I do the kind of work that I feel comfortable doing." The integrity of her practice protects her from much of the moral distance traditionally associated with carrying out the lawyer job.

Setting aside detachment and neutrality, as Carol says, "to be there for the client when they need you," an attorney is still often unable to prevent harm, to give as much as the client needs. This is the major problem for women who bring their care orientation into the attorney role--how to deal with the stress of caring within the context of the profession. While all lawyers describe the pressure of meeting deadlines, attending to details, billing and collecting from clients, those who maintain a strong care orientation identify an anguish which comes from empathetic perception of unmet human needs. Beth tells how involvement exposes an attorney to the client's hurt.

> I have never done a custody battle yet that I haven't gotten totally involved in. When I lose them I'm totally bummed out . . . because I obviously believe in those cases, that my client really loves those children, is the better parent for those children . . . When you lose it's just as devastating for the attorney, for me, as it is for the client. And then I'm left--it's like they're so consumed with their own devastation that I'm always left in an empty courtroom with my devastation, by myself.

This emotional vulnerability is one reason why lawyers erect barriers of detachment and objectivity. The price of involved concern may be more than they are able or willing to bear.

Women most persistently high in care statements experience the greatest tension due to their inability to meet clients' needs. Their language of personal cost is graphic. "I bleed for clients, I really do." "I wanted to be there for the client all the time, but it was making me crazy." "You've got to be much more than an attorney--you've got to be a psychologist, you've got to be a mother, you're playing multiple roles. You're giving a lot of energy out--it's really emotionally draining." These attorneys stand in the emotional as well as the legal shoes of their clients. They take personal responsibility for the consequences of professional relationships. Since such courtroom lawyers see a parade of human problems daily, reaching out to each in turn can be overwhelming.

In response to such pressure, women attorneys who reshape roles must also change their understanding of responsibility and care. Rather than compartmentalizing care or suppressing it in their lives, they comprehend the limits of their ability to give and to take on the problems of others. After eight years in practice, Carol describes the major sources of tension in her work and the need to protect herself from her own demand to give.

> It's very hard to sit and listen to someone whose child has been kidnapped. I mean that's stressful, it's horrible. You go home at night and you worry, where's the child and how's my client, and is she going to kill herself and you know, that is very hard. I eventually last year had my number unlisted because I had so many people calling me at home because they were hysterical and I feel guilty about it because I, I wanted to be there for the client all the time, but it was making me crazy. I would come to work the next day and I wouldn't have slept or I'd still be upset from talking to people all night on the phone . . . And I can't give that much. It's too much.

Carol encounters the limits of her own selflessness and reassesses what it means for her to be responsible as a lawyer.

> It used to be my attitude was that somehow I was responsible for that client's troubles. The minute the client came in to see me I became responsible for everything that happened--in an abstract way, but yet responsible. And it did not matter how hard my efforts, the child being kidnapped occurred anyway. That particular incident was so stressful for me because of that factor, because of taking on the responsibility. And I realized with a couple of cases that I really didn't have the control over every client I would like to have, to make sure that they did everything they should do so their case worked out okay. Once I admitted that to myself, I realized that if I didn't have the control, I also didn't have the responsibility because if the person isn't going to listen to me, I can't do anything about that. I started kind of letting go a little bit and realizing that as long as I did everything I could do, as long as I communicated, and as long as I felt for that person and tried to solve that person's problem, and if I knew honestly that I had done every single step that I could do, that it was the best I could do, and if they still turned around and gave their kids back to their ex-husband because they were upset that night, that's not my fault.

Recognizing her lack of power to control what happens to other people, Carol places boundaries around her feelings of personal responsibility. Her limitation of responsibility allows her to feel care without guilt and pain each time a negative result occurs.

Hillary also finds unbounded responsibility exhausting. A lawyer for handicapped people, she was "approaching burn out in terms of my practice" because she heeded inner imperatives learned from socialization to the female role. The already demanding norms of the "good woman" become impossible when taken into a law office.

> I think I had to deal with an upbringing which I think a lot of women have, which is it's my job to take care of people, and it's my job to make everything okay. I had to go through a process of realizing there's no way that I can make everything okay or take care of people and that the people had done some incredible things to get their lives to the point that they were at, and that I could not undertake that as my job to fix it, or to do it. I had to go through a real conscious process of trying to free myself of that expectation.

Modifying her expectations of herself, Hillary limits the reach of her responsibility. Like Carol, she does not withdraw from clients, but changes her understanding which allows her to relate to them in an empathetic but realistic manner.

> I think, almost ironically, I have maybe a more caring relationship with clients now because I don't feel the burden of responsibility. I feel that I can acknowledge that there is a lot of pain, or can acknowledge that is a terrible situation--"you are in a real mess and we'll see if we can start breaking it down into small pieces and working on sorting that out"--and I guess acknowledging that, I think that I do end up having a pretty personal relationship with most of my clients.

The change in her understanding of responsibility allows Hillary to "deal with the expressed concern but not take it on as your own," which means that she need no longer "find myself going home at night and agonizing over cases for the most part." She is able to respond empathetically to problems rather than to feel responsible for them.

For these women who integrate care into their law practice, shifts in the meaning of responsibility coincide with changes in their understanding of morality. They recognize that always putting other people's needs ahead of their own leads to self-sacrifice and hurt: "It will kill you," "it will eat you up as a person." When considering human need, the supply always exceeds the ability to respond. Faced with realistic limits on how much they can give, these women assert the right to respect for their own needs--"my human needs are as important as the client's needs." They reorder their understanding of care to include themselves as recipients of the care they extend to others. "I'd come home from work and spend all night on the phone. And that wasn't doing me any good . . . and that's when I decided to get an unlisted number."[5]

Despite the ideal of feminine unselfishness, these lawyers realize that they cannot hold themselves ultimately accountable for the happiness and well-being of others, just as they cannot hold others accountable for their own sense of satisfaction and professional competence. As Hillary says:

> Part of the process, I think, had to come from realizing that a client's response to the case isn't necessarily a measure of the quality of the work that was done or how much I had helped them . . . learning to give myself my own feedback and setting up my own standards in terms of what constitutes a good job for me in doing that, and realizing my own limitations began to replace looking to the client for the measure of my worth as a lawyer.

By separating their care orientation from conventions of stereotypic good women, Hillary and Carol maintain involved concern and also attenuate the stress of caring within their attorney role. However, for others, care is difficult to contain.

By its very nature, to limit care is, in part, to be uncaring. Bringing care to the office while restricting its reach is not easy. Lawyers who try this solution vary in their success at finding workable boundaries. For example, Rachel takes on an expansive responsibility to "fix" situations of broken relationships and personal hurt which she deals with in her role as a prosecuting attorney. Rachel condemns herself when her attempts fail, even though intellectually she recognizes she did the best job she could. Describing a case of child beating which occurred after she agreed, with conditions, to return the child home, she says:

> I felt very responsible, at that point, and I felt that I had done something very, very wrong by agreeing to the conditions. But I know, when you look at it logically, I wasn't wrong. I didn't do anything wrong, but I felt that way. You know, I felt that I should have been able to save this kid.

From the perspective of her role, Rachel knows that she did nothing wrong, but her moral imperatives tell her she failed to prevent harm. To the extent that attorneys integrate care into the profession and do not change the conventional understanding of feminine goodness and responsibility, they inevitably fall short of unreachable standards.

Of the lawyers we interviewed, only two described themselves as bringing care into their practice and limiting its consuming reach. Carol, a feminist domestic relations lawyer, and Hillary, doing work for the

handicapped, reshaped their roles and in so doing gained the respect of the
legal community and a sense of personal satisfaction. A present challenge
is whether their openly caring style can be employed in other areas not so
obviously adaptable to a morality of care. Will the individual initiative of
imaginative, energetic lawyers be enough, or will it require institutional
redefinition and shifts of attitude in the profession if all parts of the law
are to benefit from the attributes of a care morality?

## WOMEN'S STRENGTHS, WOMEN'S VULNERABILITIES WITHIN LAW

Care, cooperation, responsiveness, personal involvement, and lack
of aggression are often dismissed as negative stereotypes about women
in law, even by women themselves. Yet these characteristics appear as
vulnerabilities only under certain rules of the game--rules established by
generations of male lawyers. In a different context care characteristics
become attributes we would like to find in the people with whom we live
and work. Under the Zapotec ideal of justice--restoring personal relations
to equilibrium, preserving community--women's "vulnerabilities" are
strengths.[6] Care-oriented lawyers reorder the hierarchy of values in the
legal system and bring to their practice new perspectives on power, competition, self-determination, and authenticity.

Women's concern for caring and relational responsibilities can challenge the legal system to creative change. Yet, since these concerns are
often seen as liabilities within the legal profession, there is a danger that
the articulation of care concerns can be used to relegate women to marginal positions "suited" to their values. Such a limitation of women is further
supported by the association of care with women, home, and family and by
its exclusion from the public sphere. While a care orientation does make
for good family law practitioners, it is a fallacy to assume that a care perspective can make positive contributions to only a few segments of the law.
We have met care-oriented women excelling in general practice, in the pros-
ecutor's office, and in the office of the public defender. They bring reason and feeling, advocacy and responsibility to their work.

The attributes of care are valuable wherever human relationships are
at stake, which is the whole of the legal system. Restricting the availability of these characteristics limits constructive possibility. The assump-

tion that a care orientation cannot accompany the ability to be a good lawyer falls into the trap of dichotomous thinking prevalent in the legal system. Assuming a sharp division between reason and emotion, linear and associative thought, cold rationality and warm empathy reinforces the exclusion of traditionally feminine traits from the practice of law. In our research we met lawyers--women and men both--who were grappling with how to combine these attributes in their work. Just as the culture in the past has taught that these sets of traits are mutually exclusive and gender specific, in the future the message should be one of integration and compatibility. A person can be empathetic, intuitive, and understanding while also being rational, competent, and quick-witted. In the legal system, the question "is no longer either simply about justice or simply about caring, it is about bringing them together to transform the domain" (Gilligan, 1985).

Care-oriented women with whom we spoke all faced a common problem--how to enter a system alien in many ways to their most fundamental values. They showed three ways of entry and adjustment to the practice of law. All three ways are possible, but none without risk. Under the current rules of the game, care-oriented lawyers suffer difficulty because the rules are not their own. This does not mean that they cannot perform well. Lawyers we interviewed and thousands of others across the country prove that they can. It does mean that they pay a psychological price not extracted from most men--the present owners of the game. Giving up the caring self, compartmentalizing it, integrating it into an unreceptive system are all costly. Individual care-oriented attorneys will select the way most suitable to their own needs and personality.

What is a reasonable response to the fact that large numbers of people entering law find basic incompatibilities with the advocate role? One attorney suggests, "if you can't stand the heat, get out of the kitchen." A more thoughtful reply would be to ask what is wrong with the kitchen that there is so much heat? Why do so many bright, competent people find it difficult to work there? What happens if people work all day in a kitchen that is too hot? If we carefully examine the sources of stress particular to care-oriented lawyers and their strategies of adjustment, what do we learn about the legal system and about the possible changes which need to be made? A clear understanding of a problem is both a prerequisite and a guide for thinking about a solution. The next step is to determine whether the solution creates more problems than it rectifies. Given the social value of care morality, we believe that changes necessary to make the legal system more compatible with care values would substantially improve the system, so long as basic tenets of rights-oriented morality retain strength in their appropriate place. The perspective of these women attorneys and the paths they follow challenge conventional definitions of the lawyer role and raise new possibilities for a synthesis of equal justice and human caring.

## NOTES

1. Gelenter, C. "Speak Louder, Lower, Women Lawyers Told." *Seattle Times* (October 18, 1980).

2. "Women in the Law: Many Are Getting Out." *New York Times* (August 9, 1985).

3. "Open Letter to the Law School Community." By Minorities and Women at Yale Law School, unpublished document (1984).

4. Other professional women in business also replicate this pattern. See especially P. McBroom, *The Third Sex*, New York (1986).

5. These changes in women's morality correspond with a pattern of female development described by Gilligan (1982).

6. See L. Nader, ed., *Law in Culture and Society*, Chicago (1969), for a description of other cultures' justice systems. In particular, the Zapotec system's ideals are those embodied in a morality of care. Also, Miller (1976) made the point that what have been seen as women's weaknesses within a male-dominated society are, in fact, women's strengths.

## ACKNOWLEDGMENTS

Our thanks to the Russell Sage Foundation for financial support for research underlying this chapter. We gratefully acknowledge Carol Gilligan's ideas and comments on an earlier draft of this chapter.

# AFTERWORD

The research presented in this volume is based on listening to the ways people talk about morality and about themselves. Of central interest are the questions: How do people define conflicts they face and describe choices they make in the course of their daily lives? How do people speak about themselves, about others, and about the world in which they live and act? The present work is also grounded in the recognition that psychological theories of moral development, identity formation, and adolescent and adult development have for the most part been based on studies of boys and men only. Rather than asking how well women fit standards derived from studying men, we have asked what insights women's thinking contributes to psychological understanding and whether attention to girls' and women's experience generates new ways of thinking about self, morality, adolescence, and adulthood. What can be learned from girls and women? The papers collected here describe a series of approaches to this question and also provide some answers.

The hypothesis of a different voice, defined by a focus on care concerns and associated empirically with women, is born out here across a variety of circumstances and settings. Two ways of speaking about self, relationships, and morality are consistently recorded. One voice is well represented by psychologists and well developed through our educational systems. Against this background, the other voice, although recognizable, sounds different; traditionally, it has been both idealized and at the same time also characterized as deficient. Among samples of educationally advantaged North American adolescents and adults, a focus on care concerns, although not characteristic of all the women, was found to be primarily a female phenomenon. Given the evidence that both females and males understand and voice both care and justice concerns, and given that everyone by virtue of being human is vulnerable both to abandonment and oppression, the fact that care thinking tends to be voiced mainly by girls and women raises a series of questions for psychological theory and sets an agenda for education.

The current research on moral voice documents a tendency for people to silence one voice or lose sight of one set of moral concerns when describing moral conflicts. The voices of girls and women who focus on care tend to draw our attention to the overriding justice focus of contemporary American culture and psychology and the ultimate value placed on maintaining separation and independence. By resisting the detachment of justice reasoning, by taking evidence of violence at face value and as grounds for moral action, and by questioning conventions of care which are associated with idealized images of feminine goodness or female self-sacrifice, care-focused girls and women demonstrate a resistance to the conventions of thinking in contemporary American society. In doing so, they highlight the costs of silencing care concerns, not only in private life but also in professional training. Care-focused thinkers, primarily but not exclusively girls and women, recognize detachment as morally problematic and underscore the tendency in this highly technological age for people to lose sight of human connection, to overlook the ways in which people enter and affect one another's lives.

Specifically, the present research draws attention to signs of girls' resistance to detachment and disconnection in early adolescence, during the time of identity formation and the transition to adulthood. This time of shifting to adult forms of connection corresponds with the move from primary to secondary education. The dilemma posed for schools is how to promote the development of abstract thinking and higher order reasoning while also sustaining human connection and strengthening the ability to understand relationships between people. This dilemma has been evaded in contemporary psychology, and more generally in Western culture, by splitting reason and emotion, thinking and feeling, public and private, political and personal, and then aligning these divisions with the distinction between male and female. The problems in these divisions are elaborated throughout this volume, but the question remains: how to speak about differences between the sexes, including such morally relevant if stereotypic differences as the greater involvement of men with violent crime and the greater tendency of women to take care of young children. The concepts of moral voice and moral orientation which are key to the current mapping of the moral domain provide a way of representing differences which avoids simplistic views of women or men as well as the presumption of a neutral standpoint (a voiceless position) from which to make male-female comparisons.

At present, the question of sex differences marks a chasm between psychological theory and social reality. In many ways the lives of girls and women differ from the lives of boys and men in contemporary North American society. It would be surprising if such differences--in early childhood relationships, in adolescent experience, and in adult social and economic status--had no psychological ramifications. The commitment of a democratic society to an ideal of social justice based on a premise of individual equality makes evidence of differences disturbing. Within an educational system committed to the goals of equal opportunity and individual freedom, ideals of no difference are often sustained by practices of not listening and not seeing. The justification of such practices in the name of justice reasoning, the encouragement of children and adolescents to turn away from the perception of others' needs and often their own needs as well, points to a central dilemma for American education: how to encourage human responsiveness within the framework of a competitive, individualistic culture.

By listening for the voice of care as well as justice reasoning, the research gathered in this volume documents how attention to differences fosters the discovery of inclusive or creative solutions to moral conflicts, solutions which often dissolve dilemmas by responding to everyone's needs. In circumstances where difficult choices are inescapable, care focused thinkers are less likely to describe violence as an acceptable response to human conflicts and more likely to consider detachment in the face of suffering as a moral problem. Our studies of urban youth become particularly illuminating in this context.

Living in the inner city, often with a minimum of economic resources, urban teenagers remind us of the necessity for care, of the reliance of people on human resources, and the capacity of people to nurture and care for one another. Researchers who listen with a human ear, rather than relying on instruments of psychological and educational assessment, can readily hear in the voices of inner city children and teenagers what Maya Angelou calls "rich exchanges," expressing a knowledge of human psychology that is based on experience and careful observation of people. The fact that such children and teenagers are often described by psychologists and educators as knowing little or having little to share is in itself a cause for major reconsideration.

In assembling the present volume, we have made certain decisions about inclusion and exclusion. We call the attention of our readers to papers which may be of particular interest to clinical psychologists and psychotherapists and which have appeared in professional journals: Catherine Steiner-Adair's study of the vulnerability and invulnerability of high school girls to eating disorders and Dana Jack's studies of women and depression. We also alert our readers to recently completed work which provides important validation for the independence of justice and care as separate moral perspectives and for the stronger association of care thinking with ego development and identity formation in females. Here we refer to the work of Annie Rogers, relating the moral voices of justice and care to Jane Loevinger's stages of ego development, and to the work of Eva Skoe, relating the development of care reasoning in women to the development of identity as defined by Erik Erikson and measured by James Marcia. The research findings on sex differences in images of violence, noted here in the study of physician vulnerability, have received independent confirmation in the replication study conducted by Vicki Helgeson and Don Sharpsteen.

Finally, a different kind of encouragement and validation as well as new insights into women's development comes from the work of colleagues who are also creating new maps of development and new visions of psychological health and education. Most directly relevant to the present endeavor is the work of Mary Belenky, Blythe Clinchy, Nancy Goldberger, and Jill Tarule on *Women's Ways of Knowing*; Jean Baker Miller and the psychologists at The Stone Center, Wellesley College, who describe the development and psychotherapeutic treatment of women's relational sense of self; Sara

Ruddick who has introduced the concept of maternal thinking and explored its relation to peace making; Jane Martin whose book, *Reclaiming a Conversation*, examines the ideal of the educated woman; and Gisela Konopka, a pioneer in listening to the voices of adolescent girls and in taking those voices seriously. As the editors of the present collection of research reports and interpretive essays, we hope that the maps drawn here and the pathways charted will encourage and enable further explorations on the part of others.

Carol Gilligan
Janie Victoria Ward
Jill McLean Taylor

Cambridge, Massachusetts

# REFERENCES

# REFERENCES

Adelson, J. *The Handbook of Adolescent Psychology.* New York: John Wiley & Sons (1980).

Adelson, J., & Doehrman, M. J. "The Psychodynamic Approach to Adolescence." In J. Adelson, ed., *The Handbook of Adolescent Psychology.* New York: John Wiley & Sons (1980).

Adelson, J., & Douvan, E. *The Adolescent Experience.* New York: John Wiley & Sons (1966).

Angelou, M. *I Know Why the Caged Bird Sings.* New York: Bantam Books (1969).

Arendt, H. *The Origins of Totalitarianism.* New York: Harcourt, Brace (1951).

Arendt, H. *Eichmann in Jerusalem: A Report on the Banality of Evil.* New York: Viking Press (1963).

Arendt, H. *The Human Condition.* Garden City, N. Y.: Doubleday (1958).

Arendt, H. *The Life of the Mind: Thinking.* New York: Harcourt, Brace, Jovanovich (1972).

Atkinson, J. W., ed. *Motives in Fantasy, Action and Society.* New York: Van Nostrand (1958).

Attanucci, J. "Mothers in Their Own Terms: A Developmental Perspective on Self and Role." Unpublished doctoral dissertation, Harvard Graduate School of Education (1984).

Austen, J. *Persuasion.* New York: Harcourt, Brace & World (1964).

Badinter, E. *Mother Love, Myth and Reality.* New York: Macmillan (1981).

Bakan, D. *On Method.* San Francisco: Jossey–Bass (1969).

Baldwin, J. M. *Mental Development of the Child and the Race.* New York: Macmillan (1895).

Baldwin, J. M. *Social and Ethical Interpretations in Mental Development.* New York: Macmillan (1897).

Balint, A. "Love for the Mother and Mother Love" (1939). In M. Balint, ed., *Primary Love and Psychoanalytic Techniques.* New York: Liveright (1965).

Bardige, B. "Facing History and Ourselves: Tracing Development through Analysis of Student Journals." *Moral Education Forum* (Summer 1981) 42–48.

Bardige, B. "Reflective Thinking and Prosocial Awareness: Adolescents Face the Holocaust and Themselves." Unpublished doctoral dissertation, Harvard Graduate School of Education (1983).

Baruch, G. & Barnett, R., & Rivers, C. *Lifeprints: New Patterns of Love and Work for Today's Women.* New York: McGraw–Hill (1983).

Baumrind, D. "Parental Disciplinary Patterns and Social Competence in Children." *Youth and Society,* 9 (1978) 239–276.

Baumrind, D. "Sex Differences in Moral Reasoning: Response to Walker's (1984) Conclusion That There Are None." *Child Development,* 57 (1986) 511–521.

Belenky, M., Clinchy, B., Goldberger, N., & Tarule, J. *Women's Ways of Knowing.* New York: Basic Books (1986).

Benedek, E. P. "Dilemmas in Research on Female Adolescent Development." In M. Sugar, ed., *Female Adolescent Development.* New York: Brunner/Mazel (1979).

Bernard, J. *The Future of Motherhood.* New York: Dial Press (1974).

Bettelheim, B. "The Problem of Generations." In E. Erikson, ed., *The Challenge of Youth.* New York: Anchor Books/Doubleday (1965).

Bettelheim, B. *The Uses of Enchantment.* New York: Vintage Books (1977).

Bishop, Y., Feinberg, S., & Holland, P. *Discrete Multivariate Analysis: Theory and Practice.* Cambridge, Mass.: Massachusetts Institute of Technology Press (1975).

Blos, P. "The Second Individuation Process of Adolescence." *The Psychoanalytic Study of the Child,* 22 (1967) 162–186.

Blos, P. *The Young Adolescent.* New York: Macmillan (1970).

Blum, L. *Friendship, Altruism and Morality.* Boston: Routledge & Kegan Paul (1980).

Boston Public Schools. "Report to the Safe Schools Commission." (November 1983).

Bowlby, J. *Attachment and Loss* (3 vols.). New York: Basic/Harper Colophon (1969, 1973, 1980).

Bromley, D. B. "Natural Language and the Development of the Self." *Nebraska Symposium of Motivation* (1977) 117–167.

Bronfenbrenner, U. *The Ecology of Human Development: Experiments by Nature and Design.* Cambridge, Mass.: Harvard University Press (1979).

Broverman, I., Vogel, S., Broverman, D., Clarkson, F., & Rosenkrantz, P. "Sex-Role Stereotypes: A Current Appraisal." *Journal of Social Issues*, 28 (1972) 58–78.

Brown, L. "When Is a Moral Problem Not a Moral Problem?" Unpublished manuscript, Harvard Graduate School of Education (1986).

Brown, L., Argyris, D., Attanucci, J., Bardige, B., Gilligan, C., Johnston, K., Miller, B., Osborne, R., Tappan, M., Ward, J., & Wilcox, D. "A Guide to Reading Narratives of Moral Conflict and Choice for Self and Moral Voice." Unpublished manuscript, Harvard Graduate School of Education (1987).

Brown University, Office of the Provost. "Men and Women Learning Together: A Study of College Students in the Late 1970's." (1980).

Bruch, H. *The Golden Cage: The Enigma of Anorexia Nervosa.* Cambridge, Mass.: Harvard University Press (1978).

Burdwick, J., Douvan, E., Horner, M., & Gutman, D. *Feminine Personality and Conflict.* Belmont, Calif.: Wadsworth (1970).

Bussey, K. & Maughan, B. "Gender Differences in Moral Reasoning." *Journal of Personality and Social Psychology*, 42(4) (1982) 701–706.

Camus, A. *The Plague.* New York: Random House (1948).

Chekhov, A. *Collected Plays.* New York: Penguin (1964).

Chodorow, N. "Family Structure and Feminine Personality." In M. Rosaldo & L. Lamphere, eds., *Women, Culture and Society.* Stanford, Calif.: Stanford University Press (1974).

Chodorow, N. *The Reproduction of Mothering: Psychoanalysis and the Sociology of Gender.* Berkeley, Calif.: University of California Press (1978).

Chodorow, N. "Feminism and Difference: Gender, Relations and Difference in Psychoanalytic Perspective." In H. Einstein & A. Jardine, eds., *The Scholar and the Feminist*, Vol. 1, *The Future of Difference.* Boston: G. K. Hall (1980).

Cohen, J. "A Coefficient of Agreement for Nominal Scales." *Educational and Psychological Measurement*, 20 (1960) 1.

Cohler, B. & Grunebaum, H. *Mothers, Grandmothers, and Daughters.* New York: Wiley-Interscience Publications, John Wiley & Sons (1981).

Colby, A., Kohlberg, L., Candee, D., Gibbs, J., Hewer, A., & Speicher, B. *The Measurement of Moral Judgment: A Manual and Its Results.* New York: Cambridge University Press (1985).

Colby, A., Kohlberg, L., Candee, D., Gibbs, J., Hewer, A., Kaufmann, K., & Power, C. *The Measurement of Moral Judgment: Standard Issue Scoring Manual.* Cambridge, England: Cambridge University Press (1986).

Colby, A., Kohlberg, L., Gibbs, J., & Liebermann, M. "A Longitudinal Study of Moral Judgment." *Monographs of the Society for Research in Child Development,* 48 (1 & 2, Serial No. 200) (1983).

Coles, R. *The Moral Life of Children.* Boston: Little, Brown (1986).

Colt, L., Paine, J., & Connelly, F. "Facing History and Ourselves: Excerpts from Student Journals." *Moral Education Forum* (Summer 1981) 19–35.

Crisp, A. H., Palmer, R. L., & Kalucy, R. S. "How Common is Anorexia Nervosa? A Prevalence Study." *British Journal of Psychiatry,* 128 (1976) 549–559.

Cunnion, M. "Sex Differences in Problem Solving." Unpublished doctoral dissertation, Harvard Graduate School of Education (1984).

Dally, A. *Inventing Motherhood.* New York: Schocken Books (1982).

Damon, W. *The Social World of the Child.* San Francisco: Jossey-Bass (1977).

Damon, W. & Colby, A. "Listening to a Different Voice: A Review of Gilligan's *In a Different Voice.*" *Merrill-Palmer Quarterly,* 29 (1983) 473–482.

Deutsch, H. *The Psychology of Women* (2nd ed.). New York: Grune & Stratton (1945).

Douvan, E. & Adelson, J. *The Adolescent Experience.* New York: John Wiley & Sons (1976).

Dryfoos, J. *Preliminary Report to Rockefeller Foundation. Review of Interventions in the Field of Adolescent Pregnancy.* New York (1983).

Dubois *et al.* "Feminist Discourse, Moral Values and the Law--A Conversation." *Buffalo Law Review,* 34(1) (1985) 11–87.

Ehrenreich, B. & English, D. *For Her Own Good: 150 Years of the Experts' Advice to Women.* New York: Anchor Books (1979).

Eisenberg, N. & Lennon, R. "Sex Differences in Empathy and Related Capacities." *Psychological Bulletin,* 94(1) (1983) 100–131.

Eisenberg-Berg, N. "Development of Children's Prosocial Moral Judgment." *Developmental Psychology,* 15(2) (1979) 128–137.

Elder, G. H. "Appearance and Education in Marriage Mobility." *American Sociology Review,* 34 (1969) 519–533.

Eliot, T. S. *On Poetry and Poets.* New York: Farrar, Straus & Cudahy (1957).

Emde, R. N., Johnson, W. F., & Easterbrooks, M. A. "The Do's and Don't's of Early Moral Development." In J. Kagan & S. Lamb, eds., *The Emergence of Morality in Early Childhood.* Chicago: University of Chicago Press (1987).

Erikson, E. *Childhood and Society.* New York: W. W. Norton (1950).

Erikson, E. *Young Man Luther.* New York: W. W. Norton (1958/1962).

Erikson, E. *Insight and Responsibility.* New York: W. W. Norton (1964).

Erikson, E. "Youth: Fidelity and Diversity." In E. Erikson, ed., *The Challenge of Youth.* New York: Anchor Books (1965).

Erikson, E. *Gandhi's Truth.* New York: W. W. Norton (1968).

Erikson, E. *Identity: Youth and Crisis.* New York: W. W. Norton (1968).

Erikson, E. "Reflections on the Dissent of Contemporary Youth." In *Life History and the Historical Moment.* New York: W. W. Norton (1975).

Erikson, E. "Reflections on Dr. Borg's Life Cycle." *Daedalus,* 105 (1976) 1–29.

Fallows, D. *A Mother's Work.* Boston: Houghton Mifflin (1985).

Far West Laboratory for Educational Research and Development, United States Department of Education. *Educational Programs That Work* (8th and 9th eds.). Report prepared for the National Diffusion Network Division, San Francisco (1986).

Fox, P. "Good-bye to Gameplaying." *Juris Doctor,* 1 (1978) 37–42.

Freeman, S. & Giebink, J. "Moral Judgment as a Function of Age, Sex, and Stimulus." *The Journal of Psychology,* 102 (1979) 43–47.

Freud, A. "The Role of Bodily Illness in the Mental Life of Children." In *The Writings of Anna Freud,* 4. New York: International Universities Press (1968) 260–279.

Freud, S. "Three Essays on the Theory of Sexuality," VII (1905); "On Narcissism," XIV (1914); "Some Psychical Consequences of the Anatomical Distinction between the Sexes," XIX (1925); "Female Sexuality," XXI (1931). In J. Strachey, ed. and trans., *The Standard Edition of the Complete Psychological Works of Sigmund Freud.* London: Hogarth Press (1953–1974).

Friedan, B. *The Feminine Mystique.* New York: Norton (1963).

Friedman, G. "The Mother–Daughter Bond." *Contemporary Psychoanalysis,* 16(1) (1980) 90–97.

Gallatin, J. *Adolescence and Individuality: A Conceptual Approach to Adolescent Psychology.* New York: Harper & Row (1975).

Garwood, S., Levine, D., & Ewing, L. "Effect of Protagonist's Sex on Assessing Gender Differences in Moral Reasoning." *Developmental Psychology,* 16(6) (1980) 677–678.

Geertz, C. *The Interpretation of Cultures.* New York: Basic Books (1973).

Gelles, R. *The Violent Home.* Beverly Hills, Calif.: Sage Publications (1974).

Gelles, R. "Violence in the Family: A Review of Research in the 1970's." *Journal of Marriage and the Family* (November 1980).

Gergen, K. J. "Social Psychology, Science, and History." *Personality and Social Psychology Bulletin,* 2 (1976) 373–383.

Gibbs, J. & Wideman, K. *Social Intelligence.* Englewood Cliffs, N.J.: Prentice-Hall (1982).

Gibbs, J. C. & Schell, S. B. "Moral Development 'versus' Socialization: A Critique." *American Psychologist,* 40(10) (1985) 1071–1080.

Giele, J., ed. *Women in the Middle Years.* New York: Wiley–Interscience Publications, John Wiley & Sons (1982).

Gilligan, C. "In a Different Voice: Women's Conceptions of the Self and of Morality." *Harvard Educational Review,* 47 (1977) 481–517.

Gilligan, C. "Woman's Place in Man's Life Cycle." *Harvard Educational Review,* 29 (1979).

Gilligan, C. *In a Different Voice: Psychological Theory and Women's Development.* Cambridge, Mass.: Harvard University Press (1982).

Gilligan, C. "Adult Development and Women's Development: Arrangements for a Marriage." In J. Giele, ed., *Women in the Middle Years.* New York: Wiley–Interscience Publications, John Wiley & Sons (1982).

Gilligan, C. "The Conquistador and the Dark Continent: Reflections on the Psychology of Love." *Daedalus* (Summer 1984) 75–95.

Gilligan, C. "Exit–Voice Dilemmas in Adolescent Development." In A. Foxley, M. McPherson, & G. O'Donnell, eds., *Development, Democracy, and the Art of Trespassing: Essays in Honor of Albert O. Hirschman.* Notre Dame, Ind.: University of Notre Dame Press (1986).

Gilligan, C. "Remapping the Moral Domain: New Images of the Self in Relationship." In T. C. Heller, M. Sosna, & D. E. Wellbery, eds., *Reconstructing Individualism.* Stanford, Calif.: Stanford University Press (1986).

Gilligan, C. "Reply" (to critics). *Signs,* 11(2) (1986) 324–333.

Gilligan, C. "Female Development in Adolescence: Implications for Theory." Unpublished manuscript, Harvard University.

Gilligan, C. & Attanucci, J. "Two Moral Orientations: Gender Differences and Similarities." *Merrill–Palmer Quarterly,* in press.

Gilligan, C., Bardige, B., Ward, J., Taylor, J., & Cohen, G. *Moral Identity Development in Urban Youth.* Final Report to the Rockefeller Foundation (1985).

Gilligan, C. & Belenky, M. "A Naturalistic Study of Abortion Decisions." In R. Selman & R. Yando, eds., *New Directions in Child Development: Clinical-Developmental Psychology,* 7. San Francisco: Jossey-Bass (1980) 69–90.

Gilligan, C., Brown, L. M., & Rogers, A. G. "Psyche Embedded: A Place for Body, Relationships and Culture in Personality Theory." In A. Rabin *et al.*, eds., *Studying Persons and Lives.* New York: Springer, in press.

Gilligan, C., Johnston, D. K., & Miller, B. *Moral Voices, Adolescent Development, and Secondary Education: A Study at the Green River School,* Monograph #3, GEHD Study Center (1987).

Gilligan, C., Langdale, S., Lyons, N., & Murphy, J. *The Contribution of Women's Thought to Developmental Theory: The Elimination of Sex Bias in Moral Development Research and Education.* Final Report to the National Institute of Education. Cambridge, Mass.: Harvard University Press (1982).

Gilligan, C. & Murphy, J. "Development from Adolescence to Adulthood: The Philosopher and the Dilemma of the Fact." In D. Kuhn, ed., *New Directions in Child Development: Intellectual Development Beyond Childhood,* 5. San Francisco: Jossey–Bass (1979) 85–99.

Gilligan, C. & Wiggins, G. "The Origins of Morality in Early Childhood Relationships." In J. Kagan and S. Lamb, eds., *The Emergence of Morality in Early Childhood.* Chicago: University of Chicago Press (1987).

Gilligan, M. & Luchsinger, M. L. "Intimidated? Or Intimidator?" *Women Lawyers Journal,* 72 (Winter 1986) 1–2, 22.

Glaser, B. G. & Strauss, A. L. *The Discovery of Grounded Theory: Strategies for Qualitative Research.* Chicago: Aldine (1967).

Gottman, J. M. "How Children Become Friends." *Society for Research in Child Development Monograph,* 48(3) (1983).

Gutmann, D. "Psychological Naturalism in Cross–Cultural Studies." In H. L. Raush & E. P. Willems, eds., *Naturalistic Viewpoints in Psychological Research.* New York: Holt, Reinhart & Winston (1969).

Gutmann, D. "Parenthood: A Key to Comparative Study of the Life Cycle." In N. Datan & L. Ginsberg, eds., *Life–Span Developmental Psychology: Normative Crisis.* New York: Academic Press (1975) 167–184.

Haan, N. "Hypothetical and Actual Moral Reasoning in a Situation of Civil Disobedience." *Journal of Personality and Social Psychology,* 32(2) (1975) 255–270.

Haan, N. *A Manual for Interpersonal Morality.* Berkeley, Calif.: University of California, Institute for Human Development (1977).

Haan, N. "Two Moralities in Action Contexts: Relationships to Thought, Ego Regulation and Development." *Journal of Personality and Social Psychology,* 36 (1978) 286–305.

Haan, N. "Gender Differences in Moral Development." Paper presented at the American Psychological Association meetings, Los Angeles (1985).

Haan, N. *On Moral Grounds.* New York: New York University Press (1985).

Hallowell, A. I. *Culture and Experience.* Philadelphia: University of Pennsylvania Press (1955).

Hamburg, B. "Early Adolescence: The Specific and Stressful Stage of the Life Cycle." In G. Coelho, D. A. Hamburg, & J. E. Adams, eds., *Coping and Adaptation.* New York: Basic Books (1974).

Hamilton, V. *Narcissus and Oedipus.* London: Routledge & Kegan Paul (1982).

Harragan, B. L. *Games Mother Never Taught You.* New York: Warner Books (1977).

Heffner, E. *Mothering.* New York: Doubleday (1978).

Helgeson, V. & Sharpsteen, D. "Perceptions of Danger in Achievement and Affiliation Situations: An Extension of the Pollak and Gilligan Versus Benton *et al.* Debate." *Journal of Personality and Social Psychology,* 53(4) (1987) 727–733.

Hellman, D. "Analysis of Violence in the Boston Public Schools: Incident and Suspension Data: A Report to the Safe Schools Commission." Boston (November 1983).

Hirschman, A. O. *Exit, Voice, and Loyalty: Responses to Decline in Firms, Organizations, and States.* Cambridge, Mass.: Harvard University Press (1970).

Hoffman, M. "Empathy, Role-Taking, Guilt, and Development of Altruistic Motives." In T. Likona, ed., *Moral Development and Behavior.* New York: Holt, Rinehart & Winston (1976).

Hoffman, M. "Sex Differences in Empathy and Related Behaviors." *Psychological Bulletin,* 84(4) (1977) 712–722.

Holstein, C. "Irreversible, Stepwise Sequence in the Development of Moral Judgment: A Longitudinal Study of Male and Females." *Child Development,* 47 (1976) 51–61.

Ibsen, H. *The Complete Major Prose Plays.* New York: New American Library (1964).

Inhelder, B. & Piaget, J. *The Growth of Logical Thinking from Childhood to Adolescence.* New York: Basic Books (1958/1983).

Iskrant, A. & Joliet, P. V. *Accidents and Homicide.* Cambridge, Mass.: Harvard University Press (1968).

Jack, D. "Attachment, Loss and Depression in Women." Unpublished qualifying paper, Harvard Graduate School of Education (1981).

James, W. *The Varieties of Religious Experience* (1902). New York: Collier (1961).

Johnson, M. & Strom, M. "Facing History and Ourselves: Holocaust and Human Behavior." *Organization of American Historians Newsletter.* (November 1985).

Johnson, W. R. *Darkness Visible: A Study of Vergil's Aeneid.* Berkeley, Calif.: University of California Press (1975).

Johnston, D. K. "Moral Problem Solving: A Pilot Study of Adolescents' Ability to Use Both Moral Orientations." Unpublished manuscript, Harvard Graduate School of Education (1983).

Johnston, D. K. "Two Moral Orientations, Two Problem-Solving Strategies: Adolescents' Solutions to Dilemmas in Fables." Unpublished doctoral dissertation, Harvard Graduate School of Education (1985).

Johnston, D. K. "Two Problem-Solving Strategies Exemplified in Moral Problem Solving." In progress.

Josselson, R. "Psychodynamic Aspects of Identity Formation in College Women." *Journal of Youth and Adolescents,* 2(1) (1973) 3–52.

Josselson, R. *Finding Herself: Pathways to Development in Women.* San Francisco: Jossey-Bass (1987).

Kagan, J. "Acquisition and Significance of Sex Typing and Sex Role Identity." In M. L. Hoffman & L. W. Hoffman, eds., *Review of Child Development Research,* 1. New York: Russell Sage Foundation (1964) 137–167.

Kagan, J. "A Conception of Early Adolescence." *Daedalus,* 100(4) (1971) 997–1012. Also in J. Kagan & R. Coles, eds., *Twelve to Sixteen: Early Adolescence.* New York: W. W. Norton (1972).

Kagan, J. *The Nature of the Child.* New York: Basic Books (1984).

Kagan, J. & Moss, H. A. *Birth to Maturity.* New York: John Wiley & Sons (1962).

Kagan, J. & Lamb, S., eds. *The Emergence of Morality in Young Children.* Chicago: University of Chicago Press (1987).

Kant, I. "Groundwork of the Metaphysic of Morals" (1785). In Paton, trans., *The Moral Law.* London: Hutchinson & Co. (1948).

Kaplan, B. "Genetic Dramatism: Old Wine in New Bottles." In S. Wagner & B. Kaplan, eds., *Toward a Holistic Developmental Psychology.* N. J.: Lawrence Erlbaum Assoc. (1983).

Kaufman, M. *Evolution of Psychosomatic Concepts: Anorexia Nervosa, a Paradigm.* London: Hogarth Press (1965).

Kegan, R. *The Sweeter Welcome: Martin Buber, Bernard Malamud and Saul Bellow.* Needham Heights, Mass.: Wexford (1977).

Kegan, R. *The Evolving Self: Problems and Process in Human Development.* Cambridge, Mass.: Harvard University Press (1982).

Kingston, M. H. *The Woman Warrior: Memoirs of a Girlhood among Ghosts.* New York: Alfred A. Knopf (1976).

Kluckhohn, C. & Murray, H., eds., *Personality in Nature, Culture and Society.* New York: Alfred A. Knopf (1948).

Kohlberg, L. *Education for Justice: A Modern Statement of the Platonic View.* Ernest Burton Lecture on Moral Education. Cambridge, Mass.: Harvard University Press (1968).

Kohlberg, L. "Stage and Sequence: The Cognitive Developmental Approach to Socialization." In D. Goslin, ed., *The Handbook of Socialization Theory and Research.* Chicago: Rand McNally (1969) 347–480.

Kohlberg, L. "From Is to Ought: How to Commit the Naturalistic Fallacy and Get Away with It in the Study of Moral Development." In T. Mischel, ed., *Cognitive Development and Epistemology.* New York: Academic Press (1971) 151–235.

Kohlberg, L. "Moral Stages and Moralization: The Cognitive-Developmental Approach." In T. Lickona, ed., *Moral Development and Behavior: Theory, Research and Social Issues.* New York: Holt, Rinehart & Winston (1976).

Kohlberg, L. *The Philosophy of Moral Development: Moral Stages and the Idea of Justice: Essays on Moral Development,* 1. San Francisco: Harper & Row (1981).

Kohlberg, L. "A Reply to Owen Flanagan and Some Comments on the Puka-Goodpaster Exchange." *Ethics,* 92(3) (1982) 513–528.

Kohlberg, L. *The Psychology of Moral Development: Essays on Moral Development,* 2. San Francisco: Harper & Row (1984).

Kohlberg, L. & Gilligan, C. "The Adolescent as a Philosopher." *Daedalus,* 100(4) (1971) 1051–1086. Also in J. Kagan & R. Coles, *Twelve to Sixteen: Early Adolescence.* New York: W. W. Norton (1972).

Kohlberg, L. & Kramer, R. "Continuities and Discontinuities in Childhood and Adult Moral Development." *Human Development,* 12 (1969) 93–120.

Kohlberg, L., Levine, C., & Hewer, A. "Moral Stages: A Current Formulation and a Response to Critics." In J. Meacham, ed., *Contributions to Human Development Monograph Series,* 10. Basil, Switzerland: S. Karger (1983).

Konopka, G. *The Adolescent Girl in Conflict.* Englewood Cliffs, N.J.: Prentice-Hall (1966).

Konopka, G. *Young Girls: A Portrait of Adolescence.* Englewood Cliffs, N.J.: Prentice-Hall (1976).

Kundera, M. *The Unbearable Lightness of Being.* New York: Harper & Row (1984).

Kutash, I., Kutash, S., Schlesinger, L., et al. *Violence: Perspectives on Murder and Aggression.* San Francisco: Jossey-Bass (1978).

Ladner, J. *Tomorrow's Tomorrow.* New York: Anchor Books (1972).

Ladner, J. *Final Report to the Mayor's Blue Ribbon Panel on Teenage Pregnancy Prevention.* Washington, D.C. (1985).

Lamb, M., ed. *The Role of the Father in Child Development.* New York: John Wiley & Sons (1981).

Langdale, S. *Conceptions of Morality in Developmental Psychology: Is There More than Justice?* Unpublished qualifying paper, Harvard Graduate School of Education (1980).

Langdale, S. "Moral Orientations and Moral Development: The Analysis of Care and Justice Reasoning across Different Dilemmas in Females and Males from Childhood through Adulthood." Doctoral dissertation, Harvard Graduate School of Education (1983).

Langdale, S. "A Re-vision of Structural-Developmental Theory." In G. Sapp, ed., *Handbook of Moral Development.* Birmingham, Ala.: Religious Education Press (1986).

Langdale, S. & Gilligan, C. *The Contribution of Women's Thought to Developmental Theory.* Interim Report to the National Institute of Education. Cambridge, Mass.: Harvard University (1980).

Laufer, W. S. & Day, J. M., eds. *Personality Theory, Moral Development and Criminal Behavior.* Lexington, Mass.: Lexington Books (1983).

Lee, H. *To Kill a Mockingbird.* New York: Fawcett Popular Library (1960).

Lessing, D. *The Summer Before the Dark.* New York: Alfred A. Knopf (1973).

Lever, J. "Sex Differences in the Games Children Play." *Social Problems*, 23 (1976) 478-487.

Lever, J. "Sex Differences in the Complexity of Children's Play and Games." *American Sociological Review*, 43 (1978) 471-483.

LeVine, R. "Anthropology and Child Development." *New Directions for Child Development*, 8 (1980) 71-86.

LeVine, R. *Culture, Behavior, and Personality* (2nd ed.). Chicago: Aldine de Gruyter Publishing (1982).

LeVine, R. "The Self in Culture." In R. LeVine, ed., *Culture and Personality* (2nd ed.). Hawthorne, N. Y.: Aldine de Gruyter (1982).

LeVine, R. "The Self and Its Development in an African Society: A Preliminary Analysis." In B. Lee, ed., *New Approaches to the Self.* New York: Plenum Press, in press.

Levinson, D. *The Seasons of a Man's Life.* New York: Alfred A. Knopf (1978).

Lightfoot, S. L. *The Good High School.* New York: Basic Books (1983).

Loevinger, J. *Ego Development: Conceptions and Theories.* San Francisco: Jossey-Bass (1976).

Loevinger, J. *Scientific Ways in the Study of Ego Development.* Worcester, Mass.: Clark University Press (1979).

Lyons, N. "Seeing the Consequences." Unpublished qualifying paper, Harvard Graduate School of Education (1980).

Lyons, N. "Manual for Coding Responses to the Question: How Would You Describe Yourself to Yourself?" Unpublished manuscript, Harvard Graduate School of Education (1981).

Lyons, N. "Conceptions of Self and Morality and Modes of Moral Choice: Identifying Justice and Care Judgments of Actual Moral Dilemmas." Unpublished doctoral dissertation, Harvard Graduate School of Education (1982).

Lyons, N. "The Manual for Analyzing Responses to the Question: How Would You Describe Yourself to Yourself?" Unpublished manuscript, Harvard Graduate School of Education (1982).

Lyons, N. "Two Perspectives: On Self, Relationships and Morality." *Harvard Educational Review,* 53(2) (1983) 125–145.

Maccoby, E. "Social Grouping in Childhood: Their Relationship to Prosocial and Antisocial Behavior in Boys and Girls." In D. Olwens, J. Block, & M. Radke–Yarrow, eds., *Development of Antisocial and Prosocial Behavior: Theories, Research and Issues.* San Diego: Academic Press (1985).

Maccoby, E. & Jacklin, C. *The Psychology of Sex Differences.* Stanford, Calif.: Stanford University Press (1974).

Marcia, J. "Identity in Adolescence." In J. Adelson, ed., *Handbook of Adolescent Psychology.* New York: John Wiley & Sons (1980).

Marshall, M. *The Cost of Loving.* New York: Putnam (1984).

May, R. *Sex and Fantasy.* New York: W. W. Norton (1980).

McClelland, D. C. *Power: The Inner Experience.* New York: Irving (1975).

Mead, G. H. *Mind, Self, and Society.* Chicago: University of Chicago Press (1934).

Miller, J. B. *Toward a New Psychology of Women.* Boston: Beacon Press (1976).

Miller, J. B. "Women and Power." *Work in Progress,* 1. Wellesley, Mass.: Stone Center Working Paper Series (1982).

Miller, J. B. "The Development of Women's Sense of Self." *Work in Progress,* 12. Wellesley, Mass.: Stone Center Working Paper Series (1984).

Miller, J. B. "What Do We Mean by Relationships?" *Work in Progress,* 22. Wellesley, Mass.: Stone Center Working Paper Series (1986).

Mishler, E. "Meaning in Context: Is There Any Other Kind?" *Harvard Educational Review,* 49(1) (1979) 1–19.

Mishler, E. *Research Interviewing.* Cambridge, Mass.: Harvard University Press (1986).

Murdoch, I. *The Sovereignty of Good.* Boston: Routledge & Kegan Paul (1970).

Murray, H. A. "Thematic Apperception Test Manual." Cambridge, Mass.: Harvard College (1943).

Nadelson, C., Notman, M., & Previn, D. W. "Medical Student Stress, Adaptation, and Mental Health." In S. C. Schreiber and B. B. Doyle, eds., *The Impaired Physician.* New York: Plenum Medical Books (1983).

National Institute of Education. "Violent Schools--Safe Schools: Safe School Study," 1. Report to Congress by Secretary Joseph Califano, Jr. (January 1978).

Neumann, E. *The Great Mother.* Princeton, N.J.: Bollingen Foundation, Princeton University Press (1955).

Niebuhr, H. R. *The Responsible Self.* New York: Harper & Row (1963).

Notman, M., Salt, P., & Nadelson, C. "Stress and Adaptation in Medical Students: Who Is the Most Vulnerable?" *Comprehensive Psychiatry,* 25(3) (1984) 355–366.

Nunner–Winkler, G. "Two Moralities: A Critical Discussion of an Ethic of Care and Responsibility versus an Ethic of Rights and Justice." In W. Kurtines & J. Gewirtz, eds., *Morality, Moral Behavior, and Moral Development.* New York: John Wiley & Sons (1984) 348–361.

Offer, D. *The Psychological World of the Teenager: A Study of 175 Boys.* New York: Basic Books (1969).

Offer, D. & Offer, J. *From Teenage to Young Manhood.* New York: Basic Books (1975).

Orchowsky, S. & Jenkins, L. "Sex Biases in the Measurement of Moral Judgment." *Psychological Reports,* 44 (1979) 1040.

Orwell, G. *An Orwell Reader.* New York: Harcourt Brace (1949).

Osborne, R. "Good–Me, Bad–Me, True–Me, False–Me: A Dynamic Multidimensional Study of Adolescent Self–Concept." Unpublished doctoral dissertation, Harvard Graduate School of Education (1987).

Ovid. *The Metamorphoses.* M. Inness, trans. London: Penguin (1955).

Parke, R. D. *Fathers.* Cambridge, Mass.: Harvard University Press (1981).

Perry, W. *Forms of Intellectual and Ethical Development in the College Years.* New York: Holt, Rinehart & Winston (1968).

Piaget, J. *The Child's Conception of the World* (1929). Totowa, N.J.: Littlefield, Adams, & Co. (1979).

Piaget, J. *The Rules of the Game.* London: Routledge & Kegan Paul (1932).

Piaget, J. *The Moral Judgment of the Child* (1932). New York: Free Press (1965).

Piaget, J. "The Mental Development of the Child" (1940). In *Six Psychological Studies.* New York: Vintage Books (1967).

Piaget, J. *To Understand Is To Invent: The Future of Education.* New York: Grossman/Penguin (1973).

Pipp, S., Shaver, P., Jennings, S., Lamborn, S., & Fischer, K. "Adolescents' Theories about the Development of Their Relationships with Parents." *Journal of Personality and Social Psychology* (1985) 991-1001.

Polanyi, M. *Personal Knowledge.* Chicago: University of Chicago Press (1958).

Pollak, S. "A Study of Gender Differences in Violent Thematic Apperception Test Stories." Unpublished doctoral dissertation, Harvard Graduate School of Education (1985).

Pollak, S. & Gilligan, C. "Images of Violence in Thematic Apperception Test Stories." *Journal of Personality and Social Psychology,* 42 (1982) 159-167.

Pollak, S. & Gilligan, C. "Differing about Differences: The Incidence and Interpretation of Violent Fantasies in Women and Men." *Journal of Personality and Social Psychology,* 45 (1983) 1172-1175.

Pollak, S. & Gilligan, C. "Killing the Messenger." *Journal of Personality and Social Psychology,* 48 (1985) 374-375.

Pratt, M., Golding, G., & Hunter, W. "Aging as Ripening: Character and Consistency of Moral Judgment in Young, Mature, and Older Adults." *Human Development,* 26 (1983) 277-288.

Pratt, M., Golding, G., & Hunter, W. "Does Morality Have a Gender? Sex, Sex Role and Moral Judgment Relationships across the Lifespan." *Merrill-Palmer Quarterly,* 30 (1984) 321-340.

Ravitch, D. "Decline and Fall of Teaching History." *New York Times Sunday Magazine* (November 17, 1985).

Rest, J. *Development in Judging Moral Issues.* Minneapolis, Minn.: University of Minnesota Press (1979).

Rogers, A. "The Question of Gender Differences: A Validity Study of Two Moral Orientations." Unpublished manuscript, St. Louis, Mo., Washington University (1988).

Roscoe, B. & Callahan, J. "Adolescence Self Report of Violence in Families and Dating Relations." *Adolescence,* 20(79) (1985) 545-553.

Rutter, M., Baughan, B., Mortimore, P., Ouston, J., & Smith, A. *Fifteen Thousand Hours.* Cambridge, Mass.: Harvard University Press (1979).

Sarbin, T. R. "Role Theory." In G. Lindzey & E. Aronson, eds., *Handbook of Social Psychology,* 1. Reading, Mass.: Addison-Wesley (1954) 223-258.

Sartre, J. P. *Existentialism and Humanism.* London: Methuen (1948).

Sassen, G. "Success Anxiety in Women: A Constructivist Interpretation of Its Source and Its Significance." *Harvard Educational Review,* 50(1) (1980) 13–24.

Schatzman, L. & Strauss, A. L. *Field Research: Strategies for a Natural Sociology.* Englewood Cliffs, N.J.: Prentice–Hall (1973).

Schwartz, D., Thompson, M., & Johnson, C. "Anorexia Nervosa and Bulimia, the Socio–Cultural Context." *International Journal of Eating Disorders,* 1 (1982) 20–36.

Selman, R. *The Growth of Interpersonal Understanding: Developmental and Clinical Analysis.* New York: Academic Press (1980).

Selman, R. & Jaquette, D. "Stability and Oscillation in Interpersonal Awareness: A Clinical Developmental Approach." In C. B. Keasy, ed., *Twenty–Fifth Nebraska Symposium on Motivation.* Lincoln, Nebr.: University of Nebraska Press (1977) 261–304.

Sherman, J. A. *On the Psychology of Women: A Survey of Empirical Studies.* Springfield, Ill.: Charles C. Thomas (1971).

Siegel, S. *Nonparametric Statistics for the Behavioral Sciences.* New York: McGraw–Hill (1956).

Skinner, M. "The Last Encounter of Dido and Aeneas 6.450–476." *Vergilius,* 29, The Vergilius Society (1983).

Skoe, E. E. & Marcia, J. E. *The Development and Partial Validation of a Care– Based Measure of Moral Development.* Unpublished paper (1988).

Snarey, J. "Cross–Cultural Universality of Socio–Moral Development: Critical Review of Kohlberg Research." *Psychological Bulletin,* 97(2) (1985) 202–232.

Snarey, J., Kohlberg, L., & Noam, G. "Ego Development in Perspective: Structural Stage, Functional Phase and Cultural Age–Period Models." *Developmental Review,* 3 (1983) 330–338.

Snarey, J., Reimer, J., & Kohlberg, L. "The Socio–Moral Development of Kibbutz Adolescents: A Longitudinal Cross–Cultural Study." *Developmental Psychology,* 21 (1985) 3–17.

Stack, C. *All Our Kin.* New York: Harper & Row (1974).

Stein, D. *The Interpersonal World of the Infant.* New York: Basic Books (1985).

Steiner–Adair, C. "The Body Politic: Normal Female Adolescent Development and the Development of Eating Disorders." Unpublished doctoral dissertation, Harvard Graduate School of Education (1984).

Steiner–Adair, C. "The Body Politic: Normal Female Adolescent Development and the Development of Eating Disorders." *Journal of the American Academy of Psychoanalysis,* 14(1) (1986) 95–114.

Stern, D. *The Interpersonal World of the Infant.* New York: Basic Books (1985).

Strachan, N. "A Map for Women on the Road to Success." *American Bar Association Journal,* 70 (May 1984) 94–96.

Straus, M. A. "Sexual Inequality, Cultural Norms, and Wife Beating." *Victimology,* 1(1) (1976) 54–70.

Straus, M. A. "Measuring Intrafamily Conflict and Violence: The Conflict Tactics (CT) Scales." *Journal of Marriage and the Family* (February 1979) 75–88.

Straus, M. A., Gelles, R., & Steinmetz, S. *Behind Closed Doors: Violence in the American Family.* New York: Anchor Press (1980).

Strom, M. S. & Parsons, W. *Facing History and Ourselves: Holocaust and Human Behavior.* Watertown, Mass.: Intentional Educations (1982).

Strom, M. S. & Parsons, W. "Students Learn the Pain of Thinking." *Social Education* (1983) 197–198.

Sugar, M., ed. *Female Adolescent Development.* New York: Brunner/Mazel (1979).

Surrey, J. "The Self-in-Relation." *Work in Progress,* 13. Wellesley, Mass.: Stone Center Working Paper Series (1984).

Suttie, I. *The Origins of Love and Hate.* New York: The Julian Press (1935).

Templeton, S. "Comparative Human Infancy Project: Maternal Self-Perception Interview." Unpublished manuscript, Harvard Graduate School of Education (1980).

Terris, D. "Reading, Writing and Weapons: How Boston Schools Make Learning Safe." *Boston Globe Magazine* (March 2, 1986).

Trilling, L. "On the Modern Element in Modern Literature." In I. Howe, ed., *The Idea of the Modern in Literature and the Arts.* New York: Horizon Press (1967).

Turiel, E. "Conflict and Transition in Adolescent Moral Development." *Child Development,* 45 (1974) 14–29.

United States Federal Bureau of Investigation. *Uniform Crime Reports: Crime in the U.S.* Washington, D.C.: United States Government Printing Office (1983).

Vaillant, G. *Adaptation to Life.* Boston: Little, Brown (1977).

Virgil. *The Aeneid.* R. Fitzgerald, trans. New York: Random House (1983).

Vygotsky, L. S. *Mind in Society.* M. Cole *et al.,* eds. Cambridge, Mass.: Harvard University Press (1978).

Walker, L. "Sex Differences in the Development of Moral Reasoning: A Critical Review." *Child Development,* 55 (1984) 677–691.

Walker, L. "Sex Differences in the Development of Moral Reasoning: A Rejoinder to Baumrind." *Child Development,* 57 (1986) 522-527.

Ward, J. V. "A Study of Urban Adolescents' Thinking about Violence Following a Course on the Holocaust." Unpublished doctoral dissertation, Harvard Graduate School of Education (1986).

Weil, S. "Human Personality." In G. Panichas, ed., *The Simone Weil Reader.* New York: David McKay (1977).

Weitzman, L. "Sex Role Socialization." In J. Freeman, ed., *Women: A Feminist Perspective.* Palo Alto, Calif.: Mayfield Publishers (1975).

Wiggins, G. "Thoughtfulness as an Educational Aim." Unpublished manuscript, Harvard Graduate School of Education (1987).

Willard, A. K. "Self, Situation, and Script: A Psychological Study of Decisions about Employment in Mothers of One-Year Olds." Unpublished doctoral dissertation, Harvard Graduate School of Education (1985).

Winnicott, D. W. *The Family and Individual Development.* New York: Basic Books (1965).

Winnicott, D. W. *Playing and Reality.* London: Tavistock Publications (1971).

Wolf, D., Rygh, J., & Altshuler, J. "Agency and Experience: Action and States in Play Narratives." In I. Bretherton, ed., *Symbolic Play: The Development of Social Understanding.* New York: Academic Press (1984) 195-217.

Wolfgang, M. *Patterns of Criminal Homicide.* New York: John Wiley & Sons (1966).

Woolf, V. *Jacob's Room.* New York: Harcourt Brace (1922).

Wylie, R. C. *The Self-Concept* (revised ed.). Lincoln, Nebr.: University of Nebraska Press (1974).

Youniss, J. *Parents and Peers in Social Development.* Chicago: University of Chicago Press (1980).

Youniss, J. & Smollar, J. *Adolescents' Relations with Mothers, Fathers, and Friends.* Chicago: University of Chicago Press (1985).

# INDEX

# INDEX

322 Mapping the Moral Domain

Murdoch, Iris, 22–23, 43, 120, 151
Murphy, Michael, 44n1
Murray, H., 223

Nader, L., *Law in Culture and Society*, 288n6
Niebuhr, H. Richard: *The Responsible Self*, 18n1, 44n5
Nietzsche, 113
Nuclear threat, 142, 156, 157

*Obedience* (film), 97, 99, 102, 104
Oedipal conflicts, 148, 216
 *See also* Freud, Sigmund
Orwell, George: *On Gandhi*, 245

Parsons, William, 89
Perry, William, xxviii
Physicians, 245–262, 292
Piaget, Jean, 22, 49, 82–83, 90, 91, 108, 117, 137n1
 on cognitive development, xi–xii, xiv, 66, 112, 113
 on "heteronomous" morality, xxxv, 168
 on relationships, 24, 114
 clinical method of, 37, 52, 248
 on children's games, 112, 129–130, 264
 on adolescence, 127, 130–131
 and altruism in childhood, 133
 on peer interaction, 134
 and egocentrism, 135–136, 166
 on moral vs. intellectual development, 138n2
Pipp, S., xiii
Polanyi, Michael, xx, 66
Pollak, Susan, 245–262
Problem-solving, xxi–xxii, xxiii
 strategies for moral, xx, xxi–xxiii, 66–69
 and connection, 238
 *See also* Fables
Psychoanalysis, 209, 229
Psychology: and questions of interpretation, i, viii, xxvii
 language of, ii, ix, xxiv, xxxii
 and sex differences, iv, 112
 and education, xii
 of love, 4, 5–7, 9–10, 14, 16
 and philosophy, 43
 of relationships, 43, 208, 223
 moral, 129
 self-concept research in, 208
 of child development, 228

Psychotherapy, ii, x, 156, 208

Racism, 176, 178
Ravitch, Diane, xii
Rawls, John, 125, 133
Reagan, Ronald, 150
Relationships: parent/child, viii–ix, xiii, 5, 144, 145, 149, 151, 152, 166, 167, 202, 216
 and moral reasoning, 118–137, 151
 and co-feeling, 122–123
 and voice, 153–154
 mother–infant, 202–203
 and self, 202–204, 207, 210, 213–223
 marital, 214
 and power, 246
 and femininity, 272–275, 276
 *See also* Care Focus
Response orientation, 35–36, 38–42, 50–66
 definition of, 44n5
 absence of, 150
 *See also* Care Focus
Responsibility, xiii, 4–5, 7–8, 16, 44n5, 78, 96, 98, 108, 127
 and connection, 7, 151–152, 281
 and self, 201, 216
 and care, 284, 290
Rights orientation, 35, 50–66
 *See also* Justice Focus
Rogers, Annie, 292
Role theory, 201–223
Ruddick, Sara, 292–293
Rutter, Michael, xxx
Rygh, J., 125

Sarbin, T. R., 201
Sartre, Jean-Paul, 117, 132
Self: and morality, iii, xxiii, 4, 8, 22–32, 36–43, 44n1, 129, 144, 145
 women's sense of, x–xi, xvii, 32, 204–207
 and relationship, xiii, xxiv, xxv, 122
 images of, 3–18, 22, 144
 autonomous, 6, 146
 and gender, 8–9, 17–18, 25, 43, 44n1, 204, 246
 objective vs. subjective, 33, 34, 40–43, 124, 201–203, 205
 connected, 33–34, 40–43, 153, 154, 155, 203–204, 213
 study of, 201, 208
 and role, 202–223